NO DEBATE

CAUT SERIES TITLES

Universities at Risk: How Politics, Special Interests, and Corporatization Threaten Academic Integrity. Edited by James L. Turk. 2008.

Free Speech in Fearful Times: After 9/11 in Canada, the US, Australia, and Europe. Edited by James L. Turk and Allan Manson. 2006.

Time's Up! Mandatory Retirement in Canada. Edited by C.T. (Terry) Gillin, David MacGregor, and Thomas R. Klassen. 2005.

Disciplining Dissent. Edited by William Bruneau and James L. Turk. 2004.

Let Them Eat Prozac. David Healy. 2003.

Counting out the Scholars: How Performance Indicators Undermine Colleges and Universities. William Bruneau and Donald C. Savage. 2002.

The Olivieri Report: The Complete Text of the Report of the Independent Inquiry Commissioned by the Canadian Association of University Teachers. Jon Thompson, Patricia Baird, and Jocelyn Downie. 2001.

The Corporate Campus: Commercialization and the Dangers to Canada's Colleges and Universities. Edited by James L. Turk. 2000.

Universities for Sale: Resisting Corporate Control over Canadian Higher Education. Neil Tudiver. 1999.

NO DEBATE

THE ISRAEL LOBBY AND FREE SPEECH AT CANADIAN UNIVERSITIES

JON THOMPSON

James Lorimer & Company Ltd., Publishers
Toronto

James Lorimer & Company Ltd., Publishers, acknowledges the support of the Ontario Arts Council. We acknowledge the financial support of the Government of Canada through the Canada Book Fund for our publishing activities. We acknowledge the support of the Canada Council for the Arts, which last year invested $20.1 million in writing and publishing throughout Canada. We acknowledge the Government of Ontario through the Ontario Media Development Corporation's Ontario Book Initiative.

Canada Council
for the Arts

Conseil des Arts
du Canada

Cover design: Meghan Collins

Library and Archives Canada Cataloguing in Publication

Thompson, Jon H.
No debate : the Israel lobby and free speech at Canadian universities / Jon Thompson.

(CAUT series)
Includes bibliographical references and index.
Issued also in electronic format.
ISBN 978-1-55277-656-8

1. Academic freedom--Canada--Case studies. 2. Freedom of speech-- Canada--Case studies. 3. Lobbying--Canada--Case studies. 4. Zionists-- Political activity--Canada--Case studies. 5. York University (Toronto, Ont.)--Case studies. 6. Arab-Israeli conflict--Case studies. 7. Universities and colleges--Political aspects--Canada--Case studies. 8. Higher education and state--Canada--Case studies. I. Title. II. Series: Canadian Association of University Teachers series

LC72.5.C3T56 2011   378.1'2130971   C2011-905893-6

James Lorimer & Company Ltd., Publishers
317 Adelaide Street West, Suite 1002
Toronto, ON, Canada
M5V 1P9
www.lorimer.ca

MIX
Paper from
responsible sources
FSC® C016245

Printed and bound in Canada

Contents

FOREWORD

John le Carré has taken us behind the curtain of police and security agencies to show, albeit in fictionalized accounts, the reality of intelligence work and how it is shaped by human passions and self-interests—quite unlike official accounts. His work is terribly important for those of us who value civil liberties because he exposes how vulnerable such liberties are in the day-to-day operations of agencies that ostensibly exist to protect our democratic way of life.

In this book, Jon Thompson fulfills a similar function with respect to the real-life vulnerability of academic freedom—the freedom former York University president Harry Arthurs correctly described as "*a* central, arguably *the* central value, of university life."[1] Arthurs speaks for most in the academic world, when he said "anything which interferes with [academic freedom] has to be justified by reference to prior or higher values. I can think of very few, other than perhaps the protection of human life: certainly not institutional solidarity; certainly not institutional reputation."[2] Academic freedom is espoused as a central tenet in virtually every North American university's policies and has statutory protection in many countries outside of North America.

But as Thompson and his colleagues showed in their careful investigation of the landmark case of Dr. Nancy Olivieri, a distinguished professor of medicine at the University of Toronto and Toronto's Hospital for Sick Children, academic freedom can be undermined by commercial greed, hostile colleagues, donation-hungry institutions, and administrative inertia and fear. Thompson's *The Olivieri Report*[3] also showed how a small

band of ethical academics stuck with Olivieri until she was fully vindicated through their work and that of the University of Toronto Faculty
Association and CAUT.

In *No Debate*, Thompson takes on a larger task by looking at the reality
of academic freedom when it comes face to face with Middle Eastern politics, particularly those critical of the Israeli government. During the cold
war years in the 1950s, universities' defence of academic freedom largely
melted in the heat of virulent anti-communism.[4] Arguably, we are seeing
some of the same behaviours now toward those who are critical of Israeli
government policy, particularly in relation to the Palestinians.

Thompson's investigation was prompted by what took place before,
during, and after a conference with the seemingly innocuous title "Israel/
Palestine: Mapping Models of Statehood and Paths to Peace," which was
organized by members of the law faculties at York University and Queen's
University. The organizers' academic work deals with issues of statehood,
constitutional law, comparative law, human rights, rights of refugees and
other minorities, and ethnography. They felt a conference looking at two-
state and one-state solutions to the crisis in Israel and Palestine would be
a productive exercise—especially as they planned to bring a large number
of scholars, many from Israel, to explore the various options.

The organizers recruited an international advisory board of scholars
knowledgeable in the field, got the endorsements of their two universities,
and won a peer-reviewed conference grant from the Social Sciences and
Humanities Research Council of Canada (SSHRC).

Then their troubles began. Canadian pro-Israeli lobby groups raised
concerns with the sponsoring universities, as did some individual faculty
and university donors. At one point it appeared as if the conference would
be cancelled or moved off campus. Members of the advisory group came
under pressure to withdraw.

Then, in an unprecedented move, Canada's minister for science and
technology contacted the president of SSHRC—the arms-length funding
agency for the social sciences and humanities—to suggest that the decision
to fund the conference be reviewed. On hearing the news, CAUT asked to
meet with the president of SSHRC, but he declined, although, contrary to
SSHRC policy, he did insist that the organizers provide additional material.

Amidst protests led by the Jewish Defence League and in the presence
of a large number of university security personnel, the conference did
go ahead, but the controversy continued long afterward. York University
brought in former Supreme Court justice, Frank Iacobucci, to review

the organizing of the conference, advise on the responsibilities of those involved, and give York advice for future events. York's law school faculty association refused to participate in Iacobucci's review, indicating that the way the university was proceeding was "a possible threat to academic freedom, not an affirmation of it."

Thompson was asked by CAUT to look into all this. Specifically, he was asked to examine whether the academic freedom of the conference organizers and the integrity of educational work were threatened by the actions of the York administration, SSHRC, and others; to draw conclusions from the experiences of this conference with respect to the vulnerability of academic freedom and the integrity of educational work; and to make recommendations as to policies and procedures that will safeguard academic freedom and the integrity of educational work.

Thompson has done that. What emerges in *No Debate* is a complex tale of a genuine intellectual quest for a solution to one of the world's most challenging problems—achieving a just peace between Israel and Palestine. It is also a tale of academic naiveté, brass-knuckle international politics played out openly and behind the scenes in Canada's academic world, personal ambition, political gamesmanship, organizational rivalries, disregard for academic freedom by some, and a strong commitment to it by others.

No Debate gives readers a unique look behind the curtains of the academic world. It gives them an understanding of the fragility of academic freedom and the need for courage in its defence. Thompson also provides background on the political issues and on academic freedom.

Universities have a unique role in democratic societies as one place, often the only place, where ideas, theories, products, and inventions can be examined from all angles and where fashion, conventional wisdom, popular thought, or powerful interests cannot shut down inquiry. Yale University President Kingman Brewster described this well in a speech forty years ago: "This spirit of academic freedom within the university has a value which goes beyond protecting the individual's broad scope of thought and inquiry. It bears crucially upon the distinctive quality of the university as a community. If a university is alive and productive it is a place where colleagues are in constant dispute; defending their latest intellectual enthusiasm, attacking the contrary views of others. From this trial by intellectual combat emerges a sharper insight, later to be blunted by other, sharper minds. It is vital that this contest be uninhibited by fear of reprisal."[5]

As Thompson has shown, this ideal is at risk. Almost any inquiry of importance faces those who want to shut it down. *No Debate* tells a story of academic freedom triumphing in the short run, but it is not clear it will also triumph in the long run. The forces threatened by open inquiry are often very powerful and do not accept defeat easily.

—James L. Turk

1

OVERVIEW

SUMMARY OF EVENTS

Israel/Palestine: Mapping Models of Statehood and Paths to Peace was a conference held June 22–24, 2009, on the Glendon College Campus of York University, sponsored by York University, Queen's University, and the Social Sciences and Humanities Research Council of Canada (SSHRC). The conference was organized by two professors and a doctoral student in Osgoode Hall Law School at York University and a professor in the Faculty of Law at Queen's University, and they were assisted by an eleven-member international advisory board.

A controversy began in the autumn of 2008 when the conference was announced and it escalated during the spring of 2009, as pro-Israeli government groups and individuals opposed to the conference exerted increasing pressure on the organizers, on the administrations of the two universities, on the granting council, and on the Government of Canada to have the event cancelled or its program significantly altered. The members of the organizing committee at York University began to experience very strong pressure in mid-April 2009, and in response they sought advice from the Canadian Association of University Teachers (CAUT) on ways to protect their academic freedom. Pressure on the universities and the organizers continued to mount in May and June 2009 when, among other things, the conference and York University were denounced by Israel lobby organizations in public statements and in communications with federal government agencies.

The controversy widened and intensified in early June, with an unprecedented interference by a federal government minister into the functioning of the granting council, followed by an extraordinary intervention by the granting council with the conference organization. These brought prompt action by CAUT and by many faculty members at York, Queen's, and other universities, in protest against the ministerial and SSHRC actions. Senior administrators at both York and Queen's universities acted to defend the conference and to ensure it would proceed.

Although the conference was held as scheduled and with the program as planned by the organizers, concerns regarding academic freedom and academic integrity remained, and CAUT commissioned this Inquiry.

TERMS OF REFERENCE AND PROCESS OF THE INQUIRY

The Inquiry was asked to

- examine whether the academic freedom of the conference organizers and the integrity of educational work were threatened by the actions of the York administration, SSHRC, and others

- draw conclusions from the experiences of this conference with respect to the vulnerability of academic freedom and the integrity of educational work

- make recommendations as to policies and procedures that will safeguard academic freedom and the integrity of educational work.

CAUT announced this Inquiry on September 2, 2009, setting out these terms of reference and inviting written submissions from certain organizations and individuals, as well as from "any other interested parties." A list of the individuals and organizations that accepted the invitation and provided briefs or other documents is given in Appendix X (http://www.caut.ca/thompson-report/appendix-x.aspx).

I also spoke with a number of persons, including representatives of organizations, in connection with whom documentation had been received, to obtain clarification or additional information. Several lengthy interviews were recorded with the knowledge and agreement of the participants.

The four members of the conference organizing committee spoke about their experiences during 2008–2009 at a conference held at Flavelle House,

University of Toronto, January 29–30, 2010, in a six-person panel discussing "Academic Freedom in the Canadian Legal Academy: Israel/Palestine and Discussions on Paths to Peace." I attended this session and spoke there with each of the organizers.

Substantial collections of documents were obtained from York University and from SSHRC as a result of requests under provincial and federal freedom-of-information legislation, respectively. The material obtained through these processes was in addition to submissions the university and SSHRC made directly in response to the CAUT invitation. Relatively small collections of documents were obtained from relevant departments or offices of the federal government through a similar process.

Information from a variety of publications also was used: scholarly books and articles; articles and reports written for general audiences, including some from newspapers, magazines, and websites; and media releases by various organizations or agencies.

BACKGROUND TO THE CONTROVERSY

The controversy around the conference was fuelled by allegations that it was an anti-Semitic event. I found such allegations to have been incorrect and unfair. They were based on strongly held opinions instead of facts. The allegations also were consistent with a long-standing political position of the State of Israel, to the effect that any significant criticism of Israel or its policies may be regarded as anti-Semitism. Foreign Minister Abba Eban, for example, said in a speech on July 31, 1972, "One of the chief tasks of any dialogue with the Gentile world is to prove that the distinction between anti-Semitism and anti-Zionism is no distinction at all. Anti-Zionism is merely the new anti-Semitism."[1]

The controversy intensified over several months, with increasingly numerous public and private expressions of opposition to the event by Israel lobby organizations, their supporters, and other individuals who were concerned about the conference topic or about some of the speakers.

The term "the Israel lobby" is used in this report in a manner similar to its usage in the American context by Professors John Mearsheimer and Stephen Walt in their 2007 book with that main title. They called the charge of anti-Semitism "the Great Silencer."

The Israel lobby has focused considerable attention on university communities in the United States, according to Mearsheimer:

Universities are the one place in the United States where Israel
tends to get treated like a normal country. Although Israel has
many defenders on college campuses, it also gets criticized there
for its past and present behaviour in ways that rarely happen in
the mainstream media or among politicians and policymakers
inside the Beltway. Many hard-line supporters of Israel find this
situation intolerable, which causes them to work very hard to
stifle criticism of Israel and American support for Israel, and
instead to promote a positive image for Israel on campuses.
To achieve this end, they seek to limit the number of critics of
Israel in the academy, and marginalize—or even better, silence—
existing critics.[2]

Much of the campaign against the conference focused on one of the possible statehood models for Israel/Palestine on the conference agenda—the
one-state, binational model, in which all citizens would enjoy equal rights.
A related source of controversy was inclusion on the program of some
speakers, both Jewish and non-Jewish, who were well known as promoters
of this model, or as critics of current policies of the State of Israel in regard
to Palestinians. However, at times the two-state model has been controversial and, just when the conference was held, media reports indicated that a
two-state model involving a viable, fully independent Palestinian state was
again controversial in some quarters.

The controversy reached its highest level in early June when a minister in
the Harper government interfered with SSHRC and his office issued a media
release suggesting the agency's grant to the conference might be placed in
jeopardy. This was an action unprecedented since SSHRC was established
as an arm's-length agency in the late 1970s. When CAUT learned of this,
it promptly protested to SSHRC and made the government's interference
and SSHRC's response public issues. Subsequently, SSHRC announced
that the grant would stand as originally awarded through its peer-review
process.

In wider contexts during recent years, aspects of the social sciences and
humanities have been under political and philosophical attack. In the
United States, where this has been more conspicuous and more severe,
there also have been efforts to dismiss or deny tenure to several professors
in these disciplines, but the phenomenon is international. The Harper
Conservative government's unprecedented interference with SSHRC in
response to complaints about the agency's grant to the conference occurred

in this broader context. This government has several times taken actions or changed policies in ways that suggest its view of the proper role of government is quite different from the views of either Progressive Conservative or Liberal governments of recent decades. Its domestic and foreign policies and its actions suggest it is more strongly influenced than its predecessors not only by the American variant of neoliberalism, but also by the American variant of another ideology, neoconservatism.

Controversy around the social sciences or humanities is not new. A century ago, dismissal actions involving professors in these disciplines provided an impetus for the founding of the American Association of University Professors (AAUP). Scholars in economics and philosophy took the lead in drafting its influential 1915 *Declaration* on academic freedom, which spoke, among other things, of "the special dangers to freedom of teaching in the domain of the social sciences" in universities and colleges. The AAUP document emphasized the importance of academic freedom to the healthy functioning of modern democracy.[3]

Campaigns against events, research, or scholars in the social sciences or humanities may be regarded as manifestations of a political phenomenon Professor Ze'ev Sternhell called the anti-Enlightenment tradition.[4] It extends back to the eighteenth century, when studies and discussions that ultimately led to the establishment of many modern academic disciplines were gaining wider attention, and has appeared in various ways and at various times since. A recurrent feature of this reactionary tradition is opposition to social and political equality rights for all citizens—including women and minority groups. Professor Jonathan Israel, who has written extensively on the Enlightenment and reactions against it, observed:

> Among the most divisive and potentially perplexing of all basic concepts introduced by the Radical Enlightenment into the make-up of modernity, and one of the most revolutionary in its implications was, and is, the idea of equality.[5]

A recent observation by Sternhell illustrates Israel's general point. He wrote that Theodor Herzl "understood the danger that hung over the Jews of Europe as soon as the liberal order began to totter, and that anti-Semitism was only one aspect of the great battle against the Enlightenment."[6]

Criticism of the conference began in early autumn 2008, shortly after the vision statement and call for papers were published. By spring 2009 there were many protests to York and Queen's universities. These included email messages and telephone calls from members of their alumni and some members of their own faculties, a denunciation of York University and the conference by the Canadian Council for Israel and Jewish Advocacy, repeated denunciations by B'nai Brith Canada and the Jewish Defence League of Canada, and a full-page B'nai Brith newspaper advertisement denouncing York University. Protests were also made to SSHRC and to the Harper government, which interfered with SSHRC, and SSHRC then made an extraordinary demand of the conference organizers.

Such reactions—against an academic event in which the State of Israel or its policies would be critically discussed, or against individual academic critics—had occurred several times in the United States during recent years. However, other than the particular topic and the specific sectors of the public exercised by discussion of ideas, similar controversies had occurred earlier. An instance of historical importance erupted in 1940, over the appointment of Bertrand Russell to the College of the City of New York. As described in Chapter 8, Christian groups and their supporters denounced the appointment because of Russell's long-standing advocacy of full social and political equality for women. The opponents embarked on an extensive, aggressive political and legal campaign to have the appointment revoked, and they succeeded.

In addition to its scope and intensity, the 1940 campaign against the Russell appointment has another parallel with the 2009 campaign against the York/Queen's conference—interference by governmental entities. In the Russell case, this came in the form of action by the city government and by the courts. Governmental actions against academics later became widespread in the United States, during the decade and a half of the era of McCarthyism. A number of anthropologists were among the academics harassed by the FBI or the legislative committees hunting for alleged political subversives. This was in part because activist anthropologists had been promoting to the general public the scientific view that race was a social construct. Some of these scholars were also leftists politically, but subsequently released FBI files documented the agency's additional specific interest in their opposition to racism. For example, anthropologist Ashley Montagu was dismissed by Rutgers University, ostensibly for public criticism of Senator McCarthy, but the FBI continued to monitor his anti-racism activities for many years afterward.

In the 1890s and for several decades afterward, a number of economists were in the vanguard of social and political change. They challenged laissez-faire doctrines, argued that the state should protect the interests of the general public and not only those of the wealthy, and "looked upon the study of economics as a way of defending public interests."[7] In more recent times, many economists have been in the vanguard of a movement that is having the effect of taking American society back toward the 1890s, through promotion of another doctrine, neoliberalism, which also is a construct of social scientists.

Thus times change, and so do academic disciplines. The historiography of Israel/Palestine and the wider Middle East is another example. It is the subject of active research and current teaching in Israel and elsewhere, but in parts of North American society there still prevails what the late Professor Tony Judt called "widespread ignorance" about Israel/Palestine, maintained by a "taboo" against critical discussion.[8]

The importance of academic freedom was emphasized by York University President Mamdouh Shoukri and Board Chairs Marshall Cohen and Paul Cantor in their public statement in defence of the conference, issued a week before it opened. Noting that the conference topics were discussed in Israel and elsewhere, the York administrative leaders said, "There is no reason why they should not be discussed in Toronto."[9]

However, the controversy over the conference suggests that many people, including some York University professors, do not have an adequate understanding or appreciation of the right to academic freedom in the Canada of our time. Many people also are either unaware of, or do not agree with, the results of some research on Israel/Palestine during recent decades, in such disciplines as history, political science, literary criticism, anthropology, and archaeology, including studies on the role of myth, tradition, and ideology in the political life of Israel/Palestine.

As disciplines develop and evolve, inevitably, as in any human enterprise, some scholarship is unduly coloured by tendentiousness, or even, occasionally, spuriousness. Either detection of unduly tendentious scholarship or exposure of spurious scholarship may bring denunciations or attempts at retaliation in one form or another. This is another reason why the right to academic freedom is important.

OUTLINE OF THE REPORT

Examples of research in the social sciences and humanities relevant to matters under review in this Inquiry are outlined in Chapters 2 and 3. Chapter 2 looks at influential research that has challenged received opinion and at aspects of the Israel lobby in the United States and in Canada, including

efforts to limit academic debate. Historical and recent discussions on one-
and two-state models for Israel/Palestine are outlined in Chapter 3.

Events pertaining to the conference and the controversy are reviewed
in Chapters 4, 5, 6, and 7: planning; funding support; the controversy as
it was manifested, especially in regard to events at York University; the
involvement of the government and SSHRC; and the conference itself and
subsequent discussion of it.

Chapter 8 outlines the historical development of the right to academic
freedom currently enjoyed by Canadian professors, in part to clarify the
difference between the effective conception of this right in Canada as compared to that prevailing in the United States, and in part to emphasize its
fragility and the constant need for vigilance and robust means of protection. It also examines how recent political changes have undermined liberal democratic structures that were developed during the several decades
following the Second World War. The implications are diverse and profound, and their increasingly adverse effects on universities, academic freedom, and academic integrity are of particular interest here. Prospects for
restoring a measure of political balance, strengthening academic freedom,
and protecting academic integrity depend on a wider appreciation—inside
the academy as well as outside—of the confluence of political currents
that brought about these electoral shifts in the United States, Canada, and
elsewhere.

Chapter 9 includes a discussion of actions and statements by certain
university administrators and by members of the conference organizing
committee, as well as discussion of the involvements of the government
and SSHRC. The report on the controversy written by Frank Iacobucci
for York University also is discussed. My conclusions related to the terms
of reference of the Inquiry are presented in that chapter. Chapter 10 lists
lessons to be drawn from the events and makes recommendations.

Cited email texts are reproduced as they were provided to this Inquiry.

2

RESEARCH IN THE SOCIAL SCIENCES AND HUMANITIES

THE SOCIAL SCIENCES AND HUMANITIES RESEARCH COUNCIL (SSHRC)

In Canada, three federal agencies provide financial support for research in universities on a peer-review basis: the Canadian Institutes for Health Research (CIHR), the Natural Sciences and Engineering Research Council (NSERC), and the Social Sciences and Humanities Research Council (SSHRC). They are arm's-length agencies, receiving annual funding though the budgets of the government ministries through which they report to Parliament (Health Canada in the case of CIHR, and Industry Canada in the cases of NSERC and SSHRC).

NSERC and SSHRC were created through Bill C-26, which came into force on May 1, 1978. The legislation arose from a review (1968–1973) of the state of research and development in Canada by the Senate Special Committee on Science Policy, chaired by Senator Maurice Lamontagne. The committee recommended that responsibility for supporting university research be transferred from existing agencies—the National Research Council in the case of science and engineering, the Canada Council in the case of social sciences and humanities—to two new agencies, and that the mandates of the older councils be revised. CIHR was created in 2000, through legislation transforming the Medical Research Council.

It is clear from the record of discussions on Bill C-26 in Parliament and in its committees that SSHRC and NSERC were to be arm's-length agencies. During second reading on December 13, 1976, James Faulkner, Minister of State for Science and Technology, said:

We have very much kept in mind [...] the environment of
continuity and freedom which is required for the fullest exercise
of creativity in research. That is why we are fully committed
to retain the "peer review system"; we will not jeopardize the
expertise and independence with which the councils support,
and scholars perform, research. At the same time, we have
sought to provide mechanisms by which eminent scholars in
the disciplines being supported will oversee the granting process
and will advise the government as to how university research
may more effectively support national goals. I hasten to add
that any approach which seeks arbitrarily to impose specific
objectives or priorities on the research community from outside
will not be a productive one and will not be instituted.[1]

Before Bill C-26 was referred to the Standing Committee on Miscellaneous
Estimates during the second reading, Progressive Conservative MP Ray
Hnatyshyn requested clarification and assurance that the term "agent of Her
Majesty" in the bill did not imply the possibility of "interference with the
Council,"[2] and the Trudeau government subsequently gave such assurances.

The current government of Prime Minister Stephen Harper has stated
that SSHRC, in particular, is an arm's-length agency. For example, included
in a list of points ("Media Lines") approved by the Privy Council Office
in October 2009 for public distribution (in response to questions about
the SSHRC grant to the York/Queen's conference in June) is the statement:
"Let me assure you that the government is committed to the principle of
academic independence and the independent, arm's-length, peer-review
process for assessing applications for research grants."[3]

The president of SSHRC also confirmed, in a letter to the executive director of CAUT dated June 16, 2009, that SSHRC is an arm's-length peer-
review agency. In the same vein, Tony Clement, the Minister for Industry
Canada, wrote in reply to a letter from a person concerned about the York/
Queen's conference:

I would like to assure you that maintaining a fair and efficient
system of peer review at the federal granting councils is very
important to us. Peer review helps to ensure that we fund
the best initiatives and that the process of adjudication is
objective. [...] I am fully supportive of SSHRC's commitment to
independent peer review, its grant policies and procedures, as

well as its ethical and legal standards.[4]

These assurances were issued after the government's interference with SSHRC, so their value may reasonably be questioned. All of the three granting agencies are governed by a council, headed by a chair and a president. During the events pertaining to the York/Queen's conference, Thomas Kierans was the chair of SSHRC and Chad Gaffield the president. A full list of the council members can be found at www.sshrc.ca.

IMPORTANCE TO SOCIETY

For many years all three Canadian research granting councils have been underfunded in relation to their counterparts in other advanced countries. Of the three councils, SSHRC has the smallest annual budget, and it has long been an aspiration of the SSHRC research community to obtain increased funding.

Various reasons have been suggested for the funding disparity between SSHRC and the other two councils. Some say research in medicine and science is inherently more expensive to conduct, so CIHR and NSERC need larger budgets. Others say that the disparity results mainly because almost everyone can name a few advances in science, engineering, or medicine that have brought widely appreciated benefits (military advantage, corporate profits, improved health, or personal convenience), whereas such advances and benefits are harder to identify in the social sciences and humanities.

Still others say that research in the social sciences and humanities is largely irrelevant or, worse, dangerous. For example, newspaper columnist Margaret Wente wrote, "some research, especially in the sciences and medicine, matters a great deal to the advancement of society. But a vast amount of it—especially in the humanities and social sciences—does not."[5] In his 2005 Goethe Prize lecture, Israeli writer Amos Oz alleged that the social sciences have had a pernicious effect on our world:

> Somewhere in the nineteenth century, not long after Goethe's demise, a new mode of thought made its way into Western civilization that put Evil to one side and even negated its very existence. This intellectual innovation came to be known as "the social sciences." [...] In the eyes of this school, uncompromisingly rational, optimistic, wonderfully sophisticated—psychology, sociology, anthropology and the economic sciences—Evil does

not exist. And in fact neither does Good.[6]

Thus Oz brought together two of the main currents of the growing anti-Enlightenment sentiment of our time: opposition to the social sciences, and nostalgia.

The modern disciplines of the social sciences and humanities evolved from developments in the Age of Enlightenment that, on the contrary, *did* lead to identification of evils, notably those related to social inequality or political powerlessness, such as racism, colonialism, sexism, and religious persecution. They also contributed to development of ways to combat such evils, along with criteria for defining good. Thus research in the humanities and social sciences matters a great deal to the advancement of society. By way of contrast, in the lost paradise of the religious world apparently lamented by Oz, evils such as anti-Semitism were not identified as such. In Christendom, anti-Semitism often was encouraged, and at other times not significantly discouraged—as instances from the Mainz massacre of 1096 to the Kishinev pogrom of 1903 and on through the Holocaust demonstrate.

Research in the social sciences or humanities can help bring about social or political change that is sorely needed, or can help consolidate positive transformations already well advanced. It can also be a harbinger of change before there is widespread appreciation of the need. Often such change is highly controversial and strongly resisted—and bitterly resented when it occurs.

EXAMPLES OF RESEARCH

I would like to highlight three examples of influential research relevant to this Inquiry, each of which challenged conventional wisdom or shed new light on an important topic not fully explored.

An American Dilemma. As noted in Chapter 1, a statehood model for Israel/Palestine in which all citizens would have equal rights was a source of controversy for the York/Queen's conference. Equality rights have long been controversial and have been the subject of academic study. One of the most significant and far-reaching research projects in any academic discipline in the twentieth century was on equality rights and the effects of severe inequality in a specific context. It was conducted by the Swedish political economist Gunnar Myrdal, who was commissioned because he was an outsider to the particular field of study, independent, and noted for his high standard of scholarship.

Published in 1944 as *An American Dilemma: The Negro Problem and*

Modern Democracy, Myrdal's study described the appalling social, political, and economic conditions of African-Americans, analyzed the causes, and proposed ways of addressing the problems. It concluded:

> The main international implication is [...] that America, for its international prestige, power, and future security, needs to demonstrate to the world that American Negroes can be satisfactorily integrated into its democracy.[7]

The study was commissioned by a private foundation, the Carnegie Corporation, which had been funding research in eugenics, a field of study then widely considered to provide a scientific basis for racism. However, by the late 1930s there was a growing appreciation that America's treatment of its black citizens was undermining its growing aspirations for international leadership.

Myrdal was recruited from Sweden, even though "there was no lack of competent scholars in the United States who were deeply interested in the problem and had already devoted themselves to its study."[8] The board of the Carnegie Corporation sought "as the responsible head of the undertaking someone who could approach his task with a fresh mind, uninfluenced by traditional attitudes or by earlier conclusions."[9]

Myrdal's extensive report was widely read and influential. It helped inspire the American civil rights movement, and was cited in the landmark school desegregation ruling by the United States Supreme Court (*Brown v. Board of Education*, 1954). To some extent, the ground had been prepared for its public reception by the scientific work of Franz Boas and his school of anthropology at Columbia University. The 1942 book *Man's Most Dangerous Myth: The Fallacy of Race* by Boas's former student Ashley Montagu, "established and popularized the anthropological framework of race as a social construct."[10]

Myrdal's report was followed in the international context by the 1948 UN *Universal Declaration of Human Rights*, and the 1950 UNESCO *Statement by Experts on Race Problems* (drafted by prominent biological and social scientists—including Montagu and Myrdal). The *Statement by Experts* declared racism immoral.

During the quarter century following publication of *An American Dilemma*, prodigious efforts by many courageous individuals, civil rights organizations, and successive American governments to address problems Myrdal had identified met with widespread resistance, including

sometimes murderous violence. Nevertheless, significant democratic integration was achieved during this period.

The changes brought about in the decades following Myrdal's report
were profound, including the development of a substantial black middle
class and, most recently, election of the first black citizen as president.
However, a strong political reaction against such changes began to develop
in the 1970s, and it went on to form a substantial component of the political constituency now known as the conservative movement.[11]

None Is Too Many. An example of research helping to consolidate a
social transformation already well advanced is the study *None Is Too Many*
by historians Irving Abella and Harold Troper, work that was supported by
SSHRC. Published in 1983, a year after enactment of the *Canadian Charter
of Rights and Freedoms*, this work gave special point to the provisions of
Section 15 (1) on equality rights and freedom from discrimination.

Abella and Troper documented the failures by western countries,
Canada among them, to assist European Jews in escaping from the Nazi
regime, while the intense persecution that began in the 1930s progressed
through the Holocaust. The authors showed that indifference to the plight
of European Jews was due to widespread anti-Semitism.

The book contains many compelling illustrations, including the spring
1939 voyage of the *St. Louis* with more than nine hundred German Jews
on board who hoped to find refuge in the Americas. After every country in
Latin America refused entry, the United States Coast Guard was "ordered
to make certain that the *St. Louis* stayed far enough off shore so that it
could not be run aground nor any of its frantic passengers swim ashore."
Canada was their last hope, but senior government officials also refused
entry, on the basis that "Canada had already done too much for the Jews,"
and that, "the line must be drawn somewhere." As a result, "the Jews of
the *St. Louis* headed back to Europe, where many would die in the gas
chambers and crematoria of the Third Reich."[12]

During the war, the Canadian government was informed by groups
representing Jewish citizens, as well as by the British and American governments, of the mass extermination of Jews by the Nazis, and was made
aware that even modest interventions could help save lives. For instance,
a 1944 telegram to the Department of External Affairs sent by Samuel
Bronfman of the Canadian Jewish Congress said:

> Implore Canadian government to instruct Canadian
> representative [to the Intergovernmental Committee on

Refugees] to offer some measure of participation in rescue
scheme for our compatriots trapped in Nazi area and for rescue
of children in those and contiguous countries. Indifference to
the fate of these refugees will fully sign their death warrants.[13]

Despite being provided with such information, the Canadian government remained largely unresponsive, in part because of anti-Semitic
sentiment among the majority of the voting public and in part because of
the personal views of senior officials. Abella and Troper concluded, "The
Jewish community was not an important part of the domestic power equa-
tion. It had no leverage."[14]

Anti-Semitism continued to be widespread in the Americas and Europe
even after the extent of the Holocaust became known, with the result that
British-controlled Palestine was the only viable refuge for many of the
European Jews who had survived. After the establishment of the State of
Israel in 1948, and changes in social and political circumstances in North
America over the next few decades, Jewish organizations eventually did
develop significant political leverage in the United States and Canada, and
influential pro-Israel lobbying organizations emerged.

The Israel Lobby. John J. Mearsheimer and Stephen M. Walt's 2007 book
The Israel Lobby and U.S. Foreign Policy may be a harbinger of a significant
transformation still in its infancy. Their thesis is that central elements of
America's foreign policy have for too long been excessively influenced by
a loose but powerful coalition of individuals and groups they called the
Israel lobby. They concluded that "the lobby's political clout and public
relations acumen have discouraged U.S. leaders from pursuing Middle East
policies that would advance American interests and protect Israel from
its worst mistakes. The lobby's influence, in short, has been bad for both
countries."[15] They presented a straightforward solution: "Treat Israel as a
normal state [... such as] France, Thailand, or Mexico."[16]

The views set forth by Mearsheimer and Walt were not original.[17] The
novelty lay in their being expressed by conservative academics occupying
prestigious posts, who otherwise supported the main thrust of American
foreign policy in the post–World War II era. They described in meticulous-
ly referenced detail the components of the lobby (certain Jewish-American
organizations, such as the American Israel Public Affairs Committee,
along with some prominent Christian evangelicals and influential neoconservative politicians, and their supporters), its modes of operation
in Washington and in universities across the country, the reasons for its

extraordinary influence, and its political effects.

The origins of the book illustrate both its harbinger aspect and the operation of the lobby. In late 2002, with the war on Iraq looming, Mearsheimer and Walt were invited by the *Atlantic Monthly* (a magazine long in sympathy with establishment views) to write an article on the Israel lobby. They agreed, and the article was developed "over the next two years in close collaboration with the *Atlantic's* editors," but when they submitted it, "to [their] surprise," the magazine refused to publish it.[18] Later, the *London Review of Books* (*LRB*), whose editor, Mary-Kay Wilmers, is Jewish, did publish it.

The article appeared in the *LRB* issue dated March 23, 2006, and simultaneously the authors posted a fully documented version as a working paper on the website of Harvard's John F. Kennedy School of Government, where Walt was then dean. "The response to the essay was breathtaking. By July 2006, the Kennedy School's website had recorded more than 275,000 downloads [...] the essay initially generated a firestorm of criticism from [...] the lobby, and we were denounced as anti-Semites by the Anti-Defamation League and by op-ed writers" in various newspapers, including the *Wall Street Journal*.[19] Over the course of 2006, a serious debate emerged, as a "growing number of people seemed to realize this subject needed airing."[20] Mearsheimer and Walt then decided to expand the article into a book, to provide more detail on the lobby's operation and to answer their many critics more comprehensively. They described the frequent, casual, yet devastating use of "smear tactics" by some individuals and groups in the lobby, notably the charge of anti-Semitism, which they call "the Great Silencer."[21] For example, when former US President Jimmy Carter's book *Palestine: Peace Not Apartheid* appeared in 2006, he was denounced as an anti-Semite, and his views were compared to those of a leader of the Ku Klux Klan.[22]

In their 2006 working paper, Mearsheimer and Walt had outlined the lobby's tactics:

> No discussion of how the lobby operates would be complete
> without examining one of its most powerful weapons: the
> charge of anti-Semitism. Anyone who criticizes Israel's actions
> or says that pro-Israel groups have significant influence over
> U.S. Middle East policy—an influence that AIPAC celebrates—
> stands a good chance of getting labelled an anti-Semite. In fact,
> anyone who says that there is an Israel Lobby runs the risk of
> being charged with anti-Semitism, even though the Israel media

themselves refer to America's "Jewish Lobby." In effect, the Lobby boasts of its own power and then attacks anyone who calls attention to it.[23]

The issue is not lobbying *per se*. Mearsheimer and Walt accept that "most of [the Israel lobby's] tactics are reasonable and simply part of the normal rough-and-tumble that is the essence of democratic politics":

> Unfortunately, some pro-Israel individuals and groups have occasionally taken their defence of Israel to illegitimate extremes, attempting to silence individuals who hold views they dislike. This endeavour can involve intimidating and smearing critics of Israel, or even attempting to damage or wreck their careers.[24]

They also wrote that "the charge of anti-Semitism remains a widely used weapon for dealing with critics of Israel, especially in the United States," and listed the reasons for its effectiveness: i) anti-Semitism has "led to great evils in the past, including the monstrous crimes of the Holocaust, and it is now utterly discredited in most segments of society"; ii) "smearing critics of Israel or the lobby with the charge of anti-Semitism works to marginalize them in the public arena"; and iii) "this tactic works because it is difficult for anyone to prove beyond all doubt that he or she is not anti-Semitic, especially when criticizing Israel or the lobby. Proving a negative is hard to do under any circumstances."

Furthermore, "The accusation is likely to resonate among American Jews, many of whom still believe anti-Semitism is rife," because of their awareness of historical persecution, "magnified by the role that the Holocaust plays in the attitudes of a significant number of Jewish Americans," so that many "still worry that virulent anti-Semitism could return at any time." Summarizing, the authors stated:

> Let us be clear: anti-Semitism is a despicable phenomenon with a long and tragic history, and all people should remain vigilant against its resurgence and condemn it when it arises. [...] But it is essential that we distinguish between true anti-Semitism and legitimate criticism of Israeli policy, because blurring them makes it harder to fight true bigotry and makes it more difficult to intelligently discuss U.S. foreign policy.[25]

Several scholars have observed recurring claims of resurgent anti-Semitism—sometimes called the new anti-Semitism or the real anti-Semitism—in the United States and elsewhere. Mearsheimer and Walt have documented that such claims have been "alarmist," and that supporters of Israel "have a history of using fears of a 'new anti-Semitism' to shield Israel from criticism."[26]

In a talk given in 2002, Noam Chomsky observed that the use of the charge of anti-Semitism for political purposes was not new:

> With regard to anti-Semitism, the distinguished Israeli statesman
> Abba Eban pointed out the main task of Israeli propaganda [...]
> is to make it clear to the world there's no difference between
> anti-Semitism and anti-Zionism. By anti-Zionism he meant
> criticisms of the current policies of the State of Israel. So there's
> no difference between criticism of policies of the State of Israel
> and anti-Semitism, because if he can establish 'that' then he can
> undercut all criticism by invoking the Nazis and that will silence
> people. We should bear it in mind when there's talk in the US
> about anti-Semitism.[27]

Canada, too, has an Israel lobby, similar to its much larger American counterpart in composition and methods of operation. Under the successive governments of Paul Martin and Steven Harper, Canadian foreign policy became more closely aligned with that of the United States than in any other time during the preceding half-century. During the same period, the Canadian Israel lobby became more significant in this country and its political leverage is now substantial.[28]

ATTACKS ON ACADEMIC FREEDOM

In the broader North American context, neither the concerted opposition to the York/Queen's conference on Israel/Palestine nor the particular ways in which it was manifested were new. In 2007, several prominent American scholars (three historians, a sociologist, and an anthropologist) formed an Ad Hoc Committee to Defend the University and organized a petition as a way of responding publicly to attacks on academic freedom.[29] The petition stated:

> In recent years, universities across the country have been targeted

by outside groups seeking to influence what is taught and who can teach. To achieve their political agendas, these groups have defamed scholars, pressured administrators, and tried to bypass or subvert established procedures of academic governance. [...] These attacks threaten academic freedom and the core mission of institutions of higher education in a democratic society. Unfortunately and ironically, many of the most vociferous campaigns targeting universities and their faculty have been launched by groups portraying themselves as defenders of Israel. These groups have targeted scholars who have expressed perspectives on Israeli policies and the Israeli Palestinian conflict with which they disagree. To silence those they consider their political enemies, they have used a range of tactics such as:

- unfounded insinuations and allegations, in the media and on websites, of anti-Semitism or sympathy for terrorism or 'un-Americanism';

- efforts to broaden definitions of anti-Semitism to include scholarship and teaching that is critical of U.S. foreign policy in the Middle East and of Israel; [...]

- and demands in the name of "balance" and "diversity" that those with whom they disagree be prevented from speaking unless paired with someone whose viewpoint they approve of.[30]

The petition also noted that, "A study by a Harvard sociologist last summer found that 'a greater percentage of social scientists today feels their academic freedom has been threatened than was the case during the McCarthy era,'" and concluded, "It is time to defend the norms of scholarship and the best traditions of the academy."[31] It urged scholars to undertake a public information campaign with administrators, students, and the general public on the importance of academic freedom.

IDEOLOGY IN SCHOLARSHIP

Some critics of the York/Queen's conference expressed views to the effect that Zionist ideology, or its implications, or political agendas based on it, could not be subjected to criticism beyond certain limits. Some critics denounced certain conference speakers as ideological. Ideologies, along with individual biases, are inevitable in scholarship—even in disciplines such as mathematics or physics—and in human life in general. Every ideology—no matter how significant or fruitful—has its limitations.[32]

Whether significantly influenced by particular ideologies or not, scholars may differ on interpretation or explanation of essentially the same set of facts or circumstances. For example, historians A. J. P. Taylor and Hugh Trevor-Roper held strong and strongly differing views on the rise of Hitler and the origins of the Second World War, but both perspectives were illuminating. Historian Fritz Stern, who had reviewed many of Taylor's works "with meticulous appreciation," said that "to argue with his work was a bracing exercise."[33] The recent trilogy *The Third Reich* by Richard J. Evans and the 2011 book *Nazi Empire* by Shelley Baranowski show that these topics are of continuing scholarly interest and controversy.

There has also been controversy over Jewish history and the history of Zionist ideology, sparked in part by works of historians Ze'ev Sternhell, Gabriel Piterberg, and Shlomo Sand, all of whom have published works challenging academic orthodoxy. For example, Sternhell wrote:

> The view that Jewish history is a separate area of study has already had many negative results, but in twentieth-century history and especially the history of Zionism, its consequences have been truly appalling. Very often this approach has paralyzed any real critical sense and any effort at comparative analysis, has perpetuated myths flattering to Israel's collective identity, and has led many historians of Zionism to lock themselves up in an intellectual ghetto where there are no means of comparison or criteria of universal validity. Such exclusiveness can lead to ignorance.[34]

Sometimes biases or ideologies—whether inadvertent or otherwise—can adversely affect the development of a discipline or the public interest. For example, scientific discoveries such as oscillating chemical reactions, moving tectonic plates, or the bacterial origins of many peptic ulcers were initially denied by leading authorities despite compelling empirical evidence. In extreme cases, biases or ideologies can facilitate scholarship that is not simply tendentious but spurious.

Among the sometimes adverse external influences on some disciplines

is the availability of large funding resources from public or private sources
for research work promoting or subservient to specific political or commercial agendas. The corruption of substantial parts of modern academic medicine by the influence over and, increasingly, control of clinical trials by private, for-profit corporations has been widely discussed in books and articles
published during the past decade by experts, as well as through reports in
the media. Another current phenomenon is the growing body of misleading
scientific literature minimizing the dangers of climate change, funded by
petrochemical and related industries. This is a development similar to the
large body of misleading scientific literature funded by the tobacco industry
that minimized the health risks of smoking. The attempt by the George W.
Bush administration to silence climatologist James Hansen (an employee
of a federal government agency) was another aspect of such phenomena.

There are historical examples of coercion by the state: Lysenkoism in
biology and agriculture in the USSR of Stalin, and the influences of Nazism
on many disciplines in Germany under Hitler, are well known. However,
tendentious research supporting state agendas need not be overtly coerced—
many German scholars willingly embraced Nazism. More generally, some
scholars have willingly served as "intellectual managers," internalizing state
propaganda and promoting it, as Noam Chomsky has noted:

> As these examples [from American foreign policy studies]
> illustrate, there are few limits to the capacity of respected Western
> intellectuals to interpret brutality, atrocities and racist horrors as
> exemplifying the highest values and noblest intentions.[35]

There also are influences internal to a discipline, such the hegemonic
influences of senior figures or academic organizations on the career
progress prospects of individuals. Although such influences are normally
benign, in some instances the result has been retarded or arrested development of a field. The adverse effects such influences have sometimes had—
in disciplines as diverse as psychiatry and economics—have been sufficiently significant as to attract critical discussion by distinguished scholars.[36] Finally, there also are individual and collective biases not necessarily
related to coercions or rewards in direct or obvious ways, and these may
contribute to incorrect findings. A recent article in the New Yorker outlined
a substantial number of instances in which published findings in behav-
ioural sciences (such as psychiatry or ethology)—acclaimed when they first
appeared—were later found not to be reproducible.[37]

3
ONE- AND TWO-STATE MODELS

ONE STATE OR TWO?

Subsequent to the 1993 Oslo Accords between the government of Israel and the Palestine Liberation Organization (PLO), under which the Palestinian National Authority (PNA) was created, international discourse focused on a two-state model for Israel/Palestine.[1] Under the Accords, Israel was to grant increasing levels of self-government to the PNA in the West Bank and the Gaza Strip over several years, while negotiations commenced on a range of critical issues, such as borders. In the minds of many, this solution would result in two viable, sovereign states: Israel and Palestine, with territory of the latter comprising the West Bank (including East Jerusalem) and the Gaza Strip, except for modest, mutually agreed upon adjustments to borders as they had stood prior to the Six-Day War of 1967.

A massacre of worshippers in a mosque in Hebron in 1994 and the assassination in 1995 of Israeli Prime Minister Yitzhak Rabin (committed by Jewish Israeli extremists) did not augur well for a peace settlement. Several years after these events, with prospects for a two-state solution still unrealized, there developed a growing interest in the question of whether a single, secular, bi-national state would be feasible—the type of one-state model emphasized by the organizers of the York/Queen's conference. This was not a new idea. Before 1947, when the United Kingdom announced it would withdraw from the Mandate of Palestine and the United Nations decided on partition, some members of the Jewish community in Palestine had been promoting the concept of a single, bi-national state. Their minority view did not prevail, but they put forward cogent arguments now being revisited in the international scholarly community.[2]

COMPETING IDEOLOGIES

The controversy over the York/Queen's conference (and similar controversies over academic events in the United States and elsewhere) can reasonably be viewed as involving competing ideologies: Zionism versus equality rights. As earlier noted, the latter concept arose out of the intellectual environment of the Enlightenment, when universal human rights were first cogently articulated and promoted. Zionism also arose (partially) from the Enlightenment. As historian Arno J. Mayer observed:

> The theorists and public intellectuals of the Enlightenment of
> the eighteenth and nineteenth century were sensitive to the
> disabilities affecting, respectively, French Protestants and Russian
> Jews. [...] The battle against religious intolerance was a vital part
> of the battle against autocracy and obscurantism.[3]

One of the Enlightenment's consequences from the French Revolution onward was the emancipation of Jewish people, first in France, but later also in some other parts of the West, including Germany during the late nineteenth and early twentieth centuries. In France, the Constituent Assembly gave civic rights to some Jewish populations in early 1790, a month after it gave them to Protestants, and extended these rights to remaining Jewish populations in 1791. As historian Georges Lefebvre observed, the French Revolution emphasized equality rights to a greater extent than the earlier revolutions in England and America.[4]

Enlightenment ideals influenced Theodor Herzl, the father of modern political Zionism, who envisaged "a democratic state and open society" based on some Western models of his time. In this vision of a secular state "there was little, if any, place for the Arabs of Palestine."[5] Recent scholarship suggests additional intellectual and cultural influences on Herzl, including the organic nationalism of Central and Eastern Europe, and Protestant traditions. Noam Chomsky has written that "Christian Zionism long precede[d] Jewish Zionism."[6]

Farther east in Europe and in Russia, where Jewish populations were larger, severe and sometimes violent repression continued—not only before, but immediately after the First World War—along with growing nationalist consciousness of the organic type. Although the Russian Revolution emancipated Europe's largest Jewish population, counter-revolutionary groups opposed to the Bolsheviks persecuted and scapegoated Jews, often accusing them of social and political radicalism and of weak allegiance to the states in which they lived. Similar events occurred in former Hapsburg domains. Arno J. Mayer observed:

> In several important respects the large-scale killing of Jews in the Russian Civil War and in the national struggles following the collapse of the Romanov and Hapsburg empires foreshadowed the mass murder of Jews during the Second World War.[7]

After consolidation of the communist regime in post–civil war Russia, and during the first few decades of the USSR, Jews were integrated into society, for a combination of political, economic, and military reasons, as Mayer outlined.

After the First World War substantial integration of Jews continued in Germany, following emancipatory trends from the late nineteenth century, and a number of the political, scientific, cultural, and economic leaders of the Weimar Republic were Jewish. However, Jewish people were increasingly scapegoated by conservative reactionaries nostalgic for the pre-war *Reich*. The assassination of foreign minister Walter Rathenau was an early manifestation of strong anti-Semitic currents in post-war German society. Mayer (who has written extensively on the persistence of pre-war European political elites during the inter-war period) noted that in Germany "the cleavages in the power elites," between "flexible conservatives and intransigent reactionaries," eventually led to "an uneasy relationship with outright counterrevolutionaries." As a result, "Rather than disavow or denounce the theory and practice of nascent fascism, the old elites condoned and encouraged it in light of their own needs and interests."[8]

Then came the rise of Hitler, whose government—after its swift and brutal suppression of the political left—moved on to the persecution of German Jews. This campaign was accompanied by sporadic but growing violence against them, progressing to systematic mass murder across Europe and the occupied USSR during the Second World War. Ze'ev Sternhell has noted the efforts after World War II by certain conservative Western intellectuals to minimize the role conservative reactionaries and political elites, along with religion, played in the rise of Nazism:

> By making Nazism a reflection of communism and a legitimate
> response to the Bolshevik danger, by cutting it off from its
> ideological and cultural roots, by laying undue stress on the
> role of the Führer, Nazism could be virtually excised from the
> [German] national history.[9]

Mayer noted key political factors during the months when Hitler was offered and accepted the position of chancellor and formed a coalition government:

> The most crucial of these contingencies was the deep-seated
> convergence of interests between, on the one hand, the cartel
> of traditional conservatives and reactionaries, and, on the
> other hand, Hitler and the National Socialist movement. [...]
> a combination of anti-communism and ultra-nationalism
> constituted the brick and mortar for the factitious collaboration
> between Nazism and conservatism in both civil and political
> society.[10]

Both Mayer and Fritz Stern have noted the sophisticated use Hitler made of German national symbols, myths, and traditions, including religious beliefs. Mayer's study led him to conclude that "by and large, Germany's Christian churches acted to consecrate Hitler's crusade against the east," and he suggested the code name Barbarossa for the campaign against Soviet Russia "was heavy with symbolic significance."[11] Stern observed:

> God had been drafted into national politics before, but Hitler's
> success in fusing racial dogma with a Germanic Christianity
> was an immensely powerful element in his electoral campaigns.
> Some people recognized the moral perils of mixing religion
> and politics, but many more were seduced by it. It was the
> pseudo-religious transfiguration of politics that largely ensured
> his success, notably in the Protestant areas, where clergy shared
> Hitler's hostility to the liberal-secular state and its defenders, and
> were filled with anti-Semitic doctrine. [...] resentment against
> a disenchanted secular world found deliverance in the ecstatic
> escape of unreason. German elites proved susceptible to this
> mystical brew of pseudo-religion and disguised interest.[12]

Elsewhere, Stern outlined similarities between the world-view promoted by Hitler and that of Kaiser Wilhelm II, who regarded the First World War "as a struggle between good and evil," declaring, "'God wants this struggle and we are His instruments.'" After it became clear that the war had been lost, the Kaiser concluded there had been betrayal. "Until his death in exile in 1941, the Kaiser spread venomous poison where he could: the Jews were to blame, as were the socialists—he alone was right. [...] he saw in Hitler the new man chosen by providence, a savior after the treachery that had caused Germany's defeat."[13]

Mayer identified factors in the rise and successes of the Zionist program, from Europe in the 1890s to the Middle East from the 1920s onward:

> Zionism was born out of violence, not God or a golden vision: the physical and psychological violence of the pogroms in czarist Russia, and the rhetorical violence surrounding the Dreyfus Affair in Republican France and Karl Lueger's related municipal reign in Imperial Vienna; then, the physical, psychological, and symbolic violence of the Zionist settlement in Arab–Muslim Palestine, a variant on the polymorphous violence of imperialist Europe's increasingly contested civilizing mission overseas.[14]

Scholars have sought to characterize and explain the current political culture of the State of Israel. The complexity of the past and present may be illustrated by the views of Sternhell. He strongly defends Enlightenment principles as essential for the preservation of modern civilization:

> Fascism was an extreme expression of the Anti-Enlightenment tradition; Nazism was a total assault on the human race. Here one sees the significance that the rejection of universal values and humanism, that cornerstone of Enlightenment thought, can have for a whole civilization. For the first time, Europe endowed itself with regimes and political movements whose aim was nothing less than the destruction of the culture of the Enlightenment, its principles and its intellectual and political structures.[15]

Sternhell also strongly defends liberal Zionism and the establishment of the State of Israel within its pre-1967 borders, concluding from the historical events summarized above that "the conquest of the land was thus an existential necessity."[16]

BRITISH WAR AIMS AND THE BALFOUR DECLARATION

During the First World War, the British government made three successive commitments regarding post-war disposition of territory of the Ottoman Empire: in 1915, a promise to Sharif Hussein of Mecca to support an independent Arab state (the McMahon–Hussein correspondence); in 1916, an agreement with France to divide the Middle East into British and French spheres of influence (the Sykes–Picot agreement); and in 1917, a promise to use "its best endeavours" to facilitate the establishment "in Palestine of a national home for the Jewish people [...] it being clearly understood that nothing shall be done which may prejudice the civil and religious rights of existing non-Jewish communities in Palestine" (the Balfour Declaration).

Briefly, the 1915 promise to Sharif Hussein was made in order to encourage an Arab revolt against the Ottoman Empire, and the Sharif fulfilled his part of the bargain. However, in the same year Britain, France, and Russia began discussions on an arrangement under which they would carve up Ottoman territory into zones under their control or influence. An agreement was reached in 1916, negotiated mainly by Sir Mark Sykes and François Georges-Picot for Britain and France, and, with minor amendments, assented to by Russia. Aspects of this initially secret agreement began to leak out from French and British sources in spring 1917, and in May the new Russian government led by A. F. Kerensky effectively withdrew from it. The successor Bolshevik government published details of the Sykes–Picot agreement in December 1917. Meanwhile, Chaim Weizmann and Nahum Sokolow, the leading proponents in Britain of Theodor Herzl's Zionist program, had achieved in discussions with the British government what they regarded as a success: the declaration by Foreign Secretary A. J. Balfour. The declaration was approved by the British War Cabinet at the end of October and published several days later.

Palestine was in the intersection of Ottoman territory allotted through these three commitments, and there have been political and scholarly disagreements about their meaning—and relative priority—ever since.[17] Jonathan Schneer provided a detailed account of the three commitments in *The Balfour Declaration*. He also described efforts by Prime Minister David Lloyd George to pursue a fourth arrangement: a proposal for a separate peace with the Ottoman government, an offer his emissary, wealthy arms dealer Basil Zaharoff, conveyed in early 1918. The proposal included a substantial bribe to Ottoman leader Ismail Enver (Enver Pasha) and continued Ottoman control over Palestine. Such arrangements had been opposed by some government officials (Sykes, Curzon, Balfour) when first

discussed seriously in late 1917, but "British officials made sure that neither Weizmann nor Hussein heard anything about them."[18]

In January 1918, notwithstanding Foreign Office opposition, the prime
minister authorized Zaharoff to convey the offer to Enver Pasha. The offer
ultimately was not accepted, so that the Balfour Declaration "seems to
have just missed the side track," and "what might have happened then is
anybody's guess."[19] Israeli historian Benny Morris summarized the background of British considerations leading to the Balfour Declaration and
its relation to the Sykes–Picot agreement: "The sorry state of the Allies in
1917 [...] was a major factor propelling Britain to issue [...] the Balfour
Declaration," citing the lack of Allied progress on the Western Front,
concerns that Russia would abandon the war, and "a desire to prod the
United States into a fuller commitment to the Allied cause," along with
a desire "to counter French claims to Palestine." He added the clarification that "Britain and France came to believe that rallying American Jews
to their cause would help bring the United States into the war and keep
Russia involved." Morris also cited a comment by Edward Mandell House,
an advisor to President Woodrow Wilson: "It is all bad and I told Balfour
so. They are making the [Middle East] a breeding place for future war."[20]

TWO DIFFERENT ONE-STATE MODELS

A leading proponent of the one-state binational model in the pre-partition
era was Rabbi Judah L. Magnes, an American who had immigrated to
Palestine in 1922, and became one of the founders of Hebrew University.
Along with Martin Buber, Ernst Simon, and others, Rabbi Magnes was a
prominent member of the Brit Shalom (Covenant of Peace) organization
and, later, of Ihud (Union), "Zionism's premier associations of public intellectuals, dedicated to promoting Jewish–Arab understanding and a confed-
eral state on the model of Switzerland, Belgium or Canada."[21] He also was
Ihud's chief spokesperson before the United Nations Special Commission
on Palestine (UNSCOP) in 1947. Writing of "these dissidents" sixty years
later, Mayer summarized their view: "From the outset their cosmopolitan
humanity moved them to warn, on both moral and pragmatic grounds,
of the unwisdom of first disregarding and disdaining Palestinian Arabs,
and eventually condemning them as irreconcilable, benighted enemies."[22]
When asked by UNSCOP why he opposed partition, Magnes explained
that "the creation of two states would make for chronic hostility between
the two states, as well as between the majority and minority within each

state,"[23] and he predicted that partition would soon lead to outright "warfare between Jew and Arab."[24]

During the 1920s and 1930s the "polar opposites of the emergent Binationalists, led by Magnes," were the Revisionists (so called because of their wish to revise the mandatory borders), led by Ze'ev Jabotinsky.[25] Until his death in 1940, Jabotinsky was one of the most politically effective spokespersons for the Jewish community in Palestine under the British Mandate.[26] Jabotinsky, a native of Odessa, had studied in Bern and Rome, and on his return to Russia had become a writer and an activist for Jewish rights. During the First World War he went to the Middle East as a correspondent for a Moscow newspaper. In response to violence against Jews in Palestine by Turkish forces, he formed a unit of Jewish volunteers who fought with distinction in the British Army. He later disagreed with Zionist leaders such as Chaim Weizmann over conceptions of a Jewish state. Specifically, "Jabotinsky strongly opposed the partition of Palestine," and favoured an "immediate declaration of the Jewish right to political sovereignty over the whole of this area [of the original 1920 Palestine Mandate]."[27] In 1925 he formed a new political party, the World Union of Revisionist Zionists, to promote these aims.

However, Jabotinsky was in agreement with Weizmann and other Zionist leaders in that they were western oriented and followed Theodor Herzl in assuming "that the support and protection of a great power were absolutely indispensable in the struggle for statehood."[28] Avi Shlaim wrote that Jabotinsky also "believed in the cultural superiority of Western civilization," and that "Zionism was conceived by Jabotinsky not as the return of the Jews to their spiritual homeland but as an offshoot or implant of Western civilization in the East."[29] Thus the Revisionists were proponents of a one-state model, but of a different type than envisioned by the binationalists. Mayer summarized the role of Jabotinsky and his proposal as follows: "The prime mover of ultra-Zionism articulated in secularized and traditional words and concepts, Jabotinsky called for a unitary Jewish state from the Mediterranean Sea to beyond the Jordan River, thus including all or part of the lands of the recently fashioned Hashemite desert kingdom."[30] Jabotinsky also predicted that Palestinian Arabs would defend their ancestral land and would "not accept Zionism [until] confronted with an iron wall of Jewish bayonets."[31]

Shlaim wrote that Jabotinsky's concept of an "iron wall" was often misunderstood, even by his own followers:

For him the iron wall was not an end in itself but a means to the end of breaking Arab resistance to the onward march of Zionism. Once Arab resistance had been broken [...] it would be time to start serious negotiations. In these negotiations the Jewish side would offer the Palestinians civil and national rights [...] he recognized that the Palestinian Arabs formed a distinct national entity and [...] he accordingly considered them entitled to some national rights, albeit limited ones [...].[32]

From the mid-1920s onward, in addition to strong political divisions among Zionists, there was periodic violence involving Jews, Arabs, and British forces. However, by 1937, at the Twentieth Zionist Congress, with deteriorating conditions for Jews in much of Europe and escalating violence between Jews and Arabs in Palestine, the majority supported the pragmatic approach advocated by Chaim Weizmann and David Ben-Gurion, leader of Labour Zionism, in favour of the partition of Palestine.

In 1947, in the circumstances that had developed internationally and in the Middle East during the thirty years since the Balfour Declaration, UNSCOP recommended partition. The subsequent 1948 war resulted in a new State of Israel within boundaries recognized by the United Nations. Chronic hostility endured and outright warfare occurred several times between Israel and neighbouring states, or between Israel and Palestinian groups. Six decades later, no specific means of resolving the conflict has been discovered.

CONTROVERSIAL TOPICS

At various times during the past several decades, controversy has attended one or both of the one- and two-state proposals. The one-state, bi-national model has never enjoyed wide support among the populations of Israel/Palestine. The two-state model was highly controversial for some years prior to the Oslo Accords. For example, in 1985 Israeli Prime Minister Shimon Peres expressed the view that a Palestinian state would "threaten Israel's very existence."[33] Even after 1993, many in Israel, including its current prime minister, Benjamin Netanyahu, remained strongly opposed to any two-state model that would entail a viable sovereign Palestinian state. Christian Zionists, among Israel's most numerous and fervid supporters in North America and western Europe for the past three decades, are vehemently opposed to a two-state solution.

Since the Oslo Accords, American government leaders have promoted the concept of a two-state model. In December 2000, near the end of his second term in office, President Clinton made his final attempt to mediate a settlement between the government of Israel and the PNA. In July, at the request of the Israeli prime minister, Clinton had convened a summit meeting between Israeli Prime Minister Ehud Barak and PLO Chair Yasser Arafat at Camp David, Maryland. The summit process failed for a variety of reasons, and the Israeli and Palestinian sides have blamed each other ever since. Shlaim has given a summary of the reasons, notably:

> Both [Barak and Arafat] had serious internal problems. Barak's coalition was crumbling and he arrived at the conference at the head of a government on the edge of collapse. Arafat was under pressure not to yield on the Palestinian demand for an Israeli withdrawal from the whole of Arab East Jerusalem. The city was the core issue at the summit and the main stumbling block.[34]

Such constraints were understood, but the Clinton administration and the two parties nevertheless made an effort because of the international, as well as regional, importance of finding a means to bring lasting peace. The importance was emphasized, two months after the breakdown at Camp David, by a renewed round of provocations, violent reaction, and violent counter-reaction, resulting in many deaths and serious injuries. "Against this grim background Clinton made one last attempt," in December 2000, "to bridge the gap between the sides," and "presented his ideas for a final settlement."[35]

Shlaim outlined the Clinton proposal as follows:

> Israel was to withdraw altogether from Gaza and from 94–96 per cent of the West Bank. There was to be an independent Palestinian State but with limitations on its level of armaments. The guiding principle for solving the refugee problem was that the new state would be "the focal point for the Palestinians who choose to return to the area." With regard to Jerusalem, "the general principle is that Arab areas are Palestinian and Jewish ones are Israeli."[36]

There was sufficient interest in Clinton's proposal that negotiations between the parties resumed on this basis, at Taba in Egypt, in late January

2001. Progress was made during a week of talks, despite continuing difficulties over the status of East Jerusalem and other matters. However, an
agreement was not reached and neither the new Israeli government, led
by Prime Minister Ariel Sharon, nor the new American administration
of George W. Bush was prepared to continue along this possible path to
peace.

During the period from 2001 to 2009, which coincided approximately
with the period of the Bush administration in Washington, coalitions led
by the Likud and, later, Kadima parties were in power in Israel, headed
by prime ministers Ariel Sharon and Ehud Olmert. There were renewed
rounds of extreme violence, and more land in East Jerusalem and the West
Bank was allotted by Israel to Jewish settlers, although Israel withdrew
settlements from the Gaza Strip.

Yasser Arafat died in 2004 while under a protracted Israeli military siege
and the Palestinian leadership was subsequently in disarray. However,
in a democratic PNA election in 2006 that had been encouraged by the
USA and its allies, the PLO was defeated by the Hamas Party, which thus
became one of the rare democratically elected governments in the Arab
world. This result might have been the basis for renewed peace talks, had
the United States and its allies not immediately denounced and sanctioned
the Hamas government as a terrorist organization. A power struggle ensued
between Hamas and the PLO. This was followed by the massive military
assault in December 2008–January 2009 by Israel on the Gaza Strip, where
Hamas was strongest, resulting in many civilian deaths and injuries and
extensive destruction of infrastructure. The military assault was followed in
turn by a nearly total Israeli blockade of the Strip, in which Israel enjoyed
the effective support of Egypt. Many observers considered that prospects for
a two-state solution receded, rather than advancing, in this period.

As additional background to the renewed interest in discussing both the
one-state and two-state models and various hybrids, the positions of the
leading political figures are relevant, because those who had been in power
a decade earlier were again in power at the time the Toronto conference
at York University was held. At the turn of the century the Israeli government had been led, successively, by Benjamin Netanyahu (prime minister,
1996–1999) and Ehud Barak (prime minister, 1999–2001). Mayer summarized their positions:

> While both Netanyahu and Barak were reconciled to the
> establishment of some form of Palestinian autonomy, neither

entertained the prospect of a fully sovereign and independent state. The Palestinian leaders could never be co-equal negotiating partners, and remained only supplicants to be propitiated with trivial concessions. Netanyahu and Barak did differ on how much to concede to the Palestinians in terms of territory and political rights, and on some aspects of settlement policy; but they were equally extreme in their refusal to envisage any curtailment of the de facto outposts of Greater Israel.[37]

In 2009, Netanyahu was again prime minister, with Barak serving as minister of defence. There was no evidence that either leader had significantly changed his position from the years 1999 to 2001. Moreover, the new Likud-led coalition government included politicians considered to be farther to the right than Netanyahu, such as Foreign Minister Avigdor Lieberman, leader of the Yisrael Beiteinu Party.

WHY WAS OPPOSITION TO THE CONFERENCE FOCUSED ON THE ONE-STATE MODEL?

Opposition to the York conference was focused on one of the two main subthemes, the one-state bi-national model. Many opponents said they were concerned such a model would mean Israel would no longer exist as a Jewish state; that is, Israel would become a state in which *all* citizens, Jewish or otherwise, would enjoy equal legal status and rights. Despite such assertions, it remains somewhat unclear why this aspect should have been the main focus of opposition, given that during the intense phase of the controversy—April through June 2009—the leadership of the government of Israel was strongly opposed to establishment of a viable sovereign Palestinian state. It may be impossible to answer this question definitively. Recently, Ilan Pappé noted that, "the official discourse in the West is that a very reasonable and attainable solution is just around the corner if all sides would make one final effort: the two-state solution."[38] He assessed this view as unrealistic:

Nothing is further from the truth than this optimistic scenario. The only version of this solution that is acceptable to Israel is the one that both the tamed Palestine Authority in Ramallah and the more assertive Hamas in Gaza could never ever accept. It is an offer to imprison the Palestinians in stateless enclaves in return for ending their struggle.[39]

Three years earlier, political commentator Henry Siegman, a former executive director of the American Jewish Congress, wrote:

> Israel's disingenuous commitment to a peace process and a two-state solution is precisely what has made possible its open-ended occupation and dismemberment of Palestinian territory. And the Quartet—with the EU, the UN secretary general and Russia obediently following Washington's lead—has collaborated with and provided cover for this deception by accepting Israel's claim that it has been unable to find a deserving Palestinian peace partner.[40]

A few days before Pappé's article was published, an article by Moshe Arens appeared in the newspaper *Haaretz*, in effect reinforcing Pappé's assessment from the opposite end of the Israeli political spectrum. Arens, who had served as minister of defence and minister of foreign affairs in Likud governments, and as ambassador to the United States, wrote that those hoping for a two-state solution were "likely to be sorely disappointed," because PNA President Mahmoud Abbas was not in a position "to implement any commitments" in negotiations with Israel, due to the facts that he was not recognized by Hamas, which controlled the Gaza Strip, and that his political support in the West Bank was "questionable."[41]

Arens discussed another solution, namely extension of permanent Israeli sovereignty over the whole of the West Bank, combined with an offer of Israeli citizenship to its Palestinian population, and more effective action by the government of Israel to integrate its current population of Muslim citizens into the wider society, together with those from the West Bank who chose to become citizens. He recognized this proposal would "pose a serious challenge to Israeli society," but said it nevertheless "merits serious consideration."[42] In summary, because he considered a two-state solution unlikely, Arens proposed a one-state solution along lines similar to the type of state promoted by Ze'ev Jabotinsky decades earlier. In this article, Arens did not make any suggestion regarding the Gaza Strip.

Finally on this question, remarks by Richard Falk, United Nations Special Rapporteur for the Occupied Palestinian Territories, are of note:

> I think one needs to look in new directions to be hopeful about an eventual, just outcome of the Palestinian struggle. That new

direction depends on the mobilization of global civil society around this struggle as the symbolic struggle of our present period and one that does rest on the premises of what I've been calling the legitimacy war. This requires that we disabuse ourselves of the two-state illusion and at the same time that we be careful not to mindlessly endorse a one state that would reproduce within the borders of a single state exploitative and oppressive structures that now exist in the form of the occupation. In other words, [...] after 42 years one can consider the occupied territories to be effectively annexed. But this is a de facto one state already. It exists. The question is how do you democratize it. You can't democratize it without eliminating its ethnic identity. It has to be a state that serves the diverse peoples, the diverse religions that live within its borders.[43]

REVIVAL OF INTEREST IN THE ONE-STATE MODEL

The late Edward W. Said, the most prominent public intellectual of the Palestinian diaspora, promoted a revival of the one-state model with a 1999 article in the *New York Times*. A decade earlier, Said had played an important role in helping to persuade the PLO leadership to recognize Israel's right to exist and to express a willingness to accept UN Security Council Resolution 242. Even though he condemned the subsequent 1993 Oslo Accords as a betrayal of Palestinian interests—and an arrangement negotiated between a very weak PLO and a very strong Israel—Said supported the two-state model for a period of several years. However, eventually, "disappointment with Oslo and with the Palestinian leadership that was associated with it led naturally and logically to the fourth and final stage in the evolution of Edward Said's thinking on solutions to the Palestinian-Israeli dispute—advocacy of a bi-national state."[44]

Among the first to follow Said in public discussion of the one-state model was the late Tony Judt, a prominent public intellectual of the Jewish Diaspora. In 2003 he published an essay in the *New York Review of Books* (*NYRB*) titled "Israel: The Alternative." His reason for doing so was that "the two-state solution—the core of the Oslo process and the present 'road map'—is probably already doomed."[45] He faulted Israel for this, because it had undermined and humiliated the Palestinian leadership, and also the United States for not using its influence to restrain Israel: "The depressing truth is that Israel's current behaviour is not just bad for America, though it surely is. It is not even just bad for Israel itself, as many Israelis silently acknowledge. The depressing truth is that Israel today is bad for the Jews."[46]

Israel is a democracy in which a large number of citizens do not enjoy full rights, "Hence its present dilemma," Judt wrote.[47] He explained that although the one-state model is opposed by the great majority of Israel's Jewish citizens, the alternatives being contemplated by some of Israel's political leaders—such as ethnic cleansing of Palestinians from their historic lands—might be even more fraught with difficulty. A similarly pessimistic assessment of the alternatives for Israel was given by Mearsheimer and Walt, although they themselves did not believe the one-state model was feasible.[48]

In a subsequent issue of *NYRB*, Judt reported on readers' responses to his one-state article:

> Much of the American response verged on hysteria. Readers
> accused me of belonging to the 'Nazi Left,' of hating Jews,
> of denying Israel's right to exist [...] and 'being party to
> preparations for a final solution.' [...] The most distressing
> aspect of the American reaction is not so much the taboo on any
> discussion of Zionism as the widespread ignorance to which that
> taboo has given rise.[49]

Both at the time and subsequently, Judt's article served as a catalyst for international discussion of the one-state model. *NYRB* printed several responses by experts for and against his view, along with his reply to the critics. An article titled "The One-State Solution," by political scientist Virginia Tilley, appeared in the *London Review of Books* a month after Judt's *NYRB* piece. A conference focusing solely on this model of state-hood for Israel/Palestine was held in November 2007 at the School of Oriental and African Studies (SOAS), University of London, sponsored by the SOAS Palestine Society.

More recently, Benny Morris published a book discussing both the one-state and the two-state models. He disputed Judt's analysis and faulted the Palestinian leadership for the failure of the two-state solution to be realized, concluding that "a two-state settlement [...] is unlikely" but "remains the only sound moral and political basis for a solution."[50] Despite having reached this conclusion, in the final three pages of the book he sketched a rather different solution—a new "Arab state [...] that fuses the bulk of the West Bank and East Jerusalem and the east bank, the present-day Kingdom of Jordan"—the realization of which may be fraught with difficulty, as he himself acknowledged.[51]

4

CONFERENCE PLANNING AND SUPPORT

THE CONFERENCE ORGANIZERS

The conference was organized by Professors Bruce Ryder and Susan Drummond (Osgoode Hall Law School, York University), Professor Sharryn Aiken (Faculty of Law, Queen's University), and Mazen Masri, a doctoral student at Osgoode Hall. The research and teaching interests of Ryder, Drummond, and Aiken lie in intersecting areas that include questions of statehood, constitutional law, comparative law, human rights, rights of refugees and other minorities, and ethnography, all of which are relevant to issues facing Israel and Palestine. Ryder was Masri's doctoral research advisor and Drummond was a member of the advisory committee for Masri's research program. Aiken and Drummond had worked in Israel for periods of time, and Masri is a citizen of Israel who had lived there most of his life.[1]

In autumn 2007, Ryder and Drummond initiated a reading group on the one-state model, with several graduate students, including Masri. The idea of holding a conference to compare models of statehood emerged, and Aiken was invited to join with Ryder, Drummond, and Masri in organizing such a conference.

Planning for the conference began in late 2007. The initial working title for it was "Imagining a Bi-National Constitutional Democracy in Israel/Palestine." As conference planning evolved in 2008, the conception of it was transformed into a comparison between one-state and two-state models with a new working title, "Israel/Palestine: One State or Two."

AN ACADEMIC EXERCISE

The organizers planned an academic exercise in a positive sense of the term. The theme involved efforts to identify possible means of resolving the Israel/Palestine problem, an important and long-standing unsolved problem in international relations, with diverse human and intellectual dimensions. This is the type of challenge that attracts academics and other scholars with expertise in a variety of disciplines.

The central purpose was to generate a serious, scholarly debate on possible models for statehood among well-informed advocates of the different models: one bi-national state, two states, and hybrid arrangements. Legal, historical, cultural, sociological, and religious dimensions would be explored through talks, panel discussions, and film presentations. The organizers went to great lengths to ensure a broad representation of views among conference participants, as well as a broad range of relevant academic disciplines. The controversy around one of the models made broad representation particularly desirable, even though not essential.

From direct personal experience in Israel and Canada, as well as from published reports, all members of the organizing committee were well aware—from the outset of their planning process—that the one-state bi-national model was highly controversial. They also were aware that a viable two-state model was strongly opposed by many in Israel. As experienced academics, however, they knew that approaches toward solutions to difficult problems can emerge from open discussion by experts, coming together to present ideas and analyses and to discuss them freely in an academic setting. Of course, no one expected that a widely acceptable solution to such a complex problem would emerge from a single academic conference. As is typical in such matters, and as set out in their grant application to SSHRC, the organizers aspired to shed light on the issues and to encourage future work.

SUPPORT FOR THE CONFERENCE

The Advisory Board. To assist in the endeavour, the organizers recruited a large and diverse International Advisory Board consisting of "internationally recognized scholars and intellectuals."[2] Without great difficulty they were able to persuade Palestinian and Israeli scholars living in the Middle East, and scholars from the Palestinian and Jewish diaspora communities living outside Canada, to serve on the Advisory Board. Among the early members of the Advisory Board were Ali Abunimah (an intellectual and political activist of the Palestinian diaspora, and a proponent of the one-state model) and Professor David Kretzmer of Hebrew University (an authority on international human-rights law and a former member of the UN Human Rights Committee). In contrast, they had great difficulty in attracting any Canadian Jewish scholar to serve in this capacity, despite efforts extending over several months, because, as they were informed by scholars they approached, there was strong pressure against participation from elements of the Canadian Jewish community. However, in August 2008, Professor Ed Morgan of the Faculty of Law, University of Toronto, agreed to join the Advisory Board.[3]

University Support. Aiken's university, Queen's, was the first to confirm financial support for the conference, even though it would be held at York University. Subsequently, the dean of Osgoode Hall, Professor Patrick Monahan,[4] agreed to provide support in the form of salary for a part-time research assistant. In addition, he suggested to the organizers that they apply to the special fund (U50) established on the occasion of the fiftieth anniversary of the founding of York University and said that, as dean, he would support such an application.

U50 Support. An elaborate framework had been established in 2005 for the planning and implementation of U50 events in 2009. This included processes for reviewing applications for financial support of events that would receive official U50 designation, and for provision of administrative support in the successful cases.

The application for York U50 support was presented to Monahan in early spring 2008 by Drummond and Ryder on behalf of the conference organizing committee. It was reviewed and signed by the dean on April 11, and he then submitted it to the U50 Committee on behalf of the organizers, in accordance with U50 procedure. At this stage of its development the project focused primarily on the one-state model, as reflected in the draft title for the conference, "Imagining a Bi-national Constitutional Democracy in Israel/Palestine," but would also include discussions on the two-state model and its prospects for realization.

The application approved by Monahan included a vision statement (U50 Event Proposal) in which the organizing committee stated:

> We are a group of two Osgoode faculty members, a member of Queen's University Faculty of Law, and an Osgoode doctoral candidate. [...]

The purpose of the conference is to explore the possibility that a single bi-national constitutional democracy in Israel/Palestine may be the most promising path to future peace and security in the region.

A growing number of scholars are reaching the conclusion that the chances of reaching a just two-state solution are increasing remote. [...]

The existing one state scholarship is devoted primarily to convincing those with an aversion to even considering the idea. Specific issues of constitutional design have not been explored in any depth. While these matters can be decided only by the people of Israel/Palestinian in future negotiations, this conference aims to envision in specific terms the possible constitutional dimensions of a future single state. [...]

The conference aims to open a series of principled conversations among scholars with a commitment to the equality of all peoples and in particular, the equal rights to dignity and fundamental justice for Jews and Palestinians. Drawing on the experiences of other multinational constitutional democracies—such as Canada and South Africa—the conference will explore the possibility that a state shaped by federalism, equal citizenship and respect for linguistic, cultural and religious rights could provide better protection than the current situation to the long-term security of all peoples in the Middle East. [...]

The scope and ambition of the conference as it is conceived promises to generate a high profile, highly prestigious conference on a topic of widespread topical interest. [...]

Holding an academic conference on such a challenging and provocative topic provides an opportunity for York University to showcase the thoughtfulness, rigour, and spirit of adventure that characterizes its academic community.[5]

The application included a detailed draft conference program, a budget, and a list of possible funding sources and commitments to date. In particular, the organizers would apply for a "SSHRC conference grant." The application also included biographical summaries of the seven members of the International Advisory Board who had agreed to serve by that time in April, among them Abunimah and Kretzmer.

The application was successful and, like all other successful U50 applicants the organizers of this event were required to sign a Memorandum of Understanding (MOU) pertaining to U50 support, with the head of their academic unit co-signing. In this case, the MOU was signed by Ryder and Monahan. Although several pages long, the MOU dealt mainly with administrative matters aimed at assisting organizers to mount successful events.

The organizers also secured support from several other York University sources, including the Jack and Mae Nathanson Centre on Transnational Human Rights, Crime and Security; the Office of the Vice-President Research and Innovation; and the Faculty of Graduate Studies. The commitments of support from York and Queen's would be noted in the organizers' application to SSHRC for additional support in mid-autumn 2008.[6]

In July 2008 the organizers reserved space for the conference on York's Glendon College campus, considering it ideal because of its facilities and its being closer to downtown Toronto than the main campus. At the time of year when the conference would be held, there normally would be no competing major functions at Glendon. For U50 events, space reservations were additionally coordinated through the assistance of U50 staff. This arrangement was made for the York/Queen's conference by Sarah Brathwaite, U50 Manager of Implementation, the person specified in the MOU for such purposes.

Evolution in the Proposal. During the period following the U50 application in April, the organizing committee decided to broaden the range of discussion, by giving the one-state and two-state models approximately equal prominence, both in the conference title and the program. This was on the advice of Israeli members of their Advisory Board who had informed the organizers that a conference focused primarily on the one-state model would be unlikely to attract many participants from Israel. The title was changed to "Israel/Palestine: One State or Two" and the vision statement was revised accordingly.

The Call for Papers. The organizers issued an international call for papers, with the revised title and vision statement, in September 2008 for the conference to be held in June 2009, and they set up a public website.[7]

The published vision statement (Statement of Purpose of Conference) opened by saying:

The purpose of this conference is to explore which state models offer promising paths to resolving the Israeli–Palestinian conflict, respecting the rights to self-determination of both Israelis/Jews and Palestinians. [...]

Despite the current diplomatic focus on the two-state model, the continued failure to achieve peace in the region highlights the necessity of rigorously examining whether the two-state approach is indeed the only way, or the best way, beyond the impasse. The horrific toll division and violence takes on Jews and Palestinians adds moral urgency to the need to explore alternative political futures in the region.

The conference seeks to systematically measure models based on two states or a single binational state, federal and con-federal approaches, and other models in between and beyond. The framework of the conference invites robust academic critique of the deficiencies, promise, and perils of the range of prospective models of statehood.[8]

In other words, the published vision statement clearly stated that orthodoxy would be challenged in the conference. The tentative vision statement in the U50 application had also been explicit about challenging orthodoxy. The key difference in the two proposals was that in the second one, approximately equal prominence would be given to the currently orthodox model (two-state) and the currently unorthodox model (one-state).

Approximately one hundred and twenty submissions were received in response to the call for papers, and during the next several months the organizers and the Advisory Board selected and confirmed approximately fifty speakers. The selection was based on assessment of the scholarly merit of the submitted abstracts and their relation to the conference themes, as well as of the scholarly background of potential speakers as reflected in their CVs.

INITIAL OPPOSITION

Concerns of Professor Morgan and Others. After the call for papers was issued, concerns about the conference were raised by increasing numbers of members of the Jewish community in Toronto, including several York faculty members. In an email to Sharryn Aiken on September 27, Ed

Morgan referred to these and said, "I've been taking a lot of criticism from elements of the Jewish Community about allowing my name to be on the advisory committee [the International Advisory Board]."[9] He also said that he remained ambivalent about his involvement and had agreed to serve "because of, frankly, my respect for Bruce Ryder and yourself (plus, I should add, David Kretzmer, who was already on the advisory committee when I agreed to join it)."[10] Nevertheless, Morgan continued his involvement and assisted the organizers in resolving an issue raised several days later by Professor Benjamin Geva of Osgoode Hall.

Professor Geva's Concerns. On October 2, 2008, Geva sent an email to Dean Monahan (copied to Morgan, Ryder, and Drummond, among others) raising concerns and questions about the conference. These included concerns that "the mainstream Peace Camp is committed to the two-state solutions," that "the 'one-state solution' has become a code word disguising a call for the destruction of Israel," and that the one-state model might lead to "repatriation of the 1948 Palestinian refugees to their old homes in Israel," along with questions as to:

> Whether it was appropriate for Osgoode Hall and the U50 Committee to support a conference discussing such a controversial topic as the one-state model;

> Why other territorial conflicts (such as in Sri Lanka or in the former Yugoslavia) were not included in the program;

> Why other regional statehood options, such as "a Jordanian–Palestinian Federation," were not included in the program;

> Whether the conference may inadvertently give support to extremists, including those who would destroy Israel.[11]

These objections were similar to those raised by others during the ensuing months.

However, over the next couple of weeks, following a suggestion by Morgan, discussions among Geva, Morgan, Ryder, Drummond, and other interested York faculty members focused on the conference title as a source of controversy. The result was a new title: instead of "Israel/Palestine: One State or Two," it would be, "Israel/Palestine: Mapping Models of Statehood and Prospects for Peace."[12] In an email dated October 18, 2008, Professor

Geva agreed this was a good choice and wished the organizers well in the conference endeavour. In an email the following day, Dean Monahan thanked his Osgoode colleagues for their efforts in resolving the concern in a collegial manner. He also wished the organizers well, adding, "This is a very important initiative and I am hopeful with good will on all sides that it will make a significant positive contribution to our understanding of the issues raised."[13]

The JDL Boycott Warning. On October 4, 2008, Meir Weinstein, National Director of the Jewish Defence League of Canada (JDL), sent an email warning to the President of York University, Mamdouh Shoukri,[14] in regard to the June 2009 conference. The email letter was copied to the Canadian Jewish Congress (CJC) and others. In it the JDL referred to the conference website and said:

> This conference should not be sponsored by York
> University. […] The Jewish Defence League of Canada is
> discussing the possibility of leading a campaign against York U,
> calling for boycott, divestment and sanctions. It is my hope that
> such a campaign will not be required, but we refuse to stand by
> and allow Jewish students to feel threatened.[15]

On October 5, 2008, the JDL sent a second copy of the same email message to President Shoukri, with the difference that the CJC was omitted from the copy list. On October 9, Drummond sent a copy of this version of the JDL boycott warning to Dean Monahan.[16] Later that day, the dean sent an email message to the president, enclosing a copy of the JDL email and commenting on the conference. He wrote:

> I recognize that this conference will certainly be controversial
> and attract a good deal of attention. I just wanted you to know
> that I have met on a number of occasions with the two Osgoode
> faculty members who are on the organizing committee, and that
> I plan to work closely with them to ensure that the conference is
> balanced and scholarly in its approach.[17]

Shoukri replied to Weinstein on October 24, acknowledging receipt of his communication and adding, "Thank you for getting in touch."[18]

The Bil'in Seminar. One of the seminars scheduled in an Osgoode Hall series, Putting Theory into Practice (PTTP), in autumn 2008 was on international legal issues pertaining to the construction by a Quebec-based company of housing units for an Israeli settlement in the occupied Palestinian territories, near the village of Bil'in. Masri had assisted in the organization of this seminar, proposing it in late August through Associate Dean Peer Zumbansen. It was scheduled for October 30. One of the two speakers would be a civil litigation lawyer who had filed a lawsuit in Quebec on behalf of the village, and the other a legal researcher for a Palestinian human-rights group. The two speakers were also scheduled to make a similar presentation at Harvard, McGill, and the University of Toronto.

On October 5, Professor Geva sent an email to Dean Monahan (copied to Ryder and Drummond) objecting to this seminar. On the following day, the dean's office sent an email message to Masri asking for background information on the speakers, the lawsuit, and details of the proposed talks in the seminar. Later that day, Zumbansen emailed Masri saying, "It may well be that we, due to the politically heated nature of the topic, have to complement the two litigators with an adequate representative of a differing view."[19] In other words, the associate dean suggested that balance was lacking and should be arranged before the event could proceed.

Masri provided the requested information, and a week later Zumbansen replied, saying that "After deliberations at the Law School, we want to postpone the pttp [PTTP] talk from October 30 to the Winter term. We believe it will be a much more worthwhile event if prepared with more lead time."[20] Masri responded that, in view of the schedules of the two speakers he had proposed, such a postponement might in effect result in their being unable to participate.

Subsequently, Drummond and Professor Craig Scott, Director of the Nathanson Centre, took up the matter. A compromise was reached, ensuring that the Bil'in seminar would be held on the date and largely in the format originally announced, but with the addition of Scott as moderator for the presentation.

The Dean's Request for Removal or "Balancing" of Masri. On October 9, 2008, Ryder and Drummond met with Monahan at his request. In asking them to meet, he referred to the controversy over the conference, and sent to them in advance of the meeting a copy of an article in *Toronto Life* magazine discussing a series of controversies at York University in recent years related to Israel and Palestine. In the meeting, the dean proposed that Masri be removed from the organizing committee, giving as his reasons that removal of Masri would improve the optics of the conference (or words to that effect), and that Masri was only a graduate student.[21]

Ryder and Drummond objected that this would be unreasonable academically, as well as unfair personally to Masri. The dean then proposed that, alternatively, the organizing committee be augmented by the addition of a fifth member, who would "balance" Masri's presence on the committee. Specifically, he suggested that Professor Morgan, or someone like Morgan, would be a good choice for the fifth member. Ryder and Drummond objected to the dean's alternative proposal as well.[22]

On the following day (October 10) they sent a three-page memo to Monahan outlining organizational progress to date and explaining in some detail their reasons for not agreeing to a change in the composition of their committee, and specifically for not agreeing to the removal of Masri. In essence, the conference proposal had been developed over many months by the two of them, together with Aiken and Masri, and the four were now a coherent team. The existing committee could already have been regarded as balanced, in at least some aspects of the sense mentioned by the dean in proposing that that Masri be removed, or in the alternative that Morgan or someone like him be added.[23] In this memo they reminded the dean that they had the assistance of a broad-based advisory board composed of experts in the various topics on the conference program. (This group was now larger than the seven-member board listed in the U50 application that the dean himself had approved, now including Morgan and several other more recent additions.)

Dean Monahan's request that the committee membership be adjusted— by removing Masri, or by "balancing" him with someone like Morgan— cannot reasonably be seen as merely a casual suggestion made in a conversation, because in the late afternoon of October 10, 2008, following his meeting with Ryder and Drummond, he sent them an email saying:

> Fyi. When I meet with the President and the VPA [Vice-
> President Academic] I will be indicating that I have requested an
> adjustment in the membership of the organizing committee. Plse
> let me know what you decide to do in that regard.[24]

The dean's email message included a chain of three emails: his own; one by the president's executive assistant, Irene Fezza, sent to him that afternoon; and a copy of the JDL boycott warning (the version dated October 4). Fezza's email to the dean (copied to Harriet Lewis, the university's staff legal counsel, and others) said, "I will be in contact with your offices to arrange a meeting next week to discuss the note below [the JDL boycott warning]."[25]

In their October 10 memo, Ryder and Drummond confirmed they were aware of opposition to the conference in some elements of the Jewish community and the need for community liaison work. Ultimately, they themselves undertook this task, together with Aiken, and they made substantial efforts to meet with conference opponents from both on and off the York campus, to explain the nature of the conference and its academic soundness. During a period of many weeks, Aiken met mainly with community groups from off campus and individuals on campus, while Ryder and Drummond met mainly with individuals and groups on the York campus.

Aiken had discussions with several Canadian Jewish faculty members at other universities, as well as with several York faculty members. The latter included Professor David Dewitt, with whom she, Ryder, and Drummond had discussions about the conference extending over many months. During this period the organizers several times also invited him to participate in the conference.

Aiken also met with senior representatives of CIJA, CJC, and JDL. Aiken informed this Inquiry she had been reluctant to meet with JDL representatives, because of their organization's public reputation. However, Bernie Farber, chief executive officer of CJC, strongly encouraged her to meet with the JDL and, on this basis, she agreed.

Professor Morgan Withdraws. Morgan reported that "In mid-October I had several meetings with Bruce Ryder and Sharry Aiken in which I explained to them my decision to withdraw from the conference advisory committee."[26] Nevertheless, discussions regarding his participation continued for a few weeks before he definitively withdrew, as indicated by an email exchange between Morgan and Ryder on November 9, 2008.

Morgan wrote that the conference on the one-state model in November 2007, held at the University of London, "appears to be virtually the same conference" as that being planned for York University in June 2009.[27] In his reply, Ryder explained there were substantial differences. For instance, unlike the London conference, "Ours is a conference aimed at critically interrogating, from a scholarly perspective, one state and two state proposals and other models of statehood in between and beyond. Ours is aimed at generating a scholarly debate between proponents of various options [...] the London conference was by and for one state partisans."[28] He emphasized his appreciation of Morgan's participation and encouraged him to continue.

However, by this time Morgan had publicly aired his concerns about the conference, first in an article in the *Canadian Jewish News* on October 23, followed by a very similar article in the *National Post* on November 4. In his *National Post* article, titled "Fight Bad Speech with Good Speech," he wrote that although "the notion of the 'one state' is deployed by Israel's enemies as a rhetorical tactic to undermine the Jewish state," he had initially decided "that we should at least engage the debate rather than shut it down," and so had agreed to join the Advisory Board for the conference.[29] However, subsequently, some of the organizers and Advisory Board members had been proposing speakers active in groups he considered inappropriate for an academic conference, such as those involved in "boycott Israel" campaigns.

Morgan also wrote:

> For a conference such as Osgoode's to succeed, one needs
> speakers who genuinely grapple with the issues of political
> and legal theory and do so out of good faith, not cynicism.
> Personally, I have proposed keynotes—former Israeli chief justice
> Aharon Barak and novelist Amos Oz among them—who will
> demonstrate that having a distinctively Jewish national character
> does not undermine the possibility of liberal democracy, and
> that when it comes to the "two state" model, the Palestinians
> would do well to try to emulate the Israeli combination of
> national distinctiveness and a liberal ethic.[30]

He concluded the article with the statement, "if the event continues the trend of giving boycotters a platform for anti-Israel grandstanding, I will not be there."[31] He did withdraw from the Advisory Board and later commented that, "For their part, Bruce and Sharry continued to ask me to submit a paper to present at the conference, which I declined."[32]

THE SSHRC CONFERENCE GRANT

The Application. In autumn 2008, the organizers applied to SSHRC's Aid to Research Workshops and Conferences in Canada Program for a conference grant of $20,000 (not a workshop grant).[33] It was signed on October 28, 2008, by Bruce Ryder as the Applicant, with Sharryn Aiken, Susan Drummond, and Mazen Masri listed as members of the Organizing Committee. The application was approved and forwarded to SSHRC by York University's Office of Research Services. The summary description on the application form said:

The aim of the conference is to juxtapose the two models for resolving the Israeli/Palestinian conflict in a rigorous and thoughtful manner. The current political situation in the Middle East makes the revisiting of these challenges crucial and relevant. The conference will open avenues to explore whether a two-state solution or a single constitutional democracy in Israel/Palestine offers the most promising path to future peace and security in the region. Despite the current diplomatic focus on the two-state model, the continued failure to bring peace to the region highlights the necessity of rigorously examining all options for a resolution of the conflict, including both two-state and one-state models. Situating discussions in an academic, interdisciplinary context, this conference invites scholars working in a wide range of disciplines including law, gender studies, geography, economics, political science, and the arts. Uniquely, this is the first university-sponsored conference in recent history held on this challenging and provocative topic. Canada's difficult struggles with multiculturalism and bi-nationalism, as well as its history of involvement in the Middle East, make the conference setting the ideal location to host such a conference. Further, such a conference will allow Canadian students and scholars to interact and participate in academic discussion with leading international scholars on themes such as binationalism, multiculturalism and the conflict in the Middle East. [...]

Selected papers from the conference will be published in an edited volume with a leading academic publisher to stimulate further discussion and research. [...]

The conference will be a rare opportunity for graduate students in Canadian universities to interact intellectually with some leading world experts on the Israeli–Palestinian conflict. [...] One of the key members of the four organizing committee members is a graduate student. [...]

Students will also be involved in the preparation of the conference report [...]. This will be an excellent learning opportunity for students, and will involve them in the details [...]

from the early stages of planning a conference to its fulfillment
followed by dissemination of its proceedings.[34]

The application also outlined the role of the conference's international
advisory board in developing the program and in ongoing activities in
preparation for the conference
The usual types of information were provided on the form, including
a program for a two-and-a-half-day conference, the call for papers, a list
of academic disciplines involved, and budget details listing support committed by York and Queen's,[35] along with estimates of expenditures. The
application form gave the expected number of speakers as thirty and total
number of participants as 150. It said that the location would be York
University's Glendon College (which had been booked in summer 2008
for the June 2009 conference). Also included on the form were three lists
of presenters/speakers: those who were confirmed and for whom SSHRC
funding would be used to pay their expenses, those who were confirmed
and for whom SSHRC funding would not be used to pay their expenses,
and those who were possible presenters or possible graduate-student participants but who were not yet confirmed.[36]
The Award. The application was assessed by SSHRC through its
independent peer-review system. In March 2009, Ryder was notified that
a grant of $19,750 had been awarded (close to the maximum for confer-
ences of its size). The SSHRC notification included standard information
for applicants on the assessment results, including the comments made
to SSHRC by its Adjudication Committee. Ryder was informed that the
Adjudication Committee had rated his application very highly among
those in that round of competition, and that:

It found the program to be well designed and the subject matter
to be highly relevant. The committee appreciated the range
of institutions participating and the excellent potential for
discussion opportunities.[37]

5
INTENSIFYING CONTROVERSY: MARCH–MAY 2009

A PRECURSOR

A controversy similar to the one over the conference but on a smaller scale emerged in February 2009, in connection with a seminar series titled "Academic Boycotts and Contemporary Conflicts," held at the York Centre for International and Security Studies (YCISS). The director of YCISS, Professor Robert Latham of the Department of Political Science, informed this Inquiry that he had been asked to issue a public statement on behalf of the Centre condemning the international call for an academic boycott of Israel. He discussed this with colleagues in the Centre and they concluded there was a substantive academic question involved, although two colleagues disagreed. Thus, instead of issuing a statement, the Centre organized a seminar series in which representatives of both sides of the issue could present their views. A doctoral student in YCISS, Genevieve LeBaron, was assigned to coordinate the series as part of duties associated with her teaching assistantship.

The Invitation to Omar Barghouti. It was announced in February that the first speaker in the series would be Omar Barghouti, who would address the topic, "Boycotts as Civil Resistance: The Moral Responsibility of Intellectuals," on March 2.[1] Professor Latham informed this Inquiry that Barghouti, a leading spokesperson for the boycott campaign directed at Israel, was selected to be the first speaker because it happened that he would be in Toronto then for another event. He already was listed on the conference website as a speaker at the York/Queen's conference in June.

Following this announcement, Latham received a large number of emails protesting against the decision to invite Barghouti, many of which were copied to President Shoukri. Latham and Shoukri met to discuss the matter, and agreed that the seminar should proceed despite the protests.

President Shoukri Defends Academic Freedom. On February 26, Shoukri addressed the university senate on a number of important matters, including the difficult financial circumstances universities were facing and the importance of universities to society. He also discussed other recent difficulties at York, as well as recent successes. In his address, the president mentioned core university values, such as "Freedom of speech—*especially* for those with whom we disagree," and "social justice," adding, "Social justice is for everyone, or it is for no one. York has a history of social activism, but the events of the past weeks—intimidation and shouting each other down—have nothing to do with social activism."[2] He gave examples illustrating how the academy serves as a place where difficult issues can be discussed freely, including the topic Barghouti would address on campus on March 2:

> Next week, the York Centre for International and Security Studies is hosting an event that will examine the idea of academic boycotts. Speakers will explore the topic in a reasoned way in an academic forum. These two examples share one common element: faculty involvement. Our faculty needs to be involved in leading these conversations. Students look up to their professors. They look to you for direction. You are in a position to mentor and guide them and to teach them how to talk about things that anger us, but without anger, without hate, without fear. I am asking you to help us fix our community, because this truly is our problem.[3]

The Views of Professor David Dewitt. Professor David Dewitt, York's Associate Vice-President Research (Social Sciences and Humanities) attended Barghouti's YCISS talk on March 2.[4] During the discussion period at the end of the talk, he introduced himself as a founder of the Centre, and said he regretted that YCISS was hosting Barghouti. He added that he would continue to work on developing academic contacts with Israeli universities, and outlined his conception of academic freedom.

Professors Bruce Ryder, Susan Drummond, and Sharryn Aiken had a number of discussions with Dewitt about the York/Queen's conference during 2008–2009, because he had relevant expertise, research administrative responsibility in the SSHRC areas, and strong connections with the Jewish community. The office of the Vice-President Research was one of the conference sponsors, and the organizers repeatedly invited Dewitt to participate as a speaker. When controversy over the conference intensified in April and May, he made suggestions to the organizers about revising the program, and he was consulted a number of times by Osgoode Hall Dean Patrick Monahan.

Beginning in early March, Dewitt criticized the conference in communications with the organizers. For instance, in an email message to one of them on March 1, the day before Barghouti's talk, Dewitt wrote:

> I am increasingly of the view that this [conference] could
> easily become an opportunity simply to try to discredit and
> delegitimize the State of Israel and its efforts to consolidate a
> Jewish liberal democratic ethos and government, in the midst of
> expanding and strengthening Islamic fundamentalism.[5]

In the same email message, he said he had reviewed material on the conference website and that, in addition to his own concerns, he was aware of "harsh criticism" of the conference by colleagues of his in North America, particularly because some announced participants would be advocating the one-state model. Dewitt also expressed the view that Drummond lacked "relevant credentials" to organize such a conference.[6]

Other Speakers in the YCISS Series. The second speaker was Edward S. Beck of Walden University in Minneapolis, who spoke on March 10 on "Academic Boycotts as the Creation of Counterproductive Efforts for Peace and Antithetical Constructs to Academic Freedom."[7] The third and final event in the series was a panel discussion on May 11 involving four speakers, titled "A Debate on the Academic Boycott of Israel." The speakers were: on the anti-boycott side, Professor Howard Adelman (York University) and Professor Clive Seligman (University of Western Ontario); and on the pro-boycott side, Professor Alan Sears (Ryerson University) and Professor Abigail Bakan (Queen's University).

The invitations to anti-boycott speakers were arranged through Canadian Academic Friends of Israel (CAFI).[8] Originally, a Palestinian doctoral student at York had been invited to speak instead of Bakan. However, very strong opposition to the doctoral student was mounted by some organizations and individuals, who considered the student an activist. YCISS was advised that no anti-boycott speakers would agree to be on the YCISS panel with this doctoral student. As a result, Bakan was invited instead.

CRITICISM OF THE CONFERENCE IN MARCH 2009

Organizational Progress. From the end of November onward, the organizers had been posting a list of confirmed speakers on the conference website and updating the list as more names were added. By mid-March 2009, thirty-eight speakers had been selected and confirmed (of a projected final total of approximately fifty). The selection process required each prospective speaker—whether invited by the organizers in consultation with the members of their Advisory Board, or a respondent to the international call for papers—to submit a title and an abstract for his or her proposed talk. This requirement was uniformly enforced. This Inquiry was informed of an instance in which a prominent Jewish Israeli writer and peace activist declined to submit an abstract, and in consequence did not participate in the conference.

The confirmed speakers included Palestinian and Israeli scholars living in the Middle East, and scholars from the Palestinian and Jewish diaspora communities. Because of the controversial nature of the subject matter, the organizers worked diligently to recruit speakers from diverse political, cultural, and geographic backgrounds, as well as those representing a range of academic disciplines.

They made these efforts because they hoped to engage participants in a wide-ranging discussion, with a view to making a contribution toward identifying solutions to one of the most complex and difficult international problems, as described in the grant application to SSHRC. Ultimately, they did recruit a wide range of scholars, although not a complete range. For example, there were none representing some of the more extreme currents of Palestinian or Israeli political thought. They had difficulty in recruiting scholars from the Canadian Jewish community, but nevertheless several did speak at the conference.

Criticism by Two Potential Conference Participants. As mentioned above, from the beginning of March onward, Dewitt, who had been consulted on the conference and invited to participate, raised strong concerns with the organizers to the effect that their conference could become a platform for raising fundamental criticisms of the State of Israel. His concerns were focused on certain of the confirmed speakers—in particular, on proponents of the one-state model.

On March 20, Professor Howard Adelman sent a memo captioned "Explaining My Withdrawal from the Conference"—unaddressed, but widely circulated by email.[9] In it he explained that he had been very reluctant to participate, but eventually was persuaded to agree, based on two conditions: that the conference would be scholarly, and that it "would not be used to bash Israel."[10] He said that a few days earlier he had reviewed the list of confirmed speakers and read their abstracts. Although he found that "a clear majority of the scholars are reputable and do excellent work and whether I agree or disagree with them, I respect their work," he decided to withdraw because of "the inclusion of five papers of unequivocal Israel bashers in the neo-colonialist and apartheid language mode."[11] Adelman also expressed disappointment that the list of speakers did not include what he would have regarded as a sufficient number of strong proponents of the two-state model.

The JDL Email Campaign. During March, the JDL escalated its opposition to the conference. In October, JDL National Director Meir Weinstein had sent a warning to President Shoukri that if the university did not cancel the conference, then it might lead to "a campaign against York U, calling for boycott, divestment and sanctions." On March 5, Weinstein sent out a message distributed through email lists, directed to donors, among others. It said:

> In June, York University in honour of their 50 years, will sponsor an International Conference that calls for the end of Israel as a Jewish State. This must be opposed. We are asking all donors to York University to pull their contributions unless this conference is cancelled. [...] And they boast on their website the following: "[the conference] was awarded a grant by the Social Sciences and Humanities Research Council of Canada."[12]

On March 22, Weinstein issued an open letter to President Shoukri that he expressly copied to certain Members of Parliament, such as Jason Kenney and Irwin Cotler, along with Senator Jeremiah Grafstein and the leaders of the Canadian Jewish Congress and B'nai Brith. Captioned "Hate on Campus and International Conference? at York University," the letter said, "This is of great concern to the Jewish Community. [...] We have been witnesses to many anti-Jewish mobs in the streets and on campus."[13] On March 26, Shoukri's office sent a copy to Dean Monahan with the request, "Given that this academic conference is being hosted within Osgoode, could I ask you to reply to Mr. Weinstein and copy the President's Office on your response?" and the dean replied, "Ok fine. Will do."[14]

Professor Abella Writes to the President. In late March, York Professor Irving Abella (historian, J. Richard Shiff Chair for the Study of Canadian Jewry, and a co-author of *None Is Too Many*[15]) was in communication with President Shoukri about the conference. The dates of their email correspondence were made available to this Inquiry, but not the content.[16] It was around this time that AVPR Dewitt informed the organizers that Abella was actively opposing the conference.

THE CAFI/CJS CONFERENCE, MARCH 8–9

A conference titled "Emerging Trends in Anti-Semitism and Campus Discourse" was held at the Munk Centre, University of Toronto, on March 8–9, 2009. It was sponsored by the Canadian Academic Friends of Israel (CAFI) and the Centre for Jewish Studies of the University of Toronto (CJS). Among its participants were Professor Ed Morgan, National Chair of CAFI and a member of the conference organizing committee, and Professor David Dewitt, who chaired a session. The keynote speakers were Irwin Cotler, a Liberal Member of Parliament, and Lord Parry Mitchell, a member of the House of Lords. Miriam Ziv, Ambassador of the State of Israel to Canada, gave an evening address on March 8.

Professor Gerald Steinberg, who later emerged in the vanguard of opponents of the York/Queen's conference, was one of the two speakers in a session titled "The Manipulation of Human Rights Discourse: Orwellian Inversions, Group Defamation and Genocidal Affirmations." Most of the speakers were academics, but several speakers were from non-academic organizations. The latter included Senator Jeremiah Grafstein; Len Rudner, Ontario Regional Director for the Canadian Jewish Congress; and Jacques P. Gauthier, Vice-Chair of the International Centre for Human Rights and Democratic Development (also known as Rights and Democracy).

The relevance of the CAFI/CJS conference to the controversy over the York/Queen's conference is that observations regarding the latter made by its critics (such as the fact that some speakers were not academics, or that the program of speakers was not balanced) could reasonably have been made also regarding the former, yet no comparable controversy arose in regard to the CAFI/CJS conference. Of course there is no general requirement that all speakers at an academic conference be academics, or that the program be balanced. The organizers of conferences have the academic freedom to devise their own program. That a controversy arose over one of these two events but not the other is discussed in a recent article by Mazen Masri.[17]

DEAN MONAHAN DEFENDS THE YORK/QUEEN'S CONFERENCE

Organizational Success. Despite the concerns of Dewitt and Adelman, and opposition by some in the Canadian Jewish community, recruitment of conference speakers continued and by the beginning of April there were more than forty confirmed speakers. Thus, with nearly a full complement of speakers, and the SSHRC grant secured, along with substantial support from York and Queen's, the organizers appeared to be in a good position to mount in June the type of international conference for which they had received the support. Certainly, they themselves were quite confident in the impending success of the conference, and they explained this to the dean when they met with him on April 2.

CIJA Concerns Forwarded to the Dean. On April 1 an email message captioned "Osgoode Hall—One/two state conference in June," was forwarded to Dean Monahan. Enclosed with it was an email thread, each item of which had the same caption. The item appearing immediately below the message to the dean was sent by Susan Davis, executive vice-president of the Canadian Council for Israel and Jewish Advocacy (CIJA) to "David Dewitt," and copied to "iabella" at "yorku.ca," but the text is redacted on the copy released to CAUT under Ontario freedom-of-information legislation (FIPPA).[18]

However, the remainder of the email thread was made available. This was an email message addressed to "Dear UOC members" and signed "Susan." It is reasonable to infer that "UOC" as used here was the acronym for the University Outreach Committee of CIJA. The text of the message gave the link to the conference website, and said that "UOC met with one of the organizers last autumn to express concern that the very construct would lead to an Israel-bashing exercise with little room for academic debate," but that "the approach did not change." The message continued, "With his permission I am attaching a note from Prof. Howard Adelman who was listed as a presenter at the conference. Howard asked that his name be removed from the conference program and his reasons are attached." The message concluded, "I am going to share this with a few Osgoode Hall graduates and I suggest that you do the same. Note that Queen's is also a sponsor." The attached document was Adelman's memo, dated March 20, 2009.[19]

Monahan's email reply (to a person whose name was redacted on the copy released to CAUT) was brief, but suggested he was not unduly concerned about the conference at this stage. He wrote, "Thanks I will see what has been happening with this. Seems to be a few bumps in the road."[20]

Immediately before the dean sent this message, he wrote to Ryder and Drummond:

> I have received a copy of the memo from Howard Adelman withdrawing from the conference. It would be helpful for me to understand how the planning has evolved, so that I will be in a position to respond to these concerns in an informed manner. Should we try to chat about this in the next few days?[21]

The Organizers' Progress Report. Ryder replied to Monahan on April 1, agreeing to meet and adding:

> It is a shame that Howard decided to withdraw, especially since, as he put it in the memo [...] "the organizers should be congratulated for attracting a large number of first-rate scholars." Indeed even more speakers have been confirmed since he decided to withdraw. We now have over 40 confirmed speakers with abstracts posted on the website [...] including a number of excellent senior scholars based at Israeli universities. We're very pleased with the way things have been shaping up [...] our goal from the outset has been to promote a debate between a broad range of different perspectives on the conflict.

In the meeting on the following day, Monahan, Ryder, and Drummond discussed conference matters, including issues raised by Adelman's widely circulating memo of March 20. The dean asked for details on the conference planning and organization, and in response the organizers sent him a two-page memo summarizing their efforts to make the conference a success. Among other things, their memo said:

> The speakers will present a range of perspectives on models of statehood – some are strong advocates of one and two state models, others advocate positions between and beyond, while still others emphasize the durability of the status quo. [...] With the impressive roster of internationally recognized scholars who

are committed to participating in this conference, we have every
expectation that the conference will generate a scholarly output
of the highest caliber. [...]

We wish to reiterate that we remain open to hearing concerns
and suggestions of ways that the conference might be improved.
Our goal is a conference that is a fair and dispassionate
intellectual inquiry into the issues. It is one of our deepest
aspirations that the conference reflect favorably upon the ability
of laws schools and universities to wrestle with vexatiously
difficult topics with sensitivity, scholarly rigour, and intellectual
dispassion and compassion.[22]

It is of note that the organizers' memo also informed the dean that "we
decided not to invite journalists, judges or politicians to participate in the
conference."[23]

Discussion among the Board Chair, President, and Dean. It is clear from
an email thread on April 11 and 12 that none of President Shoukri, Dean
Monahan, or the chair of the board of governors, Marshall Cohen, was
unduly concerned about the conference or the attendant controversy. On
April 11 (at 6:58 AM), the dean sent an email message to the president,
saying that the conference was continuing "to attract some controversy,"
and noting that Professor Adelman had recently withdrawn from it, "on
grounds that it was not taking a sufficiently balanced approach to the
issues."[24] Monahan continued:

This [withdrawal] has attracted some attention within the
community and, because of the other [earlier] events involving
students, may create a knee-jerk reaction in the community.
About a week ago I asked the organizing committee to prepare
a report for me on the status of the conference. I am attaching
their report from your information. In general, I am satisfied
that this conference will involve a balanced exploration of some
very difficult and challenging issues, and we have nothing to
apologize for in regards to this conference.[25]

The president forwarded the dean's message to Cohen the next morning.
Cohen replied, saying he had read a copy of Adelman's March 20 withdrawal
memo, given to him a few days earlier by an acquaintance. He added:

When I read the memo the next day, it didn't seem to me to be much different from the usual academic infighting that goes on all the time at York and at all universities. [...] Patrick [Monahan] seems to have done all the right things. [...] That said, if this is the next big community push (now that IAW [Israel Apartheid week] is over), we shld not wait for the deluge before reacting. Consider whether we need a pro-active approach—i.e. a meeting w the community leaders to convey the message that Patrick laid out in his reply to [redacted] and in his email to you. We need to look like we have thought about the situation even if our conclusion is not what the community wants to hear. We also need to get the facts on the table before these campaigns gain momentum.[26]

Shoukri forwarded Cohen's message to Monahan, saying:

Frankly, I am of two minds. On one hand, it is wise to anticipate these reactions and deal with them before they become problems. On the other hand, this is becoming a full time job. The community need to trust us. I like your response to [redacted]. We should stay with the message.[27]

The Dean's Response to a Critic. It is reasonable to infer that the "message" to which Cohen and Shoukri referred (in the April 12 emails quoted above) was the one contained in the email Monahan sent to a conference critic on the previous day, and copied to the president. The critic had written to the dean in response to the anti-conference campaign email sent out by JDL on March 5. In his reply to the critic, Monahan addressed the JDL comments and defended the conference:

Further to our exchange yesterday, in my view the [JDL] email you received is a totally inaccurate and unfair characterization of this conference. It is not calling for anything, and certainly not the end of Israel as a Jewish state. It is, rather, a serious academic conference that will feature over 40 speakers from around the world, including many from Israeli universities. The purpose of the conference, as is explained on the conference website, is to explore whether there are new solutions that might be explored in the middle east in an attempt to find

peaceful solutions to the conflict there. This will involve
the exploration of controversial ideas, and I know that the
conference has been controversial within some elements of the
community here in Toronto. But a serious academic institution
has to encourage free inquiry, as long as the debate is balanced
and not skewed in one direction or the other. I believe that this
conference will do that. [...]

I encourage you to look at the website and see for yourself the
range of opinion that is going to be canvassed at the event.

The fact that it received a grant from an independent committee
at the SSHRC is evidence of the scholarly character of the
conference. [...] In fact the SSHRC committee, which is made
up of scholars from other universities, gave the conference the
highest possible ranking as a scholarly conference. I do not
know why your correspondent would take that as something to
criticize.[28]

In summary, the dean's two emails of the morning of April 11 supported
the conference. Moreover, on Sunday, April 12, in reply to the comments
by Shoukri and Cohen, the dean wrote:

At this point I think we continue to monitor the situation. [...]
I think the problem we are having is that with the other events
that have taken place recently, we are not given the benefit
of the doubt on these questions. But I don't think we should
initiate any discussions with the broader community at this
point.[29]

To this advice, the president replied, "Agreed. Thanks."[30]

RISING PRESSURE AND A BIFURCATION

Two days later (Tuesday, April 14), the complexion of events changed dramatically. Cohen emailed Shoukri, saying:

Further to my message to you over the weekend, I am growing
increasingly concerned that, rightly or wrongly, this is inflating

into a huge issue. It's too complicated to work through by e-mail exchanges. Can we talk about it asap? (If you want a 3 way conversation with Patrick on the call, that's ok too.)[31]

In response, Shoukri emailed Monahan, enclosing Cohen's message and saying:

> The pressure from the Jewish community is growing regarding the june conference. Mickey would like to have a 3-way call to discuss.[32]

The president's assistant, Irene Fezza, then sent a message to the dean with times when Shoukri would be available (5:30 or 6:00 PM the next day, April 15, or 8:00 AM on the day following).

Mid-afternoon on April 15, Cohen sent an email message to Shoukri and Monahan:

> After a sleepless night fretting about the mapping conference, I prepared the comments you see below. This is more intrusion then I am usually guilty of, but I care and I am concerned. Hopefully I am all wet, but just in case. ... We are fighting both maybe a little reality and a lot of (mis)perception. As always, the what to do is your decision. And there are probly a dozen more or better things you can up with. Anyway I finally decided to send it to you both so we can have a more focussed discussion later today Do what you think is best just don't shoot the messenger.[33]

With this email message to the president and the dean, Cohen enclosed an email memo to himself from mid-morning. He wrote:

> Bottom line is that I think there is a gathering storm out there and I think we need to prepare for it. This situation worries me far more than recent events, but coming on top of recent events, it has tsunami proportions. If I sound a little panicky, it's because I am—not my normal style but there it is. Hopefully, I am all wrong about this.

> First, what I am hearing in the Jewish Community:

This is a biased, Israeli bashing, one state solution,
verging on anti-semitic conference. [You have heard
this too]

The moderate organizations in the community will
soon start their campaigns to reach our parents,
donors etc etc

The more extreme groups will march and protest [JDL,
maybe B'nai Brith]

This is different than recent events—IAW was every
universities problem, the Ferman incident was
unexpected.[34] This conference we blessed, we know
it's coming, and we are letting it happen. This is a
York event.

This is another Durban in the making and York will
be forever tagged with it.

From those who care about York, – this conference is bad news
in and of itself, but on top of recent events, it will be a disaster.
[...] So what to do.

First, some principles:

We should not defend the indefensible. By this I
mean you guys shld get really comfortable that the
conference is what it purports to be. I think you shld
[sic] speak to Adelman, Abella and anyone else who
might have insight from the Israeli perspective to
understand whaty the concern is and whether it has
any basis.

Second, we should defend the defensible, once you get
comfortable that the conference is being misunderstood.
By this I mean we shld get very proactive and try to
defuse the situation. Freedom of speech and academic
freedom are essential to what we are

Here are some thoughts of my own. They may be non starters
and they will certainly be met w [sic] a 1000 objections, but I
wld ask you to measure them against the tsunami alternative
that may await us. We are between a rock and a hard place and
managing and mitigating the risks is all we can do.[35]

Among the suggestions made by Cohen in this memo were the following:

1] I wld seriously consider moving the venue off campus.
If this blows up on us then it occurring on campus will
overwhelmingly exacerbate the impact on York. [...]

2] You need to met w the Jewish community leadership to
carefully explain our position [...]

5] can we populate the audience with observers &/or participants
to ensure a balanced dialogue [...]

All these ideas have a price tag attached but the alternative may
be even costlier.[36]

In his communication to the president and the dean, Cohen had suggested that Professor Abella be consulted, among others. However, on
the day before (April 14), there had already been email correspondence
between the dean and Abella about the conference.

INVOLVEMENT OF PROFESSOR ABELLA

The organizers were aware that opposition to the conference was growing
on campus, as well as off campus. Around the end of March or the beginning of April, they were informed that Irving Abella was a leading oppon-
ent, as Drummond noted to Dean Monahan on April 15:

As I think Bruce and I mentioned, we met with David Dewitt
a couple of weeks ago. He suggested that we meet with Irving
Abella who, David indicated, was leading the campaign against
the conference. Bruce and I promptly contacted Irving to set up a
meeting with him to see if we can address his concerns.[37]

Drummond enclosed with this email message to the dean a copy of one she had sent that morning to AVPR Dewitt, saying, "Bruce Ryder and I have followed up on your suggestion that we make contact with Irving Abella regarding our conference (I cc'd you on the email I sent to him). Irving indicated that he is back in Toronto next week and we will make arrangements to get together upon his return."[38] She had asked Dewitt whether he could "be of some assistance to us in suggesting scholars that we might approach for a particular spot on the conference," namely, a "high caliber speaker" who would address "the pros and cons of the two-state model"—especially from a pro-two-state perspective—in a panel of two speakers (the other speaker would address mainly the one-state model) that would open the conference on the first morning.[39] She also repeated the organizers' invitation to Dewitt to participate in the conference.

In her message to the dean, Drummond added that "The [enclosed] letter to David [Dewitt] is just one of the many, many we have sent out both over the last two weeks and from the very beginning of conference organizing roughly one and half years ago."[40]

There is evidence that Monahan was already aware that Abella had concerns about the conference, at least one day before Drummond sent her email message of April 15 to him. An index of records obtained by CAUT from York University includes two entries for email threads involving Abella. The contents were not released, but brief descriptions are available in records provided by the university. The first record is for an email thread between President Shoukri and Abella, dated March 27, 2009, captioned "Re: Conference at York," while the second is for an email thread between the dean and Abella, dated April 14, 2009, with the same caption.[41]

The information available confirms that April 14, at 4:40 PM, Abella sent to Monahan an email message about the conference to which he attached his March 25 message to the president. The dean replied to Abella during the evening of April 14.

On April 15, Monahan sent an email message to Abella, captioned "Speak more about conference." The dean copied this message to Justice Rosalie Abella at her Supreme Court of Canada email address. He wrote:

Irv I have looked at the website in more detail and understand better the concerns. I want to get involved now in a more direct way and would like to speak with you, this evening if possible. Where can I reach you?[42]

After speaking with Professor Abella, Monahan reported to Shoukri and Cohen on the conversation:

I spoke to Irv this evening and he tells me that he can't speak at the conference b/c he is speaking at an Aspen Conference at that time and, in any event, this is not an area of his expertise. I pressed him on it but that is his position. However he did say that he thinks David Dewitt would be a good speaker and also that David could assist us in getting others who would be helpful. I now have a list of other names of potential speakers suggested by Irv that we can approach, perhaps though David or with his assistance. I will get the list of names typed up tomorrow and sent around.[43]

During the next few weeks, Monahan consulted a number of times with Dewitt on matters related to the conference. At the dean's request, Dewitt contacted a number of scholars in an effort to assist with finding speakers both he and the dean would consider suitable. The dean was, in particular, "trying to add a keynote speaker who will be a strong defender of Israel," as he replied to conference critics on April 24.[44] The conference organizers also kept up their own efforts to find such a speaker. Organizers informed this Inquiry that this continued to be a difficult task for everyone involved in the effort, not least because some prospective speakers with appropriate credentials were coming under the same types of strong community criticism regarding participation as Professor Ed Morgan had mentioned to Sharryn Aiken in September 2008.

DEAN MONAHAN AND AVPR DEWITT CRITICIZE THE CONFERENCE

Criticism by York Administrators. Beginning in mid-April 2009 and during the course of the next four weeks, both Dean Monahan and AVPR Dewitt criticized the conference in strong terms in communications with Professors Ryder and Drummond, as well as in communications with each other. The substance of the comments to the organizers and the manner in which the administrators expressed them caused them to feel they were being subjected to inappropriate pressure. It was acknowledged in correspondence among senior York officials that pressure was being exerted on the organizers by Dean Monahan.[45]

The comments to the organizers came in the form of a series of suggestions, proposals, and demands regarding the academic content and organization of the conference, as well as its location and timing. At various times the sense of pressure intensified. The comments eventually included a challenge by Monahan as to the academic credentials of Professors Ryder, Drummond, and Aiken to mount such a conference. Some of the comments were made in email messages, others in meetings, and the last one in a telephone call on the evening of May 12.

Aiken experienced nothing whatever of this kind at Queen's, where senior administrators—including the dean of law and the principal—were at all times fully supportive of her and the conference, notwithstanding the fact that they, too, were receiving protests from on and off campus.

By April 15 both the dean and AVPR Dewitt had come to the view that the opposition to the conference, from on and off campus, was due at least in part to faulty design of the conference program. They each made academic assessments of the program content, attributed fault to the organizers, and made proposals for changes to the academic content of the program in efforts to bring about a solution to the perceived problem or problems.

However, Monahan and Dewitt initially promoted different approaches. The dean's view was that the program lacked balance, and the primary thrust of his approach was to try to attract additional speakers known to be strong supporters of the two-state model and to reorganize the program so as to feature such speakers. The AVPR promoted a more radical approach, in effect to "disinvite" the majority of the already confirmed speakers so that the program thereby truncated would have only about a dozen "worthy" speakers.

After April 15, when they received Dewitt's email message outlining his proposal, the conference organizers declined to discuss conference organization with him. Thereafter his involvement and influence on events came through his communications with Monahan, who relied on him for academic advice on the program and for assistance in efforts to recruit the types of speakers the dean felt were needed to balance the program. The sense of pressure felt by the organizers at York was intermittent during the period from April 15 to May 12, when it reached its maximum intensity. On occasions when they considered administrators' comments to be inappropriate interference, they resisted. On other occasions, when they considered suggestions by administrators to be appropriate or not unreasonable, the organizers agreed and expressed appreciation for the assistance.

The April 15 Interventions by Dean Monahan and AVPR Dewitt. By mid-April there were approximately fifty confirmed speakers. On April 15, Monahan and Dewitt sent email messages to Ryder and Drummond expressing concerns about the conference. The dean's first email of April 15 was sent in the late morning, before he received the detailed email message that day from Marshall Cohen, but after the email from the president on April 14 to arrange a discussion in response to "pressure from the Jewish community," and after his email exchange with Irving Abella on April 14.

The dean sent this message to Ryder and Drummond only four days after his April 11 email defending the conference program, citing the SSHRC grant, and inviting one of his correspondents to "look at the website and see for yourself," and only three days after he had suggested to the president there was no need for immediate action. However, the dean had changed his assessment. He now wrote to Ryder and Drummond that:

> There are increasing concerns emerging over the June conference. Over the last ten days or so I have received a variety of calls or emails from individuals both in and outside of the University expressing concerns over what is described as a lack of balance in the speakers and papers that are being prepared for the conference. In reliance on the [April 3] memorandum you prepared for me I have consistently indicated that my understanding is that these fears are unfounded and that in fact the conference will be a balanced look at some difficult issues in the region. However in light of the fact that these concerns are persistent and in fact increasing I have now taken some additional time to review the website and in particular the papers that are described as having been confirmed for the conference. I must say that I have some serious concerns over a variety of aspects of the papers that I see both in terms of the content of specific papers as well as the overall volume and direction that many contributors appear to be taking to these issues. [...] I must say though that this is becoming a significant

issue and I am concerned about the impact it will have on a
variety of fronts. I look forward to speaking with you about this
in the near future.[46]

Plainly, the dean had now made his own academic assessment of the
suitability of some of the talks to be given at the conference, following communications between himself and Abella, and after reading the
abstracts on the conference website. Also, as he indicated, he was prompted
to read them at least in part because of "calls or emails from individuals
both in and outside of the University." He made such an assessment even
though he was not an expert on the topics of the conference, as Ryder and
Drummond knew, and as he himself subsequently acknowledged to them,
and as he also acknowledged to AVPR Dewitt.

Half an hour later, Drummond sent the email message to Dean
Monahan in which she mentioned that Dewitt had recently indicated that
Abella "was leading the campaign against the conference." In the early
afternoon Ryder responded to Monahan by email, saying he would be
happy to meet and adding:

> We've heard these concerns persistently from the outset of
> conference planning, and have responded by meeting with
> everyone who has openly expressed their concerns to us,
> by listening seriously to their concerns, and by sending an
> invitation to every academic speaker who has been suggested to
> us. We remain open to any and all suggestions.[47]

Dewitt, in his email of April 15 (5:52 PM)—sent to the conference
email address, MappingModels, and copied to Drummond's faculty email
address—said that some confirmed speakers, "by their past actions have
been tarnished by ideology and polemic," and from this assessment he
concluded the organizers' "well-meaning effort to unpack the challenges
facing both Israelis and Palestinians is being hijacked."[48] He added:

> Balance and objectivity here are not appropriate criteria for
> what I understand has been your intent. As you and I discussed,
> I personally see nothing wrong with asking some very tough
> and fundamental questions about "models of statehood or of
> national aspirations" so long as it is very clear that we are not
> entertaining the elimination of the Jewish national homeland

or questioning the legitimacy of the State of Israel or its right to
live within secure and recognized boundaries. Alas, I continue
to think that this baseline has been crossed. Under these
circumstances, I continue to be unable to participate and I also
can't really provide you with anyone who might be appropriate
for what you—quite understandably and appropriately—want to
lead off the conference.[49]

Dewitt mentioned the names of five prominent scholars (four in Israel,
one in Canada) who would have appropriate stature, but who would not
participate in the conference.

In this email message, Dewitt also proposed a major change to the conference, presumably one that would bring the program over to his side of
the line he had drawn earlier in the same email message. He wrote:

since you already seem pretty confident that you have about
a dozen or so strong contributions by recognized and worthy
individuals, why not notify all that due to financial constraints
(and everyone now knows about those!) the program has had
to be reduced to a shorter time (one day perhaps or day plus a
morning) for the presentation of those 12 or so papers, and only
those individuals will receive financial support and be on the
program. Others are certainly invited to attend in the audience
and to participate from that vantage point, but not to present.[50]

In other words, he suggested to the organizers that they reduce the conference program from two and a half days to one or one and a half days,
reduce the more than four dozen confirmed speakers down to "about a
dozen or so strong contributions by recognized and worthy individuals,"
and that they give "financial constraints" as their reason for doing so.
Dewitt added that, despite such a major change:

You should be able to fulfil your academic responsibilities to
SSHRC.[51]

That evening (9:44 PM), after he had spoken with Abella, Monahan
replied to Ryder's message:

I do appreciate the fact that you have issued invitations to a wide

variety of people from different perspectives. But it is not enough
to say that you have invited people. You will be judged on who
is actually speaking. If you look at your website and review
the abstracts I have to tell you that this comes across as not
particularly balanced. We can discuss this more on Friday. This
is provoking a major reaction in the community, that will then
provoke a counter-reaction from other groups. The conference
will be lost in the cross fire. When we speak I want to impress
on you the seriousness of the situation that we (both you and
the university) is facing. This is shaping up as a major event that
could spin very badly out of control. You need to understand
that.[52]

Thus, once again, the dean expressed an academic assessment on the
basis of posted conference abstracts, this time after having been again in
communication with Professor Abella. Yet, as already noted, he himself
was not an expert in the relevant topics. Also, as he himself had informed
Shoukri and Cohen in an email message, this was not an area of Abella's
expertise.

THE YORK UNIVERSITY CONFERENCE VENUE AT ISSUE

The Glendon Reservation Cancelled. In July 2008 the organizers had reserved
space on the Glendon campus for the conference. On March 2, 2009, in an
email message to Professor Ryder, U50 Manager of Implementation Sarah
Brathwaite said:

> We have recently finished reconfirming space for U50
> events taking place February–May, and are now going to be
> reconfirming space for events taking place June–September.
> Before reviewing the space requirements for your conference
> with the Registrar's Office and Pascal at Glendon can you please
> review the information below and let me know if any changes
> are required.[53]

On this basis Ryder assumed that the Glendon reservation was being
reconfirmed. However, on April 14, 2009, Brathwaite told him that a
scheduling conflict had arisen, with the result that the Glendon space was
no longer available. He was informed that, because of the protracted strike

by the university's contract academic staff (approximately three months, from late fall to early winter), events related to Convocation had been delayed until late June and these would be given priority over the conference. The U50 office had instead reserved facilities for the conference at the main campus on Keele Street.

Ryder protested on behalf of the organizing committee, noting that the original reservation had been made the previous summer and that confirmed speakers and other participants were already being booked into Glendon residences or nearby hotels. In an email reply to Brathwaite on April 14, he wrote:

> I remain stunned about the possibility that we won't be able to hold our conference at Glendon. According to the info on the York website, Glendon convocation will be held on June 30th, the week after our conference.[54]

Brathwaite replied that the Glendon space was required for pre-Convocation set-up, as well as for a board of governors meeting and reception/dinner event on June 23. However, she offered to try to negotiate a resolution with the Glendon College administration. The next day, April 15, Professor Ryder was informed by Pascal Lewin at Glendon that, according to his records, there should be no problem in keeping the original conference reservation.

The Proposal to Move the Conference Off Campus. Ryder and Drummond met with Dean Monahan on April 17 (as requested in his April 15 email messages to them). The dean repeated the concerns he had expressed in his April 15 messages, and urged them to secure additional speakers who would be prominent advocates of the two-state model. In addition, he informed them that they would likely not be allowed to hold the conference on any York University campus. He gave them to understand that this was the wish of the board of governors.[55] It is clear from a report of this meeting that he himself wrote (cited below) that, regarding denial of a campus venue to the conference, the dean was conveying information from communications he had had with the president and the chair of the board on or about April 15.[56]

Later on April 17, Monahan sent the following meeting report to Cohen (Chair of the Board of Governors), President Shoukri, and Stan Shapson (Vice-President Research and Innovation):

I met with the organizers (Bruce Ryder and Susan Drummond)
today to impress upon them the seriousness of the situation
and had a productive discussion. First, they have welcomed
my offer to assist in recruiting additional speakers to provide
some balance. I am wondering, Stan, whether you have spoke
to David D about his own participation as well as his assistance
in recruiting others. Second, they are open to moving the
conference off-site to a hotel, subject to cost. I am having
someone investigate the availability of a modestly price hotel
option. Mickey you raised this idea—do you think it worth it to
invest the additional money needed to move it off-campus? By
the way, as of now it is scheduled for Glendon, not the main
campus. I expect the incremental cost would not be large. Let me
know what you think.[57]

Cohen replied that day as follows:

On the question of moving, I wld suggest we handle it as Plan B.
That is to say, if we get comfortable that it is balanced and that
people perceive it to be so [i.e. no marches etc], then no need
to move it to a hotel. But if there is any doubt, and given that
the incremental costs don't seem excessive, I wld move it. Ergo,
can we book something as insurance and then decide in a week
or two when we see how things are going. Then at most, we
might lose our deposit but that wld be an insurance premium
well worth paying. [the interesting thing, if I read your note
right, is that the organisers don't seem bent out of shape at the
suggestion. I can only assume that you put the fear of all 3 gods
involved here into them! Good work][58]

The Board Chair's "Durban II" Concerns. Cohen's level of concern
appears to have been heightened on April 21 by media coverage that morning of the World Conference against Racism (sometimes referred to as
the Durban Review Conference or, by critics, as Durban II) being held in
Geneva (April 20–24, 2009).[59] On April 21 he sent Shoukri and Monahan
an email message captioned "Durban 11," saying:

The story in today's papers about "Durban 11," which I assume
you have both seen, is what worries me about the upcoming

Mapping Conference. Assuming we get enough pro Israel speakers to "balance" the program, we may still not be out of the danger zone. What do we do if one of the speakers launches into what amounts to or comes close to a racist diatribe?

Yes we can argue that at a university academic conference, free speech must be tolerated but that argument will get drowned out in the media circus that will erupt. Some attendees will walk out, but some will stay and applaud, as was the case in Geneva and we, as sponsors and [physical] hosts will be caught in the middle of an argument we can't win. So, the issue becomes—is there anything we can do to ensure that no speaker wanders off the range—i.e. they stick to their abstracts. Can the conference organisers enforce some discipline on the speakers—and are they strong enough to do so? Can we disinvite known hate mongers, if we have any on the program? Is this censorship? Do we need an ombudsman in attendance at all times to preserve civility [Roy McMurtry?] I don't have an answer but someone needs to think about this and be prepared.

Again, apologies for continuing to pester you guys about this, but yesterday's events will just heighten everyone's interest in and fears about the conference.[60]

Shoukri replied, in more measured terms:

My expectation, based on early assurance, is that the participants are reasonable people who have strong views about the issue. In that sense, I do not expect them to cross the line. It is always possible that some may. It is also possible that some from the other side may draw a line that is easily crossed. Either way, it is not hard to imagine a scenario in which some people walk out in protest. Based on the above, I like your idea of an ambudsman-like in attendance. He may not be acting like a sensor but at least can interfere if things get out of hand or can be a reliable source of info on what really happened. I wonder if Roy will be willing to do that. Can he or John McCamus be asked to chair one of the sessions where troubles may occur?[61]

Later that afternoon, Monahan also replied:

> I met on Monday [April 20] with Stan [Shapson] and David
> Dewitt and we are working on a plan to try to rework the
> agenda and mitigate the damage. David and I are meeting with
> the organizers on Thursday morning [April 23] to explore the
> possibilities and try to find a path forward. Rather than detail
> our thoughts now (some of which may not be possible or
> attainable), I want to meet first with the organizers and see what
> might have a chance of working. I will get back with an update
> once we have had that meeting.[62]

It is of note that the dean was of the view that there was "damage" to be
mitigated and that he was involving Dewitt in what he viewed as a mitiga-
tion process. As he reported to Shoukri and Cohen on April 25, the organizers declined to agree to the presence of Dewitt in the April 23 meeting,
because Dewitt had already, in his April 15 email message to them, drawn
a line, and they were opposed to any further involvement by him in conference planning.[63] Whether Dewitt's line was one "easily crossed" (to use
Shoukri's phrase) was, by this point, immaterial, because he suggested to
them on April 15 that they had already crossed it. This also was the email
in which Dewitt had suggested they substantially truncate the conference
program, a suggestion the organizers considered inappropriate.

The Search for an Off-Campus Venue. In the meeting with the dean, as
the dean had reported to the board chair and others, the organizers did
express a willingness to move the conference off campus—if that really
was necessary—but indicated they had no funding for hotel or similar
accommodation. Monahan suggested to them that York University could
consider providing additional funds. Over the course of several days, with
the assistance of Osgoode Hall staff-person Matthew Murray, a number of
possible off-campus venues were contacted, but options for a large conference on relatively short notice were limited.

Contact with CAUT. The organizers informed this Inquiry that they
found these developments—the apparent cancellation of their reservation of conference space on the Glendon campus and, worse, the
dean's information that they likely would be denied any York campus
venue because of the purported wish of the board of governors—very
distressing. They consulted a senior Osgoode Hall colleague for advice,
and he suggested, among other things, that they contact the Canadian

Association of University Teachers (CAUT) for possible assistance. Drummond then contacted James Turk, the executive director, and in a conference call shortly thereafter with the three York members of the organizing committee, Turk assured them of active CAUT interest on the basis that academic freedom might be at risk.[64] From this point in April onward, the organizers consulted with CAUT on developments as they arose. In addition, they kept a detailed record of discussions in future meetings with Monahan, and they also began to strongly resist moving the conference venue.

Suggestions by Dean Monahan on Conference Changes. Ryder and Drummond met with the dean again on April 23 (8:30 AM). They agreed to suggestions by the dean that efforts be made to secure additional keynote speakers and additional plenary speakers, and the program be rearranged so as to feature such speakers—provided the full organizing committee concurred, and the additional speakers met relevant academic criteria. In the dean's view, these would be speakers who would restore the balance he now regarded as lacking. For his part, the dean agreed to assist in contacting additional speakers and to provide the required funding for them. Also during this meeting, Ryder and Drummond asked Monahan for his assistance in re-securing the Glendon College venue, and he agreed to help.

Monahan, Ryder, and Drummond came away from this meeting with different understandings of the basis for the discussion and its conclusions. The two conference organizers separately informed this Inquiry that they considered they were being offered suggestions by the dean that might help further strengthen what they regarded as an already strong conference program, and they were willing to give these suggestions full and fair consideration in discussions with their co-organizers, in light of appropriate academic criteria. As for the issue of a campus venue, Glendon in particular, they saw no good reason, academic or administrative, for a change—and they so informed the dean in the meeting, as he himself noted in an email message to his administrative superiors two days later.[65] Specifically, they did not regard the April 23 discussion as being tantamount to bargaining or exchanging program changes in return for a campus venue.

Monahan's understanding was outlined in an email message to Ryder and Drummond on May 10, written after their collective efforts to recruit an additional keynote speaker—the one agreed on by all three of them— were unsuccessful. The dean considered that the organizers had not lived up to an agreement with him, because in this email he wrote:

> So adding a new speaker as a keynote was a very important and
> constructive decision on your part. I was encouraged by your
> agreement with this, and based on that, (as well as on the idea of
> plenary sessions to highlight the strongest scholars), I facilitated
> the securing of the space in Glendon for the conference.[66]

The dean appears to have given AVPR Dewitt a similar understanding in
regard to the April 23 discussion with Drummond and Ryder, because in
an email message to the dean on May 11, Dewitt referred to "the agreement
you thought you had with them."[67] It is Monahan's position, as stated to
this Inquiry, that he was not bargaining or exchanging program changes in
return for a campus venue:

> I supported the organizers in their desire to remain on the
> Glendon Campus, and did not attempt to bargain the availability
> of space for changes in the program.[68]

Re-instatement of the Glendon Reservation. The material role of Dean
Monahan, if any, in "the securing of the space in Glendon"—in his own
view, this was his part of an agreement he had with the organizers—is
unclear to this Inquiry. This is because email correspondence among senior administrative staff records that President Shoukri had already, on or
before April 20—three days before the April 23 discussion between the
dean and the two conference organizers in which the purported agreement
was made—directed that the Glendon College venue be secured for the
conference. On April 20, Ijade Maxwell Rodrigues, senior executive officer
in the Office of the President, had emailed Harriet Lewis, university secretary and general counsel, saying:

> The President has asked that I get in touch with you about
> having the Board of Governor's meeting [...] moved from
> Glendon College to either Keele or Downtown. He would like
> to make sure the Osgoode conference stays at Glendon and
> that the Board meeting is not held in the same location as the
> conference. Would you please let me know where the meeting
> will be moved to?"[69]

Also on April 20, Pascal Lewin emailed Professor Ryder to confirm that Glendon Convocation set-up would not conflict with the conference space.

In a communication to this Inquiry on February 11, 2011, Monahan stated that he had not received a copy of the April 20, 2009, email message from Maxwell Rodrigues to Lewis and was "unaware of its existence at the time."

Later on April 23 (12:47 PM), Ryder received an email message from U50 Project Director Cindy Bettcher confirming that the conference could proceed at Glendon, as originally planned, because the other events planned for the same space had been relocated.

On April 25—five days after senior staff-persons in the president's office were, at his request, "mak[ing] sure" that the conference would stay at Glendon—Dean Monahan reported in an email message to President Shoukri and Board Chair Cohen on his April 23 discussions with Ryder and Drummond. He summarized the suggestions he had made to them in regard to keynote and plenary speakers, and indicated they had agreed to these. (As noted above, the position of Ryder and Drummond was that they had agreed only to discuss the dean's suggestions with their committee colleagues in light of appropriate academic criteria.) The dean continued:

They have gotten their backs up on the idea of moving off campus. They say they booked the space at Glendon long ago and there is no legitimate academic reason for moving it now. They also say it would be embarrassing to them b/c the location has been advertized (including in the U50 booklet) and it would be hard for them to explain why it is being moved. Ryder (who is the more reasonable of the two) was particularly exercised on this point. With the changes discussed above, I have indicated they can go ahead at Glendon.

They also don't want to shorten down the conference. This was a suggestion from David Dewitt (with whom they ultimately refused to meet [on April 23], but that is another long story I can share if you want), but I don't think it makes a lot of difference whether it is 1.5 days or 2.5 days. The key is to get this kind of rebalancing that will ensure that the conference is a legitimate academic conference.[70]

In the same email, the dean went on to describe the tenor of the April 23 meeting:

> I have to say that I pushed them very hard, even to the point where Drummond on Thursday [April 23] said that I was pressuring them inappropriately and infringing their academic freedom. She suggested that they may have to raise the matter with CAUT and with the Faculty Association. I don't think that will happen, but I just wanted to indicate that I have to be very cautious now in making suggestions, as opposed to demands. It is still a work in progress, but there definitely is progress.[71]

DEAN MONAHAN DISCOUNTS HIS OWN SIGNATURE

From early April onward, Dean Monahan was receiving messages from individuals opposed to the conference, some of which he referred to as "angry emails."[72] In a reply to a conference critic on April 24 he said, "There are certainly major problems with this conference. I have become involved in a significant way in the last two weeks, in an attempt to ensure that there is balance in the discussion at the conference," adding that this was "extremely challenging," in light of "issues of academic freedom that are at play here and that have to be approached very carefully."[73]

In the same reply, he discounted Osgoode Hall sponsorship of the conference, which he himself had approved as dean, signing the organizers' U50 application:

> As for the issue that it is "sponsored" by Osgoode, the organizers applied to a York committee to be designated as a York 50th event, which meant that they got some money from a fund created to celebrate the 50th anniversary of York. I supported their application, based on the vision statement. And really I had no other realistic choice but to support them. I supported every application that was put forward by my faculty members. (There were 7 applications and all of them got money from the York 50th fund.) So that is what "sponsorship" consists of. (They also got a grant from SSHRC, but I wasn't involved in that.) I wanted to give you guys a sense of the challenges I am facing here, and the attempts I am making to address them. I do not expect you will be happy. I am not happy about it.[74]

DEAN MONAHAN RELIES ON AVPR DEWITT'S EXPERTISE

During the period from late April to mid-May, the dean actively enlisted the assistance of AVPR Dewitt in finding additional prominent scholars as speakers and also sought his advice on other matters pertaining to the conference, as demonstrated by email correspondence between them. The dean involved Dewitt even though, as Monahan himself acknowledged on April 25 to the president and the board chair, the organizers did not desire any further involvement by the AVPR in conference program discussions, following Dewitt's email message to them on April 15.[75] However, as requested by Monahan, Dewitt was in contact with several scholars, inviting them to consider speaking at the conference or to suggest the names of others who might be interested, and he reported their replies to the dean. Monahan also consulted with Dewitt on other matters pertaining to the conference program.

An instance of Monahan's reliance on Dewitt's opinions on the academic content of the conference can be seen in an email message dated May 2. In it, the dean said to the AVPR:

> See below from Bruce [Ryder]. As you will see, he is asking to keep this strictly confidential at this point. It is therefore absolutely essential that if you share this information (and not his actual email) with anyone you must have 100% guarantees from them of confidentiality. Don't let me down on this. We have a chance to shape this in the right direction, but just one chance.[76]

On May 1, Ryder had written to Monahan to provide a "Conference Update" and it was this email message the dean forwarded to Dewitt. Ryder reported that the organizing committee had scheduled a four-hour meeting for May 8 to discuss "re-arranging the draft program with more plenaries to highlight our best speakers," adding that the importance of this was "underlined again in a conversation that Susan and I had with Irving Abella over coffee yesterday."[77]

Ryder informed the dean that the committee would be considering which confirmed speakers would be given prominent roles, in plenary sessions or otherwise, and he mentioned six members of the conference's Advisory Board, "Abunimah, Bevenisti, Farsakh, Kretzmer, Lustick, Smooha," along with "a handful of other senior scholars (possibilities include Adam, Bisharat, Gans, Rabinowitz, Rouhana, Todd and the newly

signed-on Marc Ellis, Director, Centre of Jewish Studies, Baylor U). [...]
We'll keep you posted."[78] He concluded with a request:

> In the meantime, can we agree to keep our conversations
> about prospective speakers and the conference program strictly
> confidential? We are grateful for your input and feedback, but
> fearful of ways in which others might continue to misconstrue—
> and even actively seek to undermine—our efforts.[79]

The confidentiality request arose from the fact that the organizers had
been informed by several Jewish scholars who had been invited to participate and who initially had agreed, that they had come under strong community pressure to withdraw, to the extent of feeling compelled to withdraw. Moreover, when, at the suggestion of Dewitt, Ryder and Drummond
met with Abella on April 30 to discuss his concerns, they were surprised
when he told them he knew they had very recently invited Professor
Michael Bell to speak. To their knowledge, only Monahan, the members of
the organizing committee, and Bell himself were aware of this.

ADDITIONAL KEYNOTE SPEAKERS

Professor Bell Invited. During his meeting with Ryder and Drummond on
April 23, Dean Monahan had proposed that Michael Bell, an expert on
the Middle East at the University of Windsor, be invited as an additional
keynote speaker.[80] His name had not previously occurred to the organizers, but they agreed, welcoming the suggestion because Bell had served as
Canada's ambassador to Israel and to other countries in the Middle East,
was well versed in the political complexities of the region, and was highly
regarded academically.

Later that day, Ryder sent the dean an email message confirming that all
four members of the organizing committee had met and agreed Bell should
be invited as a keynote speaker. Monahan replied:

> Bruce I think you should send the letter of invitation to Michael
> asap and then I will follow up with him myself. You should
> copy me on the letter. I agree that Michael would be excellent.
> Let's hope we can persuade him to do it.[81]

The four members of the organizing committee wrote to Bell on April

27, outlining the aims of the conference, and offering him the same honorarium as the keynote speaker already confirmed, Jeremy Webber. The invitation also said:

> While we would leave the choice of topic to your discretion,
> it would certainly be of interest if you could offer a principled
> defence of a two-state model that addresses why and how such a
> model is still feasible in the current context.[82]

The invitation offered to Bell his choice of time slot on the program and assured him he could speak on a topic of his own choosing, instead of the one suggested.

Monahan was copied on the organizers' email transmission to Bell and he promptly forwarded it to AVPR Dewitt, indicating he planned to call Bell the next day to encourage him to accept. Later that evening, Dewitt replied to the dean, encouraging him to follow the organizers' invitation with a telephone call to Bell. He wrote of "the weight his name carries among both Israelis and Palestinians inside and out of governments and academe," and continued:

> Michael Bell is, in my view, very well placed to unpack such
> arguments [for and against various two-state models], examine
> alternatives, and I would guess whether for principles or for
> pragmatic politics, argue why a two-state solution is the only
> possible path should peace and security be the shared goal.[83]

Dewitt suggested to Monahan that Bell should be given information about the controversy surrounding the conference, adding:

> Michael must be informed about the "third tier" participants/
> presenters, and appreciate that there may be some attention
> given to this meeting and especially to those who are seen to
> be one staters in favour of undermining/destroying Israel, Israel
> apartheid and "Zionism as Racism" types, but the other one-
> staters who see the necessity of "cleansing" Israel of all Arabs and
> perhaps even all non Jews, Arab or other.[84]

Monahan again emailed Dewitt on the evening of April 27, saying:

I spoke to [redacted] this evening and, quite frankly, it is very discouraging to discuss this with him. He is not impressed with Bell, saying he is not seen as a defender of Israel; he also says (in response to my request to identify 10-12 speakers who should be featured in the plenary session) that there aren't really any speakers in the list at all. When I pressed him he did mention Lustick and Benvenisti, but grudgingly.

In any event this is not my area and I need some guidance as to whom we should be seeking to include in (and, conversely, to exclude from) the plenaries. I'm hoping you can help me with that. [redacted] just isn't helpful at all, quite frankly, and I find it (more than) a bit frustrating.[85]

Thus, in the first paragraph of this late evening message to Dewitt, the dean acknowledged, in effect, and independent of whatever his intent may have been, that his approach—adding balance to the program—might not be met with the degree of success he appeared to expect when he began promoting it with the conference organizers by email on April 15 and in their meeting on April 17. Also of note is the dean's acknowledgement of his own lack of credentials in the conference topic—"this is not my area"— and his request to Dewitt (who did have relevant credentials) for assistance in making proposals to the organizers as to speakers that should be given prominence in the conference program.

Although the name of the person with whom Dean Monahan had spoken that evening was redacted in the copy of the email message released to CAUT, the fact that he was in communication with this person so soon after the organizers sent the invitation to Bell suggests the dean considered this person's opinion on conference matters to be important. Another point to note is the dean's explicit reference to involvement of Professor Ian Lustick in the conference.

Monahan himself spoke with Bell several times in the week or so after April 27 in an effort "aimed at persuading him to participate as a keynote speaker."[86] However, on May 7 Bell informed the dean he had not succeeded in rearranging his schedule so as to make this possible.

MPs Rae and Cotler Considered. In the April 23 meeting with Ryder and Drummond, when the dean had proposed Bell as a keynote speaker, he also had proposed Bob Rae, a Liberal member of parliament and former NDP premier of Ontario, and Irwin Cotler, a Liberal member of parliament and former federal minister of justice, as possible keynote speakers.[87] The organizing committee considered these possibilities and initially informed the dean that, "our strong preference is for Michael Bell, [...] If Michael turns us down, our second choice would be Bob Rae, and our third would be Irwin Cotler."[88]

However, by the time Bell declined, members of the organizing committee had become concerned that Rae and Cotler, although distinguished, were currently serving politicians, so that inviting them could result in demands that representatives of other federal parties be invited. In their view, this would risk turning an academic conference into a more political event. In early April they already had informed the dean in writing that they had decided not to invite politicians to speak.[89] However, when they initially agreed to consider Rae and Cotler—in an early morning meeting in the dean's office on April 23—they were still under the impression, given to them by the dean in a meeting on April 17, that the dean could be influential in a decision by the board of governors whether to deny or grant a campus venue for the conference, and that the outcome could depend on their response to the dean's proposals on the conference program. It was not until later on April 23 that they learned from U50 staff that the Glendon campus reservation had been reinstated.[90]

Ryder communicated to Monahan the concern about serving politicians, in an email exchange on May 8, the day after Bell confirmed he would be unable to speak. The dean replied:

> Forget Rae and Cotler. They won't do it. Not even close. It's a non-issue. Let's think of some serious academics. How about Alan Dowty, at Notre Dame? He is very respected and widely published. We don't have much time now.[91]

Professors Lustick and Bisharat Confirmed. The conference was now only a month and a half away from opening, and the organizers also appreciated that time was running out. They decided—without consulting Dean Monahan—to ask two confirmed speakers with outstanding scholarly reputations to be additional keynote speakers. The first to be confirmed was Professor Ian Lustick (political science, University of Pennsylvania), a former president of the Association for Israel Studies and a member of the Council on Foreign Relations. In addition to being an internationally distinguished scholar, Lustick satisfied another criterion proposed by Monahan for the second keynote speaker—he was pro-Israel.[92] Soon thereafter, the organizers confirmed that Professor George Bisharat (Hastings College of Law, University of California), an expert on the Palestinian legal system under the Israeli occupation, would be the third keynote speaker.[93]

Dean Monahan's Message to the Organizers, May 10. The organizers informed Monahan that they had settled on Lustick as a second keynote speaker. The dean responded in a lengthy and strongly worded email message to Drummond and Ryder on Sunday, May 10,[94] expressing great disappointment that they had used up a keynote slot without consulting him further:

> This is not what we agreed in my office. More importantly, from my perspective, by using up the additional keynote slot on an existing speaker, you now have made it virtually impossible to attract any additional major scholars to the conference.
>
> Even more troubling is the fact that you have already gone ahead and invited Lustick as a keynote, without any further consultation or discussion with me.[95]

The dean also wrote:

> I thought we had agreed that, regardless of the reasons, there is a problem with the overall balance in the speakers and it was therefore important to add at least one other speaker who would be a strong advocate of a two-state solution. [...]
>
> I was encouraged by your agreement with this and, based on that, (as well as on the idea of plenary sessions to highlight the strongest scholars), I facilitated the securing of the space in Glendon for the conference.[96]

In the same message, the dean also objected to the fact that Drummond and Ryder had requested a meeting with the president to be held in his absence.[97] He continued, "I have to tell you that at this point I very much doubt that I will be able to personally support the conference" because "the necessary balance" had not yet been achieved, but he added, "Despite all this I remain open to working with you and attempting to assist you."[98]

AN AGREEMENT BETWEEN THE DEAN AND THE AVPR, MAY 11–12

Continued Reliance by the Dean on the AVPR. During the period May 9 to May 12 there were several email messages between AVPR Dewitt and Dean Monahan regarding the conference. On May 9, Dewitt wrote:

> Just to let you know that I've contacted four scholars each from a different university (one an American in the US; two Israelis; another a South African/Israeli jointly with a major northeastern US university) with the list of possible plenary speakers as well as the website of the conference. I hope to hear back soon and then will give you whatever information and advice I can based on their responses. Hold tight for what could be a continuing turbulent ride...[99]

Also on May 9, President Shoukri sent an email message to Monahan, asking whether he (the president) should personally ask Dewitt to present a paper at the conference. The dean replied:

> I'm not sure this would be fair to David since the topic of the conference is not really in his area and in any event the organizers have not been demonstrating the required flexibility. I am still going to try to work with the organizers and see if we can make any progress.[100]

On May 10, Dewitt sent an email message to Monahan and Vice-President Stan Shapson, enclosing an announcement by the Koffler Centre for the Arts about action taken in regard to a controversial art exhibit. Monahan replied by email, saying:

> Thanks David. I was told by Bruce Ryder that UMass recently held a conference on one-state vs two-state proposals for the Middle East and that it came off w/o protest. He also told me that the conference speakers were generally favourable to one-state options. Do you know of this event and do you have any further background or comments?[101]

On the following afternoon (May 11) Dewitt forwarded to Monahan comments on the UMass conference "from one of [his] contacts," who wrote:

David—many of the same names were are listed in the UMass
program—this is apparently a travelling road show, and since
some are on the organizing committees, the question arises
regarding the origins of the York program. Who pushed this
through the system and sold this to gullible academics and a
government research body?[102]

Earlier on May 11, Dewitt forwarded by email to Monahan, "a draft of
an op ed that [redacted] a very well known senior Israeli academic who
often writes in various Canadian and US newspapers, plans on submitting to one of G&M, Star, Citizen, or Post," and also, "sending it to Jason
Kenney and Irwin Cotler in the context of the SSHRC funding issues."[103]
The dean replied later that day:

> I'm meeting tomorrow morning with Susan and Bruce. Can I
> show them this piece, without indicating how it came to me?"[104]

To this question, Dewitt replied in an email message that opened with
the request, "Patrick, PLEASE DO NOT SHARE THIS," and in which he
wrote in response to the dean's question:

> I think not. Even without telling them from whom it came,
> they will suppose it is either from me or from someone else
> with whom you are connected within a group of individuals
> interested in undermining them. Let them see it in the
> newspapers if/when it appears. I also think that given what I
> understand to be their views and how they have not kept one or
> more aspects of the agreement you thought you had with them,
> it puts you in an unfavourable position.[105]

Later in this same email message, Dewitt described to Monahan the
YCISS panel discussion on academic boycotts held that afternoon on campus. Dewitt wrote:

> I was pleased that things weren't worse, and I thought the chair did
> rather well in managing the situation. However, it convinced me
> even more that this conference planned for June is a very bad idea,
> and so clearly stacked in one direction that even if I were in town
> I'd not bother attending. I'd be too embarrassed and annoyed,

and I don't need either, and certainly would be unlikely to defend York for convening it (again, not around the issue of being critical of Israel or Israeli state policy, but the use of the vehicle of an academic meeting as a pretense for something else).[106]

Monahan replied to Dewitt early the next morning (May 12), before the meeting he was to have with Ryder and Drummond:

> Ok, I will not share it, but will use the substantive points as the basis of my discussion. We will see where they are at. They may be feeling the pressure. I sent them a strong email over the weekend and Susan's email reply to me was a bit cryptic. But the armour may be cracking.[107]

In summary, both Dewitt, Associate Vice-President Research (Social Sciences and Humanities), and Monahan, dean of Osgoode Hall Law School, had been informed it was likely that not only would the conference be criticized in a major daily newspaper, but that the peer-reviewed SSHRC grant also would be criticized in communications to a senior government minister and a prominent Opposition member. Yet they agreed not to forewarn the conference organizers.

Correspondence between AVPR Dewitt and Professor Steinberg. In the collection of documents obtained by CAUT from York University under Ontario freedom-of-information legislation, the name of the author of the draft op-ed article and the text of it were redacted. Monahan and Dewitt later confirmed to this Inquiry (on February 11, 2011) that the author was Professor Gerald M. Steinberg. However, neither they nor York University has released a copy of the text of this draft op-ed article.

Steinberg is well known as the founder and president of NGO Monitor (www.ngo-monitor.org). It is apparent from articles by Steinberg or NGO Monitor, posted on their websites or published elsewhere, that they have taken on a function somewhat analogous to that of Daniel Pipes and his Campus Watch organization in the United States: namely, denouncing persons or organizations they regard as critical of Israel or its policies, and conducting campaigns against events or organizations they regard as not in Israel's interests. Israeli political commentator and former Mossad agent Yossi Alpher, writing in the *Forward* in late 2009, made the following observations:

NGO Monitor [...] is not sticking to its Web site's slogan of "promoting critical debate and accountability of human rights NGOs in the Arab Israeli conflict." Rather, it seems dead set on eliminating human rights monitoring of Israel entirely and smearing anyone who supports this vital activity. In so doing, NGO Monitor is running roughshod over some important organizations that are working to maintain Israel's integrity in the context of its ongoing occupation of the West Bank.[108]

In late May and early June, three op-ed articles strongly attacking the conference were published on websites based in Israel, and the third of these was published also in the *National Post*. The author of all three was Steinberg. The three articles were not identical, but were variants of each other, with certain aspects common to all three. For example, some confirmed speakers were denounced in all three variants as "activists," and Ali Abunimah and Jeff Halper were explicitly named as such in all three.

NEW PRESSURES, MAY 12

Professors Ryder and Drummond of the organizing committee met with Dean Monahan around 9:00 AM and had a lengthy discussion. The dean reiterated concerns about perceived lack of balance in the program and the community opposition to the event. He then criticized details of the program in terms they had not previously heard from him, and challenged their credentials. He also proposed an approach to solving what he considered to be the imbalance problem—one that appeared to have similarities with the approach AVPR Dewitt had proposed to the organizers on April 15 and they had rejected at the time.

Detailed Criticisms of the Program and the Organizers. During the discussion, Monahan said he was very concerned about the quality of the confirmed speakers (or words to that effect). He expressed the view that some of them were not serious academics (or words to that effect), and that some were "activists" or "polemicists," or both. He specifically mentioned Ali Abunimah and Jeff Halper as being in this ostensibly undesirable category. He added that some of the confirmed speakers were graduate students, and suggested he had expected more established academics.

It is relevant to note that Ryder and Drummond had no knowledge that Monahan had in hand a copy of Professor Steinberg's draft op-ed criticizing the conference, the one he had received from Dewitt. (At the time—May

12—the dean had informed Dewitt that he would use the substance of the op-ed in this meeting. In his February 2011 brief to this Inquiry, Monahan confirmed he had done so.)

At this point, Drummond reminded the dean of the conference proposal that had actually been reviewed and approved by him in April 2008—it was focused on the one-state model and not intended to be balanced between the one- and two-state models. The organizers and their advisory board had subsequently revised the proposal, so as to focus on a comparison of one-state and two-state models.

Monahan then asserted that none of Ryder, Drummond, and Aiken had the relevant academic credentials to organize a conference on models of statehood for Israel/Palestine, and he expressly noted that Masri was a graduate student. Drummond and Ryder disagreed with his criticisms and offered reasons why they considered them inappropriate. (No such criticisms were ever expressed by Dean William Flanagan, Dean Monahan's counterpart at Queen's.)

In this meeting, Monahan acknowledged to Drummond and Ryder that he himself was not an expert in this area, confirming what they already knew. Also, he several times invoked the name of David Dewitt as a scholar knowledgeable in the area, whose opinions he valued in matters pertaining to the conference and whose opinions he suggested they also should value.[109] He also suggested Dewitt should be present in any meeting they might have with the president.

The Dean Proposes Postponement. Later in his meeting with the organizers, Monahan proposed that the conference be postponed, effectively until autumn. He further proposed that the organizers use the extra time for discussions with Dewitt and Professor Howard Adelman concerning the list of speakers, with a view to making such compromises in the program as might accommodate the concerns of these two York professors. The dean acknowledged that he knew that Dewitt and Adelman were strongly opposed to the presence of some of the confirmed speakers on the program—all three persons present in this meeting had read Adelman's March 20 memo explaining why he had withdrawn from the conference, and all three knew that Dewitt had proposed disinviting about three-quarters of the total number of confirmed speakers. Drummond and Ryder already (in April) had informed the dean that they wished no further involvement by Dewitt in discussions about the conference program, as a result of his email message to them on April 15. Yet the dean not only urged postponement on them but also urged that some of the delay be used in an effort to accommodate Dewitt and

Adelman. The dean also suggested that the president himself would want the organizing committee to meet with Dewitt and Adelman in an effort to reach a compromise on the program.

Drummond and Ryder did not accept these proposals. It was not practical to postpone a major international conference less than two months before it was scheduled to be held. Postponement could well result in permanent cancellation. The second proposal was inappropriate in their view, for the reasons noted in the preceding paragraph. Finally, in the same meeting, the dean requested that the organizers delay posting the final draft program on the website, to give time for further discussion. They did not agree and posted the program publicly the next day, May 13.

The CIJA Call to Action. Around mid-day on May 12, the Canadian Council for Israel and Jewish Advocacy (CIJA) issued a statement denouncing the conference. In addition to the public posting of the statement electronically, copies were sent to the board and executive committee of CIJA's University Outreach Committee (UOC), together with an email message from CIJA's manager of communications, Catherine Morrow. Morrow informed the UOC that:

> After months of discussions we must now alert our community that it is time for a public statement regarding the conference, *Israel/Palestine: Mapping Models of Statehood and Paths to Peace* at York University. Given that we have Jewish students at York from right across Canada, we regard this as a national issue. We ask that this be circulated widely on behalf of CIJA.[110]

A copy of the CIJA communication to its UOC, together with the text of its public statement, was sent to Dean Monahan early that afternoon by AVPR Dewitt.[111]

The CIJA statement said that the conference would be exploring the one-state model, "the imposition of which would spell the end of Israel as a Jewish state." It raised concerns about some of the speakers, "who are recognizable for their roles as organizers and outspoken proponents of 'Israel apartheid week' and the Israel boycott movement," and concluded the conference would "certainly not" be "one of high academic integrity or good scholarship."[112]

The statement called on supporters of CIJA to write letters of protest to President Shoukri and Dean Monahan. It provided suggested wording for the letters, including, "Events like this should not have the sanction of the university," and "These events lead to an increased sense of insecurity for those who should feel free to express their support for Israel."[113] This was the first public statement against the conference by CIJA. As noted earlier, another Israel lobby organization, the Jewish Defence League of Canada (JDL) had issued a boycott warning to President Shoukri on October 4, 2008, that was widely circulated, and on March 5, 2009, JDL had sent out an email statement asking York donors to cease donations if the conference were not cancelled.

Responses to CIJA by Academics. Two Osgoode Hall professors, Leslie Green and Craig Scott, publicly responded to the CIJA statement. Green explained succinctly the nature of a university and the essence of academic freedom, and concluded, "The CIJA should be ashamed of itself for calling for the shut-down of an academic conference of this kind."[114]

Scott posted a more detailed response. He analysed "the explicit and implicit structure of what passes for argumentation in the CIJA statement," and noted that, "there is seemingly no awareness how ironic (perhaps even hypocritically ironic) the CIJA position is [...] by exerting pressure on York University and the conference organizers to boycott in some fashion the 'wrong' kind of Israeli academic (and others, too, of course)."[115] He concluded:

> In contrast to what CIJA expects, York University should respect the academic courage (and defend the academic freedom) of the organizers of this conference and not bend before the gusts of external censure. If York were to give in to political pressure of this sort, in the process abandoning a core mission of a university to support scholars such as this conference's organizers (as well as the attendees), it would deserve to be laughed off the world stage of serious universities. Its reputation would likely be damaged for years and a lack of faith in the University leadership would be generated amongst the large majority of the scholars at York, some of whom might well not hesitate to seek out opportunities to move to a less compromised institution. For these reasons, I have faith that the University will continue to do the right thing.[116]

Dean Monahan Repeats his Postponement Proposal. During the evening of May 12—following his meeting with Ryder and Drummond that morning and the mid-day release by CIJA of its public statement—Monahan contacted Ryder by telephone. He expressed opposition to allowing the conference to be held as scheduled, in very strong terms, repeating his proposal from that morning that the conference should be postponed until autumn. The dean also suggested that when the organizers met the following day with the president, Shoukri might himself repeat and support some of the proposals he (Monahan) had been making, including postponement. As in the meeting with Monahan that morning when Drummond also was present, Ryder did not agree to the dean's postponement request.

Dean Monahan Informs President Shoukri. Shortly after his telephone conversation with Ryder, Monahan sent an email message to the president, captioned "June conference—possible solution." In it the dean informed Shoukri that he had asked the organizers to agree to a postponement of the conference, and that they had refused:

> Mamdouh I think the organizers are not going to agree to postpone the conference. I spoke with one of them [Ryder] this evening and he was very hostile to the notion. I don't think it will fly with them. And we can't force them to delay it. That will only hurt us.[117]

The "possible solution" Monahan proposed to the president was to "issue a [public] disclaimer of some kind," to the effect that:

> [T]his is an independently organized academic event [...] since the university does not generally endorse the particular opinions of faculty members [...] then we would just let them proceed with their event as they wish, without attempting to make any further changes.[118]

In essence, the dean's proposed new "solution" to what he been regarding as a problem ("damage" to be "mitigated," as he described it earlier) during the past four weeks was to the effect that the university disavow any responsibility for the conference. This was similar to, but weaker in terms of defending the event than, the position he had expressed to an individual conference critic by email on April 11.[119]

A Night of Anxiety for the Organizers. After Monahan's evening telephone call with Ryder had concluded, the organizers heard nothing further from the dean until the meeting with President Shoukri on the following day. He did not send any message to them, and so they knew nothing of the advice he had emailed to the president following Ryder's refusal to agree to postponement. Drummond recalled the night as follows:

The phone call from the Dean in the evening of May 12—the
day of our meeting with him and hours before a meeting on
May 13 we had scheduled with the President and the Dean—left
us with profound uncertainty about where things stood. We
were uncertain about whether sponsorship by the law school,
the university and 50th anniversary celebration committee would
all be pulled if we did not agree to a "postponement." We were
unsure about whether funding that had already been committed
by these groups would also be withdrawn, leaving us with
participants' already booked airfares and hotel accommodation
to pay. Given that the university had already come close to
rescinding our use of the campus venue that we had booked
the previous summer, we were in fact left deeply anxious about
whether we could continue to hold the conference at all in these
circumstances.[120]

PRESIDENT SHOUKRI REASSURES THE ORGANIZERS, MAY 13

In an email message to the president dated May 8 (copied to the dean),
Drummond and Ryder had requested a meeting with him to discuss their
concerns over events related to the conference. Dean Monahan had been
suggesting to them that his concerns about the conference were shared by
the president. The dean had emailed the president early on May 9, advising that he "not meet with them at this stage" of discussions regarding the
conference, and adding:

> This [meeting request] I interpret as an attempt to do an end-
> run around me and perhaps to complain to you about me. I
> have not mentioned to them that I have been discussing the
> conference with you.[121]

Notwithstanding the dean's advice, on May 13 Shoukri met with all
three York organizers—Drummond, Ryder, and Masri—with Monahan
also present. Dewitt was not present. The organizers went to the meeting
in a state of apprehension. However, to the surprise and relief of the organizers, the president raised none of Dean Monahan's criticisms or proposals.
In particular, the president did not propose postponement of the conference, nor did he propose any program changes, or make any proposal to
reach a compromise with Dewitt and Adelman.

Instead Shoukri expressed a firm institutional commitment to academic freedom in general and with respect to the conference in particular. He also expressed personal understanding and encouragement to the organizers, along with regret that they might at any time have been left with the impression that the university was not firmly committed to academic freedom.

PROFESSOR LUSTICK RESPONDS TO THE CIJA STATEMENT, MAY 13

Professor Ian Lustick, who now, in addition to being a member of the Advisory Board for the conference, was scheduled to be one of the three keynote speakers, sent an email message to the conference email address commenting on the CIJA statement. He copied President Shoukri and Dean Monahan on the message. In it, he wrote:

> The CIJA statement on the upcoming conference [...] is a part of
> a pattern of misguided, so-called 'pro-Israel' attempts throughout
> North America to suppress debate, run away from challenges,
> and ignore serious questions confronting Jews and Palestinians
> in the Middle East. In this particular case [...] the statement
> is formulated in an unusually egregious way that directly and
> unashamedly defies the principles of freedom of speech and of
> unfettered intellectual disputation.[122]

He then quoted a key passage in the CIJA statement: "The organizers have procured a few balanced speakers of high repute, but this is certainly not enough to characterize the conference as one of high academic integrity or good scholarship as would befit a first-class institution,"[123] and explained its inappropriateness:

> The implication here goes far beyond the (illegitimate) demand
> that an event at a university be cancelled because the demander
> does not agree with something that will be said; to a demand
> that all events should be cancelled except for those featuring an
> unspecified percentage, perhaps a majority, of speakers that the
> demander actively approves of as "balanced."[124]

Lustick continued:

> There is one and only one criterion that any self-respecting

college or university can use when judging whether to host an event or speaker. That criterion cannot have anything to do with the substance of what will be argued, but only whether what will be said or done will contribute to the ability of members of the community to improve their arguments and their analyses. Any other criterion places power in the hands of particular groups with particular opinions and agendas to decide what is right, what is worth considering as possibly right, and what is illegitimate to even question.[125]

Lustick concluded with the observation that the type of demand issued by CIJA "threatens the principle of intellectual freedom at its core."[126]

Dean Monahan immediately forwarded Lustick's email to AVPR Dewitt, saying:

See below from Ian Lustick. This confirms the wisdom of the approach we are going to take on this.[127]

PRESIDENT SHOUKRI ADDRESSES CONCERNS OF DONORS

Meanwhile, President Shoukri was being called upon to address concerns of supporters of the university displeased by the upcoming conference. On May 12, in an email exchange with Paul Marcus, president and CEO of the York University Foundation, Shoukri agreed to meet with a supporter who had sent an email message addressed to him. The message said:

Dear President Shoukri: I have not had the pleasure of meeting you in person but by way of introduction, my husband [redacted] has been proud to be one of York University's major donors. [redacted] and I have been following with great dismay the situation at York as it pertains to Jewish students. Frankly we are frightened and appalled by what we have heard. I recently had lunch with a professor of Jewish Studies at York who told me that she considers her top priority as an educator to be: "protecting her students against violence." This is totally unacceptable as I'm sure you would agree. I have now learned that the university is planning yet another Israel-bashing conference in June entitled: Israel/Palestine: Mapping Models of Statehood and Paths to Peace. It seems obvious that such

pseudo-academic conferences whose true and sole purpose is
to denigrate and demonize the state of Israel will only add to
the atmosphere of fear and academic intimidation that has
already been established at York. It saddens me that my husband
has donated [redacted] to an institution which has so boldly
positioned itself as an enemy of tolerance and understanding.
As recently as last month [redacted]. But such donations will
now end until we are convinced that we are indeed supporting
a liberal and academically free institution where all students,
regardless of faith or heritage, may feel free to express themselves
intellectually without fear for their physical safety. I urge you
to reconsider the sanctioning of anti-semitic conferences on
campus.[128]

Shoukri replied to Marcus the same day, saying:

Paul: Happy to meet with them. I hope you can arrange that.
That said, you know I am sensitive to the donations issue. If I
meet with them, I will be very firm on the issue of donations.
We will do everything possible to fight anti-semitism as a
principle not because of donations. Reference to donations
makes a just cause cheaper than necessary.[129]

AVPR DEWITT CONTINUES TO ADVISE DEAN MONAHAN

During this period, Dean Monahan continued to receive opinions on the
conference from, or through, AVPR Dewitt. For instance, on May 13 the
AVPR forwarded to him the text of an email message, "from a very distinguished Israel scholar whom I have known for 20 years," who had written
to him that:

The problem is the insufferable one-sidedness of the conference.
There is not one really mainstream Israeli in the entire list. It
could very well be that it is so obviously lopsided that more
centrist folk refused to participate. [...] Bottom line, the problem
is not with the qualifications of any one of the speakers, but the
congregation of an almost entirely one sided crowd to engage in
what is obviously going to be an Israel bashing festival with no
real scholarly debate. [...] The organizers are motivated by their

own war against Israel and that is what this is really about. All the rest is camouflage. This in essence is not a scholarly exercise but political advocacy under the guise of scholarship—the high jacking of academe to promote the undoing of Israel. The world abounds today with evidence that flies in the face of the one state idea (Belgium, Czechoslovakia, Yugoslavia, Sri Lanka) yet none of these are even discussed. [...]

Whoever wants to give this a hand should know what he/she is really doing.[130]

CONSIDERATION OF A YORK RESPONSE TO CIJA

An Evolving Discussion. In the days immediately following May 12, there were discussions among the organizers, York media relations staff, and senior university administrators on whether and how to respond to the CIJA statement. Some of these discussions can be followed on email threads extending from May 13 to May 21, when York issued a presidential statement. For example, on May 14, in a message copied to Dean Monahan, President Shoukri asked chief marketing officer Richard Fisher, "Should we respond to this? particulary the inaccuracy of the statement on aim of the conference."[131] Both Fisher and Monahan replied, suggesting the organizers should respond. The dean added, "Mamdouh should issue a broader statement on academic freedom at the appropriate time along the lines of the draft I circulated earlier today."[132]

The conference organizers were willing to issue a statement. However, the discussions on a response to CIJA included a media-relations person, Jane Shapiro, from the firm of Hill and Knowlton. In the course of an email thread, Shapiro initially recommended against any formal public response (suggesting that instead that individual emails protesting the conference be replied to individually), even after receiving an email message on May 15 from Fisher, who wrote:

Patrick is hot to trot on issuing a statement early next week as he is getting about 50 emails a day on the subject. the draft is attached. I have explained to him the reasons why but he's buying in to the drama a bit I think.[133]

However, views evolved, in part because some of the email messages to

Shoukri and Monahan were from conference supporters, such as a person who wrote on May 18 that she had read the CIJA statement and:

> I am therefore taking the opportunity to urge you not to capitulate to the CIJA's attempt to intimidate York University into withdrawing its support for this event. As a Jewish academic, it pains and disappoints me to see a Jewish organization attempt to silence academic freedom [...] The Canadian Council for Israel and Jewish Advocacy does not speak for me.[134]

Monahan forwarded this favourable message to Fisher and Shapiro, saying:

> One of a number from the other side of the fence. She and many others like her are expecting us to say something about this. Silence is not an option.[135]

Monahan had been proposing a response in the form of an op-ed by Shoukri in the *Globe and Mail*, but Shapiro was not in favour of an op-ed. By mid-evening on May 18, the dean agreed that an op-ed was not the best option. He insisted, nevertheless, that there must be a public statement by the president. Three hours later, Shoukri replied, saying:

> Attached is my revised version. I intended to focus on the principles and as such I included my definition of academic freedom at the beginning. I also tried to make it more balanced in the eyes of the Jewish community without compromising our principles. I also hope that the conference organizers can see in it the support they need.[136]

A Further Communication from Professor Steinberg. AVPR Dewitt was among those who had been consulted by Monahan on an earlier draft of what was to become the presidential statement. On May 14 the dean had forwarded a copy with the request, "David further to our call yesterday have a look at this, on a confidential basis, and give me your comments."[137] On the morning of May 20, the day before the presidential statement was posted on a university webpage, the dean again emailed Dewitt, saying:

> The Pres will be putting out a statement today that will make

it clear that the listing on the U50 events calendar does not indicate support for the views expressed at the conference. Here is a draft of what is coming.[138]

Earlier that morning (May 20), Dewitt had emailed Shapson and Monahan, enclosing a multi-page text that is redacted on the copy released to CAUT, with the message "FYI; see below." The name of the author also is redacted. However, the email caption was not redacted and it read, "Fw: Corrected op-ed submission: York University's anti-Peace Conference: Immoral, Naïve, or Both?"[139] This was the same title as that of an article published electronically by Professor Gerald Steinberg, bearing the date May 21, 2009. Among other things, the posted May 21 article said that the announced conference would be as "equally ludicrous" as a conference "featuring supporters of the [FLQ] terrorists who killed officials in Canada in 1970," or one "in which the main speakers were Al Qaida and Taliban activists." It said also that, "many of the invited guests [speakers] are radical political and ideological activists [...] Most have little or no connection to academic research."[140]

PRESIDENT SHOUKRI PUBLICLY DEFENDS ACADEMIC FREEDOM, MAY 21

The final version of York's response to the May 12 CIJA statement was posted on the president's webpage on May 21 as a public statement by President Shoukri. This was about a week after the president had expressed the university's commitment to academic freedom privately to the conference organizers, in the presence of Dean Monahan. Shoukri's statement said:

Freedom of inquiry by faculty and students is central to the mission of the academy. [...]

The freedom of independent scholars to organize events such as conferences on matters of legitimate academic inquiry goes to the very heart of academic freedom. It would be entirely inappropriate for the university administration to intervene in or to take responsibility for the academic content of such events, provided that they do not offend Canadian law, are consistent with the obligations cited above and deal with issues that are appropriate for academic debate.

Within those general parameters, the choice of topic, of who
is to speak, and of what is said at the event lies squarely with
the individual academics who organize and/or participate in it
and no one else. The university provides a forum for the robust
exchange, but does not align itself with a particular set of views
or positions.

Some have complained that the conference should not form
part of the University's 50th anniversary calendar of almost
100 events. However, this would have involved excluding a
conference because of its subject matter, which would in itself
have been a fundamental violation of academic freedom.[141]

The president also addressed the topic of academic boycotts. Noting that
the topic had recently been debated in a forum at York (the YCISS seminar
series discussed earlier), he said:

Universities at their very core are free institutions that must be
open to the widest range of ideas, arguments and debates. Thus
the concept of a boycott, which would prescribe a blacklist, is
antithetical to the very purpose of a university. [...]

On this basis, York University has consistently opposed the call
to boycott Israeli universities; our position is clearly outlined in
the President's statement on the autonomy of universities.[142]

He concluded:

Like democracy, academic freedom is untidy, ungainly and
often inconvenient, but it remains our best defence against
the intellectual paralysis that is the hallmark of totalitarian
societies.[143]

Thus the president made it clear that the conference would be held at
York University as scheduled. Subsequently, Israel lobbying organizations
in Canada, and many of their individual supporters and other conference
opponents, intensified the campaign to discredit the conference and prevent it from occurring, notwithstanding Shoukri's public commitment.

STEINBERG'S REACTION TO THE PRESIDENT'S STATEMENT, MAY 22

As noted above, Professor Gerald Steinberg had published electronically a strongly worded article against the conference that was dated May 21. A version of this had been in limited circulation earlier and, in particular, Steinberg had sent an article bearing the same title to AVPR Dewitt on May 20.

On May 21, immediately after President Shoukri's statement was posted on the York website, media-relations staff-person Keith Warnoch sent an email message to several university officials—including the president and Dean Monahan—confirming this. Several minutes later, the dean sent an email message to AVPR Dewitt and VPR Shapson, captioned, "President's message on academic freedom posted." In it, the dean wrote:

> See below. David as per our discussion can you follow with GS?
> Thanks.[144]

The next day (May 22), Steinberg posted an article about the conference on his website at Bar-Ilan University. He had first emailed it (at 3:29 AM) to Dewitt as a "Draft for comment before blog posting: 22 May 2009." Dewitt forwarded the draft to Monahan and Shapson, saying, "FYI. Don't know where he intends to post this."[145] In his February 2011 submission to this Inquiry, Dewitt stated the he did not provide comments to Steinberg on the draft.

The revised article was titled "YORK UNIVERSITY VS. ISRAEL; 'ACADEMIC FREEDOM' OR ACADEMIC FARCE?" It was similar in some respects to the article posted on May 21, although the titles were somewhat different. In the May 22 article, Steinberg denounced not only the conference, but also the president's statement and, in effect, the president himself. Both the May 21 and May 22 versions used strong language. For example, the May 22 article said, "the [academic freedom] defense [of the conference] offered by the President of York University is a farce," and added that such a conference would transform the university "into a macabre circus that sells hatred, martyrdom and murder. In a free society, the circus, like the university, is open to all—as P.T. Barnum observed, 'There's a sucker born every minute.'"[146] A version of this (May 22) article, with some editing, was published by the *National Post* on June 9, under a different title.

In April 2010, after she obtained copies of the email correspondence cited above (pursuant to requests under Ontario freedom-of-information legislation) Drummond contacted President Shoukri, requesting an explanation as to why Steinberg, Monahan, and Dewitt appeared to be involved in a consultation at this juncture. The president replied:

> I was made aware of the draft of the Steinberg op-ed by the
> Provost [Monahan] last May. In discussion with the Provost,
> I authorized the sharing of my statement with Professor
> Steinberg who I believed might share some of the values of
> academic freedom which I had expressed. I hoped Steinberg
> might consider modifying his proposed article; specifically, that
> he might soften his attack on the university's decision to support
> the conference. Of course that is not what he chose to do. I hope
> this helps clarify that issue.[147]

The basis for Shoukri's hope that there was a non-negligible prospect that Steinberg might consider softening his characterizations of the conference is unclear.

REACTION TO PRESIDENT SHOUKRI'S STATEMENT BY B'NAI BRITH AND JDL

Response by B'nai Brith. Also on May 22, B'nai Brith issued a news release, denouncing the conference and the president's statement:

> This sham of a conference, which questions the Jewish State's
> very right to exist, promises to be a veritable "who's who" of
> anti-Israel propagandists [...] This is not an issue of academic
> freedom, despite the great lengths the University is going to try
> to paint it in that light. [...]
>
> We question why an event that promotes hatred and encourages
> the destruction of the Jewish State would connect in any way to
> York University's 50th anniversary celebrations.
>
> We call on York University professors, students, benefactors, alumni
> and members of the public at large to demand that York cease
> becoming a breeding ground for encouraging anti-Jewish hatred.[148]

Complaint by JDL to Industry Canada. On May 25, JDL sent a complaint about the conference to Industry Canada, the government department through which SSHRC reports to Parliament. It later emerged (from documents obtained under federal and provincial access-to-information legislation, and a public statement by a minister) that a number of individuals and groups registered complaints with SSHRC, or government ministers, or both, about the conference and the SSHRC grant.

AN ALTERNATIVE BALANCING PROPOSAL, MAY 26

On May 26, President Shoukri and Vice-President Research Shapson met with a person representing a "Committee in Support of the Speaker Series at York," who proposed that the university sponsor "a three-part speakers' series involving world-class scholars," to address topics concerning "Islam, Fundamentalism and Canadian Values," as a response to what this person regarded as a "dangerous and one-sided environment" at the university.[149] He said that there was an "atmosphere of anti-Jewish intimidation and even violence at York. York's reputation for anti-semitism is unfortunately a globally recognized fact."[150]

The proposed series was to consist of events with the following titles and speakers: 1. "Women in Islam"—Ayaan Hirsi Ali and Irshad Manji; 2. "Human Rights in the Islamic World"—Nazanin Afshin-Jam, Ali Alyami, and Elliot Abrams; 3. "Islamic Extremism and the Continuing Threat to the West"—Daniel Pipes.[151]

In the meeting, the president explained that he disagreed with the Speaker Series proponent's characterization of the atmosphere at York and that he considered the proposal inappropriate. In an email message the following day, the Speaker Series proponent objected to Shoukri's response, "Your response to this proposal [...] was to disparage the qualifications of these speakers and to deny that the president of the university should have any role in supporting such an event."[152]

President Shoukri replied that evening:

> York is absolutely committed to fighting all forms of anti-Semitism or racism and I have clearly stated my personal position on this in many public statements. [...] As a university president, one of my key roles is to protect the fundamental value of academic freedom, even if I do not necessarily agree with the views being expressed—providing of course that they do not violate Canadian Laws, or promote hatred or violence. With regard to our meeting, there appears to be a misunderstanding on several points:

A university is above all an academic community and the
responsibility for organizing academic conferences resides
squarely with individual academics. As such, the willingness
of an external group or individual to fund a conference or a
lecture series cannot be the main justification for holding it. The
conference needs to be grounded in, with and from an academic
unit or a group of faculty members. [...]

Whenever such a condition is satisfied [...] the selection of
speakers also needs to comply with the principles of academic
freedom, which is a matter for academics to evaluate. My
personal view on any speaker is simply not relevant to this
process.

May I ask that you share my response with those to whom you
have copied your note so that they may fully understand the
nature of our meeting and my position on the issues raised.[153]

THE DEAN EXPLAINS ACADEMIC FREEDOM

On May 12, Dean Monahan had received an email message opposing the
conference. Among other things, the message said:

This conference is a not a worthy meeting for York University/
Osgoode. The University should not sanction this type of event.
There have already been problems at York that have intimidated
Jewish students and will increase their insecurity. The organizers
of this conference are the proponents of "Israel apartheid week"
and the Israel boycott movement.[154]

Two weeks later (May 27), the dean replied:

In fact, the freedom of individual, independent academics to
organize academic events such as conferences on subjects of their
choosing—within certain limitations—goes to the very heart of
academic freedom. It would be inappropriate for the university
administration to intervene in or to take responsibility for the
academic content of such events. [...] There are almost 100
events and initiatives that make up the [York] 50th anniversary

calendar, and the university has no stake in the academic content of any of them. At the same time, it would be unthinkable to exclude a conference *because* of its subject matter. York University's President, Dr. Mamdouh Shoukri, recently issued a statement dealing with the importance of academic freedom, and its relationship to the planning of this conference. [...]
I have included a copy of this statement for your reference.[155]
(Emphasis in original)

RENEWED INVITATION TO PROFESSOR DEWITT, JUNE 1

On June 1, Sharryn Aiken emailed David Dewitt, repeating the invitation to participate in the conference that had been extended to him several times earlier in the year by members of the organizing committee. She said that three speakers, in regard to whom Professor Howard Adelman had raised objections, had since withdrawn, and that several other speakers had been recruited. She also said that Ian Lustick and George Bisharat would be additional keynote speakers. (Aiken, along with the other organizers, was unaware that during the previous month Dean Monahan had been consulting in detail with Dewitt on speakers and other matters pertaining to the conference.)

Aiken added:

> I appreciate that there continues to be concerns about this conference in the community—but we are determined to prove the naysayers wrong. This conference is steadfastly committed to the principles of civil dialogue and debate—values which I believe are core to academe—as well as to the Jewish faith.[156]

In his reply later that day, Dewitt again declined the invitation, adding that he would be out of town when the conference opened. (He did, however, attend part of the third day of proceedings, on June 24, having returned to Toronto by then.)

PUBLIC RELATIONS AND SECURITY

Public Relations. The university assigned a team of communications experts to work with the organizing committee on public relations for the conference. It included York staff members Richard Fisher, Chief Marketing and

Communications Officer, and Alex Bilyk, Director of Media Relations, along with Jane Shapiro from the firm of Hill & Knowlton. Their initial meeting with Ryder and Drummond was held on May 12, and they remained involved until the conference concluded.

During this period, Shapiro and the York communications staff were consulted on a range of matters, and there sometimes were disagreements. A notable disagreement between Shapiro and the organizers over strategy involved the matter of media access to the conference itself. She proposed to limit adverse publicity by preventing media access to the conference. The conference organizers proposed to encourage favourable publicity by opening conference sessions to reporters. It is apparent from records of their discussions that the organizers were concerned that Shapiro and the university's communications experts did not fully understand and appreciate the principles of academic freedom, while Shapiro and others were concerned that the organizers did not fully understand and appreciate the methods of public relations.

Eventually, on June 4, Dean Monahan was consulted, and he supported the communications experts on the basis that permitting full access to reporters would unavoidably alter the character of the event, in ways that would be outside the control of academics. The organizers agreed, reluctantly, to accept the dean's advice. As a result, media reporters were barred from conference sessions. This decision itself, however, became a source of media attention and controversy during the conference.[157]

There were also disagreements regarding whether and how to respond to public attacks on the conference, such as the June 9 *National Post* article by Professor Steinberg ("York University sinks deeper into the mire"), and a possibly defamatory statement issued by B'nai Brith on June 12. As a result, when the Steinberg article appeared in the *National Post*, the organizers—without consulting the communications experts—arranged for Professor Lustick to submit a reply article, and the organizers engaged a defamation lawyer at their own expense in connection with the B'nai Brith statement.

Security. Extensive preparations were made for security during the conference, especially as the actual dates for it (June 22–24) approached and the opposition to it by Israel lobbying organizations, their supporters, and other anti-conference individuals was increasingly manifested through email campaigns, on blogs, and in media releases or commentaries. There had been loud demonstrations and counter-demonstrations on the York campus by pro-Israeli and pro-Palestinian groups in connection with other events in the recent past, and there were concerns that similarly disruptive events might occur at the conference, especially because JDL Canada had been saying it would mount demonstrations.

In response to these concerns, York University engaged the Toronto Police Service, in addition to a private security firm, and extra time was arranged for campus security personnel. Initially, it had been suggested the conference organizers should be responsible for the costs of extraordinary security. However, it was soon appreciated that the organizers had no budget for security and the university agreed to cover these costs (which for Toronto Police and the private security firm were in excess of $10,000, each).

6

INVOLVEMENT OF THE FEDERAL GOVERNMENT AND SSHRC

COMPLAINTS TO FEDERAL AGENCIES

As early as March 2009, at least one element of the Israel lobby in Canada sent complaints about the conference to federal politicians. On March 5 the Jewish Defence League's national director, Meir Weinstein, had distributed an email message to supporters, opposing the conference. On March 22, Weinstein sent an open letter to York President Mamdouh Shoukri with copies to Jason Kenney, a senior minister in the Canadian government; Senator Jeremiah Grafstein; the CJC; B'nai Brith; and other organizations and individuals.[1]

Available records indicate that, following President Shoukri's public statement of May 21, Israel lobbying organizations and their supporters began focusing more attention on the Canadian government and on SSHRC, while continuing to complain to York University administrators and also to Queen's University administrators.

On May 25, mid-morning, an internal SSHRC email message captioned, "Extremely urgent, complaint that SSHRC funds an anti Israel conference," from Communications Manager Trevor Lynn to several other staff-persons said:

> Hi, I have just been sent a complaint, received by Industry
> Canada, from the Jewish Defence League that SSHRC has
> funded this conference and that the advisors of this conference
> have made objectionable statements. We'll need to look into
> this matter so any help is appreciated.[2]

Lynn's email included the text of the JDL email complaint to Industry Canada. It began by saying a federal agency (SSHRC) was sponsoring an "International Anti Israel Conference that will take place at York University June 22–24," and noting "major Jewish groups have issued statements against this conference."[3] It cited the CIJA statement of May 12 and one by B'nai Brith on May 22. The JDL email made the following request of Industry Canada:

> This Conference goes against the Official Federal Government position on Israel. There is still time to pull Government support from this anti Israel Conference. Can you please speak out and take action.[4]

In this message the JDL national director illustrated his group's concern by denouncing six members of the conference's International Advisory Board, with a paragraph devoted to each: Ali Abunimah, Islah Jad, Leila Farsakh, David Kretzmer, Ian Lustick, and John B. Quigley. For example, Weinstein said Kretzmer "is a professor at Hebrew University and calls for War Crimes trials to be used against Israel Government officials," while Lustick "has hosted [Dr. Norman] Finkelstein several times at Penn, is a far leftist, anti-America and unabashedly anti-Israel," who "wrote in the anti-American, anti-Israel magazine, The Nation," that the invasion of Iraq in 2003 was "not driven by a particular threat," such as "Al Qaeda."[5]

As an initial response that day (May 25), SSHRC communications staff began drafting a list of "Key Messages" about the conference and its SSHRC grant. In an email thread beginning in early afternoon, Lynn sent a draft with five key points to his communications colleagues, director Ursula Gobel and advisors David Holton and Julia Gualtieri, with the covering note, "OK, here's my stab at it, I am open to comments. We'll have to move very fast to have these ready for the Minister."[6]

Gobel replied:

> Think we need to add reference to research excellence that supports building of knowledge and understanding on cultural, social ... issues. Also make it clear that sshrc is not a Sponsor of the Conference.[7]

Lynn then replied, "Unfortunately, we are listed as a sponsor on their site so not really sure how to finesse that one."[8] Additional points were added in the course of the afternoon, and revised lists circulated among staff.

In a late-afternoon reply to Lynn, copied to others, director Craig McNaughton wrote:

> The [JDL] note that came over from IC [Industry Canada] says that SSHRC is named as a sponsor of an 'anti-Israel conference'... it might be worthwhile simply pointing people to the vision for the conference at http://www.yorku.ca/ipconf/vision_eng.html without commentary or interpretation. I think most will find the objectives there reassuring. For example:
>
>> - The purpose of this conference is to explore whether a two-state solution or a single constitutional democracy in Israel/Palestine offers the most promising path to future peace and security in the region.
>>
>> - The conference will open a series of principled conversations among scholars with a commitment to liberal democracy and to the equality of all peoples and in particular, the equal rights to dignity, security and fundamental justice for Jews and Palestinians. The objective is to create an inclusive and respectful forum that promotes genuine debate and dialogue. To this end, conference speakers will be selected to represent a range of opinion, including proponents of one and two state models for Israel/Palestine.[9]

The list of Key Messages about the conference and its SSHRC grant included statements such as:

- "The Social Sciences and Humanities Research Council is the arm's length federal agency that that promotes and supports university-based research and training in the social sciences and humanities";

- "SSHRC [...] facilitates knowledge sharing and collaboration across research disciplines [...]";

- "SSHRC's peer-review process is 'up to the best practices and highest international standards' [...] according to an independent Blue-Ribbon Panel report."[10]

During the next couple of weeks, in another internal response by SSHRC staff, a multi-page table was drawn up from information on the conference website. The table listed the names of confirmed speakers/presenters and their institutional/organizational affiliations. It also indicated whether their names were included on the grant application to SSHRC in November 2008. Names of individuals "being criticized by various organizations" were shaded in grey on the table.[11]

A second SSHRC table reported summary statistics from the first table. For example, "31 of the 56 speakers listed on the conference Web site were named in the original [SSHRC] application; 25 were not," and of the latter twenty-five, the table indicated their origins (six Canadian faculty, five American faculty, five Israeli faculty members (from Haifa, Tel Aviv, and Hebrew universities), one faculty member from the United Arab Emirates, one faculty member from Europe, four graduate students, and three others representing organizations. The second table also reported, "at least 10 of those speaking were named in articles critical of the conference," and of these ten, five were listed in the original [SSHRC] application, while four of the remaining five were members of the conference's International Advisory Board. This suggests that SSHRC had obtained complaints about the conference from sources additional to the JDL protest letter to Industry Canada (which had listed the six names noted earlier).[12]

INTERFERENCE BY MINISTER OF STATE GOODYEAR, JUNE 4

SSHRC documents confirm that on June 4 the Minister of State (Science and Technology), Gary Goodyear, spoke with the president of SSHRC, Chad Gaffield, regarding the conference.[13] A press release by the office of Minister Goodyear, dated the next day (June 5), presented an account of the discussion. It said:

Approval of this [SSHRC] funding was based on an initial proposal that did not include detailed information on the speakers at the conference. Since funding was provided, the

organizers of the conference have added a number of speakers to
their agenda.

Several individuals and organizations have expressed their grave
concerns that some of the speakers have, in the past, made
comments that have been seen to be anti-Israeli and anti-Semitic.
Some have also expressed concerns that the event is no longer an
academic-research-focussed event.[14]

Therefore, I have spoken to the president of the Social Sciences
and Humanities Research Council to bring these concerns to
his immediate attention and asked that Council give them full
consideration. In particular, I asked that the Council, once they
have seen this information, to consider conducting a second
peer review of the application to determine whether or not
the conference still meets SSHRC's criteria for funding of an
academic conference.[15]

This action was unprecedented in the more than three decades since
SSHRC was established by an act of Parliament as an arm's-length agency.
It involved a direct ministerial challenge to the award of a grant through
the council's peer-review process, and a ministerial request for a second
peer review, despite the fact that SSHRC policy contained no provision for
such action. The action SSHRC took in response was also unprecedented.

Neither York University nor the grant holder, Professor Bruce Ryder, was
notified immediately of Minister Goodyear's statement. SSHRC notified
York University on June 8, but did not contact Ryder until June 10. Others,
however, were notified immediately—an email message on June 5 from
Gary Toft of Industry Canada to his counterpart Trevor Lynn of SSHRC,
conveying the ministerial statement, said:

Trevor, please see the statement below that is being provided
to Canadian–Jewish media, based on the conversation that the
minister had with Dr. Gaffield.[16]

Less than an hour after receiving this email message, Lynn sent the
following email message, captioned "Extremely urgent," to Gaffield and
several senior SSHRC staff:

> Hi, Industry Canada will be releasing the following statement
> forthwith. I spoke to Phil and he indicated that this is an
> appropriate statement and they do not wish to change it at all.
> He said that this is a serious issue and was so serious that it will
> make it hard for the Minister to recommend increased funding
> for SSHRC in the next budget. He said the Minister respects peer
> review 100% but thinks that it is appropriate to publicly ask us
> to consider a second peer review. If you want speak with Phil call
> 943 xxxx. This is going out very soon.[17]

More than three months later, SSHRC issued a statement that Lynn's
email was "inaccurate," and Lynn himself declined to elaborate.[18] In any
event, the documents released under Access to Information and SSHRC's
public record of actions during the relevant period of time suggest the message delivered to SSHRC on behalf of the government was stern.

SSHRC RESPONDS TO THE MINISTER'S REQUEST

June 5 was a Friday, and there is no record (available to this Inquiry) of
SSHRC office activity on the weekend of June 6–7. On Monday, June 8, in
an email thread, the question, "Did Minister Goodyear send out a press
release on York university conference friday?" is asked at 9:20 AM, and the
reply at 9:40 AM said, "No, he didn't."[19] However, a more precise answer
would have been that the press release was sent out, to Jewish–Canadian
media and Israel lobby groups only, on Friday, June 5—as Gary Toft of
Industry Canada had stated in his email message early that afternoon to
Trevor Lynn.

Thus on Sunday, June 7, on the blog *Israpundit.com*, under the heading,
"JDL gets traction against York U.," writer Ted Belman reported that "[t]
he JDL, under Meir Weinstein, started a campaign six months ago to shut
down the conference. [...] I am very happy to say he is getting traction."
Comments were followed on the blog page by a copy of the full statement,
dated June 5, by Minister Goodyear.[20]

On Sunday evening, a copy of the minister's statement—the one being
circulated during the weekend by Jewish–Canadian media and Israel lobby
groups or their supporters—was forwarded to CAUT Executive Director
James Turk. He immediately sent an email message to Chad Gaffield, saying, "This is a highly unusual request for a federal minister to make to the
President of SSHRC."[21] He asked Gaffield to confirm the accuracy of the

statement, a copy of which he enclosed. Throughout the week of June 7, in phone calls and emails to Gaffield and by issuing public statements, Turk protested the interference of the minister and the response of SSHRC to it.

During the morning of Monday, June 8, SSHRC Vice-President Gisèle Yasmeen sent to York Vice-President Research Stan Shapson a copy of the statement by Minister Goodyear in an email captioned, "FYI As Discussed."[22] Early that afternoon, York Associate Vice-President Research David Dewitt forwarded a copy of the minister's statement to Shapson.

In the late afternoon of the same day, Dewitt sent another email message to Shapson, forwarding a four-page article issued by NGO Monitor (the organization headed by Professor Gerald Steinberg), dated June 8. Dewitt wrote, "Please see the attached document which Gerald Steinberg has sent to me. I gather he has sent this to the SSHRC and to the PMO [Prime Minister's Office]."[23] The attached article was titled "York University's Israel/Palestine Conference: Speaker Political Profiles—Behind the Academic Facade." Shapson sent this on to Yasmeen at SSHRC the following morning.

The article began with a brief denunciation of the conference, and then provided a list of fifteen conference speakers, together with a paragraph about each one, summarizing the reasons that individual was considered undesirable. This list was considerably longer than the JDL list sent to Industry Canada on May 25, but the JDL list was not a subset of the longer list—the only person on both lists was Ali Abunimah.[24] For example, Professors David Kretzmer and Ian Lustick were on the JDL list but not on the NGO Monitor list.

Also on June 8, B'nai Brith sent out a Community Action Alert to its Jewish Canada network. It said, "Subsequent to our appeal to the Government on this matter, the Hon. Gary Goodyear [...] released a statement on the conference that is reproduced below."[25] The Action Alert noted that "the [minister's] statement stops short of announcing a funding withdrawal [of the SSHRC grant]," and went on to ask readers to write to the minister to convey their thanks and appreciation for his action to date, as well as to

> Urge the Minister to direct SSHRC to immediately withdraw
> its funding from this sham of a conference that seeks to
> delegitimize the Jewish State and its supporters here at home.[26]

Meanwhile, SSHRC staff-persons were considering possible courses of action, in response to the minister's request and the protests against the conference that SSHRC had received directly. The internal SSHRC email records provided to CAUT suggest that SSHRC staff-persons understood there was no existing policy designed to accommodate interference by a minister of the Crown in a decision made through the peer-review adjudication process of their arm's-length agency. (They also had another, different problem—the minister's intervention came at a time when they were very busy preparing for meetings of the SSHRC executive committee and council—and it was difficult to find a convenient time to meet.)

Among the events of June 9 was the publication by the *National Post* of Professor Steinberg's op-ed article denouncing the conference. The text of earlier versions of it had been available on websites in May. Two days later, the *National Post* published an op-ed article by Professor Lustick, defending the conference.

In the afternoon of June 9, the university's government-relations officer, Maria Papadopoulos, sent an email message to President Shoukri, Dean Monahan, and others, captioned "FYI – confirmation of Goodyear's statement – not just JDL petitioning," and saying:

> I have spoken with the Ministers Director of Communications
> about the release. He told me that the release stemmed from
> a conversation that the Minister has had with a number of
> people [who] are concerned about the scope and the speakers
> at the conference. I told him that I was concerned about the fact
> that the Ministers office did not provide us with a copy of the
> statement, nor were they forthcoming with information when
> I contacted their office. In addition, the Ministers Director of
> Communications referred me to the SS[H]RC, as opposed to
> answering any of my questions. Very strange indeed.[27]

An early-morning SSHRC email thread on June 9, involving Director Craig McNaughton, Vice-President Gisèle Yasmeen, and Executive Vice-President Carmen Charette, discussed applicable policy. The thread began with a message from McNaughton to Yasmeen, in which he sent her a copy of SSHRC's Non-Discrimination Policy. The only immediately relevant aspect of this policy is that it leaves discretion in the hands of the peer-review committees, subject to general non-discrimination provisions. In reply, Yasmeen asked:

Do we oblige our conf applicants to have an event with balanced
views ie folks both for and against stuff or does this come up in
the review or do we just not have a policy on that.[28]

In his reply to Yasmeen's question, McNaughton wrote:

No Policy – I would say a question like that is one for peers to
decide as a function of their assessment of the scholarly quality
– eg in relation to the criterion on "appropriateness and quality
of the conference's scope and program in relation to its theme or
themes"

As it turns out, they [the organizers] do advocate a balanced
approach (from the conference website):

"Mindful of the fraught context in which debates relating
to Israel/Palestine unfold, the conference aims to open up
measured and thoughtful conversations on the range of possible
paths out of the current impasse."

BTW, I just noticed this statement on their website (http://www.
yorku.ca/ipconf/):

"The scholarly goals of the conference are premised on the
intrinsic value of civil dialogue and debate. Our commitment to
ensuring that neither anti-Semitism nor any other form of racism
has any place in this forum informs both the conference and all
aspects of its planning process."[29]

In summary, he appeared to suggest that the conference met existing
SSHRC policies.

An email thread mid-day on June 9, between SSHRC Corporate
Secretary Christine Trauttmansdorff and Vice-President Charette, began
with Trauttmansdorff sending a copy of Minister Goodyear's statement
and saying, "I assume you are well aware of this [statement] but neither
Erin [Skrapek, Corporate Operations Coordinator] nor I were … so I'm just
covering bases," to which Charette replied, "Yes we are. I meant to send to
you. We have ben dealing with this since yesterday morning. Can hardly
keep up." Trauttmansdorff then wrote, "I can imagine – this puts it all in a

rather different light."[30]

An email thread later that day among several SSHRC staff-persons began with a message from Charette to Trauttmansdorff and others, saying:

> We will need to think through a process to deal with this situation. [...] I am thinking of a analogous approach to an ethical or integrity case. We could either use a committee or council or put together a group. We do not have a lot of time however so we need to keep this in mind. The university is looking at how it has evolved from the poit of view of minor and major change. Craig [McNaughton] is also looking at it. [...] I seek your views given the recent work on integrity looking at models to deal with cases brought forward. Let's discuss tomorrow.[31]

Later comments in this email thread include, "the oinly available tine is noon given OMC and SMC in the morning. Sorry but this is top priority."[32]

The June 9 email from Charette suggests that a misconduct investigation was an option under discussion, an interpretation confirmed by a message from Skrapek to Yasmeen and McNaughton on June 10 saying, "Attached are some sample letters sent to institutions requesting investigations into allegations of misconduct, as per our research integrity policy."[33] An email thread on June 14 initiated by Trauttmansdorff indicates another option being considered; it was captioned "Criminal Code Primer," and provided links to "A couple of web site that provide explanations of the Criminal Code provisions on hate crimes."[34]

Legal implications of cancellation of the SSHRC grant appear to have been explored. On Sunday June 14, SSHRC Corporate Secretary Trauttmansdorff sent an email message to Heather Beaton in Industry Canada Legal Services, captioned "Urgent Request for Legal Advice," and attaching a number of documents pertaining to the conference, among them Minister Goodyear's statement.[35] The text of the message is redacted on the copy released to CAUT, but a reply to Trauttmansdorff from Beaton on June 16 forwarded a message dated June 15 from Natalie Girard of the Department of Justice with the caption, "FW: Withdrawal of SSHRC Funding for York University Conference on Israeli–Palestinian Issues – Charter Considerations – Protected B."[36] Girard's advice was summarized by Beaton (redacted in the copy released to CAUT), and in response Trauttmansdorff wrote to Charette and Yasmeen, "Overall this is good news ... with some new perspectives introduced. [...] I don't think it will change anything we're doing this week."[37]

In the period June 9–11, SSHRC issued three media releases, one each day, with significant differences in their wording. The first said: "SSHRC confirms that the Minister of State for Science and Technology spoke to the President of SSHRC on June 4, regarding the upcoming conference at York University."[38] The next said, "SSHRC [...] has requested that the grantee identify any changes to the conference since the time of application."[39] The last, dated June 11, said:

> In accordance with these [post-award] procedures, SSHRC will be determining whether or not there have been significant changes to the conference since the application was submitted in November 2008. In keeping with regular practices, SSHRC is doing due diligence to ensure that policies and procedures are respected.[40]

In summary, in the face of the allegation by CAUT (on June 10) that SSHRC, under pressure from the minister, was breaching its own written policy, the Council invoked a "practice" of "due diligence," to explain its actions.

The public at large learned of the minister's intervention with SSHRC on June 10, when the *Globe and Mail* published a news story. The article mentioned the minister's request for a second peer review of the conference, and reported that CAUT was calling for his resignation, because he had interfered in the work of an arm's-length agency.

The procedural device SSHRC selected for its approach to Professor Ryder, the applicant, was related to, but at variance with, the guideline requiring that SSHRC be informed in advance of the conference in the event of major changes. This same guideline stated that no pre-conference notification to SSHRC was required in the event of minor changes, and it provided substantial latitude as to the interpretation of the term "minor." For minor changes, the SSHRC policy required only post-conference notification.[41]

Director McNaughton drafted a letter on June 10 for review by other SSHRC staff. The draft asked Ryder, "Could you confirm whether or not there have been significant changes in your conference plan? Would you be able to let us know by end of day tomorrow?"[42] Shortly after preparing this draft, at 3:16 PM EDT, McNaughton sent Ryder an email message asking him to call. McNaughton sent a final version of the letter to Ryder at 5:22 PM EDT. The version sent included a more comprehensive request for information about changes and a more precise deadline; "please identify any changes in your conference since the time of your application, by close of business tomorrow."[43]

Also on June 10, CAUT Executive Director Turk emailed SSHRC President Gaffield (in response to SSHRC's June 10 media release) saying, "We find your revised position to be wholly unacceptable," because its demand that the organizers "account for [even] minor program changes now [prior to the conference being held]" would "be violating your own procedures and legitimating the unethical and inappropriate political intervention by Minister Goodyear."[44] Turk described the step that would have been in accordance with SSHRC's policies and procedures, in contrast to what SSHRC actually did:

> [T]he only appropriate question for the conference organizers
> is whether they have made "major program changes (such as
> changing the theme or focus of the event)." If their answer is
> "No", that must be the end of the matter for SSHRC until they
> submit their report at the conclusion of the grant.[45]

Although Professor Ryder was at the time attending a conference in South Africa and was given only about twenty-four hours to respond, he provided the requested information in a two-page letter to McNaughton the following day, June 11. He was assisted by Professors Drummond and Aiken, Vice-President Shapson, and Dean Monahan in drafting the letter.[46]

Ryder's letter to McNaughton stated, "Let me begin by saying that there are no major changes to the conference. I am happy to provide additional information to substantiate this position," and he then described changes that had been made, stating that all of them were "minor" in accordance with the usage of this term in the SSHRC post-award policies.[47] He added, "The Dean of Osgoode Hall Law School and the Vice-President Research and Innovation are in agreement with our assessment."[48]

Among the details provided in Ryder's letter were those specifically addressing the issue most prominently figuring in the protests of conference opponents, as well as in Minister Goodyear's statement:

> The names of 37 conference speakers appeared on the grant
> application, and the names added to the program have increased

the capacity of the conference to meet its scholarly objectives to fulfill SSHRC criteria. [...]

The scholarly aims of the conference remain unchanged in their essence and indeed have been strengthened by our efforts since the submission of the grant application last November.[49]

SSHRC had provided no clear indication to Ryder as to what would be done concerning the information he was asked to send. This gave rise to additional concerns, especially after Drummond learned from Shapson on June 12 that SSHRC would be reviewing the information by a process that had not been specified. She wrote to McNaughton on June 13 with a series of questions, including questions about the review process, the policy basis for it, and "Who is conducting the review? What are their qualifications?"[50]

Drummond received no response from SSHRC. On or before June 12, however, SSHRC had decided against the second peer review of the grant application the minister had asked it to consider. SSHRC so informed CAUT, and it then informed the presidents of its local associations of this decision and asked them write to SSHRC expressing concerns that still remained. The first such letter in the SSHRC files released to CAUT was one by Professor Catherine Christie, president of the Queen's University Faculty Association (QUFA), saying, "QUFA understands that you have refused Minister Gary Goodyear's request to initiate a second peer review process [...] In the name of academic freedom, we thank you."[51] Her letter continued with an expression of disappointment that SSHRC had requested a pre-conference report from the grant holder, contrary to its own written policy, which she quoted.

During this period, Minister Goodyear and SSHRC continued receiving many email messages demanding cancellation of the SSHRC grant. The minister's office encouraged its correspondents to address their concerns to SSHRC. An email message from Carmen Charette to President Gaffield on June 14 said, "I have been receiving many emails through the weekend. Here is one example for your information."[52] A number of these included lengthy passages copied from a statement against the conference sent out by B'nai Brith over its Jewish Canada network a few days earlier.

Beginning on June 12 and during the following days, SSHRC received many letters from academics supporting the conference and protesting SSHRC's demand for a pre-conference report from the organizers. These included an open letter by the CAUT executive committee and the letter by the QUFA president on June 12, and a letter by Professor Arthur Hilliker, president of the York University Faculty Association (YUFA) on June 16. On June 14 a large group of faculty members in Osgoode Hall sent an open letter to SSHRC, and soon after that other letters of protest were sent from across Canada.

Meanwhile, during the June 13–14 weekend, several senior SSHRC staff-persons were drafting both a letter to Ryder and background notes for a meeting on June 15 of SSHRC's executive, governance, and nominating (EG&N) committee. These staff-persons included Corporate Secretary Trauttmansdorff, Vice-Presidents Yasmeen and Charette, and Director McNaughton.

A draft (dated June 13) of the letter to Ryder included the sentence:

> It is important that the Council be able to respond to recent
> public concerns around your conference and we appreciate being
> able to rely on yourself as the grantee to permit an informed
> response.[53]

Responding to this draft on June 14, Trauttmansdorff recommended that this sentence be omitted, for two reasons. First, the members of the council "don't have a formal role in the process, nor have we asked them to insert themselves in this case," and:

> Second, I am a little worried that the sentence suggests that
> SSHRC and Council have a pre-determined role or responsibility
> vis à vis responding to concerns raised about grants. In the
> normal course of things, questions or concerns about projects
> we fund are directed to the grant holder and the institution and
> that's the end of it. This case is outside the norm.[54]

The final version of the letter did omit the sentence questioned by Trauttmansdorff when it was sent to Ryder the next day.

A lengthier commentary on material for the letter being drafted—a one-page note from McNaughton to Yasmeen (undated but apparently from that weekend)—clarifies the extent to which this case was being handled "outside the norm." McNaughton wrote:

> I reviewed my original draft to Ryder and Christine's redraft and
> would suggest a further revision [...] that will help clarify the

nature of our action. [...] I think we need to address the issue
raised by CAUT of asking the grantee to respond within 24 hrs.
by thanking him for his collaboration.

Then we need to explain why the speed was needed: we needed
his (collaborative) response as grantee to allow us to respond
to public concerns about his conference. It does not matter that
the Minister relayed the concerns (save in the sense that his
statement complicates matters in relation to principles of arm's
length and peer review); the reality is there are serious public
concerns which we believe need to be addressed as a function
of our overall accountability to Parliament, the public and, for
that matter, our mandate to promote SSH in Canada.[55] The
implication is that we would do the same with any grant and
with any group if we judged the public concerns serioius and
credible.

We also need to refer to the agreement by Shapson and
Monahan. Our first available recourse is to check with the
applicant that all is well; our second is to check with the
institution(s) involved. Beyond these two moves, SSHRC
as a research granting council (reliant on peer review and a
highly decentralized management of grant funds) has limited
recourse.[56]

SSHRC's actual reply was sent to Ryder in a letter from McNaughton on
June 15. It said:

We have reviewed your letter of June 11, 2009. Thank you for
informing us that the changes in your upcoming conference are
minor in nature, consistent with the provisions outlined in the
Grant Holder's Guide for the Aid to Workshops and Conferences
Program – and for informing us that the Dean of Osgoode Hall
Law School and the Vice-President Research and Innovation are
in agreement with you.

We accept this assurance that planning for the conference is
proceeding in a manner consistent with the provisions of the
Grant Holder's Guide for the program.[57]

Also on June 15, SSHRC issued another media release on the conference. This statement included the information provided to Ryder in the letter quoted above, and it also said:

> SSHRC has accepted their [the grant holder, the Osgoode Hall dean, and the York vice-president research] assurance that planning for the conference is proceeding in a manner consistent with provisions of the Grant Holder's Guide for the program.[58]

Thus, contrary to its public statement issued June 11 (quoted above, from the SSHRC website), SSHRC itself did not "determine" whether the changes made to the conference since the grant application was submitted were minor or major. Instead, it "accepted" the assurance of the grant holder and the agreement by the dean and vice-president with his report.

On Sunday, June 14, Trauttmansdorff had sent an email message transmitting "background notes" on the York conference to Thomas Kierans, chair of SSHRC's EG&N committee and chair of its governing council, for the EG&N meeting the next day. The message was copied to President Gaffield. In addition to general information on the conference grant and SSHRC policies, the background notes included the information communicated on June 15 to Ryder by McNaughton, along with excerpts from President Shoukri's public statement on academic freedom issued May 21. The background notes also said:

> Public discussion and media reports about the conference included allegations that the program had changed significantly, i.e. that SSHRC policy had been breached in that approval of these changes had not been sought. Exercising due diligence and following established procedures for alleged breaches of agency policy, SSHRC contacted the grant holder, advised him of the allegation, and asked him to identify any changes in the conference since the time of the application.[59]

Thus, once again, in the face of the June 10 allegation by CAUT that SSHRC itself—not the grant holder—had breached its own policy and procedures, senior SSHRC administrators advanced "due diligence" as a justification for the action taken, as they had in the media release issued on June 11.

ACTIONS BY CAUT, JUNE 7–15

CAUT Executive Director James Turk's email message to SSHRC President Chad Gaffield on June 7 asked him to confirm details in the statement by Minister Gary Goodyear being circulated by Canadian Jewish groups that weekend. SSHRC formally replied on June 9, with an emailed copy of its media release of that date. The next day, June 10, CAUT issued a media release:

> [CAUT] is calling for the resignation of Minister of State Gary Goodyear following his unprecedented efforts to interfere with funding for a major academic conference. [...] For a minister to intervene in an effort to derail an academic conference on behalf of special interest groups is simply unacceptable, and compromises the integrity and public purpose of universities.[60]

During this period, while it was still unclear whether SSHRC might cancel its grant to the conference in response to the pressure from the minister and the demands of Israel lobby groups, both CAUT and the Nathanson Centre at York offered to assist the organizers financially if SSHRC funding were withdrawn.

Throughout the week of June 7, there was a series of formal and informal communications between CAUT and SSHRC, including the June 10 letter from Turk to Gaffield. The information that SSHRC had decided it would not proceed to conduct a second peer review of the application, and that it would instead demand an immediate and detailed pre-conference report from Professor Bruce Ryder, emerged from these exchanges.

A further CAUT response to SSHRC's actions was the issuance of an open letter to Gaffield on Friday, June 12, by all members of the CAUT executive committee. The letter said:

> We are deeply troubled by your response to Minister of Science and Technology Gary Goodyear's complaint to you about the conference on Israel/Palestine being held at York University later this month. Your action of requiring the conference organizers to immediately provide you with a list of all changes to their program since their grant was awarded violates SSHRC's own policies and legitimates the Minister's unprecedented and unacceptable political intervention in SSHRC's peer-reviewed granting process. In short, your response was not to stand against

the Minister's action but to bow to it. [...]

In an apparent effort to please the Minister, you chose to disregard SSHRC's Grant Holder's Policy that specifies any changes other than a major change to the theme of the conference are to be provided in the organizers' report of activities submitted at the conclusion of the grant. Instead, you demanded the information now so as to comply with the Minister's request. [...]

At the very least, you owe an apology to the conference organizers for your failure to protect the integrity of the granting process of SSHRC. You need publicly to assure the Canadian academic community that your bowing to political pressure will not happen again. If you cannot or will not do this, we question your fitness to continue in your present position.[61]

Gaffield replied to the CAUT open letter on June 16, saying:

Let me emphasize that the peer review of the grant-in-aid application has never been in question at SSHRC following the award decision in January 2009. As stewards of public funds, SSHRC is expected and committed to look into concerns about how awards are being administered. [...] In this case, the result is that SSHRC – as well as the public – has timely assurance that conference planning is proceeding in a manner consistent with the provisions of the Grant Holder's Guide for the program. In other words, we have all been served well by our independent peer review process, policies and procedures, to which SSHRC is unwavering in its commitment. Thus, I am fully satisfied that our handling of the matter, as an arm's length agency, is consistent with relevant SSHRC policies and procedures and with our responsibilities as stewards of public funds under the mandate of the SSHRC Act.[62]

Months later, on September 30 (two days after the SSHRC media release of September 28, saying that Communications Manager Trevor Lynn's "extremely urgent" June 5 email message to Dr. Gaffield was "inaccurate"[63]), SSHRC communications staff-person David Holton emailed a draft five-point list of "media lines" to Tania Bercier of Industry Canada. His covering note said, "Please find enclosed the media lines you requested."[64] Several days later, an emailed reply was sent by Leng Chiv of Industry Canada to Holton and his superiors Gobel and Lynn in SSHRC's communications group, with the covering note, "Attached are the PCO [Privy Council Office] -approved lines re: York conference issue."[65]

The PCO-approved Media Lines document attached to Chiv's October 5 email opened with the explanation:

> These lines are to be used as the government's response to allegations around SSHRC's funding of the conference called "Israel/Palestine: Mapping models of statehood and prospects for peace" held at York University in June 2009.[66]

The first two media lines in the seven-point PCO-approved list were the statements:

- Let me assure you that the government is committed to the principle of academic independence and the independent, arm's-length, peer-review process for assessing applications for research grants.

- The fact of the matter is that there was no ministerial interference in this process. The Minister of State's office informed SSHRC of public concerns that they had received regarding the York conference.[67]

The remaining five points were essentially the same as "key messages" prepared earlier by SSHRC communications staff, and had appeared either in SSHRC media releases of June or September, or in Gaffield's June 16 letter to Turk.

Thus, in October 2009, following an Opposition question in Parliament several days earlier, the federal government's concern was to have the public record state that:

1. The government was committed to the arm's-length status with which SSHRC had been established by Parliament, and

2. The government did not interfere in the arm's-length process pertaining to the SSHRC grant to the June conference at York University.

However, in June, following the representations made by Israel lobby groups and their supporters, the government had not only interfered with an arm's-length research-granting agency, but also had taken steps to ensure that this lobby was the first to know that it had interfered—by immediately sending Minister Goodyear's June 5 statement confirming his interference to the Canadian Jewish media, several days before its release to the general media. As noted earlier, B'Nai Brith Canada apparently understood this to be the case when it then sent out an Action Alert over its Jewish Canada email network, asking supporters to thank the minister for his announced interference, and to urge him to interfere even more strongly.

MEDIA COMMENTARIES ON THE CONFERENCE OR ITS TOPIC, JUNE 5, 9, AND 11

Article by Patrick Martin. On June 5, the *Globe and Mail* published an article titled, "Has the Two-state Ship Sailed?" by its Middle East bureau chief, Patrick Martin, discussing the various models of statehood for Israel/Palestine. He reported that although some international leaders, including American President Barack Obama, insisted on the two-state solution:

> Israel's Prime Minister, Benjamin Netanyahu, still doesn't agree, and an impressive gathering of right-wing politicians met in Jerusalem recently to back him up, outlining several reasons why the two-state solution is a failed option, no matter what Barack Obama says, and proposing several alternatives. Ironically, these Israelis have only expressed what many Palestinian thinkers have been arguing for some time: The two-state ship has sailed and it's not coming back. [...] Are there alternatives to a two-state solution? Sure there are. But a lot of people aren't going to like what they are.[68]

After noting that, "Members of Israel's right now argue that the two-state formula has been tried and failed," because "Palestinians are not capable of governing themselves."[69] Martin added:

> The fact is, most Israelis don't want Palestinians to have a real

state at all. Even the dwindling peace camp, and certainly Ms. Livni's Kadima Party, when they say they support a two-state solution, they really mean a Palestinian state that would have severe limits on its military capacity, its foreign policy and its borders. It's not much different from the self-governing "entity" Mr. Netanyahu speaks of.[70]

Martin outlined other statehood models that had been discussed over the years: one-state, various hybrids of one- and two-state models, and continuation of the status quo (Israeli occupation of Palestinian territory with Palestinians being progressively forced out of significant parts of it).

Article by Professor Gerald Steinberg. Steinberg's article on the conference, versions of which had been circulating on the Internet since May, was published by the *National Post* on June 9 under the title, "York University Sinks Deeper in the Mire." This was the day after he had sent out by email a denunciation of the conference and fifteen of its speakers on NGO Monitor letterhead.

The article in the *National Post* was shorter than, but otherwise very similar to, the one Steinberg had web-posted on May 22.[71] It opened by attacking York President Shoukri's May 21 public statement defending academic freedom and the June conference. The article said the president's reference to academic freedom was "a diversion—a straw man aimed at deflecting criticism and blocking important public debate over the role of university campuses as battlefields in the Arab–Israeli narrative wars that perpetuate the violent conflict," and then quoted with approval from the May 12 CIJA public statement against the conference.[72]

Steinberg went on to denounce at some length two of the speakers, Ali Abunimah and Jeff Halper (the first two on his June 8 list of fifteen undesirable speakers) as "virulent anti-Israel activists, with little or no connection to academic research on this subject."[73] He said that "had the event's 11 sponsors—six from York, four from Queen's university plus a government-funded research framework—exercised due diligence," they would have reached the same conclusions.[74]

From his perspective, "the defence [based on academic freedom] offered by the president of York University is a farce," while such conferences transform "the university into a macabre circus that sells hatred, martyrdom and murder."[75] He concluded with an apocalyptic warning and a branding of York University as a criminal accomplice:

> Seen from the Middle East, conferences like the one about to take place on a Canadian university campus will only serve to fuel the vicious warfare and mass terror, which has taken the lives of tens of thousands of Israelis, Palestinians and others and is escalating into nuclear confrontation. York University has now become an accomplice in this crime.[76]

Among the comments on Steinberg's article posted by the *National Post* on its website was one by Professor Craig Scott, director of the Nathanson Centre for Transnational Human Rights, Crime, and Security in Osgoode Hall. His Centre was one of the eleven sponsors of the conference, thus presumably one of those that—according to Steinberg—had failed to exercise due diligence. He wrote:

> I write in brief initial response to Professor Steinberg. I situate myself as someone who, in the face of misguided calls for boycotts of Israeli universities, sponsored the invitation to Bar-Ilan University's Faculty of Law to join a leading group of law faculties that comprise the Association of Transnational Law Schools (ATLAS)—which I am happy to report Bar-Ilan's Faculty of Law accepted. In reading Professor Steinberg's analysis (which is more a cross between a diatribe and a hatchet job), I can only be grateful that our partner is the Faculty of Law at Bar-Ilan and not a department (of Political Science) that would see fit to elect a Chair of their department with such a shallow grasp of both pertinent facts as well as fair and cogent reasoning.[77]

Article by Professor Ian Lustick. On June 11, the *National Post* published Lustick's article titled, "The Conference Must Go On," commenting on Steinberg's article, as well as on the recent statement by CIJA (May 12) and B'nai Brith's Action Alert (June 8). He wrote:

> These statements, plus these organizations' letter writing campaigns and other pressure tactics these organizations are mounting are part of a pattern of misguided, so-called "pro-Israel" attempts throughout North America to suppress debate, run away from challenges we Zionists must face. [...]
>
> Steinberg's argument that defending the conference based

on academic freedom and scholarly values is a straw man is breathtakingly specious. His organization, along with a parallel group called Israel Academia Monitor, is devoted to silencing debate, discussion and original thinking. Every month, these groups distribute dozens of e-mails urging donors to cut off funds to international organizations and Israeli universities because of conferences or research activities they consider threatening to their views on Israel's future.

B'nai Brith's statement runs along similar lines, denouncing the participants in the conference as supporting an event "that promotes hatred and encourages the destruction of the Jewish state." B'nai Brith Canada should learn from its U. S. counterpart's mistakes: In 1983, the organization had to apologize for secretly monitoring scholars it deemed enemies of Israel. Ironically, many of those scholars were early supporters of the "two state solution"—a position that is now used as a sign of acceptability by many pro-Israel organizations. Therein lies the danger of setting oneself up as the arbiter of the questions it is "legitimate" for scholars to ask. [...]

As a scholar of contemporary Middle Eastern politics I will be participating in this conference at York University for the same reason I attend any academic conference—to learn. I will learn from those with whom I agree, and I will learn even more from those with whom I disagree.

Shame on those who, in the name of academic integrity, would suppress an opportunity for colleagues to learn together about such a complex and important issue as the future of Israelis and Palestinians in the Middle East.[78]

PROFESSORS ADELMAN AND DEWITT TAKE A SECOND LOOK, JUNE 7, 8

Dean Patrick Monahan had read the June 5 article by Patrick Martin in the *Globe and Mail*, and commented to AVPR David Dewitt:

I thought that the piece was very well balanced and suggested that, at the very least, the notion of two versus one state is a topic for some debate. What was interesting was the fact (according to Martin) that even some of the Israeli right seem to be entertaining a discussion of a one state solution.[79]

Dewitt replied:

Yes, the Martin article was good, and had the initial conference website presented something similar and then managed – by invitation – the speakers, we'd likely not be facing yhe current situation. By the way, the substantive part of the conference, at least the abstracts now listed, has shown considerable improvement. Still problems, but better than before.[80]

The next day, Dewitt forwarded to Monahan the B'Nai Brith Action Alert denouncing the conference, issued earlier the same day. He commented, "Classic BB right-wing stuff playing to their constituency."[81] He then outlined his current views on the conference, as well as those of Professor Howard Adelman:

Last week I went over the conference website and abstracts carefully and concluded that the organizers have improved what was there. While I personally still have some reservations, had what it is now been presented six months ago and had they been a bit more careful in how they selected their speakers, I think much of the problems we've encountered either would not have happened or could have been managed. And I told them that last summer. [...]

I was pleased to note that entirely separately, in speaking with Howard Adelman over the weekend, he had gone through a similar exercise and came to much the same conclusion: what is there now is significantly better than before. Still problematic in some ways, but not to the extent previously and certainly within the bounds for what might now be a managed engagement of strongly differing ideas. [...] It still is not in my mind a high level/quality conference even with some very good scholars present; too uneven and still with some rather dubious individuals. Hence, Gerald Steinberg will still write what he writes, as noted in my previous email to you.[82]

Although Monahan and Dewitt already had discussed the June 5 Martin article in their email exchange the day before, Dewitt concluded this one as follows:

As an aside, I hope you had a chance to read Patrick Martin's long article in Saturday's G&M on the very topic of the conference. It was well done, and could have been a fine piece to frame the original conference call [for papers] had it been available a year ago! Oh well.[83]

PRESIDENT SHOUKRI REPLIES TO ANOTHER CRITIC, JUNE 10

On June 9, a person sent President Shoukri an email message captioned "ANOTHER SH-T STORM COMING," and saying:

This is like watching a train bearing down on my child. Do we have a death wish?? Why in hell do we have to have this stuff on our campus after all our public relations problems this year? THIS THING WILL NOT END WELL AND SHOULD BE STOPPED.[84]

Shoukri replied the next day:

I became aware of it [the conference] as we started to receive messages from the community who appeared to believe that [the] conference is promoting this particular [one-state] solution. This is not true. This is an academic conference where participants debate ideas and issues freely and the conference does not issue statements in support of any resolution. When we became aware of the concerns, Patrick Monahan and Stan Shapson encouraged the organizers to encourage more participation by people who hold other points of view. We know that the organizers tried their best and may have had some success but the campaign continued. [...] Unfortunately, there is absolutely nothing we can do at this moment. We cannot cancel the conference and cannot appear to interfere any further without triggering another serious problem by the academics all over the country regarding academic freedom. I assure you, this is a real threat.[85]

Fifteen minutes later, the president's correspondent replied:

I DON'T CARE A FIG ABOUT ACADEMIC FREEDOM. I DO CARE ABOUT YORK – AND WITH OUR PROBLEMS THIS YEAR. THIS IS TROUBLE WITH A CAPITAL T.[86]

AVPR DEWITT'S VIEWS ON ACTIONS BY THE MINISTER, SSHRC, AND CAUT

In the late afternoon of June 12, the day the CAUT executive committee sent its open letter to SSHRC President Gaffield, AVPR Dewitt sent an email message to a person whose name is redacted on the copy released to CAUT (his message was copied to Susan Davis of CIJA and blind-copied to York VP Shapson). Apparently it was in reply to a message he had received, because it was captioned "Re: Fw: CAUT's letter to the President of the SSHRC." He wrote:

I understand why CAUT has written their letter; it falls within their mandate and they need to act. Similarly, as I understand Stan and Patrick tried to explain to Sharry and Susan, the Minister acted in his mandate: to respond to his constituencies' inquiries and request information from SSHRC. SSHRC then followed their posted procedures, which was not to accede to the Minister's desire to have another peer review undertaken, but rather simply to contact the PI [Principal Investigator, i.e., Professor Bruce Ryder] and ask for confirmation that no major changes had occurred. I believe that Stan and Patrick encouraged the co-PI team to respond very briefly and to the point: that no major changes had occurred and that SSHRC would receive a full report upon completion of the conference, as required by the Council. Each party for its own political purposes has played this somewhat differently; not surprisingly I might add. There are other issues, but that will have to wait until after I return on the 23rd.[87]

Possibly he had not seen the relevant correspondence. In any case, Dewitt incorrectly stated in this email that SSHRC "followed their posted procedures" and "simply [...]contact[ed] the PI and ask[ed] for confirmation that no major changes had occurred." In a significant respect, SSHRC did not follow its posted procedures, and its demand of Ryder went beyond asking for confirmation that no major changes had occurred. This point was emphasized in the CAUT open letter.

STATEMENT BY B'NAI BRITH, JUNE 12

On June 8, B'nai Brith Canada had issued an Action Alert statement against the conference and asked its supporters to write to Minister Goodyear, urging him to direct SSHRC to cancel the grant. On June 12, it issued another Action Alert statement, using stronger language and asking its supporters to write letters of protest to SSHRC, York, and Queen's. That weekend it also published a large advertisement in the *National Post*, strongly critical of York University.

Copies of the statement were faxed to the university, with a covering letter signed by Frank Dimant, executive vice-president, B'nai Brith Canada. The letter was addressed to President Shoukri and copied to several others, including Dean Monahan and Professor Craig Scott, and said, "This conference is being convened solely to debate whether Israel has a right to exist. [...] We respectfully request that support from York University [...] be withdrawn."[88]

The statement began with headlines alleging that the conference "promises to be a 'Who's Who' of anti-Israel propagandists," and "Speakers include Holocaust deniers and those who rationalize terrorism." Its text opened with the allegation that "A virulent anti-Israel hate fest is coming to the York University campus on June 22–24, 2009," and, after listing the conference's sponsors, it continued with allegations:

> The veil of academia provided by these sponsors should not
> fool anyone. No academic body should lend its imprimatur to a
> conference where several of the speakers are actively engaged in
> Holocaust denial, rationalize terrorism, and are infamous anti-
> Israel propagandists."[89]

The statement endeavoured to justify the allegations by means of brief denunciations of seven of the speakers (five of whom, including Ali Abunimah, Jeff Halper, and Omar Barghouti, were on the NGO Monitor list of June 8), based on short, one- or two-sentence quotations attributed to each. Several of the speakers were contacted immediately by the organizers, and they replied that the statements attributed to them were erroneous, taken out of context, or otherwise misleading.

The most inflammatory allegation—the one regarding "Holocaust deniers"—turned out to be erroneous. It was supported by a specific allegation against only one speaker, Abunimah—"This same speaker, Ali Abunimah, also pushes Holocaust denial."[90] The evidence put forward by B'nai Brith was a purported two-sentence quotation attributed to Abunimah. The attribution was incorrect, as B'nai Brith later acknowledged in another letter faxed to the university. Moreover, it was an error that B'nai Brith could have detected with very modest effort, as Scott discovered by typing the two sentences into an Internet search engine. He informed this Inquiry, "I needed scarcely a minute on Google," to learn that the sentences quoted were compiled from utterances by another person, Khalid Ameyrah, but later misattributed to Abunimah.[91]

Scott emailed the results of his Google search to the conference organizers, who then contacted Abunimah. He confirmed he was aware of this incorrect allegation against him and had earlier made attempts to have it corrected, but ultimately had been unsuccessful, in that it could still be found on the Internet.[92]

The conference organizers considered the allegations by B'nai Brith to be defamatory of themselves and the sponsors, as well as of the speakers. They consulted a defamation lawyer on actions that might be taken to persuade B'nai Brith to correct the error and publicly apologize. As a result of subsequent discussions among B'nai Brith, York University, and the organizers, B'nai Brith publicly acknowledged that the allegation against Abunimah was erroneous. In its statement of retraction, it also apologized to Abunimah, the conference organizers, York University, and Queen's University, and the other sponsors, and it undertook to correct this misinformation publicly. It said that a student intern had taken the claim from a website. Apparently, neither the student intern nor more senior persons in B'nai Brith had ascertained whether it was correct.[93]

However, the B'nai Brith statement of retraction and apology was not publicly issued until over a week later.[94] As often occurs in such matters, the allegations in the original—uncorrected—version of the June 12 Action Alert caught the attention of some recipients, who responded to its call for action.

For example, on June 15 a faculty member at Queen's received a copy of the June 12 B'nai Brith statement from a faculty member at another university, who had received it from a colleague on B'nai Brith's Jewish Canada mailing list. That night, the faculty member at Queen's forwarded the June 12 Action Alert to the principal, the vice-principal, and the dean of Law saying, "I got this rather disturbing email today. We are not really involved in this outrage, are we?"[95] In reply, one of the Queen's administrators recommended that the concerned faculty member speak with their colleague Professor Aiken, as a member of the conference organizing committee. Two days later, the concerned faculty member wrote back to the Queen's administrator, saying he had now heard another side of the story and had moderated his views.

Another such example was a letter emailed to the prime minister on June 15 by an individual who enclosed the uncorrected June 12 statement by B'nai Brith, including the allegation that Abunimah was a Holocaust denier. His letter said:

> I am writing to request that individuals with proven racist activities and who are scheduled to speak at this meeting be barred from entering the country based on our established laws against racism and hate-mongering.[96]

A NEWSPAPER AD BY B'NAI BRITH, JUNE 13

B'nai Brith placed a full-page advertisement in the *National Post* on June 13. Composed as a "Report Card," it gave failing grades to York University on such "Subjects" as "Preventing anti-Israel agitators from spewing hatred," and said that the institution "is now in danger of becoming infamous for enabling rabid anti-Israel and anti-Jewish sentiment." In an email message to President Shoukri and Chief Marketing Officer Richard Fisher that morning, Dean Monahan wrote:

> See the full page ad by B'nai Brith on page A20 of the *Post* slamming York. Incredible that they would do that. They seem to be declaring war on us.[97]

Fisher replied, "They're playing to their base. They have really misstepped on the Goodyear thing and are desperately trying to bring it back to York in time for the conference."[98] The president replied, "I agree that the ad is designed to bring the issue back to York," and proposed a conference call for the following evening.[99] Monahan then wrote, "Richard and

I believe a response from the university leadership is required, since this is an unprecedented attack on the entire institution. I have asked Richard to start thinking about the outline of an appropriate response."[100]

The result of discussions during the next couple of days was a public statement, jointly signed by the president and the outgoing and incoming board chairs, issued June 15.

STATEMENTS BY YORK AND QUEEN'S LAW PROFESSORS, AND YORK DEAN

On June 14, a group of faculty members in the Osgoode Hall Law School (forty-seven in total, representing the great majority) sent an open letter to the president of SSHRC. The letter said:

> We are writing as members of the faculty of Osgoode Hall Law School at York University to express our extreme dismay that SSHRC appears to be acceding to political pressure by revisiting its decision to fund the above-noted academic conference. [...] Your decision as SSHRC President to require a special pre-conference accounting from the conference organizers, outside the normal post-conference reporting procedures for conference grants, raises the much larger question of your agency's integrity as a funder and promoter of independent university-based research in Canada.
>
> As a group we have extensive experience with the organization of academic conferences and with SSHRC granting procedures. We believe there is no basis at all for the suggestion that "major changes" were made to the plan for this conference after the grant application had been peer reviewed and funding granted. Nor do we believe that you could possibly see any basis for this suggestion. Rather, it appears that the special accounting was demanded of our colleagues in direct response to the unprecedented and entirely inappropriate political intervention of Minister Goodyear.
>
> We believe that SSHRC made a serious error in acceding to political interference in this manner. [...] By intruding into the planning of an academic event after a funding decision has been made, SSHRC's actions are likely to have a most unfortunate

chilling effect on academics considering the exploration of controversial or unpopular topics. In addition, by casting doubt on the integrity of its own procedures, SSHRC has empowered those who would devalue academic research and discourse by insisting that academic freedom be reserved only for those who happen to share their point of view.

We hope that SSHRC will very shortly stand up to defend its own granting procedures and the values of academic excellence and autonomy they are designed to protect.

The next day, a group of Law Faculty members at Queen's sent an open letter to the president of SSHRC, similar to the one sent by their colleagues in Osgoode Hall.[101]

Also on June 15, Dean Monahan sent an email message to faculty members in Osgoode Hall, outlining recent efforts by the university administration to support the conference, and adding that he "appreciate[d] the careful and reasoned arguments" in their letter to SSHRC. The dean also "commend[ed] our colleagues Bruce Ryder and Susan Drummond."[102]

STATEMENT BY THE YORK PRESIDENT AND BOARD CHAIRS, JUNE 15

President Shoukri, Board Chair Marshall Cohen, and Board Chair-designate Paul Cantor issued their joint public statement on June 15 (in response to the most recent and strongest public attack against the university by B'nai Brith, in addition to other public criticism). They began by noting that the university had recently "been singled out for public criticism from some external community groups" alleging that holding the June conference "is essentially anti-Israel and/or anti-Semitic."[103] They also noted that the criticism continued after the president's public statement of May 21:

Having considered the criticism the conference continues to generate, we believe that it is important to reiterate the University's view that the principles of academic freedom must prevail with regard to all activities undertaken under the auspices of the university, including this conference, so long as they are consistent with the obligations cited above and are consistent with Canadian law. To do otherwise would undermine the mission of the academy to provide a free and unmediated forum for serious academic discussion. We understand that the subject at the heart of the conference, an examination of the potential models for statehood that could lead to peace between Israelis and Palestinians, is one that many find difficult, sensitive and very personal. We believe that the University remains a most appropriate forum for academic debate of these issues and for a conference such as this to take place. These issues are discussed on a daily basis in all parts of the world, especially in the Middle East including Israel. There is no reason why they should not be discussed at a university in Canada.[104]

They referred to events on campus earlier in the year that had disturbed the Jewish community and the University community, and said that anti-Semitism and intolerance of any form would not be permitted at York. They added:

To that end, in March President Shoukri announced the creation of a Task Force on Student Life, Learning and Community under the leadership of the Dean of Osgoode and Provost-designate Patrick Monahan. At the time, Dr. Shoukri said, "We are committed to ensuring that our students can pursue their studies free of harassment or intimidation. This task force will take a hard look at the current environment on campus, and explore ways that we can promote open debate and the free exchange of ideas."[105]

ACADEMIC CREDENTIALS RE-EMERGE AS AN ISSUE

During the period from March through June 2009 and later, several conference critics suggested that one or more of the organizers lacked appropriate academic credentials to organize a conference on models of statehood for Israel/Palestine. AVPR Dewitt had suggested this in regard to Professor Drummond at the beginning of March, and Dean Monahan had suggested this in regard to Professors Ryder and Aiken, as well as Drummond, in mid-May. In mid-June, soon after the majority of his colleagues in Osgoode Hall issued their open letter to SSHRC in support of the conference, Professor Benjamin Geva sent letters to all of his colleagues and the president of SSHRC, outlining the reasons for his dissenting view. He prefaced the first letter (June 16) by saying that he did not dispute his colleagues' analysis of SSHRC policies, and that he was challenging neither academic freedom nor freedom of speech. He said his concerns were that:

> Though to be attended and presented by academics, as perceived, this is a strictly political conference [...] organized by two colleagues, esteemed, keen, and well-meaning as they are, but who are not experts in the area.[106]

On this basis, Geva considered it appropriate to question why SSHRC should have awarded the conference grant.

Two days later, he sent a second, longer letter to his Osgoode colleagues and the president of SSHRC, setting out his concerns more comprehensively. He wrote, "I am questioning the characterization of the conference as a research project, and as such its eligibility for research funding."[107] He proceeded to give a definition of proper academic research: "For a true academic project one needs some distance, and cannot act in a highly charged and volatile atmosphere."[108] Also, in his view, all aspects of the Middle East conflict had been discussed many times and in many places, so, "One has to be naïve to believe that any new point of research or scholarship can come out of the conference."[109]

In the second letter, Geva returned to the matter of credentials:

> I could be open to persuasion to the contrary if the conference was to be organized by experts in Middle East Studies, or even in the resolution of international conflicts in general. I will honestly say that inasmuch as our most esteemed colleagues are experts in their own area they do not fit the bill, so to speak. They may be interested in the area, and well intentioned; for me this is inadequate to qualify.[110]

He concluded with the comment that selection of this conference by the York U50 Committee as one of its sponsored events "reflects a poor judgment" by that committee.[111] He continued to have these concerns months later, as detailed in a written submission to this Inquiry.

A week after the conference, in an email message addressed to Ryder and copied to all faculty members in Osgoode Hall, Professor Martin Lockshin (Humanities, York University) appeared to express views similar to those of Geva, and also similar to some of Steinberg's views. He questioned "whether this was an academic conference, or a political exercise disguised as an academic conference (and misusing the protection of 'academic free-dom' to silence criticism of a political exercise)."[112] In a following para-graph, Lockshin proposed that to answer his question, a person needed specific credentials:

> I think a person who wants to organize a conference about
> Israel/Palestine, or a person who wants to express a view about
> whether an Israel/Palestine conference was really academic,
> should have training in the Middle East and should read Arabic
> and Hebrew.[113]

A month earlier, on May 26, the *National Post* had published an article by Lockshin in which he criticized a panel discussion to be held that week in the annual meetings of the Congress of Humanities and Social Sciences (sometimes referred to as "the Learneds"), titled, "Palestinian Solidarity on Campus: the Question of Boycott." In his view, this session lacked balance, and the scheduled speakers lacked appropriate credentials. He concluded:

> The sad truth is that there is a "privileged discourse" in our
> academy today. Under this regime, bashing Israel is legitimate—
> with or without credentials. The state of Israel—a strong and
> vibrant democracy—will survive the verbal abuse that will be
> heaped on it at the Learneds.[114]

JDL COMPLAINS AGAIN TO SSHRC

On June 21, the day before the conference opened, JDL National Director Meir Weinstein emailed a letter to SSHRC Executive Vice-President Carmen Charette. He wrote:

> I was very disappointed to read that your ministry is providing
> funding to the Anti Israel Conference that York University is
> sponsoring. [...] There is a consensus in the Jewish Community
> that this conference negates Jewish Rights and that is a
> fundamental violation of the Canadian Charter of Rights. [...]
>
> A similar conference took place last week in South Africa with
> the participation of Bruce Ryder from Osgoode Law School. [...]
> Re-envisioning Israel/Palestine http://www.hsrc.ac.za/Event-363.phtml.

This same individual, Bruce Ryder, is one of the main organizers of the conference at York University York University and we are deeply offended that your department ignored the concerns of the Jewish Community. The advisory board for the conference is filled with people that either do not accept the basic historical rights of the Jewish People or demand an Academic Boycott of Israel.

The Jewish Defence League demands the right to third party review of the application for funds.[115]

SSHRC STAFF OBSERVE FROM OTTAWA

Senior SSHRC staff-persons were following events in Toronto as they unfolded and commented on the B'nai Brith apology. In an email thread starting early on the morning of June 22, David Phipps, York's research services director, had sent to Director Craig McNaughton of SSHRC the York website link where B'nai Brith's apology was reported. Phipps remarked, "That's a relief. Fingers crossed for a peaceful conference over the next 3 days." McNaughton forwarded the email to Vice-President Yasmeen with the comment, "Useful, instructive [...]," and she in turn forwarded this to President Gaffield, Vice-President Charette, and Communications Director Gobel. Yasmeen wrote, "A must read. Too bad they didn't apologise to us, too! THX to Craig for the tip. Click on the link below." Gobel forwarded this to Communications Manager Trevor Lynn commenting, "Please include in clippings. I will let gary at IC [Industry Canada] know."[116]

7
THE CONFERENCE AND COMMENTARY ON IT

EVENTS IN AND AROUND THE CONFERENCE, JUNE 22–24

Demonstrations. York University made elaborate and expensive security arrangements for the conference venue at Glendon College, in the event of demonstrations against the conference by pro-Israeli groups and possible counter-demonstrations by pro-Palestinian groups. However, the demonstrations were peaceful and not very large, and there were no counter-demonstrations.

The only event approximating a protest altercation was between two pro-Israeli groups, as reported in an email exchange between two senior York Media and Communications staff that afternoon. In response to the question, "any protests today?" the answer was, "Two sets. Appears that Hasbora was here first noontime but that some squabble transpired that they did not want to stand in arm with JDL."[1]

Dean Monahan Cites J. S. Mill. Dean Patrick Monahan formally opened the conference with welcoming remarks on behalf of York University and Osgoode Hall. He also read welcoming remarks sent by Dean William Flanagan of the Queen's University Law Faculty.

Monahan spoke of the aims of the conference, the importance of academic freedom, and the obligations of scholars. Referring to the controversy attracted by the conference, he cited President Shoukri's public statements of May 21 and June 15, in which the university's position was set out. He mentioned *Essay on Liberty* by John Stuart Mill, which "remains the most compelling defence of the importance of free expression," and quoted a passage from it:

the peculiar evil of silencing the expression of an opinion is, that it is robbing the human race, posterity as well as the present generation—those who dissent from the opinion, still more than those who hold it. If the opinion is right, they are deprived of the opportunity of exchanging error for truth; if wrong, they lose, what is almost as great a benefit, the clearer perception and livelier impression of truth colliding with error.[2]

Monahan concluded by commending the organizers "for their efforts" in "creat[ing] an academic forum that will promote genuine dialogue on these challenging issues."[3]

The Conference Proceeded as Scheduled. The conference began with the keynote address on June 22 by Professor Jeremy Webber, and continued with a number of plenary sessions, a number of concurrent panel discussions, two more keynote addresses on June 23 and 24 by Professors Ian Lustick and George Bisharat, and screenings of several movies. The complete program is posted on the conference website, http://www.yorku.ca/ipconf/, where recordings of talks by the speakers and other information can be found.

In view of the campaign against the conference, it is of note that all fifteen of the speakers/presenters who had been denounced by Professor Gerald Steinberg on June 8 were on the final program, as were all seven denounced by B'nai Brith on May 12. In particular, Omar Barghouti, who was on both the Steinberg and B'nai Brith lists and whose invitation to speak in the earlier YCISS seminar series on academic boycotts had been protested, spoke at the conference. Of the list of six members of the eleven-person International Advisory Board denounced by JDL in its May 25 complaint against the conference to Industry Canada, four were on the final program as speakers/presenters: Professors Leila Farsakh, David Kretzmer, Ian Lustick, and Ali Abunimah.

Professor Aiken's Preliminary Report. As a member of the organizing committee, Professor Sharryn Aiken undertook to compile information from conference evaluation forms provided to participants. She provided a brief summary to York President Mamdouh Shoukri in an email message sent on August 5, adding that a full conference evaluation report would be posted on the conference website when completed, including the feedback from speakers and other participants. She wrote:

To give you a sense of that feedback now, a very large majority

of participants either "agreed" or "strongly agreed" that they
were pleased to have participated in the conference. Reproduced
below is an extract of feedback provided by a senior scholar from
a Canadian university:

> This was an important conference, dealing with a
> crucial issue. It was about as balanced as a conference
> in this area could be, given the propensity of
> participants to self-select around these issues. I
> emerged with a much better sense of the issues and
> of the fundamental stumbling blocks to a resolution
> than I had possessed going in.
>
> I know that there was controversy among some
> Canadian Jewish organizations with respect to this
> conference. What became clear, however, is that the
> Israeli participants, of whom there were many and
> of varying opinions, defined the permissible scope
> of discussion much more broadly than the diasporic
> groups. [...] Virtually all of the Israeli participants
> defined themselves as Zionist, in the sense that
> they believed deeply in a distinctively Jewish state
> (or at least an identified Jewish political unit of a
> confederal state) in Palestine. But it is clear that
> accepting such a definition of the state—essentially
> embracing a self-consciously Zionist mission in
> Palestine—is very difficult for many Palestinians.
> This is true even of those untainted by anti-Semitism
> (and I saw no evidence of anti-Semitism among the
> Palestinian participants at this conference). A number
> would certainly be committed to a state open to all,
> without a distinct identity attached to a particular
> people. There even appeared to be potential common
> ground around some kind of confederal entity
> (either structured as two states with transnational
> cooperation or as one decentralized federal state),
> with the confederal nature designed to accommodate
> the division between Jewish and Arab. But affirming
> a distinctly Jewish identity of the state was difficult

for many Palestinian participants, especially given the
presence of other groups. Getting a clear sense of this
sticking point, and considering the solutions posed in
light of it, was itself an important insight for me.[4]

The remainder of Aiken's letter was devoted to concerns she had
regarding the terms of reference for the recently announced review of
matters pertaining to the conference by Frank Iacobucci. She said she
endorsed concerns already expressed by fellow organizer Professor Susan
Drummond and by Professor Craig Scott of Osgoode Hall, because the
mandate announced was "framed in a way that will subject the conference
and its organizers to continued and inappropriate scrutiny from non-
academic, non-expert individuals representing very narrow constituencies
outside the university," adding:

> From a personal perspective, the past several months have
> been extremely painful for me as I have been on the receiving
> end of most of the very public and very vitriolic criticism of
> the conference. I was hoping that with the conclusion of the
> conference in June, this would finally be put to rest.[5]

She concluded by saying that any post-conference follow-up:

> should be concerned exclusively with issues related to
> academic freedom and an examination of the role of university
> administrators in supporting academic/policy-relevant
> conferences within the university in the face of significant
> external pressures. I strenuously object to that notion that
> there is any need to review "faculty responsibilities," the
> academic value or "success" of the conference or the work of the
> organizing committee itself.[6]

She informed the president that, for these reasons, she was "not inclined
to participate in the review in any way."[7]

Later that day, Patrick Monahan (dean of Osgoode Hall at the time of the
conference but since July 1, 2009, the Vice-President Academic and Provost)
forwarded Aiken's letter to Vice-President Research Shapson and AVPR
Dewitt. He asked them for comments on her concerns about the Iacobucci
review. Dewitt responded the next morning in the following terms:

I certainly hope that Mamdouh is taken through her missive and shown how disingenuous and wrong-headed she is about much of what she states/reports. I'd hate to think that he reads her note and assumes that she is (a) speaking the truth/fact and (b) is fair in any analysis or interpretation she offers. Both, I think, are highly questionable at this stage in her thinking.[8]

POST-CONFERENCE COMMENTARY

Statements by Israel Lobby Organizations. Immediately following the conference, several groups made statements to the effect that their opposition had been well justified by the event itself. For example, on June 26 the United Jewish Appeal Federation (UJA) and CIJA (the umbrella organization) issued a statement reporting that "CIJA assigned three observers to monitor and evaluate the event, attended by approximately 150 participants and, unfortunately, the tone of the conference confirmed our fears."[9] In their view, the conference was biased against Israel and Zionism. They concluded:

> The presentations and attitudes of participants should now convince President Shoukri that "Mapping Models" did not come close to meeting the rigorous academic criteria that he expected. [...] we believe endorsement of this conference represented a serious lapse of judgment by the university.[10]

The UJA and CIJA statement added that a more detailed assessment of the conference was in preparation.

A statement to similar effect, but in stronger terms, was issued by B'nai Brith later the same day over its Jewish Canada email network.[11]

Two days earlier, on the last day of the conference, the *Jerusalem Post* published a news story reporting, among other things, the comment:

> "What we're seeing is a hate fest," Sammy Katz, Canadian campus coordinator for the pro-Israel group Hasbara Fellowships said of the situation.[12]

Commentary in the Media. On June 28, the *Toronto Star* published a commentary on the conference by columnist Haroon Siddiqui. He explained the nature of the conference and summarized events in and around it, including the efforts by Jewish community organizations to have it cancelled. He also included comments by Professor Aiken, the one Jewish member of the conference organizing committee, who had informed him:

> I received a lot of hate mail. The extent of the vilification has been very painful. [...] I am not a self-hating Jew. [...] I am not anti-Zionist. I care about a continued safe place for Jews in Israel. [...] What is specific to the Jewish diaspora is that Israel has been instrumentalized by mainstream Jewish organizations as the primary marker of Jewish identity. Any criticism of Israel is perceived and interpreted as anti-Semitic. [...] Critical dialogue becomes deeply threatening. What is routinely discussed in Israel becomes a problem in Toronto. That's terribly wrong. In the long run it will be counterproductive. Thoughtful Jews will be put off, especially the young.[13]

On June 30, the *Toronto Star* published another commentary on the conference, written by a conference participant, Dr. Na'ama Carmi (Law, Haifa University). She was one of the two speakers in a panel discussion on "Palestinian Refugees and the Right of Return." Carmi explained that, although she had "hesitated to accept the invitation to participate," she had accepted, in "reaction to the pressure put on the conference and the Jewish Defense League's (JDL) activity against it," as well as a desire to bring a moderate voice to the discussions "and not to surrender to attempts to silence debate and curb academic freedom."[14]

Carmi continued:

> The university rightly resisted outside pressures aimed at silencing the conference. But there were attempts at the conference itself to silence unpopular views. A hostile atmosphere toward people with different views generally, and Jewish–Zionist Israelis in particular, was created. [...] The audience vocally applauded those whose views it approved. At times, those presenting a different view were subject to abuse and ridicule. For me, this reached an extreme when one interlocutor, rather than debating the substantive arguments I presented, questioned my psychological state. And all of this without any apparent attempt by the organizers to stop it.[15]

A few days after Carmi's article appeared, Professor Leo Panitch (Canada Research Chair, Political Science, York University) sent a letter to the editor of the *Toronto Star* in response.

> I am puzzled by Na'ama Carmi's claim that the York University conference on Israel/Palestine was characterized by an unacademic atmosphere. I was only there for one of the two full days of the conference (the day after Carmi spoke) but what she describes is certainly not what went on the day I was there. I attended two plenary sessions and three panels and all were characterized by a respectful academic atmosphere [...]. The only two people who showed any slight measure of disrespect the day I was there were Carmi herself and one Palestinian woman academic who were seated not very far from each other (and me as it happened) and who were both muttering under their breath at the opening plenary when things were said they didn't like. I suspected the two of them had set each other off the day before.[16]

The March 2010 report on the conference and the controversy by Frank Iacobucci published information on Carmi's participation in the conference, including the following detail:

> Professor Carmi did not follow the normal decorum at academic conferences and at times left the room abruptly, knocking over chairs, or loudly interrupted the presenters whose views she disagreed with.[17]

The October 2009 issue of the CAUT *Bulletin* published an article by Professor Dorit Naaman (Film and Media, Queen's University), a member of the International Advisory Board for the conference. She explained why a serious academic examination of alternative statehood models for Israel/Palestine was appropriate and timely:

> Democracy itself lies in the balance. The success of openly racist and anti-Arab nationalist political party Yisrael Beiteinu, led by Foreign Minister Avigdor Lieberman, brought this reality squarely into the centre of public discussion, by opponents and enthusiasts alike. [...] Jews outside of Israel cannot turn their

backs on this reality, unless they expect to leave democracy in the hands of demagogues and racists. The situation for Israelis remains painful and requires sober choices about the direction of the state.

The mainstream Canadian Jewish organizations' attempt to silence the York conference is in effect an attempt to silence discussion of this critical debate, which—ironically—is already taking place within Israel. This attempt is a disgraceful act meant to prevent Israelis, Jews, Arabs, Palestinians and others from speaking with one another in a serious academic forum. The accusations by B'Nai Brith that the York conference hosted presenters who "justify terrorism," "advocate for the destruction of the Jewish state," and "reject compromise" rely on partial quoting and false information.[18]

The September B'nai Brith Advertisement. On September 12, B'nai Brith took out a large advertisement in the *National Post* suggesting that anti-Semitic and anti-Israel hatred was commonly encountered in universities, and that students could "expect [...] harassment [...] intimidation by your professor or teaching assistant [...] Swastikas and other antisemitic graffiti all over campus."[19] The advertisement also presented a checklist of anti-Semitic incidents students should expect to encounter. The strong language was similar to that in its June 13 advertisement in the *National Post* specifically denouncing York University, but, unlike the earlier advertisement, the one in September did not name any particular university.

The Open Letter by York Faculty and Graduate Students. Several weeks after the September 12 B'nai Brith advertisement was published, a large group of York University faculty members and students issued a public statement. Headed, "Faculty and students reject the smearing of York, and uphold the University's mission to promote public debate," the statement said, "Over the course of the past year, York University has been targeted in various public spaces as a site where anti-Semitism is rife." As examples, it cited the September 12 B'nai Brith advertisement and a recent comment by Jason Kenney, MP, suggesting certain events at York resembled pogroms. It said that, "The use of such inflammatory language cannot any longer be ignored and allowed to fester," and that these "representations of the York campus—and indeed of university campuses generally—as hotbeds of antisemitism are simply untrue."[20]

THE CONFERENCE AND THE TASK FORCE ON STUDENT LIFE

In March 2009, a Presidential Task Force on Student Life, Learning and Community had been created at York University, following a series of incidents on campus involving groups of students. The preamble to its terms of reference said that these events "have raised serious concerns over whether our most cherished values and commitments are being undermined by excessive conflict, intolerance and even intimidation," and that the task force would "examine the broad spectrum of student life, the learning environment, and student community at York University."[21]

The task force was chaired by Dean (and subsequently Provost) Monahan. The other members were students or professors. The task force met with individuals and groups, received a number of written briefs, and considered policies and practices at other universities. It submitted its report to President Shoukri in August 2009, including a series of detailed recommendations on such matters as fostering dialogue and debate, availability of space for student use, space policy, student code of conduct, and communication. The president issued a statement in September, outlining steps being taken to implement recommendations in the report.

Several individuals and groups with an interest in the York/Queen's conference presented written briefs to the task force, commenting directly or indirectly on the conference. Copies of these briefs were widely circulated in electronic form. Copies of several such submissions have been provided to this Inquiry. The task force report did not discuss the conference as such, but some of its recommendations could influence the ways in which conferences on controversial topics might be considered in future. For example, the report recommended "the creation of a Standing Committee on Campus Dialogue [... to] foster and model the kind of genuine debate and dialogue appropriate to an institution of higher learning," which would "regularly sponsor balanced and high quality discussions, debates, seminars and other academic fora on pressing and timely public issues of global, national and local importance."[22] This was one of the recommendations Shoukri said was being implemented.

Aside from any influence some of the briefs commenting on the conference may or may not have had on the report of the task force, they shed light on matters pertinent to the terms of reference of this Inquiry. Thus they are discussed here.

Brief by Jewish Community Organizations. This document was prepared by an eight-member commission chaired by Elyse Lackie. The commission was established by Hillel of Greater Toronto and Hasbara at York, with the support of the United Jewish Appeal Federation of Greater Toronto (UJA) and the Canadian Council for Israel and Jewish Advocacy (CIJA). Its mandate was to "identify trends affecting the quality of life for Jewish students at York, and to make practical recommendations for improvement."[23]

The brief made a number of recommendations, organized under headings related to the terms of reference of the task force. One of the recommendations under the heading Acceptable Expression says:

> The University should rigorously define the academic standards expected of all University-sponsored conferences, insist on peer review for all conference speakers, and deny its endorsement to any conference that violate these academic standards.[24]

The three points in this recommendation are similar in substance to comments made in regard to the York/Queen's conference in public statements by Israel lobby organizations, or in Minister Goodyear's public statement in response to lobbying. For example, the first point is similar in substance to comments by JDL (March 5) and B'nai Brith (June 12), the second to a comment in Minister Goodyear's statement (June 5), and the third to comments by CIJA (May 12) and jointly by UJA and CIJA (June 26).

Other recommendations by the Jewish community organizations were the following:

- President Shoukri should issue a strong statement, instructing faculty members and teaching assistants ("teachers") not to abuse or misuse the classroom by turning it into a forum for the expression of personal political views unrelated to the subject of the course. While it is the role of a teacher to encourage critical thinking, it is not his or her role to require explicit or implicit adherence to any particular political ideology.

- The University should establish and promote a mandatory training program for all teachers on "abuse of the podium."

- The University should develop, and publicize as widely as possible, a clear and efficient complaints

mechanism for students who reasonably believe
their teachers have appropriated the classroom in
order to advance a particular political agenda.

• The University should establish a confidential
hotline for students to report "abuse of podium"
incidents.

• The University should ensure that students who
initiate such complaints against teachers are
protected from retribution or punishment.[25]

Although this may not have been the intent, wording such as "The
University should establish a confidential hotline for students to report
'abuse of podium' incidents," is reminiscent of proposals made in the
United States during the past decade by Daniel Pipes, director of a pro-
Israel organization called Middle East Forum, through its affiliated website
Campus Watch.[26]

Brief by the York/Queen's Conference Organizers. The four members of
the organizing committee—Susan Drummond, Bruce Ryder, Sharry Aiken,
and Mazen Masri—submitted a lengthy brief, dated June 29. Their brief
began by outlining the relevance of their experience to the mandate of the
task force, for example, the substantial involvement of graduate students,
and "the persistent and continuing politically-motivated assaults on the
conference, and on the personal reputations of the organizers."[27]

The organizers' brief commented on the joint brief of the Jewish community groups, which asked York University to "rigorously define the
academic standards expected of all university-sponsored conferences."[28]
The organizers outlined how academic standards are actually defined and
how they evolve, through processes involving peer review and dissent,
both of which require academic freedom. They explained that academic
standards cannot properly be set by university administrations or non-
academic lobby groups. They noted that ideas once considered controversial can become mainstream, and vice versa. They gave as an example
the two-state model for Israel/Palestine. It was highly controversial in the
1970s and 1980s, but became mainstream in the 1990s. In support of
this international understanding of academic standards, they cited two
American authorities, Professors Robert Post (Law, Yale) and Judith Butler
(Philosophy, University of California at Berkeley).

The brief then outlined the campaign against the conference by various Israel lobby groups, the interference by Minister Goodyear with SSHRC, the SSHRC response, and events on campus. It also summarized the impact of the lobbying campaign against the conference on individuals:

> The JDL protests and public vilification of an academic conference are a clear example of the inverse of CIJA's statement about an increased sense of insecurity on campus for those who should feel free to express their support for Israel. Organized insults and intimidation aimed at shutting down an academic event in a university setting have the effect of escalating the sense of insecurity for those who should feel free to openly engage in critical thinking about Israel/Palestine. As the President of York eloquently noted in his statement of June 15, "These issues are discussed on a daily basis in all parts of the world, especially in the Middle East including Israel. There is no reason why they should not be discussed at a university in Canada." Moreover, as organizers and hosts, it is embarrassing to have the Israeli scholars we invited subjected to abuse for participating in the conference.[29]

The organizers concluded:

> One lesson is abundantly clear from our lengthy experience organizing this conference: pro-Israel organizations are waging an intense campaign to shut down legitimate critical intellectual inquiry into the situation in Israel/Palestine. These organizations have disseminated crude and defamatory caricatures of events like ours aimed at fostering such critical intellectual inquiry. Using inflammatory rhetoric, they actively encouraged students and other members of the public to join protests against our conference.

> In our submission, the Task Force must take very seriously the restrictions that the activities of pro-Israel organizations seek to place on academic freedom—witness the SSHRC debacle and our conference's near-ejection from campus—and the negative consequences that ensue for a respectful learning environment for all students and faculty.[30]

The organizers' brief became widely available, and briefs submitted to the task force by others commented on it.

Brief by Professor Morgan. Professor Ed Morgan submitted a brief to the task force dated July 3, headed "Re: Anti-Israel activism at York." Part of his brief discussed the reasons why he had initially joined but later withdrew from the International Advisory Board for the conference. Another part discussed "Israel Apartheid" activities on campus.

In the concluding section, headed "Avoiding Viewpoint Discrimination," Morgan returned to the subject of the conference:

> As the testimony at the Hasbara disciplinary hearings
> demonstrates, and as the recent Osgoode conference bears out,
> the anti-Zionist, anti-Israel side of Middle East argumentation
> is the dominant view on York's campus. [...] Since it is the
> university's mission to foster knowledge, and since knowledge
> is not defined by popularity, the populist nature of anti-Israel
> causes should be a cause of some heightened administrative
> concern.[31]

Noting that the conference "came, chronologically, on the heels of a protracted sequence of 'Israel Apartheid' events this spring," Morgan said, "What might have been legitimate in isolation became toxic in the context of what preceded it."[32] He added, "In embracing the 'Israel/Palestine' conference as part of the 'York at 50' celebrations, the university came dangerously close to further institutionalizing the anti-Israel theme of so many campus events."[33]

Morgan concluded:

> [T]he decision-makers who grant permission to use York's
> facilities must be required to keep in mind the need for
> viewpoint neutrality. In order for the university to avoid the
> appearance of endorsing one side in the Middle East divide, the
> quantity and sequence of events, and not just the content of any
> one of them, must be taken into account.[34]

Brief by Professors Ehrlich, Horowitz, Lawee, and Lockshin. Professors Carl Ehrlich, Sara Horowitz, Eric Lawee, and Martin Lockshin (Humanities, York University) submitted a brief (undated) to the task force, in which they addressed the brief submitted by the conference organizing committee. The four professors wrote that "the university did well to support the organizers when outside forces attempted to stop the conference. But now that the conference has concluded, its failings should be studied."[35]

Ehrlich, Horowitz, Lawee, and Lockshin put forward several reasons to explain the "failure" by the organizers to have organized a conference that might have met with their approval. They suggested that the organizers: 1) lacked the academic credentials to "have understood the pitfalls involved in putting together a conference in Middle East studies"; 2) gave "a plat-form to speakers who advocate a boycott of Israeli scholars"; 3) chose an Advisory Board that lacked "balance" and included a non-academic "propagandist"; and 4) published a vision statement with the conference announcement (in September 2008), citing thinkers such as "Edward Said and Tony Judt," representing "only one (fairly radical) side of the discussion."[36]

Concluding that, "the conference [...] failed in its attempt to provide a genuinely respectful debate about the Middle East," Ehrlich, Horowitz, Lawee, and Lockshin then chided senior administrators of their university for not publicly stating that such a conference was "not helpful."[37] They wrote:

> The report of the conference organizers quotes (on p. 5) a very important statement from Professor Harry Arthurs: "If academic freedom implies the right of professors to make controversial statements, it also implies the right of other members of the community—including the president—to disagree, to condemn and to repudiate those statements." Consider the commendable example of President Bollinger of Columbia University who defended the free-speech right of the President of Iran to speak on his campus but publicly and forcefully excoriated his guest's views and policies. Similarly, though academic freedom protects the right of professors to organize imbalanced conferences that pain significant numbers of students, administrators can and should—while defending the rights of those professors—make it crystal clear to students and to the community at large that such a conference is not helpful, is not a positive contribution to peace and civility on campus, and represents only the conference organizers, not York University. Senior administrators at York missed an important opportunity to do this.[38]

Brief by Professor Green. Professor Leslie Green (Osgoode Hall) submitted a brief dated July 13, in which he discussed the full range of issues identified in the mandate of the task force and made recommendations on them. Included were such concerns as the space available to students for meetings and other events, inter-group conflict, and policies and practices to ensure a supportive environment. (In the quotations below, the italicization of words and phrases is that of Professor Green.)

Cautioning that the task force should not overreact "to a small number of offensive incidents that occurred during a brief period in the University's fifty-year history,"[39] Green said:

> York is not broken on *any* of the dimensions the Task Force explores. Far from it. York faces conflicts of a familiar kind, conflicts that could be handled under existing policies, and which would have faded on their own, had they not been exacerbated and inflamed by, *inter alia*, Gary Goodyear, MP; Peter Kent, MP; Chad Gaffield, PhD; B'Nai Brith Canada; the Canadian Council for Israel and Jewish Advocacy; and, sadly, a handful of York faculty and Emeritus Professors. [...] York's history shows that unless external groups exert pressure or organize boycotts, some conflict is expected and tolerated, and our internal procedures are robust enough to survive it, provided those procedures are fairly used. The challenge lies in doing so without compounding the problems.[40]

Green also commented on the briefs submitted to the task force by Morgan and by Ehrlich, Horowitz, Lawee, and Lockshin. For example, regarding Morgan's brief, he noted that:

> Morgan writes: "the anti-Zionist, anti-Israel side of Middle East argumentation [sic] is the dominant view on York's campus. [...] Since it is the university's mission to foster knowledge, and since knowledge is not defined by popularity, the populist nature of anti-Israel causes should be a cause for some heightened administrative concern."[41]

In response to these points Green observed:

> This is a confection of assertion, rhetoric, and non-sequitur.

Neither Morgan nor I know whether there is *any* "dominant view
on York's campus" about Middle East "argumentation." I rather
doubt it. And it is poor rhetorical trick to try to equate criticism
of Israel's current conduct with an attitude called "anti-Zionist,
anti-Israel." But worse of all is the creaky edifice constructed
from this crooked timber. Morgan reasons as follows: 1. Position
X is popular at York. 2. That fact that X is popular does not make
X true. 3. Therefore, the York Administration should subject
those who believe X to heightened administrative concern. The
conclusion bears no relation the major and minor premises: it
is an obvious *non sequitur*. And consider what this *non sequitur*
would licence. Suppose evolution is at York widely believed to
be the best explanation for the emergence of human kind: (1).
That admittedly does not make *evolution* correct: (2). Therefore,
(3): the York Biology Department requires "heightened
administrative concern."[42]

Morgan had made another suggestion, regarding "the quantity and
sequence of events" and "the content of any one of them." Green termed
this suggestion "rationing dissent" and commented:

Speech-rationing is also unworkable. It blithely ignores the
fundamental fact that when there is a *competition* of views, to
silence one is to help the other. [...] Which group therefore gets
to form the baseline from which the University will calculate
who is to be the target of Morgan's "heightened administrative
concern"? And who will assess the burden? What criteria will
they use?[43]

Green found the arguments of Professors Ehrlich, Horowitz, Lawee, and
Lockshin similarly unpersuasive. Commenting on the passage in their brief
in which they cited Professor Arthurs of York and President Bollinger of
Columbia, he wrote:

Again, the analogy to which the authors grope is strained. Do they
really believe there were murderous tyrants at the *Israel/Palestine*
conference, on a moral par with the President of Iran? Who? Do
they honestly think that "senior administrators" should keep a
watching brief on all peer-reviewed conferences and then "make

it crystal clear" which ones are, in their opinion, "not helpful"? Do they fail to notice the difference in power relations between the President of an Ivy League College and a despised tyrant on the one hand, and between the York President and his faculty and students on the other? (As far as I know, the President of Iran signs no one's tenure letter at Columbia.) Are the authors *seriously* recommending that the President of York make it a policy to "publicly and forcefully excoriate" unhelpful speakers' views?

If the authors are at all serious about this, they propose a very watery ideal of tolerance, one remote from our best traditions.[44]

Green contrasted the four professors' conception of tolerance "with Locke's famous argument in the *Letter on Toleration*, a central document in the formation of our concept of tolerance."[45] He added:

Equally distressing [...] is their abbreviated quotation from Arthurs (1995). [...] that statement continues, not with a call to excoriate the unhelpful, but with a plea for a large and liberal tolerance. Arthurs writes,

Does the university's duty to abstain from punishing people also mean that it has to be indifferent or silent about their behaviour? Generally speaking, I would say "yes." Indeed, *the university should err on the side of being supportive, even when it hurts.* It should defend the principle, of course, rather than the individual, and it can do this by trying to get people to see that society's long run interests are best served by allowing all opinions to be expressed, however unpalatable they may seem.

Arthurs thus stands with Locke.[46]

The final section of Green's brief was headed "More Space for Speech." He wrote:

The Task force will realise that my recommendations and observations have been fairly conservative. York is not broken;

our policies and practices serve us well; we have failed in implementation; we have sometimes made matters worse by giving in to the hecklers. But if we take our existing principles seriously, that is, *if we take them to heart*, we will be in a strong position and our students will thrive.

But let me conclude with one radical suggestion. If we are serious about free inquiry and academic freedom, and if we really want to support our students in examining the comfortable nostrums they absorbed before coming to York, then we should allow them *more* space, not less, in which to do so. We must, of course, stop saying that free inquiry is tolerable "so long as it is very clear that we are not ...questioning the legitimacy of the State of Israel..." Or any other state! (Indeed, great thinkers have written books questioning the legitimacy of every state.)[47]

THE IACOBUCCI REVIEW

Terms of Reference. On July 31, 2009, President Shoukri announced there would be an independent review of matters related to the York/Queen's conference, conducted by Frank Iacobucci of Torys LLP, a former senior academic administrator at the University of Toronto and former justice of the Supreme Court of Canada. The terms of reference asked Iacobucci to:

- review the experience with the planning, organizing and delivery of the "Mapping" conference;

- advise on the responsibilities of faculty members and University administrators in relation to conferences of this type, particularly conferences sponsored by the University;

- and to provide advice on best practices for the successful planning and execution of such events in light of York University policies and procedures pertaining to academic conferences.[48]

The president's announcement continued, "Mr. Iacobucci's review will be guided by the principles and commitment to academic freedom set forth in my two public statements on the conference [...] I have asked Mr. Iacobucci to report back to me with his recommendations by Nov. 30. His report will be made public."[49]

Background to the Review. The announcement did not state detailed reasons why the Iacobucci review was commissioned, or when the decision was made. However, Professor Susan Drummond provided this Inquiry with relevant information. She had prepared a lengthy paper titled "Field Notes from a Conference: A Case Study in the Fragility of Academic Freedom," on events related to the conference and the experience of the organizers. In the paper, actions or statements by certain individuals—Dean Monahan most notably—were criticized. Certain actions by the university administration as a whole were questioned, at least in part because (as stated in her paper) she and Professor Bruce Ryder had been given to understand by the dean that his actions and statements pertaining to the conference had prior explicit approval from the president or from the board of governors (depending on the particular occurrence).

Drummond wrote the paper in part to bring to the attention of York University a number of issues she felt should be addressed, and in part to draw public attention to the attempts by various persons and organizations to have the conference cancelled or radically altered. Accordingly, on or about July 4 she provided copies of the paper in draft form to Shoukri and Monahan. She indicated to them that she intended to have a version of the paper published at some future time, and invited comments from them.

Shoukri, Monahan, and Drummond met on July 13 to discuss her paper. In the meeting, Monahan gave her a six-page preliminary response to her paper, presenting his own view on a number of events and circumstances, in particular some of those in which he was involved. His response included criticism of the conference organizers, and the suggestion that it would be inappropriate for Drummond to publish her paper in its present form. It was in this meeting that Drummond was informed that the president had decided to commission an independent review.

An email thread between Monahan and Shoukri on July 20 indicates that Monahan was then drafting terms of reference for the review, provisionally captioned "Lessons Learned," and editing drafts labelled v6 and v7 in light of comments by the president. In regard to v6, the president commented, "I just want to avoid the impression that we are looking for something that was done wrongly."[50]

The President's View of the Dean's Involvement. On July 16, President Shoukri wrote to Drummond concerning her "Field Notes" manuscript. The letter opened by thanking her for the copy of her manuscript and saying:

I totally agree with the need for scholarly work on academic
freedom and its limitations, and on the potential threat to
academic freedom posed by special interest groups and by
political leadership. Your scholarly interest in the subject is
welcome.[51]

The president then proceeded to explain his view of Monahan's involvement in events relating to the conference:

However, we have concerns about your description of the role
of the University leadership in the period leading up to the
conference. As I mentioned the university, at all times, was
committed to protecting the academic freedom of the organizing
committee. There was no division within the senior University
administration with respect to the conference. With my complete
knowledge, the role of Dean Monahan was to attempt—while
protecting academic freedom—to examine ways to alleviate
possible concerns and to assure the external communities
of our commitment to excellence and fairness. Although the
Dean shared various suggestions with the committee, it was
always up to the committee to accept or reject his suggestions
while the university continued to provide all the logistical and
financial support to the conference at all times. I reiterated this
commitment in our May 13 meeting and in subsequent public
statements. As I mentioned, Patrick was an active proponent of
and participant in drafting these statements.

I also suggested that you may need more time to reflect on your
experience and that it would be beneficial to gain additional
distance from these events. I am grateful that you appeared to
accept this suggestion and agreed to put this project aside for the
moment while completing other work.

I truly appreciate your willingness to review Patrick's account of
some of the events and incorporate them, as appropriate, in your
next draft of the document. Your promise to share that draft with
us and provide us with an opportunity to review it in more detail
prior to publishing or distributing it is important and highly
appreciated.[52]

President Shoukri concluded his letter with a reference to the planned review of events:

> By taking a clear and strong stand on academic freedom, we
> are committing the university and its leadership to the highest
> standard. We will never deviate from this commitment. That
> is also why we are engaging an external person with the
> highest level of credibility to help us in evaluating the lessons
> learned during these events. I will be in position to share more
> information about this initiative shortly.[53]

A Clarification of Mandate. Iacobucci subsequently issued a clarification of his terms of reference, "after further discussions with President Shoukri and with his agreement."[54] He wrote:

> I wish to make it clear that my review does not in any way mean
> that I will be making findings against any individual, group,
> or organization regarding the "Mapping" conference; I am not
> conducting an inquiry into past events but rather attempting to
> familiarize myself with background information. [...] My review
> is intended to provide forward-looking recommendations on
> the holding of conferences and similar events that respect the
> University's commitment to academic freedom.[55]

Participants and Non-Participants in the Iacobucci Review. A number of York University faculty members, administrators, and support staff participated, and at least one person from off campus, Professor Ed Morgan of the University of Toronto, also participated. Of the four conference organizers, Bruce Ryder met with Iacobucci but Sharryn Aiken and Mazen Masri decided not to participate. Initially, Susan Drummond had also decided not to participate. However, several months later, following email exchanges with Iacobucci, she decided to send him a copy of the book manuscript she had developed from her unpublished "Field Notes" paper.

The executive committee of the Osgoode Hall Faculty Association (OHFA) decided not to participate. Their reasons were set out in a letter to Iacobucci, and are similar to reasons Aiken and Masri and, initially at least, Drummond gave for deciding not to participate. The OHFA executive committee wrote that:

The Osgoode Hall Faculty Association is robustly committed
to the protection and enhancement of academic freedom. [...]
The Association has serious reservations about the wisdom of
establishing an independent and external Review such as your
own. The decision of the University to proceed in this way is
a possible threat to academic freedom, not an affirmation of
it. Without in any way challenging your own competence or
good faith in undertaking this task, the Association maintains
that there are ample internal resources available to protect
and preserve academic freedom. [...] It may well be that some
positive results in promoting academic freedom at York will
flow from your Review. However, the Association is sufficiently
concerned about the overall process from which and by which
the Review and its terms of reference were established that it
does not feel it to be proper to participate in the business or
conduct of your Review at this stage.[56]

York University publicly released the report of the Iacobucci Review on
April 9, 2010. It is discussed in Chapter 9.

PANEL DISCUSSION AT FLAVELLE HOUSE, JANUARY 30, 2010

The four conference organizers—Sharryn Aiken, Susan Drummond, Bruce
Ryder, and Mazen Masri—were members of a six-person panel during
the Third Annual Conference of the Toronto Group for the Study of
International, Transnational, and Comparative Law, held at the University
of Toronto's Faculty of Law, January 29–30, 2010. The other members
of the panel, titled "Academic Freedom in the Canadian Legal Academy:
Israel/Palestine and Discussions on Paths to Peace," were Professor Richard
Moon (Law, University of Windsor) and Professor Jens Hanssen (Middle
Eastern Studies, University of Toronto). The session was chaired by Michael
Fakhri (PhD candidate in Law, University of Toronto).[57]

Each of the four organizers of the York/Queen's conference spoke on
matters pertaining to their experiences and commented on wider but related
issues. For example, Aiken said that Israel has been "instrumentalized" by
some in the Canadian Jewish community, and also that critics of Israel are
often called anti-Semites or self-hating Jews. Drummond said that the terms
of reference for the Iacobucci Review in effect focused on the conference
organizers but "said nothing about the conduct of York administrators."

Ryder said that holding the conference was a triumph for academic free-dom, adding that although in his view there were no actual violations of the academic freedom of the organizers, there were several "near misses." He illustrated this comment with a reference to the postponement propos-al by Dean Monahan in the meeting held on the morning of May 12, 2009. He added that the proposal was in effect escalated into what appeared to be a demand during a telephone call he received from the dean that even-ing, on the basis of the tone and content of the dean's remarks. He and Drummond did not agree to postponement, and they learned the next day that the president supported their position.

Later in the session, Ryder mentioned what he considered to be another near miss: the understanding given to the organizers by the dean (in a meeting on April 17, 2009) that the board of governors might not allow the conference to be held in any York University premises. He said that of the several near misses, this one was "the most upsetting" to him.

Masri said that academic freedom is especially important "when there is a power imbalance," as, for example, between administrators such as deans and faculty members or graduate students. He mentioned the incident in October 2008 when Monahan requested that he be removed from the organizing committee. He observed that Ryder and Drummond, both of whom were tenured professors, refused to agree to this request, and he was able to remain on the committee.

During the subsequent discussion with members of the audience, Ryder said that, in hindsight, a smaller conference with a narrower range of speak-ers might have avoided some of the controversy.[58] Drummond disagreed, suggesting that there would have been controversy over any conference in Toronto discussing competing statehood models for Israel/Palestine.

Professor Craig Scott (a member of the audience for the panel discus-sion) agreed with Drummond, saying that university research activities should not be determined by expressions of displeasure by persons not involved in the project, regardless of whether those displeased are academ-ics or not. He added that the claim by some at York that the organizers lacked the credentials to organize such a conference was also a serious threat to their academic freedom.

8
ACADEMIC FREEDOM

STRIKING AT THE HEART OF DEEPLY HELD BELIEFS

Everything depends on how one believes one's belief.[1]

In his report on matters pertaining to the York/Queen's conference, Frank Iacobucci asserted, "The Conference's subject matter was controversial, striking at the heart of deeply held religious and political beliefs."[2] It was ever thus. Throughout history, similar claims have been made against dissenters. Only the means of suppressing dissent have varied, as illustrated by the following cases, in addition to those discussed in this chapter:

- in 415, in Alexandria, Hypatia was murdered by a Christian mob;

- in 1600, in Rome, Giordano Bruno was burned at the stake;

- in 1656, in Amsterdam, Baruch de Spinoza was expelled from the synagogue;

- in 1917, in New York, James McKeen Cattell was dismissed;

- during 1945–1960, across the United States, many academics were dismissed and blacklisted;

- in 2008, in Jerusalem, Ze'ev Sternhell was injured by a bomb placed at his home by a Jewish West Bank settler.

Controversy can arise over matters other than religious or political beliefs, such as the safety or efficacy of a medicinal product, or the validity or usefulness of a theory in an academic discipline. But in these matters, too, there have been instances where, for example, a particular theory has been widely adhered to with a fervour resembling deeply held belief, even in the face of compelling contrary evidence.

The means used to suppress dissent are more varied and often more subtle than in the examples cited, but there sometimes are instructive similarities or parallels between academic freedom cases, even when separated by many decades, or occurring in different disciplines, or centred on different issues.

ORIGINS OF ACADEMIC FREEDOM

Unsurprisingly, several of the most informative accounts of academic freedom were written in times when it was under attack. These include *The Development of Academic Freedom in the United States*, by Richard Hofstadter and Walter P. Metzger (1955), written during the political witch hunts led by the House Un-American Activities Committee and Senator Joseph R. McCarthy; *Academic Freedom*, by Conrad Russell (1993), written in response to attacks on academic freedom and university autonomy by the Thatcher and Major governments; and *For the Common Good: Principles of American Academic Freedom*, by Matthew W. Finkin and Robert C. Post (2009), motivated in part by attacks on individual academics, and on academic freedom and university autonomy, by well-funded organizations.

These authors traced the origins of academic freedom in the West to the efforts by the medieval Church to defend its autonomy against temporal powers. The institutional claim to freedom from interference was extended gradually to individual academics as a right to dissent from either the church or the state. The transition to modern conceptions of academic freedom, such as that consolidated in nineteenth-century German universities, or the more comprehensive one understood in the United States and Canada today, extended over a millennium.

Hofstadter and Metzger cited an early instance of efforts made to defend individual academics who dissented from orthodoxy, that of John Wyclif (c. 1324–1384), of the University of Oxford:

> Since he taught a doctrine of the Eucharist that struck at the
> heart of Catholic theology and a doctrine of clerical poverty that

struck at the prevailing practices of the Church itself, it is not
surprising that the bishops should have sought to quiet him or
that they should have had the authorization of the Crown. What
was remarkable was the loyalty Wyclif commanded within the
university and the stubbornness with which it, in common with
a very large section of public opinion, defended him.[3]

The support for Wyclif endured for several years, even in the face of a
papal bull demanding he be turned over to the Bishop of London, but
eventually, near the end of his life, his school was suppressed and a period
of repression followed in the university and elsewhere.

Another singular event occurred three centuries later, in 1675, when
Charles II granted Isaac Newton a special dispensation to continue as
Lucasian Professor in Trinity College, Cambridge, even though Newton
refused to take holy orders because he adhered to the ancient heresy of
Arius, which denied belief in the Holy Trinity. Newton's extraordinary
talent may have motivated the king when he granted Newton "and all
subsequent holders of the chair exemption from holy orders" in order to
"give all just encouragement to learned men who are & shall be elected to
the said professorship."[4]

Progress was sporadic and often reversed, but by the eighteenth century
intellectual freedom in general and academic freedom in particular had
gathered wider support. This support was a product of major social and
political transformations, including the fragmentation of the Church into
major and minor sects, the development of modern nation states, the
growth of science, the expansion of trade and commerce, and the influence
of Enlightenment philosophers.

In 1732, Christian Wolff, a professor of mathematics and physics
at the University of Halle, and a leading philosopher of the German
Enlightenment, was banished, under threat of execution, by King Frederick
William I of Prussia, following allegations that his theological teachings
challenged religious orthodoxy and state power:

> Wolff's expulsion triggered a polemical explosion throughout
> Europe. More than two hundred tracts addressed the case, most
> defending Wolff in terms of the "freedom of philosophy." [...]
> Intellectual freedom was taken to have prevailed when the new
> king, Frederick William II (Frederick the Great) restored Wolff to
> Halle in 1740 as professor of public law and mathematics, vice

chancellor of the university, and Prussian privy councillor [...] The
"triumph of the Enlightenment in Prussia" was complete when
Wolff was made an imperial baron (Reichsfreiherr) in 1745.[5]

However, a period of reaction followed the death of Frederick the Great
in 1786, and a royal decree of 1788 restricted freedom of teaching and
publication. "It was under the authority of this edict that Kant was repri-
manded by Prussian Minister Wollner for having used his philosophy 'for
the purpose of distorting and deprecating several basic teachings of the
Holy Bible and of Christianity.'"[6]

After the defeat of Prussia by France in 1806, French ideas on the organization of government, including education, had a significant liberalizing influence. Notably, "As Secretary of the Department of Education and Religion
in the Prussian Ministry of Education, [Wilhelm von] Humboldt secured the
abolition of censorship for scholarly, scientific, and literary works in 1809-
10."[7] Also in 1810, Humboldt persuaded the king to establish the University
of Berlin (now Humboldt University). In this new environment, the "rector
of the University of Jena, [Johann Gottlieb] Fichte, addressed the subject of
'akademische Freiheit' (academic freedom) in 1811, by which time the term
had already begun to take on a life of its own."[8]

Nevertheless, another period of reaction followed the Congress of
Vienna and political repression of scholars continued even where religious
discrimination had subsided. But "by the time of German unification
[1871], akademische Freiheit was taken as a defining condition for higher
education, virtually as a matter of course."[9] In 1877, when Hermann von
Helmholtz assumed the rectorship of the University of Berlin, he could
extol the fact that subjects as diverse as Darwinian evolution and material-
ism in metaphysics were discussed freely on campus, even while "the most
extreme idolization of papal infallibility" was equally unhindered.[10]

Hofstadter and Metzger explained that this unfettered freedom applied
to teaching and research within the academy: "But outside the university, the same degree of freedom was not condoned. Though quite a few
German professors played prominent political roles in the nineteenth
century, and a number of these—notably Mommsen and Virchow—were
outspoken critics of Bismarck [...] it was generally assumed that professors
as civil servants were bound to be loyal, and that participation in partisan
politics spoiled the habits of scholarship."[11]

They cited the case of Leo Arons, a Privatdocent removed from his post
at Berlin for having made speeches for an opposition political party (c.

1900). The minister of education justified the action by declaring that every teacher "must defend the existing order against all attacks."[12] The Berlin philosophical faculty issued a statement in defence of Arons, demanding, unsuccessfully, that he be reinstated, but stopped short of advocating an uninfringeable right to freedom of extramural speech for professors.

Nevertheless, *akademische Freiheit* was a substantial right of university faculty in Germany, with no comparable analogue elsewhere. It had two components: *Lernfreiheit*, which "meant the absence of administrative coercions in the learning situation for students," and *Lehrfreiheit*, which "meant that the university professor was free to examine bodies of evidence and to report his findings in lecture or published form," together "with the paucity of administrative rules within the teaching situation."[13] Academic freedom, so defined, "was the distinctive prerogative of the academic profession, and the essential condition of all universities."[14]

Hofstadter and Metzger summarized the differences in the development of intellectual freedom among France, the British Isles, and Germany:

> French Encyclopedism and the English Enlightenment flourished
> outside the universities [...] whereas the great philosophers of
> England, from Bacon to John Stuart Mill, were men of affairs,
> the great figures in the heroic age of German philosophy were
> academic men. From this circumstance may be traced both the
> glory of English philosophy and the grandeur of the German
> university.[15]

It was in the English-speaking world that academic freedom later came to include freedom of extramural speech.

AKADEMISCHE FREIHEIT TRANSPLANTED AND HYBRIDIZED IN AMERICA

A substantial American academic research community developed after the Civil War, and many of the leading figures in various disciplines had attended universities such as Göttingen or Berlin, where the *akademische Freiheit* had made a lasting impression on them. The first American university based on the German model was Johns Hopkins, founded in 1876. "Of fifty-three professors and lecturers on [its] roster in 1884, nearly all had studied at German universities."[16] By the end of the century, more than a dozen other graduate schools had been established in the United States, and the numbers of graduate students and doctoral degrees had increased dramatically.

Examples of Faculty Dismissals and Community Responses. Despite the additional personal investment in research training by increasing numbers of professors, they could still be summarily dismissed for challenging orthodoxy in teaching or research, or for extramural activism. Whether established by a private donor, a state government, or a religious organization, universities were controlled by boards of trustees and presidents appointed by the boards, who considered faculty members to be employees, as in a commercial enterprise. This view was occasionally bolstered by editorials in the *New York Times* and other newspapers to the effect that "he who pays the piper calls the tune."

A number of those dismissed, or threatened with dismissal, were prominent members of the new American academic profession who had studied in Germany, or had been research students of professors with German doctoral degrees. Among these was the political economist Richard T. Ely (threatened with dismissal by the University of Wisconsin in 1894), who had obtained his PhD at the University of Heidelberg. After serving as chair of Political Economy at Johns Hopkins, Ely had been recruited to Wisconsin to direct a new School of Economics, Politics, and History. Another was the political economist and sociologist Edward A. Ross (forced to resign by Stanford University in 1900), who had studied with Ely in Baltimore. Both were incisive critics of the prevailing social and political order, whose teaching and research offended their employers. Ely rejected the doctrines of laissez-faire capitalism, and Ross was an outspoken critic of big business in general and the railway industry in particular (Stanford was founded through a donation by railway magnate Leland Stanford).

Ely was defended by colleagues at Wisconsin and elsewhere, but more importantly, Hofstadter and Metzger suggested, he had the support of the university's president, Charles Kendall Adams. They suggested also that Adams's reasons for assisting Ely were personal. Adams, who was much more conservative than Ely, was nevertheless fond of him and disliked the trustee who had initiated the action to dismiss. Ely was exonerated, and the board of trustees issued a ringing declaration in favour of academic freedom that said: "We cannot for a moment believe that knowledge has reached its final goal, or that the present condition of society is perfect. We must, therefore, welcome from our teachers such discussions as shall suggest the means and prepare the way by which knowledge may be extended, present evils [...] removed, and others prevented."[17] By contrast, Leland Stanford's widow, Jane, was successful in forcing Edward A. Ross to resign, despite the efforts of the university's president, David Starr Jordan, who endeavoured to shield Ross from her wrath.

Ross's was the second forced resignation at Stanford in two years. In 1898, political scientist H. H. Powers gave a talk on religion and Mrs. Stanford was "shocked by its heretical sophistication."[18] She demanded his removal, and although Jordan spoke in his favour, she did not relent. When Ross did not go quietly—he issued a public statement charging the university had violated his academic freedom—several Stanford professors resigned, colleagues from across the country protested his fate, and the case became a public issue. The university's response to the adverse public attention was to resort to self-justification and to charge that Ross was dismissed for the impropriety of publicly supporting a candidate in a presidential election, thereby compromising the university's neutrality, adding that they had found him to be of an unscrupulous character.

The most significant outcome of the Ross case was that the American Economic Association (AEA) established the first committee of inquiry into an academic freedom case, chaired by Professor Edwin R. A. Seligman of Columbia University. Because there was no precedent for such a process, the inquiry suffered from procedural problems and inadequate terms of reference. Nevertheless, a report was issued, which concluded that the official reasons for Ross's dismissal were inappropriate, and that there was evidence that he had been dismissed because of things he had written and said.

Disputes between faculty members and administrations, including more dismissals, continued. This led to informal discussions about the need for reform in university governance, protection for academic freedom, and fair procedures on appointment and dismissal. Many of those prominent in such discussions were social scientists, but scholars in other disciplines also participated. Addressing the AEA in 1910, Ely recalled that he and other colleagues with similar experiences "were impressed in the German university by a certain largeness and freedom of thought."[19] In addition to enjoying *akademische Freiheit*, German professors chose their own administrators from the ranks of the faculty.

American professors, like all of their fellow citizens (or at least, those with favoured ethnic or religious backgrounds), believed they enjoyed political rights, including freedom of speech in political matters, unlike their German counterparts. They believed their university employment should not be jeopardized by exercising these rights. Thus, when the American Association of University Professors (AAUP) was founded in 1915 and issued a declaration on academic freedom, it defined a larger and more robust concept than the German prototype.[20]

The Founding of the AAUP. In 1913 the learned societies for economics, political science, and sociology appointed a joint committee on academic freedom, which submitted a preliminary report the following year. In the meantime, a number of full professors at Johns Hopkins issued an invitation to colleagues at several other research universities to meet for the purpose of forming a national association. The inaugural meeting of the AAUP was held in January 1915, and philosopher and psychologist John Dewey (then at Columbia) was elected as its first president. A committee of fifteen professors was appointed to develop a formal document on academic freedom and related matters. The result, published that summer, was the AAUP's 1915 *Declaration of Principles on Academic Freedom and Academic Tenure.*[21]

The *Declaration* was a very important and ambitious document. It explained the nature of the academic profession, with its functions, duties, and responsibilities; the need for academic freedom in the public interest; the need for tenure to protect it; and the need for due process in dismissal proceedings. To a significant extent, the academic freedom enjoyed today in the United States and Canada derives from the quality of the document produced by this first AAUP committee, even though the scope of the right has been enlarged since then.

In explaining why academic freedom was for the common good, the 1915 *Declaration* spoke of "the dangers connected with the existence in a democracy of an overwhelming and concentrated public opinion," elaborating as follows:

> The tendency of modern democracy is for men to think alike, to feel alike, and to speak alike. Any departure from the conventional standards is apt to be regarded with suspicion. Public opinion is at once the chief safeguard of a democracy, and the chief menace to the real liberty of the individual. It almost seems as if the danger of despotism cannot be wholly averted under any form of government. In a political autocracy there is no effective public opinion, and all are subject to the tyranny of the ruler; in a democracy there is political freedom, but there is likely to be a tyranny of public opinion.

> An inviolable refuge from such tyranny should be found in the university. It should be an intellectual experiment station,

where new ideas may germinate and where their fruit, though still distasteful to the community as a whole, may be allowed to ripen until finally, perchance, it may become a part of the accepted intellectual food of the nation or of the world.[22]

In view of the composition of the committee, and more generally of the reasons why the AAUP was formed, it is not surprising that the *Declaration* should also say:

[I]t is not, in this committee's opinion, desirable that scholars should be debarred from giving expression to their judgments upon controversial questions, or that their freedom of speech, outside the university, should be limited to questions falling within their own specialties. It is clearly not proper that they should be prohibited from lending their active support to organized movements which they believe to be in the public interest. And, broadly speaking, it may be said [...] that "it is neither possible nor desirable to deprive a college professor of the political rights vouchsafed to every citizen."[23]

Thus, in essence, the AAUP proposed a right to academic freedom much more extensive than the German concept of *akademische Freiheit*. With such wording, the AAUP also in effect proposed a right for professors that went substantially beyond "the political rights vouchsafed to every citizen" at that time—at least in regard to freedom of speech.

However, the principles set out in the *Declaration* would have a major practical effect only when essential parts of it were widely adopted by the presidents and boards of American institutions. This did not occur until a quarter-century later when, after discussions between the AAUP and organizations representing colleges extending over a number of years, the joint 1940 *Statement of Principles of Academic Freedom and Tenure* was issued by the AAUP and the Association of American Colleges (AAC).[24] Although the 1915 *Declaration* remains significant and is a useful guide on a variety of matters, it is nearly a century old. The experience with cases over the years has broadened and strengthened the meaning of academic freedom, just as other civil rights have been broadened and strengthened—for example, the opening of the academic profession to women. Also of note is that in its initial years, the AAUP was an elite organization—only full professors with substantial research records were invited to join—because gaining acceptance for its principles was believed to require the respectability stature sometimes confers.

BERTRAND RUSSELL AND TRINITY COLLEGE

Around the time the AAUP was being formed, British academics also had acquired a modern understanding of academic freedom. It was at least as comprehensive as the one their American counterparts had adopted in 1915, but came about through different influences: the medieval traditions of their universities and the increasing acceptance of freedom of speech in civil society, due to the influence of Enlightenment thinkers and their successors, such as John Stuart Mill. Conrad Russell, an authority on British history, emphasized this when he observed, regarding the modern British legislative of definition of academic freedom, that "this wording was cast in entirely post-French Revolutionary language, and in terms of an ideal of freedom of speech which descends from Mill's *Essay on Liberty*."[25]

By the late nineteenth century there also were increasing international scholarly contacts, as American universities recruited prominent British academics to help with developing research and graduate programs, as well as with building the prestige of their undergraduate programs. There was no British analogue of the AAUP. The Association of University Teachers, formed around the same time as the AAUP, represented only non-professorial teaching staff and focused on increasing members' wages, and had no formal statement like the 1915 *Declaration*. Nevertheless, the response by academics to the dismissal of Bertrand Russell by Trinity College, Cambridge, in 1916, illustrated how British academics interpreted the concept of academic freedom.

In the first decades of the twentieth century, Russell was already one of the best-known academics in the world, due to his work in philosophy and logic, his engaging style as a public speaker and popular writer, and his political activism for women's rights, peace, and other causes. During World War I, he was an outspoken critic of British war policy and aims. In 1916, after he was convicted and fined for publishing a leaflet protesting the government's harsh treatment of a conscientious objector, the Council of Trinity College summarily dismissed him from his post as lecturer.

Despite the wartime atmosphere, controversy ensued, on the basis that the college's action was ill-founded and failed to provide due process to Russell. The protests included letters from scholars serving on active duty, and a petition signed by twenty-two Fellows of the college. However, the council's decision stood until after the war ended; in the meantime, Russell was convicted of a second offence and sentenced to six months in jail. In early 1918, he had published an article critical of American involvement in the war, and was prosecuted for having potentially damaged relations between the British and American governments.

The second conviction, on an ostensibly more serious offence, "made surprisingly little difference" to the campaign to persuade the council to reinstate him, "as none of his supporters went back on him."[26] Following a new petition signed by a majority of Fellows, including all nineteen who had served on active duty in the war and survived (four Fellows had been killed in the war), and a number of their senior colleagues—among them, Rutherford, Eddington, Hardy, and Whitehead—Russell was offered reinstatement.[27] He accepted, but later asked for a year's leave to lecture in China and Japan, which was granted. During the leave he resigned for personal reasons unrelated to the wartime controversy. However, he did return to Trinity in 1944, as a Fellow.

Despite the reinstatement offered to Russell, mathematician G. H. Hardy resigned from Trinity and moved to the University of Oxford in protest. Years later, he was persuaded to return to Trinity, and there published an account of the case. Of the council's summary dismissal of Russell, he wrote:

> They should have remembered that pacifists, and especially
> provocative pacifists like Russell, are most unlikely to get
> fair play in time of war, that many of them had already been
> convicted unjustly, and that the justice of the conviction of
> any pacifist was suspect. They should also have remembered
> that the public opinion of which they were so frightened was
> unbalanced and hysterical, and that its currents were quite likely
> to reverse themselves as soon as the war was over. [...] I do not
> accuse any member of the Council of malice or vindictiveness:
> their failure was a failure of imagination and common sense.[28]

Another example demonstrating British toleration of dissent (at least until the time of Prime Minister Thatcher and her successors) is that of economist John Maynard Keynes. Like Russell, Keynes was a towering intellectual figure in the twentieth century. Both also were in and out of academic life, although for different reasons and purposes, and both held academic positions at various times in Cambridge colleges (King's, in the case of Keynes).

Keynes, a British government advisor at Versailles, resigned from his position in protest over "the Carthaginian peace" the Allies were about to impose on Germany, on the basis that it was a recipe for European political disaster. He then published his famous *The Economic Consequences of the Peace* (1919), denouncing the terms of the treaty and setting out its implications in clear, meticulous detail.[29] He also wrote brilliant character sketches of President Wilson and Prime Ministers Clemenceau and Lloyd George as they deliberated during the Versailles negotiations—sketches that were both entertaining and devastatingly insightful. Despite this, he was again a key advisor to British and American governments in the 1930s and 1940s.

Implementation of Keynes's macroeconomic proposals helped to revive and stabilize capitalist national economies in the 1930s and in the post-war period. Also significant, in terms of his influence, denunciation of Keynesian policies was one of the organizational principles of the reactionary neoliberal school—from the 1930s onward. Until neoliberal proposals gained political acceptance in the United States around 1980, the American economy had a substantial and broad-based Keynesian component. Indeed, even after 1980, Keynesian thinking remained an appreciable part of American policy, with defence agencies funding the development costs for many technologies and the vast military budget funding employment and other economic activity. Most recently, following the international financial crisis of 2008–2009, Keynesian policies were again instituted in many countries (to varying extents) in efforts to stabilize and strengthen their national economies—even in countries with neoliberal governments, such as Germany, the United States, or Canada.

DEFENDING ACADEMIC FREEDOM IN THE UNITED STATES

In *For the Common Good*, law professors Finkin and Post presented a concise, extensively referenced description of the main features of academic freedom, explaining the right as it is currently understood in American universities. They also outlined the process whereby the concept described in the 1915 AAUP *Declaration* was enlarged and made effective. A key aspect is a system analogous to common-law jurisprudence, in place since 1915. Reports by AAUP committees of inquiry are assessed by the association's Committee A—the Committee on Academic Freedom and Tenure—which decides whether to publish them. The reports do not have legal force, but often have persuasive influence in resolution processes (formal and informal). The other key aspect of the process is that essential features of the joint AAUP–AAC 1940 *Statement* have been "incorporated into virtually all institutional policies," countrywide.[30]

Finkin and Post summarized the work of Committee A as follows:

> As the reasoned conclusions of an especially knowledgeable body, the opinions of Committee A offer an unusually rich resource for understanding the meaning of academic freedom in America. They strive to interpret a governing instrument, the 1940 Statement, which has achieved near-universal acceptance in the academic community. They do so in a disciplined, lawlike way, seeking to apply principle to context, often by reasoning from precedential analogies. [...] They are backed by a system of sanctions that, although lacking the coercive power of the state, are nevertheless consequential. [...]
>
> As a result, academic freedom has assumed a surprising uniformity of meaning throughout the United States.[31]

However, in light of events of the past decade, Finkin and Post became concerned that academic freedom had come under attacks similar to those of a century earlier, from remarkably similar sources. They cited the example of "the outrage that erupted in 2003 when the University of North Carolina decided to assign Barbara Ehrenreich's *Nickel and Dimed: On (Not) Getting By in America* as required reading for first-year students. The university was denounced by off-campus groups and some state legislators. Critics of the university's decision called the book a "classic Marxist rant" and "an all-out assault on Christians, conservatives and capitalism," and denounced the author as an atheist and a socialist.[32] At the same time, in their view, the professoriate had become dangerously complacent about its rights and protections.

Finkin and Post illustrated the evolution in the effective understanding of the concept from 1915 onward, through discussion of particular cases over the decades to the present. A feature of this evolution is enlargement of the concept, so that in more recent times professors have enjoyed wider latitude in all aspects of academic freedom.

One of their illustrations of the enlargement was a comparison. In 1931, sociologist Herbert A. Miller was dismissed by the Board of Trustees of Ohio State University after he spoke at a function in Bombay sponsored by Mahatma M. K. Gandhi. "The board's ostensible ground was that Miller's speech would give offense to the British," even though the content of it was related to his research. Linguist Noam Chomsky, by contrast, ever since the mid-1960s has been one of the most prominent and incisive critics of American foreign policy (and has criticized British and Israeli policy, too), and he also has been critical of compliant scholars. For example, in 1967, noting "the responsibility of intellectuals to speak the truth and to expose lies," Chomsky cited two instances of intellectuals who failed to live up to this responsibility.[33] Philosopher Martin Heidegger in 1933 said, in effect, that Nazi propaganda was truth, and historian Arthur Schlesinger, Jr. admitted to the *New York Times* in 1965 that he had lied to the press in 1961 about the Bay of Pigs invasion. Chomsky then proceeded to expose a series of lies and other distortions by recent American governments in support of their foreign policies. Chomsky has been a professor at MIT continuously since 1955.

Finkin and Post's discussion of intramural expression—which includes criticism of the university—illuminated an important technical difference between the AAUP–AAC and CAUT definitions of academic freedom, as well as of the enlargement of academic freedom's scope. Freedom of intramural expression is not explicitly included in the 1940 AAUP–AAC *Statement*, and so this aspect of academic freedom had to be inferred from other terms in the *Statement* and progressively developed through cases. Finkin and Post cited several instances of professors who were dismissed for criticizing the president or the board, from AAUP files dating back to 1915.

As mentioned earlier, faculty members were at first regarded as employees, with no greater job security than employees of any other private or public corporation. This issue was addressed in the United States by the insistence that, although university faculty were simply employees in law, they were more than simply employees in their university role. The 1915 *Declaration* used the term "appointees"—still in widespread use today—and the 1940 *Statement* used the additional term "officers of an educational institution." The 1940 *Statement* also says that "institutions of higher education are conducted for the common good and not to further the interest of either the individual teacher or the institution as a whole." The AAUP position is that these terms imply a right to freedom of intramural expression. Citing a series of cases on various aspects of university governance in which this principle had been accepted, Finkin and Post outlined the argument as follows:

> The common good is not to be determined by the arbitrary,
> private, or personal decree of any single individual [...] The
> common good is made visible only through open debate and
> discussion in which all are free to participate. Faculty [...] have
> an indispensible role to play in that debate.[34]

The resignation of Harvard President Lawrence Summers illustrated the enlargement of this aspect of academic freedom in recent decades. In 2005, the Faculty of Arts and Sciences passed a motion of lack of confidence in Summers's leadership, and subsequently passed (by a larger majority) a motion of censure. After another lack-of-confidence motion was scheduled for February 2006 (and was widely expected to pass), Summers announced prior to the faculty council meeting that he would be resigning from the presidency. These motions came as a result of mounting concerns over Summers's management of the institution, and were accompanied by increasingly public criticism of him by members of the faculty.

Prior to the 1960s, an outcome such as that in the Summers case would have been almost unthinkable—instead, vocal faculty critics of a president might have been dismissed, as happened on a number of occasions. Although the academic freedom of professors and the freedom of speech of citizens are different matters, universities nevertheless are part of society, and the strengthening of academic freedom may have been aided by wider societal currents, such as the increasing willingness of American courts to uphold freedom of speech. Other factors were the subsiding of the era of McCarthyism, and the growing national importance and prestige of scientific and other expertise residing principally in the universities.

FRAGILITY

In 1917–1918, the momentum toward establishing an effective right of academic freedom suffered a reversal as universities were swept up in a national wave of anti-German sentiment, and the patriotism generated by the Wilson administration to help persuade a reluctant citizenry to support America's entry into the war triumphed over all other causes. Hofstadter and Metzger summarized the effects on the academy:

> The crisis of 1917 plunged the academic profession into vast
> and unheralded new difficulties. A mob fanaticism arose that
> put every freedom in jeopardy. The American university, always

vulnerable to opinions of the community, could not escape its coercive spirit. [...] All over the nation, patriotic zealots [...] harassed those college teachers whose passion for fighting the war was somewhat less flaming than their own. Suddenly, the gains for academic freedom that had painfully and gradually been won—the greater acceptance of the principle, the beginnings of a regime of academic law—were swept aside. [...] the hard-to-learn manners of tolerance yielded to crude tribal instincts of taboo. The academic profession and its young Association confronted the almost total collapse of the moral and institutional safeguards that had been wrought in the slowness of time.[35]

A majority of AAUP leaders joined in the pro-war propaganda effort, and the association promulgated a list of four grounds on which dismissal was warranted. The first three pertained to various anti-war activities, while the fourth pertained to "professors of Teutonic extraction and sympathy."[36]

By the early 1920s, the AAUP had regained forward momentum, as increasing numbers of college and university presidents began to support its views on academic freedom. However, resistance by boards of trustees meant that formal adoption of a joint policy had to wait until 1940. Unlike events during World War I, academic freedom did not come under general attack during World War II. It was in the post-war period, especially during the decade and a half beginning in 1945, as the war ended and the Cold War began, that a second period of political repression occurred.

The repression of the early Cold War period is often referred to as McCarthyism, but it began several years before Senator Joseph R. McCarthy launched his crusade against alleged communist subversives in 1950, and it continued for several years after he was censured by the Senate in 1954. Artists, writers, and professors were among the victims of McCarthyism, and both the American Civil Liberties Union and the AAUP effectively collapsed under the weight of anti-communist sentiment.

In *No Ivory Tower*, Ellen W. Schrecker documented the impact of McCarthyism on the universities. She observed that, although "McCarthy never found any subversives," nevertheless, "McCarthyism was amazingly effective. It produced one of the most severe episodes of political repression the United States ever experienced. It was a peculiarly American style of repression—nonviolent and consensual. Only two people were killed; only a few hundred went to jail."[37]

Commonly, the professorial victims were targeted and dismissed not because of what they taught in their classrooms or published in scholarly journals—the list of victims included mathematicians and classicists, for instance—but because of their political or social activism. They were attacked for exercising their right to be engaged citizens in a democracy. Schrecker summarized the response of the universities to McCarthyism as follows:

> The academy did not fight McCarthyism, it contributed to it. The dismissals, the blacklists, and above all the almost universal acceptance of the legitimacy of what the congressional committees and other official investigators were doing conferred respectability upon the most repressive elements of the anti-Communist crusade. In its collaboration with McCarthyism, the academic community behaved just like every other major institution in American life. Such a discovery is demoralizing […] Here, if anywhere, dissent should have found a sanctuary. Yet it did not […] The academy's enforcement of McCarthyism had silenced an entire generation of radical intellectuals and snuffed out all meaningful opposition to the official version of the Cold War. When, by the late fifties, the hearings and dismissals tapered off, it was not because they encountered resistance but because they were no longer necessary. All was quiet on the academic front.[38]

Academic freedom eventually recovered from the McCarthy era, as did the AAUP. The recovery was partly the by-product of a larger phenomenon: the growing importance of higher education and research to the American political economy. The massive new government investments in universities brought greater prestige and influence, along with relative affluence, to the growing professoriate.[39] Ideological constraints did continue to operate in some disciplines, however, long after the era of McCarthyism.[40] As Chomsky observed:

> A […] complex of inducements—access to privilege and prestige, class interest, penalties for straying beyond acceptable limits, and the like—produces a systematic bias in the scholarship that is concerned with foreign policy and its formation, serving to protect the basic system of social, economic and decision-

making from scrutiny [...] It is by no means necessary to yield
to these pressures, certainly in a society that lacks the forms of
coercion and punishment found elsewhere. But the temptation
to do so is considerable, and those who choose a different path
often find that opportunities to do their work or reach more
than a marginal audience are limited or excluded.[41]

The upsurge in uncritical patriotism among many Americans after the
terrorist attacks of September 11, 2001, facilitated attacks on academic freedom by neoliberal, neoconservative, or pro-Israel organizations. Among
such organizations were those headed by Daniel Pipes and David Horowitz,
and the American Council of Trustees and Alumni. Campaigns by such
organizations have raised serious concerns, although the problems are not
yet as extensive as those of 1917–1918 or of 1945–1960.

TWO RECENT TENURE CASES

During the past decade, pro-Israel individuals and organizations have
attempted to influence several appointment and tenure processes, with
apparent success in at least one instance. Regardless of whether the academic event is a talk, a conference, a program grant, an appointment, or a
tenure assessment, if significant criticism of Israel or its policies or actions
is perceived to be involved, a concerted reaction may be expected. The
intensity of the reaction appears independent of whether the offending
criticism was made in diplomatic, circumspect terms, or in forceful, direct
terms. Two tenure cases illuminate, by analogy, aspects of the controversy
around the York/Queen's conference.

In 2007, anthropologist Nadia Abu El-Haj was assessed for tenure by
Barnard College in Columbia University, and political scientist Norman
Finkelstein was assessed for tenure by DePaul University. Both were highly
regarded by authorities in their respective fields, but their published work
was perceived by some supporters of Israel to have struck at the heart of
deeply held religious and political beliefs. Attacks on their personal character and scholarly work were launched from outside their universities
during their tenure assessments. Notwithstanding the attacks, each was
recommended for tenure by the departmental committee, but the final
outcomes were different: Abu El-Haj was granted tenure by her university
administration, Finkelstein was denied.

Only the aspects of their research work immediately relevant to the

York/Queen's conference are summarized here. Writing from an anthropological perspective, Abu El-Haj raised fundamental questions regarding the
archaeological basis for the foundational narratives of the State of Israel.
Finkelstein, among other things, determined that certain works of scholarship pertaining to Israel's territorial claims and human-rights record were
fundamentally flawed.

The Case of Nadia Abu El-Haj. Her book *Facts on the Ground: Archaeological
Practice and Territorial Self-Fashioning in Israeli Society* (Chicago: University
of Chicago Press, 2001) was widely acclaimed by experts. At the time of
publication, Abu El-Haj was teaching at the University of Chicago, where
she had good prospects for tenure. However, for family reasons, she
moved to Barnard College in 2002.

In her book, Abu El-Haj wrote, "This study is best understood as an
anthropology of science that meets an anthropology of colonialism and
nationalism,"[42] and she summarized its findings as follows:

> While at one level archaeology was a colonial discipline practiced
> in the British Raj, colonial America, and Palestine/Israel alike, it
> was not equally salient in each of these colonies. In the context
> of Israel and Palestine, archaeology emerged as a central scientific
> discipline because of the manner in which colonial settlement
> was configured in a language of, and a belief in, Jewish national
> return. In producing the material signs of national history that
> became visible and were witnessed across the contemporary
> landscape, archaeology repeatedly remade the colony into an
> ever-expanding national terrain. It substantiated the nation in
> history and produced Eretz Yisrael as the national home.[43]

In a lengthy 2008 article in the *New Yorker,* Jane Kramer reported that
"the attacks on Nadia Abu El-Haj's book began in earnest in the summer
of 2003 [...] when [Daniel] Pipes ran a review [...] in a quarterly published
by his Middle East Forum."[44] Abu El-Haj initially tried to ignore this
and subsequent attacks, in an effort to keep debate on a scholarly level.
However, after she filed for tenure assessment, a major political campaign
began, with the stated aim of persuading the university to deny tenure. It
included a website, an electronic petition signed by approximately two
thousand people (many of them Barnard graduates), and a public statement against her by a senior Barnard colleague. She was denounced as an
inferior scholar "who indulges in 'knowing misrepresentation of data,'"

and as biased against Israel. The petition was organized by a West Bank settler and Barnard alumna, Paula Stern, who said that, having read some of
Facts on the Ground, "I was horrified, because what Abu El-Haj was saying
in her introduction was just what Ahmadinejad is saying."

Kramer noted that "as many as a third of Barnard's students and a quarter of Columbia's undergraduates are Jewish. [...] A million Jews live in
New York, more than any other city in the world except Tel Aviv [...] Israel
is the cause that can raise a constituency out of an otherwise fractious, and
famously sceptical, Jewish population, and push it into a kind of collective
panic. The pressure is hardly unique to Columbia, but the university has
been a constant target."

Columbia has been a target because of its eminent long-time faculty
member Edward W. Said, and its distinguished Middle East Institute,
now headed by Rashid Khalidi, who is a historian. For many years, Said
was under frequent attack by supporters of Israel, as was the university
for continuing to employ him, but Columbia steadfastly defended him,
as well as Khalidi and others. However, Columbia has had a longer and
stronger tradition of defending academic freedom than many other major
American universities. Thus it not surprising that, despite intense public
pressure, all committees in the process recommended tenure and it was
granted to Abu El-Haj. Also of note is that, after the campaign against
Abu El-Haj began, President Judith Shapiro of Barnard (who is an anthropologist), "delivered an exemplary public rebuke to the alumnae rallied
by Stern against Abu El-Haj, telling them to beware of campaigns led by
people who 'may not be in the best position to judge the matter at hand.'"

After the favourable decision was made, two Israeli scholars published
a commentary in *Academe Online*, an AAUP publication, making the same
point as Shapiro and giving their overview on the controversy, including
their assessment of the quality of work by Abu El-Haj. Dan Rabinowitz
and Ronen Shamir of the department of sociology and anthropology, Tel-
Aviv University—the latter is department chair, the former was president
of the Israeli Anthropological Society—wrote that they used Abu El-Haj's
work in their classes, and that her book "brilliantly combines a historical
analysis with an analysis of minute, everyday life practices."[45] Regarding
the attempts by outsiders to influence the tenure assessment, they stated:

> Although we strongly believe that the significance and meaning
> of scientific works must be discussed publicly, we are equally
> convinced that formal decisions about the merit of research and

the promotion of scientists do not belong in public forums. It
is perfectly legitimate to debate the brilliance and originality
of scholarship, but science is not a form of participatory
democracy to be determined by majority opinion, public debate,
or vindications or condemnations on PetitionOnline.com. [...]
When creative minds become self-consciously preoccupied with
the political—and material—consequences of their product, they
can no longer be creative, and their thirst for truth is seriously
hindered.[46]

From their vantage point as academic experts in relevant social sciences
at a major university in Israel, Professors Rabinowitz and Shamir made
an additional observation: they suggested that "the ethnic identity of the
scholar under scrutiny" was a factor in the controversy over her work.

In Abu El-Haj's case, the scholar is of Arab descent. Her
sin is to probe into a social scientific domain—the history,
historiography, and anthropology of Israel—that is normally
defined by Jewish Israeli scholars whose tendency has always
been to position Palestinians as objects of inquiry. Abu El-Haj's
work thus perpetuates the faux pas of inverting the "proper" way
of studying Israel–Palestine.

Her violation of the norms is particularly pertinent when it
comes to the scientific gaze of anthropology, a predominantly
Western discipline that created and objectified a pristine effigy
of the exotic native as seen by westerners, an approach that
literary theorist Edward Said called Orientalizing. Abu El-Haj
belongs to a new generation of scholars—many of them
Palestinians—who, inspired by Said's legacy, insist on reversing
the Orientalizing gaze and turning Israel and Israelis into objects
of inquiry. This effort should be praised, not silenced.[47]

The Case of Norman Finkelstein. Norman Finkelstein, whose parents
were Holocaust survivors, was a doctoral student at Princeton University
interested in the theory of Zionism when a recently published book
attracted his attention: *From Time Immemorial: The Origins of the Arab–
Jewish Conflict over Palestine,* by Joan Peters (New York: Harper and Row,
1984). It was a bestseller in the United States, with endorsements by

several prominent persons (writers Barbara Tuchman and Saul Bellow, along with Elie Wiesel, among others), a great many favourable reviews (by Daniel Pipes, among others) and almost no critical reviews, and went through several hardcover printings. Peters's ostensibly well-referenced book concluded that the so-called Palestinians were all recent immigrants to the areas of the Palestine Mandate settled by Jewish people.

In the book, Peters appeared to have provided substance for the Zionist epigram "The land without a people, waiting for a people without a land," thereby solving a long-standing problem: "The trouble [had been] that the epigram was not true: Palestine already had a people. [...] The basic falsity of the slogan ha[d] remained to plague political Zionism."[48] In Noam Chomsky's view, this explained the book's American popularity:

> [...] everybody was just raving about it. Here was this book which proved that there were really no Palestinians! Of course, the implicit message was if Israel kicks them all out there's no moral issue, because they're just recent immigrants who came in because the Jews had built up the country.[49]

In contrast, when a UK edition was published the following year, British reviewers condemned the book. For example, historian Albert Hourani, a leading authority on the Middle East, concluded, "This is a ludicrous and worthless book and the only interesting question it raises is why it comes with praise from two well-known American writers." A lengthy, detailed analysis by Ian and David Gilmour in the *London Review of Books* concluded that the book was "strident, pretentious and preposterous."[50] The British reviews did not significantly dampen enthusiasm for the book or its author in the United States. However, Finkelstein conducted a careful study of the book, including all of its references, and this study became the basis for his PhD thesis. He concluded that "*From Time Immemorial* was a colossal hoax. Cited sources were mangled, key numbers in the demographic study falsified, and large swaths plagiarized from Zionist propaganda tracts."[51]

Finkelstein's findings were highly displeasing to some of his professors at Princeton; nevertheless he was awarded the degree in 1988. In 2001, he was appointed to a tenure-track position in Political Science at DePaul University, a Roman Catholic institution. By the time of his tenure review, he had published several books on the Israel/Palestine conflict. His scholarly work is well regarded by experts, including Avi Shlaim, Raul Hilberg, and John Mearsheimer.

On his website (www.normanfinkelstein.com), Finkelstein suggests that one of his other books, *The Holocaust Industry: Reflections on the Exploitation of Jewish Suffering* (New York: Verso, 2000), earned him greater enmity than his published work on the Peters book, but the work that more immediately precipitated at least part of the campaign to persuade DePaul to deny him tenure was *Beyond Chutzpah: On the Misuse of Anti-Semitism and the Abuse of History* (Berkeley: University of California Press, 2005).

Much of *Beyond Chutzpah* is devoted to a critical analysis of the book *The Case for Israel* (New York: Wiley, 2003) by Harvard law professor Alan M. Dershowitz. Soon after this bestseller appeared, with endorsements by prominent people, Finkelstein publicly criticized it in very strong terms. Subsequently, he developed the manuscript for *Beyond Chutzpah*, setting out in detail his views on *The Case for Israel* and other matters related to the Israel/Palestine conflict (such as claims that another New Anti-Semitism was prevalent). His attack on the credibility of Dershowitz's book focused on two of its central aspects: the use of sources, and Israel's human-rights record. Finkelstein summarized his findings:

> It can fairly be said that *The Case for Israel* surpasses *From Time Immemorial* in deceitfulness and is among the most spectacular academic frauds ever published on the Israel–Palestine conflict. Indeed Dershowitz appropriates large swaths from the Peters hoax. Whereas Peters falsified real sources, Dershowitz goes one better and cites absurd sources or stitches evidence out of whole cloth. [...]The point, of course, is not that Dershowitz is a charlatan. Rather, it's *the systematic institutional bias* that allows for books like *The Case for Israel* to become national best sellers.[52] (Emphasis in original)

In his 2009 book, *Israel and Palestine*, Oxford professor Avi Shlaim commented on Finkelstein's work and the campaigns against him. Regarding his analysis of Peters's book, *From Time Immemorial*, Shlaim wrote, "Finkelstein demonstrated conclusively that the book was preposterous and worthless," and regarding *Beyond Chutzpah*, Shlaim wrote, "Above all, the book is a devastating indictment of Alan Dershowitz. The most serious charge, denied by Dershowitz, is that Dershowitz plagiarised from Joan Peters, of all people."[53] Shlaim recounts the threats of lawsuits launched by Dershowitz and his lawyers and the Harvard professor's attempt to persuade California governor Arnold Schwarzenegger to intervene to prevent the book's publication by the University of Califorina Press, adding,

> The campaign against Finkelstein reached a crescendo when he
> was under consideration for tenure at DePaul University [...]
> Finkelstein had an excellent record as a publishing scholar, as a
> lecturer and as a teacher, as well as the support of the Political
> Science department. But illegitimate outside pressure evidently
> contributed to the decision to deny tenure. Alan Dershowitz
> personally intervened in this process, compiling a 60-page
> dossier against the candidate, which he sent to every faculty
> member at the university.[54]

Dershowitz continued his campaign against Finkelstein even after
he was denied tenure. In October 2007, the Oxford Union scheduled a
debate on a motion in favour of the one-state model for Israel/Palestine.
Shlaim was to be one of the speakers in favour of the one-state model,
and Finkelstein was to be one of the opposing speakers. When this
was announced, the invitation to Finkelstein was protested, and "Alan
Dershowitz was the most aggressive of the protesters."[55] A few days before
the debate, the president of the Oxford Union withdrew the invitation to
Finkelstein, with the result that Shlaim and the other speakers withdrew,
in protest against the president's action. Earlier, when the debate was being
planned, Dershowitz "had been invited to speak, but said he would participate only if he could dictate the motion and approve the other speakers—conditions which were rejected."[56]

DePaul University denied that lobbying by Dershowitz or other outsiders
influenced its decision. A negotiation followed the announcement of tenure
denial, with the result that Finkelstein submitted a resignation, while he and
DePaul issued a joint statement in which the university acknowledged he
was a prolific scholar and an outstanding teacher. This acknowledgement
and the fact that Finkelstein had already published his highly controversial book *The Holocaust Industry*, as well as his devastating analysis of the
Peters book, prior to his DePaul appointment, and that he had substantially strengthened his publication record during his years at DePaul, have
resulted in speculation as to why the administration denied him tenure.

The opposition to the York/Queen's conference mounted by Israel
lobby organizations can be seen as an extension to Canada of a phenomenon in the United States during recent decades. More than twenty years
ago, Edward Said wrote:

It is now possible to see clearly the established pattern by
which supporters of Israel do two things when they write and
organize: they reproduce the official party line on Israel, or they
go after delinquents who threaten to disturb the idyll. There
is a dialectical opposite to this pattern, however. Critics and
opponents of the Zionist lobby in civil society take as their tasks
first to decode the myths, then to present the record of facts in
as neutral a way as possible.[57]

ACADEMIC FREEDOM IN CANADA—BEFORE AND AFTER THE CROWE CASE

Canadians have benefited from adopting and often improving on developments from elsewhere. Academic freedom is an example. The development
of that right in Canada owes much to the American experience, such as the
1915 *Declaration* by the AAUP, the joint AAUP–AAC 1940 *Statement*, and
the development of policy and procedures by the AAUP. However, Canada
has a strong British tradition in many matters, and the more informal
twentieth-century concept of academic freedom in British universities also
has had a beneficial influence, as events during the early Cold War era
showed. The result today is that we enjoy a more comprehensive right to
academic freedom, with more robust protections, than in either the United
States or the United Kingdom.

Before 1958. A professor who spoke or wrote on matters considered
controversial, or who was a political activist, or simply found himself
inadvertently in the midst of a controversial matter, might be dismissed
or have his career retarded in other ways. The only effective defence
against summary dismissal was the support of influential persons, as had
been the case in the United States before the AAUP became an effective
organization.[58]

Historian Frank Underhill of the University of Toronto was a significant
figure during several decades, as a political activist, a public intellectual,
and a leader in his academic specialty. An outspoken critic of the prevailing economic and social order, he was on several occasions rebuked by
presidents of the university for articles he published in the popular press or
for political activities. For instance, in 1931, President Robert Falconer sent
Underhill a warning letter following his articles in American and British
magazines critical of the Bennett government. In 1932, Underhill's political involvement was curtailed by Falconer's successor, President Henry J.
Cody, who ordered him to resign from his membership on the executive

committee of the Ontario wing of the Co-operative Commonwealth Federation (CCF). Underhill complied on this occasion, but the following year he helped to draft the CCF's Regina Manifesto and continued as an activist for many years.

Underhill had the distinction of being denounced by three Ontario premiers: Conservative Howard Ferguson, Liberal Mitchell Hepburn, and Conservative George Drew. Underhill incurred their displeasure for maintaining that the state had a responsibility to provide medical care and other social services, and that Canada should eventually have stronger economic ties with the United States than with the United Kingdom. He also was denounced by conservative daily newspapers. That the university did not yield to recurrent demands to dismiss Underhill was on several occasions due to intercessions by senior figures in the King Liberal government sympathetic to his views.[59] Other activist academics whose supporters lacked comparable influence fared less well.

In the years immediately after World War II, the anti-communist fervour gripping the United States also infected Canada, and several Canadian academics were victims. Mathematician Israel Halperin of Queen's University was one of several rounded up in the Gouzenko spy affair of 1946, subjected to psychological mistreatment while incarcerated by the RCMP, and was later charged with criminal offences. Despite Halperin's acquittal in court, some Queen's trustees demanded his dismissal. However, Chancellor Charles Dunning persuasively argued against dismissal, saying that such action "would place a black mark beside the name of Queen's, a mark which would remain there for many a long day," with the result that Halperin remained at Queen's.[60]

Mathematical physicist Leopold Infeld resigned from the University of Toronto in 1950, in protest against infringement of his academic freedom by President Sidney Smith. Smith's actions came shortly after Infeld was the subject of a baseless allegation made in Parliament by then-Opposition leader George Drew, to the effect that Infeld had given information on the atomic bomb to the USSR. Drew made his allegations against Infeld not long after Senator McCarthy had launched his anti-communist crusade in the United States. Perhaps Drew hoped for increased popularity when denouncing Infeld, but McCarthyist tactics were not greeted with the same enthusiasm in Canada or in the United Kingdom.[61]

It is an indication of this different attitude that, between the mid-1950s and the mid-1960s, several academics dismissed and blacklisted in the United States were hired by Canadian or British universities. These

included mathematicians Louis Weisner, Lee Lorch, and Chandler Davis—
hired by the University of New Brunswick, the University of Alberta, and
the University of Toronto, respectively—and classicist Moses Finley (later,
Sir Moses Finley), who was hired by the University of Cambridge.

The Dismissal of Harry Crowe in 1958. The CAUT was founded in 1951,
but until 1958 its main efforts were directed toward improving salaries and
benefits for professors. Events arising from the dismissal of historian Harry
S. Crowe by United College (now the University of Winnipeg, then affiliated with the United Church of Canada) galvanized the Canadian academic
community. Within a few years, CAUT was transformed, defending academic freedom and promoting democratization of university governance.

Professor Crowe's offence was that, while on sabbatical leave at
Queen's, he wrote to a colleague at United College criticizing the administration—in a private letter that somehow found its way into the hands of
the principal, Wilfred C. Lockhart. Crowe's letter suggested United College
administrators were hypocritical and not to be trusted, and added that
"religion is a corrosive force."[62] His dismissal brought a call from historians at Queen's to CAUT, requesting an investigation. At the time, CAUT
had no relevant framework of its own, but it agreed to set up a committee of inquiry, and the committee adapted the relevant AAUP policies
and procedures to its purposes. The committee members were Professor
Vernon Fowke (Economics, University of Saskatchewan) and Professor
Bora Laskin (Law, University of Toronto). In the meantime, the administration publicly denounced Crowe, justifying his dismissal on the basis
of his letter and saying that "the attitude toward religion revealed by it is
incompatible with the traditions and objectives of United College."[63] In
effect, Crowe was accused of "striking at the heart of deeply held religious
beliefs," to borrow the phraseology of Frank Iacobucci.

The college faculty was sharply divided between supporters of Crowe
and supporters of the principal, and there was similar polarization in
much of Winnipeg. Sixteen members of the academic staff resigned to
protest the board's treatment of Crowe and what they saw as a disregard
for academic freedom and due process.

Fowke and Laskin submitted a ninety-page report to CAUT in November
1958. The findings were expressed in strong and direct terms. For example:

> Principal Lockhart and the Board of Regents were respectively
> tactless and arbitrary in their handling of a situation which they
> themselves had created. [...] Principal Lockhart, no less than the

Board, expected unquestioning loyalty and servility on his own terms.[64]

The Committee is struck by the unreality of the reasons for the summary dismissal of Professor Crowe given to the public by the Board of Regents in its press statement of September 20.[65]

Fowke and Laskin also found inappropriate the board's citing of religion as a reason for its action: "The Committee would observe that the administration of United College, judged by its conduct, seems to hold the view that religious belief is so fragile that it may be shattered by a breath of criticism."[66] They concluded:

The Committee's investigation leaves it in no doubt that Professor Crowe has been a victim of injustice, violative of academic freedom and tenure. The story is the sorrier because of the attempt to associate the dismissal with protection of religious principle. Rectification of the wrong done to Professor Crowe demands that the Board of Regents invite him to resume teaching duties [...] with an assurance of academic freedom and tenure as elaborated in this report.[67]

The report had a significant impact, immediately on the situation at United College, and subsequently on the professoriate, Canada-wide. A settlement was reached in December 1958 whereby the board passed a motion to withdraw the dismissal and reinstate Crowe. Crowe requested that the colleagues who had resigned be invited back, but United College refused, and in March 1959 Crowe submitted his resignation.

Crowe worked for a number of years as research director for a national labour union, but eventually returned to academic life and was dean of Atkinson College in York University at the time of his death in 1981.

After 1958. The Fowke–Laskin report did not attempt to set out a comprehensive definition of academic freedom, but it did make a number of strong statements indicating its authors had a robust conception of the right. Both the dismissal of Crowe and the Fowke–Laskin report had substantial repercussions, both immediately and long afterward.[68] CAUT appointed J. H. Stewart Reid (who had been chair of the History department at United College and one of the sixteen who had resigned to protest Crowe's dismissal) as its first executive director. It established an Academic

Freedom and Tenure Committee (analogous to the AAUP's Committee A), which has been active ever since. Laskin himself assumed a leadership role in the organization and, as vice-president and president, helped to develop CAUT into an effective voice in the academy, and helped to raise its profile in the national political context.

CAUT commissioned studies on academic freedom and tenure, of which the most significant was a review of the legal status of tenure by Queen's law professor Daniel Soberman in 1965. The recommendations in his report led eventually to Canada-wide adoption of fair procedures for the granting of tenure and for dismissal. In 1965–1966, CAUT and the Association of Universities and Colleges of Canada (AUCC) co-sponsored the Duff–Berdahl Commission on University Governance. The commission's report helped accelerate the process of consolidating faculty rights to involvement in academic decisions.

Another important result arising from the Fowke–Laskin report was that the CAUT developed and promoted a conception of academic freedom clearer and more explicit than the one set out in the American 1940 *Statement*. The CAUT definition made it clearer that academic freedom is an individual right, in the British tradition that flowed from Mill's *Essay on Liberty* and was reflected in the Trinity College faculty response to the 1916 Russell dismissal. It also explicitly included the right to criticize the university. This definition was eventually accepted by boards of governors and incorporated into faculty manuals and similar documents across Canada.[69]

Thus in Canada—in contrast to the United States—it is not necessary to argue that freedom of intramural speech is implied by other language in the definition. Laskin himself continued to promote a robust conception of academic freedom after he left the academy for the bench, as can be seen from the views he expressed in the opening pages of his report to York University in the late 1960s.[70]

By the early 1970s it was clear that important issues remained without adequate faculty involvement. For example, few universities had an effective process for negotiating salaries and benefits, or a fair and effective procedure for resolving grievances. CAUT then determined to adapt the collective bargaining process to the academy. Two decades later, almost all of CAUT's member associations across Canada operate in the manner of trade unions, even in cases (such as the University of Toronto) where they are not certified bargaining agents under a provincial industrial-relations act. As a result, academic status disputes on significant matters, including tenure, promotion, and dismissal, as well as disputes about academic freedom, may be submitted to arbitration. Arbitrators and mediators imported standards of procedural fairness from the industrial labour context and sensitively adapted them to the academy. Thus, in Canada, academic freedom and tenure are now better protected on a nation-wide basis than in any other country, and CAUT is one of the most robust organizations of its kind in the world.[71]

An Academic Legacy. After Harry Crowe's untimely death in 1981, a number of York colleagues, including Irving Abella, Howard Adelman, and David Dewitt, established the Harry Crowe Memorial Lecture series. The series was inaugurated in 1982 with a conference on anti-Semitism, and when Adelman wrote (as chair of the board of directors) to Alan Dershowitz of Harvard University with an invitation to speak, he commented:

> Harry Crowe was a unique human being and an outstanding Canadian. Though a non-Jew he was one of this country's leading supporters of the State of Israel and its most uncompromising opponent of anti-semitism and racism.[72]

In 2002, CAUT established the Harry Crowe Foundation (HCF), "to carry out education and research on the role of post-secondary teaching and research in contemporary society."[73] The HCF sponsored international conferences in 2005, 2007, and 2010 on current issues pertaining to academic freedom, research integrity, and the use of performance indicators in the academy, respectively. In 2009, CAUT Council conferred the James B. Milner academic freedom award on each of the sixteen United College faculty members who had resigned to protest Crowe's dismissal.

THE OLIVIERI AND HEALY CASES

The only two Canadian academic freedom cases to have attracted significant international media and scholarly attention occurred at the University of Toronto. The first involved Dr. Nancy Olivieri, a professor of medicine and paediatrics who conducted clinical research at the Hospital for Sick Children (HSC) and the Toronto General Hospital (TGH)—two of the university's affiliated health-care institutions. Her case became a public controversy in 1998. The second involved Dr. David Healy, who had been recruited from the United Kingdom and had received his appointment from the university's Faculty of Medicine and the Centre for Addiction and

Mental Health (CAMH), but had not yet taken up his new position. His case became a public controversy in 2001.

Olivieri and Healy were internationally recognized experts in their fields. They had published articles in leading refereed journals on serious unexpected risks of certain drugs, findings that were displeasing to and disputed by the manufacturers of the drugs. In effect, each had struck at the heart of a deeply held political belief, namely, the neoliberal doctrine that corporate profits must take precedence over public interest in such matters as health, safety, or the environment. Subsequent to publishing their findings of risks, actions were taken in regard to their employment, and each was denounced.

The Olivieri Case. Nancy Olivieri had been conducting clinical trials on deferiprone (an iron chelation drug) with thalassemia patients when, in 1996, she scientifically identified a significant unexpected risk of the drug. She then moved to fulfil her ethical obligations by revising the patient information and consent forms so as to include this new information, whereupon the drug's manufacturer, Apotex Inc., terminated the trials and issued warnings of legal action against her, should she disclose the identified risk to anyone. A controversy arose and escalated, becoming public in 1998 when, legal warnings notwithstanding, she published her findings in a leading journal.

Subsequently, actions were taken against Olivieri by the HSC, mitigated to an extent by interventions on her behalf by CAUT, authorities in her field from Oxford and Harvard, and the University of Toronto. Then, in April 2000, without prior notice to her, the HSC board of trustees held a press conference to announce that stated allegations of medical malpractice (cast as "concerns") against her were being referred to the College of Physicians and Surgeons of Ontario (CPSO). The hospital took this extraordinary measure two weeks after it and the university had jointly disciplined Dr. Gideon Koren, who had been a key witness against her during an internal HSC investigation process that had been seriously deficient in procedural fairness.

In contrast to the handling of the Olivieri case itself, at the conclusion of a joint hospital and university investigation characterized by exemplary procedural fairness, Koren was found to have committed "gross misconduct" by writing and sending anonymous and scurrilous letters against Olivieri, and in then persistently "lying" to conceal his responsibility.[74] Both institutions imposed penalties on him for professional misconduct.

Olivieri was fully exonerated by two separate independent inquiries, the first commissioned by the CAUT (report released on October 26, 2001), and the second undertaken by the CPSO (report released on December 19, 2001). The first recommended redress for Olivieri, and the second termed her actions "commendable." A year later, a mediated settlement of all matters in dispute between Olivieri and the hospital and the university was achieved. Among other things, it provided redress for Olivieri, who said it sent "a message to scientists, particularly clinical scientists, that academic freedom is worth fighting for."[75] A defamation suit and countersuit between Olivieri and Apotex remains before the courts.

The Healy Case. Prior to receiving the appointment at CAMH and the University of Toronto, David Healy had already published preliminary findings on suicidality risks of SSRI (selective serotonin re-uptake inhibitor) antidepressants, the most widely used family of antidepressants. After having received his appointment letter, Healy was invited to be one of several international speakers at a major conference hosted by CAMH. In his talk, he again mentioned the risks of SSRIs to some patients. Days later, CAMH and the university revoked the appointment, citing his talk at the conference. He later questioned this action, and the matter became public. Subsequently, Healy was denounced by the university's dean of medicine, Dr. David Naylor, who said, "The free thinker who promulgates poorly-grounded or unqualified generalizations about clinical issues is little better than the fool who thinks free speech gives him a license to yell 'Fire!' in a crowded theatre."[76] In a memo addressed to the CAMH Foundation board of directors, the president of CAMH, Dr. Paul Garfinkel, denounced Healy in similarly harsh terms. In September 2001, Healy filed a lawsuit against Naylor and Garfinkel and their institutions, alleging breach of contract and defamation. An out-of-court settlement was reached in April 2002.

Disclosure of Significant Unexpected Risks. Clinical professors of medicine have both a right to academic freedom and a professional obligation to publish findings, including findings of significant risk. They also have an ethical obligation to disclose to patients in clinical trials any scientifically identified findings of significant risk, regardless of the views of the drug manufacturer or any contractual rights to control of information the manufacturer may claim. In regard to scientific identification of significant risks, whether the clinical investigator's findings are later confirmed by other investigators is immaterial to the obligation to patients to a trial.[77]

The published findings of both Olivieri and Healy have been vindicated by subsequent scientific work and actions of regulatory agencies. In the case of Healy, American and British governments have issued warnings about the risks of SSRIs for certain categories of those with depression.[78] Apotex's iron-chelation drug that Olivieri had been investigating is still not licensed, either by Health Canada or the US Food and Drug Administration. In autumn 2009, the FDA cancelled the scheduled hearing by an expert panel that was to consider an Apotex licensing application for deferiprone. Apotex's marketing licence for deferiprone in the European Community was issued with a significant restriction that required a warning label stating that full information on its safety was not available.[79]

The Importance of Procedural Protections. These two cases occurred in faculties of medicine. At many universities in Canada and the United States, clinical professors have not been members of faculty associations and have had no effective alternative source of collective support. Thus they have not benefited to the same extent as other professors from the strengthening of the right to academic freedom, or access to grievance procedures. This was noted in a letter to the CAUT Committee of Inquiry in the Olivieri case, written by Dr. John Evans, a former president of the University of Toronto (and also a former dean of a faculty of medicine). He wrote that it would be "extremely important" to "put in place appropriate policy and instruments of conflict resolution recognizing the special circumstances of clinical faculty members and the inadequacy of labour relations grievance procedures in existence in most hospitals."[80] Since the publishing of the report of the Committee of Inquiry in the fall of 2001, CAUT has been devoting considerable resources to assisting clinical faculty members at universities across Canada to address the problem identified by Evans.

The Importance of Robust Organizations. Even though neither Olivieri nor Healy was a member of a faculty association at the time of the disputes, CAUT nevertheless intervened on their behalf and devoted considerable resources to assisting them in achieving satisfactory resolutions.[81] The result was that both have been able to continue their careers as clinical professors of medicine and to receive further recognition for their work. Olivieri received the 2009 Scientific Freedom and Responsibility Award from the American Association for the Advancement of Science, and Healy was promoted to a professorial chair in the United Kingdom. Other clinical professors in very similar circumstances in the United States and the United Kingdom have had their academic careers terminated, because no organization as robust as CAUT was able and willing to take up their cases.

BORA LASKIN AND HARRY ARTHURS ON ACADEMIC FREEDOM

In their 1958 report on the Crowe case, Fowke and Laskin gave a provisional definition of academic freedom, sufficient for their purposes:

> The privilege of a teacher in a university or college to utter and publish opinions in the course of teaching and research and to exchange opinions with faculty colleagues without liability of official censure or discipline is the commonly understood substance of academic freedom.[82]

Both from their report in general and their definition in particular, it is apparent that Fowke and Laskin conceived of academic freedom as an individual right. This conception is to be contrasted with that of some American commentators, notably Robert Post, who suggested in a 2006 essay that it was not, having based his conclusion on his reading of the 1915 *Declaration* of the AAUP.[83]

During 1968–1969, Laskin (then a Justice of the Ontario Court of Appeal) chaired a Presidential Committee on Rights and Responsibilities of Members of York University. This was a time of political ferment on university campuses in North America, Europe, and elsewhere. In his report, *Freedom and Responsibility in the University*, he made the following observations:

> Truth follows no political standard. Instead, the university should be conceived of as a vibrant shared experience in a life devoted to intellect and imagination. An essential characteristic of such an experience must be a capacity to tolerate unsettling opinions; and another must be the absence of any official doctrine or ideology. The University as a corporate community must be neutral so as to permit its members to be protagonists of widely diverse and conflicting views, except when those views are inimical to the values and purposes of the University itself.
>
> Like any community the University must continuously resolve the problem of liberty and order. But whatever be the approach in other communities, the University must in marginal cases show a preference for liberty, and risk its judgment in such cases for that preference. [...] The exaltation of order at the expense of liberty would threaten the very foundations of the University.

> If all members of the University community except one were
> of a single view, and this one member opposed that view, the
> University would have no more justification for silencing him
> than he would have, providing he had the power, for silencing
> them.[84]

These paragraphs emphasize that academic freedom is an individual
right. Laskin's understanding, shared by other leaders of CAUT in the decade 1958–1968 when it was transformed, and through to the present, is
reflected in the CAUT definition.[85]

When York University President Emeritus Harry W. Arthurs spoke on
academic freedom in a panel discussion at an AUCC meeting in 1995, he
said that:

> Academic freedom is a central value, arguably the central value,
> of university life. Anything which interferes with it has to be
> justified by reference to prior or higher values. I can think of
> very few, other than perhaps the protection of human life:
> certainly not institutional solidarity; certainly not institutional
> reputation. [...]
>
> If all of these risks attach to the exercise of academic freedom,
> on or off campus, in or out of class, what then does it mean to
> say that the university should always respect academic freedom
> whenever and wherever? It means this: that the university will
> not punish people for exercising their intellectual freedom, and
> will shield them, if it can, from attacks by others which might
> put an individual's academic status in jeopardy.[86]

Arthurs's description of academic freedom was cited by both supporters
and opponents of the York/Queen's conference. It also was cited by arbitrator Russell Goodfellow in his 2007 award in favour of the York University
Faculty Association and its member David Noble.[87] Academic freedom
is complex, and its meaning often disputed. However, as Goodfellow's
award in the Noble case illustrated, the views expressed by Laskin ("the
University must in marginal cases show a preference for liberty") and by
Arthurs (that academic freedom is "the central value of university life")
represent the modern Canadian understanding well.

In summary, the modern Canadian conception of academic freedom is more comprehensive than the conception expressed in either the 1915 *Declaration* of the AAUP or the 1940 joint *Statement* of the AAUP and the AAC, which were both written in cautious, circumspect language, reflecting the tenor of their times. However, a number of American commentators have subsequently promoted a broader conception, similar to the one prevailing in Canada.

TURGID RHETORIC

Opponents of the conference used very strong language to express their opinions, such as "virulent anti-Semitic hate fest" (B'nai Brith Canada), or "we refuse to stand by and allow Jewish students to feel threatened" (JDL Canada). CIJA used language with more subtlety, but to similar effect, in stating that events such as the conference "lead to an increased sense of insecurity for those who should feel free to express their support for Israel." B'nai Brith also claimed that some speakers were persons who "rationalize terrorism," or "actively engaged in Holocaust denial," although it later withdrew the Holocaust-denial claim.

Such reactions against events that present a challenge to received wisdom or prescribed doctrine are common and not peculiar to any social, political, religious, or other community. The invariable pattern of this type of strong collective reaction can be illustrated by comparing the controversy over the York/Queen's conference with the controversy over the appointment of Bertrand Russell to the College of the City of New York (CCNY) in 1940, in which the opposing organizations were primarily Christian, but their stated concerns and their strong language had parallels with the denunciations of the Toronto conference.

By 1940, Russell had made internationally noted contributions to mathematical logic, the foundations of mathematics, the philosophy of science, and social and political philosophy, and had been awarded honours by a number of learned societies. He had been a visiting professor at universities around the world and had given special lectures at many others. In February, by unanimous vote, the Board of Higher Education appointed him Professor of Philosophy at CCNY on an eighteen-month contract, to begin in autumn 1941.

CCNY appointed Russell to teach courses for undergraduates in logic, mathematical foundations, and the reciprocal influence of metaphysics and scientific theories. At the time, the college admitted only male students to its regular programs. (Female students were admitted to other city-sponsored institutions, such as Hunter College.) Shortly after his appointment was made public, a storm of protest erupted. It was begun by Bishop William T. Manning of the Episcopal Church, who was soon joined by a great many other persons and organizations, including councils of the Knights of Columbus, the Metropolitan Baptist Ministers Conference, and a number of prominent city politicians, both Republican and Democratic.

Russell was denounced for promoting equality rights for women and for his views on what we now refer to as lifestyle, expressed in books such as *Marriage and Morals* (1929) and in talks with titles such as "Why I Am Not a Christian." *Marriage and Morals* included chapters titled "The Liberation of Women" and "Trial Marriage," and advocated women's social emancipation. Despite many protests by distinguished academics such as Albert Einstein and John Dewey, by leaders of liberal religious denominations, and by student groups, the appointment was terminated before he actually started to teach.

The campaign of vilification of Russell even reached the New York State Legislature, which passed a resolution calling Russell "an advocate of barnyard morality," and called on the Board of Higher Education to rescind the appointment, which it refused to do. The board received warnings of inference by government if it did not revoke the appointment, including a threat by a prominent member of the city government that "he would move to strike out the entire 1941 appropriation of $7,500,000 for the upkeep of the municipal colleges."[88]

The device that brought ultimate success to the campaign was a taxpayer's suit against the Board of Higher Education in the New York Supreme Court, petitioning for an order to vacate the appointment on the basis that Russell was an advocate of immorality and an alien. It was brought by Jean Kay of Brooklyn, who "declared that she was afraid of what might happen to her daughter if she were a student at the boy's College of the City of New York and Bertrand Russell were teaching there the philosophy of mathematics and science."[89] Russell's defenders ruefully observed that his alleged offence was similar to that of Socrates: corrupting the young.

Justice John E. McGeehan found in favour of the complainant, and vacated the appointment in a decision that included the comments that, by appointing Russell, the Board of Higher Education had established a "chair of indecency," thereby exhibiting "moral standards lower than common decency requires," and that "academic freedom is freedom to do good, not freedom to teach evil."[90] The Board of Higher Education voted by a majority to appeal the decision, but in an effort to quell further political controversy, Mayor Fiorello La Guardia struck from the city budget the line item for the position to which Russell had been appointed. Subsequently, the appeal court refused to hear the matter.

The court ruling in New York encouraged actions in California, where Russell was still employed at UCLA, and in Massachusetts, where he was scheduled to teach at Harvard that autumn. However, the California courts dismissed a similar suit, and Harvard rejected a demand by a politician that it rescind Russell's appointment.

The events in New York came in the very year, 1940, when the AAUP and the AAC issued their joint *Statement* on academic freedom. In an effort to ensure that lessons would be learned from the Russell dismissal at CCNY, John Dewey and Horace M. Kallen published a collection of essays outlining the events and presenting analyses of the controversy from political, legal, philosophical, administrative, and religious perspectives. In his introduction, Dewey wrote:

> The turgid rhetoric and the dishonest abuse engaged in during the process of winning a temporary legal victory for reaction and intolerance may possibly contribute to the creation of a long black period in our intellectual life. But the extreme this reaction went to in flouting of fair play and of freedom may, on the other hand, help clear the atmosphere of foul vapors and so assist the light of intelligence to shine more brightly.[91]

The Russell case may indeed have had a salutary effect on American academe during the war years, but the black period feared by Dewey arrived immediately thereafter.

THE VULNERABILITY OF DEMOCRACY

Protecting Academic Freedom. The terms of reference of this Inquiry include a question as to whether the experiences of the York/Queen's conference have implications for "the vulnerability of academic freedom and the integrity of educational work." Academic freedom is best protected in liberal democracies, such as the United States and Canada, but only in recent decades has this right been protected consistently and effectively. A feature of modern liberal democracies is the right to free collective bargaining, and adaptation of this process to the academy was a significant factor in strengthening protections for academic freedom in the United

States and especially in Canada. Nevertheless, even in these circumstances there have been cases in both countries in which academic freedom has been seriously violated or academic integrity seriously eroded.

When a government departs significantly from liberal democratic norms of administration, academic freedom and academic integrity become vulnerable. Events in Europe and in the United States during the past century proved that liberal democracy itself is vulnerable to extreme political currents, especially when they are directed or encouraged by agencies of the state. However, the political transitions need not be swift or dramatic; the erosions of liberal democratic structures can be gradual but persistent and ultimately substantial. The Harper government has been eroding Canadian democracy in a variety of ways since 2006, by actions such as interference with arm's-length agencies. In this it has followed a trend that began in the United States.

Democracy and Oligarchy. Democracy has always been vulnerable, and today, as has been the case throughout history, it is blamed and denounced for a wide array of perceived social or political ills.

By the mid-1960s, Canada, the United States, and some other Western countries had become more liberal and more democratic than they had ever previously been, with substantial frameworks for advancing public purposes, defending the public interest, and encouraging private enterprise, while balancing oligarchic influences. But soon thereafter, increasing numbers of oligarchic elements—in the United States, the United Kingdom, France, and elsewhere—considered they had been placed in a quandary. In the United States, the discontent of oligarchic elements led to a well-financed and ultimately successful campaign by oligarchic elements of American society to, in effect, turn the clock back to a time before the Roosevelt New Deal in the United States. There have been similar developments elsewhere in the West, such as in the United Kingdom, where the post-war implementation of the social and economic programs recommended by the wartime Beveridge Report have been under sustained attack.

The campaign, which began on a small scale in the mid-1930s and was politically ineffective until around 1980, has been documented and analysed in recent years. Its main outlines were discussed in a 2004 article by Lewis H. Lapham.[92] Detailed accounts by academics and others, including works by Kim Phillips-Fein, Jacob S. Hacker and Paul Pierson, James K. Galbraith, Paul Krugman, and Linda McQuaig and Neil Brooks were published subsequently. The campaign featured extensive promotion of both neoliberal and neoconservative doctrines, and its success resulted in selective implementation of aspects of these doctrines through legislation and government policy.

During the 1970s, oligarchic transformative efforts had been more indirect than those of the 1980s and later. They were led by the Trilateral Commission, an organization of American, West European, and Japanese elites established on the initiative of David Rockefeller. It sponsored a report by intellectuals, *The Crisis of Democracy*, the substance of which Noam Chomsky summarized as follows:

> The crisis of democracy to which they refer arises from the
> fact that in the 1960s, segments of the normally quiescent
> population became politically mobilized and began to
> press their demands, thus creating a crisis, since naturally
> these demands cannot be met, at least without a significant
> redistribution of wealth and power, which is not to be
> contemplated. The trilateral scholars, quite consistently,
> therefore urge "more moderation in democracy."[93]

The Trilateral Commission's political program was successful in the United States—not least in that the president and some of the more important cabinet officers in the Carter administration were members. However, to many influential Americans the trilateral agenda was insufficiently radical. In Jacques Rancière's terms, "Both the oligarchy's quandaries and democracy's difficulties can help us to understand the intellectual manifestations of antidemocratic fury."[94] Carter was defeated by Reagan, and there were similar electoral results in other developed countries, such as the United Kingdom, around the same time or during the next decade or so.

As blends of neoliberalism and neoconservatism triumphed, the Western world embarked on a program of wealth concentration that was pursued with striking success during the next three decades. Simultaneously, the democratic structures developed during the preceding half-century came under persistent attack in the mainstream media, in parts of the academy, in publications of privately funded research organizations, and in state propaganda. The result is a circumstance in which "those who fight to retain a public service, a system of labour laws, an unemployment benefits scheme, or a pension scheme, will always be accused" of being narrowly self-interested and impeding economic progress.[95]

More generally, the common good and the public interest have been

increasingly redefined to mean private interest, a circumstance Galbraith
termed "the Predator State"—a state characterized by "the systematic abuse
of public institutions for private profit or, equivalently, the systematic
undermining of public protections for the benefit of private clients."[96] He
was describing the United States, but there is a global trend, and many
aspects of human life—and indeed much of the biosphere—have been
increasingly commodified as sources of private profit.

Collective Bargaining. Erosions of the rights of organized labour in the
United States began in the Reagan era. Initially, the groups affected were
in federally regulated workplaces, but the economic policies of the Reagan,
George H. W. Bush, and Clinton administrations had a severe adverse
effect on the major industrial unions, a trend that continued under the
George W. Bush and Obama administrations. In early 2011, American
oligarchic power was newly manifested in a concerted attack on public-
sector collective bargaining rights. In one recent instance, Republican governor Scott Walker of Wisconsin passed legislation that sharply curtailed
not only the bargaining rights but the organizational capacity of public
employees. The official justification was a state budget crisis arising from
the international financial crisis that began in 2007–2008 (a crisis caused
by the worldwide adoption of neoliberal policies in the preceding few
decades). Professor Paul Krugman wrote:

> For what's happening in Wisconsin isn't about the state budget,
> despite Mr. Walker's pretense that he's just trying to be fiscally
> responsible. It is, instead, about power. What Mr. Walker
> and his backers are trying to do is to make Wisconsin—and
> eventually, America—less of a functioning democracy and more
> of a third-world-style oligarchy.[97]

It may be recalled that the development of collective bargaining in
Canada owed much to principles embodied in American legislation and
to organizational efforts by some American industrial unions on this
side of the border. Significant weakening of collective bargaining rights
in the United States could accelerate and become more widespread. It
is not impossible that such developments could begin to influence collective bargaining in Canada in serious and adverse ways. A regressive
American-style anti-labour pattern could be established by precedent-
setting changes to labour legislation, beginning either with the federal
government or with one or more provincial governments, which then

might be emulated in other provincial jurisdictions.

Even in the absence of sweeping legislative attacks as in Wisconsin, the context of labour law generally, and collective bargaining in particular has been changed substantially in recent decades by the combined effects of neoliberalism and globalization. In a recent paper, "Labour Law after Labour," Professor Harry Arthurs observed that labour "has become marginalized as a subject of public policy making, as a concern of corporate advisors and decision makers, and as a topic familiar to ordinary citizens."[98]

Galbraith suggested that this outcome was not merely accidental or spontaneous. It was in significant measure the result of political intent that first saw practical expression during the transition from the late-Carter to the early-Reagan years. This was a time of rapidly changing political attitudes, when "conservatives around the world had come to the conclusion that it would be easier, and more effective, to destroy the union movement than to work with it in cooperation."[99]

Arthurs noted also that "the disappearance of labour as a movement and class, and the disinclination of workers to identify themselves as such, seem to have been widely recognized and, indeed, to have become self-reinforcing,"[100] and gave examples of labour's diminished importance. Moreover, in the diverse and internationalized work environments of the present, it is difficult to maintain solidarity:

> Without labour solidarity, collective bargaining legislation becomes inoperable; without public support and government engagement, labour standards legislation becomes more difficult to implement; and without effective class mobilization, the prospects for worker-friendly labour market policies, legislation and administration diminish considerably.[101]

Arthurs predicted significant evolution in the character, focus, and practice of labour law in the coming years, and outlined three broad possibilities, the optimistic ones involving an expanded scope for labour law. Depending on the path, or paths, taken, this evolution could affect the manner and possibly the extent to which academic freedom continues to be protected in Canada.

9

DISCUSSION AND FINDINGS

GENERAL OBSERVATIONS AND CONCLUSIONS

Academic Freedom. Through their collective agreements with the faculty associations QUFA and YUFA, both Queen's and York universities have agreed to uphold and protect academic freedom. Although faculty members in Osgoode Hall Law School are not members of YUFA, York University acted in a manner consistent with the academic freedom article in the YUFA collective agreement. (The controversy around certain matters involving two senior administrators is discussed below). Queen's University acted in manner consistent with the academic freedom article in the QUFA collective agreement.

The meaning of academic freedom has evolved, and the meaning of the term in Canada today is a robust hybrid of American and British conceptions. It took firm root and flourished after publication of the 1958 report by Vernon Fowke and Bora Laskin on the Crowe dismissal case. In the modern Canadian context, academic freedom is an individual right, and by extension a right of research teams composed of individuals—such as the organizing committee of the York/Queen's conference. This is clear from explicit wording in Article 10 of the York-YUFA collective agreement:[1]

> Academic freedom does not require neutrality on the part of the individual, nor does it preclude commitment on the part of the individual. Rather, academic freedom makes such commitment possible.

The role of the university as a corporate community is necessarily different from that of the individual professor—the university must be neutral so as to protect the academic freedom of individual academics. Laskin himself emphasized this principle in a report to York University a decade after publication of the Fowke–Laskin report:

> An essential characteristic of [the university] experience must be a capacity to tolerate unsettling opinions; and another must be the absence of any official doctrine or ideology. The University as a corporate community must be neutral so as to permit [...] widely diverse and conflicting views, except when those views are inimical to the values and purposes of the University itself.[2]

Among the aspects of the conference that brought the strongest expressions of protest was inclusion of the one-state bi-national model of statehood for Israel–Palestine as one of the main sub-topics. Another was the inclusion on the program of speakers—both Jewish and non-Jewish—who were well-known critics of Israel, or its policies, or Zionism. Inevitably, the conference would discuss unsettling opinions, and one or more doctrines or ideologies would be challenged by some of the speakers.

The distinction between the right of the individual (or research team) to be non-neutral and the obligation of the university as corporate community to be neutral is important to aspects of the controversy around the conference, because some critics proposed that the conference program or individual speakers should be "balanced." In other words, these critics held that the conference program designed by the research team should in some sense be neutral, or neutralized. Such criticisms were made by CIJA in its public statement, and others criticized the conference in similar terms. Professor Ian Lustick, a keynote speaker at the conference, explained the inappropriateness of the CIJA criticism in an email message sent to the organizers, and copied to Dean Monahan, President Shoukri, and Ms. Susan Davis (of CIJA).[3]

The Conference and the Controversy. The allegation by some organizations and individuals that two of Canada's leading universities and SSHRC were sponsoring an anti-Semitic event—organized by established professors and a doctoral student with the active assistance of a large advisory board that included distinguished Israeli and other Jewish scholars—was highly dubious, arguably preposterous, from the outset. Moreover, no persuasive case was put forward before, during, or after the conference. Yet this allegation was made many times, and was used as a basis for strong criticism of the organizers, the universities and SSHRC, and for government interference with SSHRC.

The campaign against the conference in Toronto was similar in tone, content, and intensity to campaigns against recent academic events (or processes) in the USA, when the topic of discussion involved Israel or its policies or actions. The common theme of the adverse reactions was that any significant academic criticism—indeed any serious criticism—of Israel or its policies or actions must necessarily be anti-Semitic and the event must therefore be denounced or cancelled, or both.

Notwithstanding the dubiousness of the allegation in regard to this conference, or its long-standing use as a political approach since the early 1970s, many persons—including influential alumni, donors, and others—and several organizations made strong representations based on it to academic administrators, to SSHRC, or to federal government ministers. The fact that there were such representations created a need for considered and diplomatic replies, because universities, SSHRC, and the government are public entities. However, a need for responses to complaints does not mean that there was a legitimate basis for these attempts to infringe the academic freedom of the conference organizers, or to impugn the reputation of the organizers, the members of their advisory board, conference participants, the university sponsors, or SSHRC, nor was there any legitimate basis for the government to interfere.

I conclude that senior administrators of both Queen's and York universities correctly took the view that the subject matter of the conference was appropriate for a university event and that the organizers had the academic freedom to design the program and select the speakers. In addition, I conclude that both universities upheld and protected the academic freedom of the conference organizers, and the academic integrity of the conference program.

I further conclude that there was every reason to have been fully confident that, had there been substance to allegations that that this event was anti-Semitic, the administrators of these universities would have taken appropriate action. I conclude also that there was no reason to have doubted the competence and integrity of Professors Aiken, Drummond, and Ryder and Mr. Masri to organize a conference that was academically appropriate.

INVOLVEMENTS OF CONFERENCE ORGANIZERS AND UNIVERSITY ADMINISTRATORS

PROFESSORS RYDER, DRUMMOND, AND AIKEN AND MR. MASRI

The organizers proposed to hold a multidisciplinary conference on a complex, difficult, important, and long-unresolved problem in international relations. They engaged in lengthy, detailed, and thorough preparations, beginning with a reading group nearly two years in advance of the conference, and including an International Advisory Board to assist with planning the program and identifying speakers/presenters. In addition to securing financial support from their universities, they were awarded a SSHRC conference grant through its peer-review process: their application was highly rated, and the grant was near the maximum for that type of research project. They successfully mounted the event for which they had received the support. In particular, no major changes were made to the program after Professor Ryder submitted the detailed funding application to SSHRC—as Ryder confirmed to SSHRC after the government interference, a statement Vice-President Shapson and Dean Monahan supported, and SSHRC accepted.

The organizers went to extraordinary lengths to explain the nature of the conference to any persons and organizations, both on and off campus, that had expressed concerns about it. They also went to extraordinary lengths to secure speakers/presenters who were well-informed on conference topics, and who represented a wide range of views concerning statehood models for Israel–Palestine. They achieved substantial balance in the views represented, even though balance was not a component of their funding application to the York U50 Committee, and also was not a SSHRC requirement.

At various times during the months before the conference, the organizers were subjected to considerable criticism and pressure, both personal and academic. The criticism continued after the conference, including opinions crystallized in Hon. Frank Iacobucci's report on the conference based on testimony he received.

I conclude that the pressures were inappropriate and the criticisms had no significant academic or administrative basis.

QUEEN'S PRINCIPAL WILLIAMS, VICE-PRINCIPAL (RESEARCH) ROWE, AND DEAN FLANAGAN

The senior academic administrators of Queen's University supported the conference throughout the controversy. They were the first to commit financial support and continued unwavering academic support, notwithstanding opposition expressed by alumni and others. They neither transmitted pressure to, nor exerted pressure on, Professor Aiken at any time. Dean William Flanagan joined with his colleagues in signing the letter of protest to SSHRC regarding its unwarranted action following Minister Goodyear's interference.[4]

YORK VICE-PRESIDENT (RESEARCH AND INNOVATION) SHAPSON

In the records available to this Inquiry, Dr. Shapson's involvement was limited and this may have been because in early April 2009 he had asked Dr. Dewitt, the Associate Vice-President Research (Social Sciences and Humanities) to represent their office in discussions about the conference. However, Shapson together with Monahan supported Ryder's report to SSHRC confirming that there had been no major changes in the program subsequent to the application to SSHRC. Internal SSHRC records available to this Inquiry suggest that this confirmation by Shapson and Monahan was considered significant by SSHRC in its decision to accept Ryder's report.

YORK PRESIDENT SHOUKRI

The host institution, York University, was subjected to more, and more varied, criticism than Queen's (for example, the full-page newspaper advertisement by B'Nai Brith of June 13, 2009, was specifically directed against York University, and the boycott warning by the Jewish Defence League of October 4, 2008, also was specific to York). President Shoukri was increasingly involved in matters pertaining to the conference from late March 2009 onward, as opposition began to mount and the controversy intensified. Responding to correspondence and telephone calls from conference critics would have been extraordinarily time-consuming for Shoukri, as well as for Monahan (the university's Information and Privacy Office confirmed that there had been hundreds of such communications, when it released "a sampling of the kinds of complaints" to CAUT).[5]

I consider it significant and—from the documentation available to this Inquiry—characteristic of the president's firm commitment to academic freedom that he resisted demands from on and off campus to prevent Omar Barghouti (who was scheduled to speak at the York/Queen's conference) from speaking in the YCISS series on academic boycotts in March 2009. Addressing the university senate in late February, Shoukri reminded everyone that freedom of speech is a core university value, "especially for those with whom we disagree," thus in effect practising principles Bora Laskin set out in his report to York University in 1969.

As is normal in universities, Shoukri dealt with many conference matters through Monahan, including the growing controversy. In an email message to Drummond on July 16, 2009, his instructions were that

> Dean Monahan was to attempt—while protecting academic freedom—to examine ways to alleviate possible concerns and to assure the external communities of our commitment to excellence and fairness. [...] it was always up to the [organizing] committee to accept or reject his [the dean's] suggestions [...].[6]

When problems arose in mid-April regarding availability of the Glendon College venue, Shoukri acted to ensure the venue was confirmed. When Monahan advised him on May 9 not to meet with the organizers, the president nevertheless agreed to meet with them. After the dean had proposed to the organizers on May 12 (both in a morning meeting and in an evening telephone call) that the conference be postponed and they refused to agree, the president personally confirmed his and the university's support for academic freedom in general and the conference in particular.

In response to communications from donors and others from off campus who were opposed to the conference, Shoukri diplomatically but firmly defended academic freedom and university autonomy. For example, his response to a conference critic on May 26 defended these principles and also supported the institutional neutrality principle enunciated by Laskin:

> [...] the selection of speakers also needs to comply with the principles of academic freedom, which is a matter for academics to evaluate. My personal view on any speaker is simply not relevant to this process.[7]

The president also issued two public statements on academic freedom and the conference, supportive of the Laskin principle.

I conclude that Dr. Shoukri consistently defended the principle of academic freedom throughout the course of events, as well as the academic freedom of the conference organizers and the academic integrity of their program.

York Board Chairs Cohen (outgoing) and Cantor (incoming)

In mid-April 2009, during a period when opposition to the conference from on and off campus was intensifying, Marshall Cohen had made suggestions to Dr. Shoukri and Dean Monahan in email exchanges about options that might be considered. These included possibly "moving the venue off campus" (which he referred to as "Plan B" in a subsequent email—thus by implication *not* Plan A), as well as seeking clarification from the organizers and from others on campus as to possible reasons for the escalating opposition and how to handle it.

However, nowhere in these exchanges did Cohen attempt to direct the president, or suggest calling in a board committee that could exercise executive power. It is clear from these exchanges that Shoukri was taking a measured view of *all* information and advice he was receiving, and that Cohen respected the president's academic and administrative authority and judgment. Notably, in one of the emails Cohen said, "Freedom of Speech and academic freedom are essential to what we are." My view of these email exchanges is that they are not atypical of the kinds of discussions that may occur regarding a significant controversy, when many ideas and options are discussed but in the end not implemented.

Importantly, both Cohen and his successor, Paul Cantor, joined with Shoukri in issuing the public statement of June 15, 2009, which stated: "The principles of academic freedom must prevail with regard to all activities undertaken under the auspices of the university, including this conference [...]. To do otherwise would undermine the mission of the academy to provide a free and unmediated forum for serious academic discussion."[8]

I conclude that President Shoukri, Vice-President Shapson, Mr. Cohen, Mr. Cantor, Principal Williams, Vice-Principal Rowe, and Dean Flanagan all conducted themselves in the best university traditions to defend academic freedom and university autonomy, in helping to ensure that an appropriate academic event was held as planned and scheduled, notwithstanding the extraordinary opposition to the event.

York Associate Vice-President (Research) Dewitt

Dr. Dewitt was involved at various times in events related to the conference, as a professor with relevant credentials, and as Associate Vice-President Research and Innovation (Social Sciences and Humanities). For instance, he was on several occasions invited by members of the organizing committee to participate as a presenter, and one component of York

University funding support for the conference was provided through his office and on his advice. In a submission to this Inquiry, dated February 11, 2011, he emphasized the "critical distinction" between the two roles. He summarized his involvements as follows:

> I offered advice when asked; brainstormed with the organizers (and with colleagues in the senior administration) when necessary. Neither I nor my colleagues in the Office of the Vice-President Research intervened or inhibited the efforts of the organizers. Ultimately, as is well known and indisputable, the event occurred with the structure, content and the participants determined by the organizers.[9]

It is Dewitt's position that, throughout these events, he was exercising his academic freedom as a professor, or endeavouring to be helpful to the organizers or to administrative colleagues by offering advice in ways that were invariably appropriate.

Dewitt characterized his commitments to fundamental principles in the following terms:

> My career has been founded on a clear commitment to academic excellence, personal integrity, public service, and a fundamental belief in the vital importance of academic freedom in order to ensure that ideas are heard and debated, however difficult that may be for some. [...] My long tenure as YCISS director, my appointment as AVP Research, and in my other roles as previously noted are testimony to my efforts to sustain these commitments.
>
> My activities related to the "Mapping Models" conference were consistent with my clear sense of my professional responsibilities and obligations. There is not a single incident which indicates otherwise. From the outset, I stated to those of the organizing committee with whom I was in contact that a serious intellectual effort to address this profoundly important topic, one with deep intellectual, emotional, and practical interests and divisions, was a worthwhile undertaking.

In regard to almost all of Dewitt's involvements, I agree that he was acting appropriately. However, his involvements in two matters are controversial:

- Certain contents of his email message to the conference organizers on April 15, 2009;

- Certain aspects of his involvement, together with Monahan, in connection with drafts of an op-ed commentary on the conference authored by Gerald Steinberg.

The Email Message of April 15, 2009

On April 15, 2009, Dewitt sent a message to the collective email address of members of the conference organizing committee.[10] This followed a meeting he had with Ryder and Drummond earlier that month, held at their request and during which the three discussed the organizers' concerns about inadequate funding and about difficulties they were encountering in recruiting speakers known to be prominent supporters of the two-state model. His April 15 message was sent "in response to their asking for help and assistance" in that meeting.

Parts of the April 15 message pertained to Dewitt's capacity as a professor with relevant credentials in regard to the conference topic, and parts pertained to his capacity as AVPR. For example, as a professor he declined to accept the invitation to participate in the conference, but he also gave advice (in the form of a "suggestion") on how the organizers might revise the program, yet still meet their obligations to SSHRC. By his own account, Dewitt not only had nominal responsibilities in regard to this conference, in his capacity as AVPR, he had in addition been "asked by VPRI, Stan Shapson, to represent our office in internal discussions about the planned event that might involve VPRI," and he added that Shapson made this request "about the same time as the April meeting with Susan and Bruce," and hence prior to his April 15 email message. He wrote that some speakers were "tarnished by ideology and polemic" and suggested that the organizers' "well-meaning effort [...] is being hijacked." He expressed the view that a "baseline has been crossed" by the program because certain types of questions concerning Israel would be discussed.

I observe that Dewitt was expressing an academic opinion on the program the organizers were well advanced in developing. (At that stage, approximately four dozen speakers had been confirmed.) There is nothing unusual or inappropriate about an academic expressing an opinion, even when strongly worded. However, Dewitt proceeded to offer advice on reorganizing the program, suggesting that they reduce the program so as to include only "about a dozen or so strong contributions by recognized and worthy individuals" and shortening the duration of the event correspondingly. The other three dozen or so already-confirmed speakers could still be "invited to attend in the audience and to participate from that vantage point, but not to present." He further suggested that the organizers explain to all concerned—including speakers who would in effect be disinvited under his proposal—that the program change would be made "due to financial constraints." In other words, he suggested that the organizers should give out a reason unrelated to the "recognition" or "worthiness" of the speakers. Dewitt further suggested to the organizers that if they made such a change to their program, they would nevertheless "be able to fulfil your academic responsibilities to SSHRC."

In summary, Dewitt offered advice to the organizers on reorganizing the program of their conference, yet still fulfil their responsibilities to SSHRC.

I conclude that, at least in this part of his email message, Dewitt was acting in his capacity as AVPR.

The nature of the responsibilities to SSHRC should be recalled. In his April 15 email message, Dewitt acknowledged their award was for a conference grant, not a workshop grant, in SSHRC terminology. Under a conference grant, "keynote speakers may be invited," but all others are to be selected from responses to the required "call for papers," as SSHRC policy stated. All speakers were selected on the basis of their knowledge, experience, and submitted abstracts, and on this basis some speakers need not hold regular university faculty positions, so long as their responses to the call for papers establish appropriate scholarly credentials, in accordance with the SSHRC policy that states that "conferences must [...] be open to all interested and qualified researchers."

Dewitt wrote in his email message that some speakers were "tarnished by ideology and polemic."But ideologies are common in scholarship and, far from necessarily tarnishing it, an ideological perspective can be fundamental to progress in a field (although it can lead in some cases to tendentious, even spurious, work). Simply to label a scholar's approach to her or his work as ideological (or even to establish that it is ideological) does not by itself establish anything about its quality. A similar comment applies to claims that a scholar's work is polemical.

However, in some instances, scholars who espouse competing ideologies or disciplinary perspectives have been known to discount the quality or substance of work by those seen to hold opposing views. Gabriel Piterberg made an observation that is ironical, illuminating, and relevant: "It is well known, of course, that that critical works about Zionism or Israel are "polemical" (or worse), whereas favourable ones are scholarly."[11]

In any case, Dewitt was free to hold and express views about the work of other scholars. The issue here is that, in the April 15 email message, he also gave administrative advice in regard to the organizers' responsibilities to SSHRC while holding a senior university administrative position with responsibilities in regard to SSHRC disciplines—and to this conference in particular.

I conclude that Dr. Dewitt's professorial assessment of quality influenced his suggestion as a senior administrator that the conference be reduced substantially both in numbers of speakers and duration of the event, because he proposed that the organizers confine the list of speakers to the "dozen or so recognized and worthy individuals." The following facts are significant:

- An SSHRC peer-review panel already had made an assessment of quality, rating the conference program highly and awarding a substantial grant.

- The original program of speakers submitted to SSHRC included the names of many potential speakers, and this list included, for example, Ali Abunimah and Uri Davis, who were on one or more lists of undesirable speakers circulated by Israel lobby organizations or other critics.

- There had been no major changes in the program subsequent to the application to SSHRC in autumn 2008, not only through the period to April 15 but through to the event itself in June 2009.

As AVPR, Dewitt had a responsibility to uphold the integrity of the SSHRC process. In his submission to this Inquiry, Dewitt wrote, "At no time did I indicate to any of the organizers that the conference they envisaged was inappropriate [...]." Against this assurance stands what he wrote to the organizers: some speakers were "tarnished by ideology and polemic"; a "baseline has been crossed"; and the organizers' "well-meaning effort [...] is being hijacked." These assertions can reasonably be seen as representing judgments of inappropriateness.

I would observe again that Dewitt, in his role as a professor as opposed to as an administrator, had the same academic freedom as any other professor to his own perspective and to the expression of his views, and also of course the freedom not to participate in the conference. Equally, the conference organizers were free to disagree with his professorial views, as he acknowledged. Had his email message been limited to academic opinions, it would not warrant more than a passing mention in this Report.

Although it may be difficult for administrators to separate their professorial views from their administrative responsibilities, it is often necessary for them to make such a separation in order to protect the academic freedom of colleagues and the academic integrity of their research projects. However difficult this may be, it is not impossible. As noted earlier, President Shoukri is on record as having emphasized the importance of such a separation of roles, and in addition as having upheld the institutional neutrality principle enunciated by Laskin.

Findings in Regard to the Suggestion that the Program be Reduced
First, the suggestion to substantially reduce the size and duration of the conference, if it had been accepted and implemented by the organizers, could reasonably have been seen as a "major change" under NSERC rules, obligating the organizers to inform SSHRC immediately. Therefore, in such event, it might have placed the grant, or at least the amount of it, in jeopardy. In addition, the suggestion, had it been accepted and implemented, could conceivably have been seen as, in effect, transforming a "conference" into a "workshop," thus potentially providing a basis for a complaint to SSHRC, either by critics of the conference or by one or more disinvited speakers. SSHRC policy says that "proposals that submit the incorrect [application] form will be deemed ineligible." In other words, a recipient of a conference grant who then mounts what might possibly be regarded as a workshop instead could, on this basis also, potentially be seen to have made a "major change" in the program.

When Dewitt put forward his "suggestion," he did not alert the organizers to potential adverse consequences. Instead he informed them that if they implemented it they "should be able to fulfil [their] obligations to SSHRC."

I conclude that Dr. Dewitt's suggestion, had it been accepted and implemented by the organizers, could potentially have resulted in difficulties with SSHRC, including the possibility of placing some, or all, of the grant funds in jeopardy. He did not draw potential adverse effects to their attention. Perhaps he did not appreciate the possible adverse consequences of his suggestion. As AVPR he should have understood the possible adverse consequences, and he had a responsibility to do so, especially since Vice-President Shapson had specifically requested that he "represent [their] office" in matters pertaining to the conference. As a result of these facts, I conclude that Dr. Dewitt's suggestion was in this respect inappropriate.

Dewitt's email message included the further suggestion that, while the dozen or so speakers whose invitation to speak should stand because they were "recognized and worthy," everyone involved should be "notified" that the program truncation was for a reason unrelated to "worthiness" or other qualitative measure, namely, "financial constraints." In summary, the AVPR suggested the organizers give out a reason that, on the plain meaning of his own words, would have been significantly inaccurate.

I conclude that in this additional respect his suggestion was inappropriate.

The organizers did not accept his suggestion. On this occasion, as on all others I am aware of, they were polite but firm. As he acknowledged in his submission to the Inquiry, they did not henceforth involve him in discussions on planning for the conference. More significantly, they expressly informed Monahan that they did not wish any further involvement by the AVPR in discussions on planning for the conference.

In his submission, Dewitt wrote, "I categorically reject the suggestion that I said or did anything to undermine their SSHRC grant." However, this statement did not address the precise point raised with him. The advice he communicated to the organizers in his April 15, 2009, email proposed a substantial change in the program that potentially could have adversely affected, or undermined, the status of their grant with SSHRC, had they accepted it, or some substantial variant of it. The fact that they did not accept it somewhat mitigates his inappropriate advice, but Dewitt should have realized his suggestion was inappropriate and should have refrained from making it. The same conclusion applies to the "financial constraints" reason for the program reduction.

Events Pertaining to the Steinberg Op-Ed Drafts, May 11–12 and May 21–22, 2009

Dr. Dewitt sent an email message to Dean Monahan with a draft op-ed article that the author planned to submit to a Canadian newspaper, and also sent it to Hon. Jason Kenney and Hon. Irwin Cotler "in the context of the SSHRC funding issues."

The op-ed author's name was redacted on the copy released to CAUT under Ontario freedom-of-information legislation, but in their submissions of February 11, 2011, both Dewitt and Monahan confirmed that the author was Gerald Steinberg of Bar-Ilan University. In his covering email message to the dean, Dewitt said that the author was "a very well known senior Israeli academic." Dewitt's email did not indicate that the author also was well known as the president of NGO Monitor (or, more precisely, the parts of the email message made available to CAUT by York University did not contain this additional information). It is not known to this Inquiry whether the dean learned of these endeavours of Steinberg from Dewitt or from some other source, or whether the dean already knew about NGO Monitor and its president.

Monahan replied later that day, saying he would be meeting the next day with Ryder and Drummond, and asking whether he could "show them this piece, without indicating how it came to me?" Dewitt responded to the dean's question on the same day, saying, "Patrick, PLEASE DO NOT SHARE THIS. [...] they will suppose it is either from me or from someone else with whom you are connected within a group of individuals interested in undermining them. Let them see it in the newspapers if/when it appears." Early on May 12, prior to his meeting that morning with Ryder and Drummond, the dean replied, "Ok I will not share it, but will use the substantive points as the basis of my discussion."[12] Dewitt's February 2011 submission acknowledged that he was communicating with Monahan as one of his "colleagues in the senior administration," in other words, in his capacity as AVPR.

The university did not release the contents of the May 11, 2009, version of the op-ed to CAUT, and so I have not seen that version. However, I have read copies of three published versions, dated May 21, May 22, and June 9. These versions shared common elements and each may reasonably be regarded as a polemic against the conference. As quoted above, Dewitt commented that the conference organizers would interpret the op-ed, if and when they saw it, as "undermining them." Therefore, it is reasonable to conclude that the May 11 version also was substantially critical of the conference.

In summary, not only would the conference likely be criticized in a newspaper op-ed, but also in a communication to a federal minister and another influential MP known to be strongly supportive of the State of Israel. Yet the AVPR and the dean agreed not to disclose this information to the organizers.

In a letter from CAUT dated December 2, 2010, Dewitt was invited to comment on issues pertaining to his May 11–12, 2009, email exchange with the dean. In his February 2011 submission, he stated: "I asked Patrick to keep Steinberg's identity confidential [...]."In fact, on May 11, 2009, he asked Monahan to keep the entire document confidential, as quoted above.

He also stated:

> I passed on his draft op-ed to Patrick because as the Dean of the sponsoring faculty of a U50 event, he was the key central administration person in this matter. He deserved to be kept informed on matters that could involve his Faculty and the University. [...] I did what was necessary and appropriate to ensure that my colleagues in the senior administration and their colleagues as the conference planners were aware of the fact that there may be an adverse op-ed piece published, thereby allowing them to be in a position to prevent unfair criticism of their work.

However, instead of ensuring that "the conference planners were aware of the fact that there may be an adverse op-ed piece published, thereby allowing them to be in a position to prevent unfair criticism of their work," Dewitt requested of Monahan: "PLEASE DO NOT SHARE THIS," and the dean agreed. Thus, in this instance in May 2009, Dewitt did not do what he himself asserted in February 2011 "was necessary and appropriate." Dewitt could have requested that his colleague disclose the content of the draft op-ed but not the identity of the author, or a summary of the substantive points but not the identity of the author. Instead, he requested that the entire document not be disclosed.

Dewitt's submission did not fully address the difference between his 2009 request to the dean and his 2011 account:

> I asked Patrick to keep Steinberg's identity confidential because there was no obvious purpose served in identifying Steinberg as the author of something only in draft and not yet public and because I did not believe I had the right to share a draft document that had been shared with me on a confidential basis from an academic colleague.

However, he wanted to do more than just keep Steinberg's identity confidential. He asked Monahan not to share the text of the draft op-ed out of concern that it might tend to identify him (Dewitt) as the dean's source.

Perhaps he was concerned that, if he was identified as the dean's source, this might identify Steinberg as the author of the draft op-ed.

Dewitt wrote that, "I did not believe I had the right to share a draft document that had been shared with me on a confidential basis from an academic colleague," yet he shared it with Monahan, who then used "substantive points" from this op-ed in his May 12 meeting with Ryder and Drummond.

Dewitt closed his account of op-ed matters with the assertion: "Knowing the identity of the author of the proposed op-ed piece would not have assisted in this undertaking whatsoever." A full assessment of this assertion would depend on knowing precisely what Dewitt meant by "assisted" and "this undertaking," but he did not elaborate. Notwithstanding this assertion, knowing that the author was Steinberg could have been of assistance to Drummond and Ryder in their May 12 meeting with Monahan, because Steinberg was not only "an academic colleague" of Dewitt, he also was president of NGO Monitor.

Later in May and in early June 2009, Dewitt again served as an intermediary between Steinberg—and also NGO Monitor—and York administrators (either Monahan or Shapson, or both). The first of these occurrences was during May 20–22, and the email exchanges pertained, among other things, to Shoukri's public statement of May 21. The second occurrence was on June 8, after the Harper government's interference with SSHRC.

Findings in Regard to the May 11–12 and May 20–22 Email Exchanges

I conclude that AVPR Dewitt had a responsibility to ensure that, in his own words, "the conference planners were aware of the fact that there may be an adverse op-ed piece published, thereby allowing them to be in a position to prevent unfair criticism of their work." He should have ensured that, at a minimum, the conference organizers were informed of the fact that there might be an adverse op-ed piece published, the gist of the draft op-ed, and the fact that the author would "be sending it to Jason Kenney and Irwin Cotler in the context of the SSHRC funding issues." This information could have been communicated directly to the organizers by Dewitt without disclosing the name of the author. It also could have been communicated to them by Dean Monahan, had Dewitt answered "yes," instead of "please do not share this," when Monahan asked, "Can I show them this piece, without indicating how it came to me?"

I conclude that AVPR Dewitt failed to live up to a responsibility of his office and, therefore, that he acted inappropriately.

Members of the conference organizing committee informed me they first saw versions of the Steinberg op-ed on websites on May 21 and 22. However, they did not learn that the author (or NGO Monitor) would be approaching federal politicians or SSHRC in connection with their grant, nor did they learn of the May 11–12 email exchange between the dean and the AVPR until many months later, after CAUT obtained documents from federal agencies and from York University pursuant to access requests under federal and Ontario legislation, and the information was disclosed to the organizers by CAUT.

In the covering email message for one of the later versions of the op-ed Steinberg sent to Dewitt (on May 22), Steinberg wrote "Draft for comment before blog posting: 22 May 2009." In this version of his op-ed, Steinberg denounced President Shoukri and the conference. In his February 11 submission, Dewitt wrote: "I did not provide any advice to Steinberg on this matter." I accept Dr. Dewitt's statement regarding "advice to Steinberg."

On June 8, 2009, Dewitt forwarded to Shapson a four-page NGO Monitor document, dated June 8, with an email note saying, "Please see the attached document Gerald Steinberg has sent to me. I gather that he has sent this to the SSHRC and to the PMO." It denounced the conference and fifteen of the speakers, with a paragraph devoted to each. Among them were: Ali Abunimah, Jeff Halper, Omar Barghouti, Uri Davis, and George Bisharat (who was one of the three keynote speakers).

Finally on matters pertaining to the involvement of Dewitt, in a letter to me in mid-February 2011, President Shoukri wrote:

> Dean Monahan and Associate Vice-President Dewitt, as members of the university's senior administration were working in a manner consistent with protecting academic freedom and the university's role as an institution of free inquiry. I hope that your deliberations will be consistent with this understanding of their role.[13]

I appreciate the president's gesture, but he provided no examples or documentation in support of his assertion concerning Dewitt and protection of academic freedom in this matter. As concluded above, in two matters Dewitt conducted his office of AVPR inappropriately: by giving certain advice (his April 15 "suggestion") to the organizers on reducing the size

and duration of their conference and on fulfilling their responsibilities to
SSHRC; and by requesting that Monahan not disclose to the organizers
any information about the Steinberg draft op ed. In the end, the confer
ence proceeded as planned by the organizers and the SSHRC grant was
maintained, but these favourable outcomes depended on the combined
influence of a number of factors, among them the determination of the
organizers, Shoukri's support, and CAUT's efforts in making the government interference with SSHRC into a public issue.

Academics, whether or not they also are administrators, may have different conceptions of academic freedom. Shoukri and Dewitt may have had
different conceptions of academic freedom, at least in regard to discussions
on some topics pertaining to Israel.

York Dean Monahan

Dean Monahan was involved in a number of developments related to the
conference and the controversy around it. He assisted the organizing committee in important ways, and on several occasions he helped to defend the
principle of academic freedom along with the conference and the university from internal and external campaigns against the event. For example,
Monahan

- reviewed, signed, and submitted the organizers' application to the
  U50 committee for funding (April 2008)

- defended the conference in email replies to at least two conference
  critics (April 11 and May 27, 2009)

- assisted the president in drafting public statements on academic
  freedom (May 21 and June 15, 2009)

- supported, with Vice-President Shapson, the confirmation Professor
  Ryder sent to SSHRC that there had been no major changes in the
  conference program (June 11, 2009)

- gave the opening remarks at the conference, welcoming participants
  on behalf of the university and Osgoode Hall and supporting the
  work of the organizers (June 22).

When Monahan provided assistance, members of the organizing committee acknowledged it and thanked him. For, example, on April 23, 2009,
Ryder wrote:

> I can't tell you how delighted and relieved we were to hear from
> Cindy Blettcher at U50 that Glendon has been confirmed as
> the location of the conference. We are enormously grateful to
> you for your continued support of the conference and for your
> willingness to work with us on making it a scholarly event of
> which we can all be proud.

On June 15, 2009, Drummond renewed the organizers' invitation to the
dean to open the conference and welcome participants, writing:

> It really would be hugely meaningful for us to have you present
> your remarks in person. And I think it would be significant
> to have someone of your stature provide a welcome to the
> conference, particularly in light of recent controversies.

I conclude that such facts demonstrate that helpful and constructive
involvement by Dean Monahan contributed substantially to the successful
mounting of the conference.

Nevertheless, there has been controversy regarding some other aspects
of the dean's involvement. Notably, there are questions as to whether in
several significant instances the dean exerted inappropriate pressures on
members of the organizing committee subsequent to expressions of concern about the event made to him or other members of the York University
administration. These instances involved statements or actions that were
perceived by members of the organizing committee as inappropriate, and
as having the potential to infringe their academic freedom and the academic integrity of their research project (the conference).

In his brief to this Inquiry, dated February 11, 2011, Monahan denied
that any of his statements or actions were inappropriate: "I categorically
reject the suggestion that any of my discussions with the organizers were
inappropriate, or that there was in any way an attempt to undermine their
academic freedom."[14]

He also stated:

> Given the collegial discussions that led to what I regarded

as a successful academic event, as well as my repeated and unequivocal support for my colleagues, I was stunned after the fact to learn that efforts were underway to develop an alternative narrative of events, a narrative that bore little relation to my own understanding. I was and am dismayed at the harm that this alternative narrative causes to the law school, to collegial relationships, and to York University itself, which is already the object of unfair criticism for the manner in which issues relating to the Middle East are discussed on campus.

In addition, he wrote that:

This Conference was an extremely challenging event for everyone involved, including the conference organizers as well as the university administration. I attempted to work collegially and constructively with the organizers to respond to concerns that arose during the course of conference planning. The organizers were free at all times to accept or reject any of the suggestions that were made. In fact the organizers accepted some suggestions but not others, and held the conference with a program they determined. While we did not always agree, the discussions throughout were collegial, respectful and appropriate.

The "alternative narrative" appeared initially in the form of Drummond's draft "Field Notes" article on the conference and the attendant controversy, copies of which she gave to Monahan and Shoukri in July 2009, not long after the conference. Subsequently, it emerged that not only other members of the organizing committee but a number of other faculty members in Osgoode Hall and the Executive Committee of the Osgoode Hall Faculty Association (OHFA) shared some or all of Drummond's concerns, as detailed in submissions and testimony to this Inquiry, or in other documents or statements referenced in this report.

For example, speaking in a panel discussion at the University of Toronto on January 30, 2010, Ryder said that there had been "near misses" in terms of potential academic freedom infringements, citing events in which Monahan had (in Ryder's view) exerted pressure on the organizers. In a letter dated April 26, 2010, to officers of the university senate, the OHFA executive committee wrote that "senior administrators were inappropriately pressuring conference organizers to make significant changes to the conference programme and speakers, to submit to internal oversight and review, or to make other modifications of the event or its planning."

These concerns contrast with the experiences of Professor Aiken. At no time did she feel any pressure was being exerted on her by or through the administration of her university.

Before proceeding to an analysis, I would note that Monahan was not the only person to have expressed considerable surprise on learning of particular developments related to the conference. For example, on April 14, 2009, Ryder also used the word "stunned" to express his degree of surprise on hearing that the conference venue had been moved from the Glendon campus to the Keele campus.[15] Members of the committee informed me they were even more surprised and concerned when, in a meeting on April 17, 2009, Monahan gave them to understand that the conference might be deprived of *any* York campus venue and that this was the wish of the board of governors.

Involvements by the Dean That Have Been Subjects of Controversy. The particular instances at issue occurred in meetings with Ryder and Drummond on October 9, 2008, on April 17 and 23, and May 12, 2009, and in a telephone call to Ryder late on May 12, or pertain to contents of certain email messages between April 15 and May 12, 2009 (inclusive) sent by the dean.

On these occasions, Monahan made certain suggestions, proposals, or requests pertaining to academic matters, or to administrative matters, or both. Specifically, the dean

- requested a change in the composition of the conference organizing committee (October 2008)

- proposed that additional speakers be added (April 2009)

- gave organizers to understand that if they did not agree to changes in the program along lines he proposed, then the board of governors might deprive them of any York University venue for the conference (April 2009)

- made adverse comments about the appropriateness of some confirmed speakers (April and May 2009)

- made adverse comments about the credentials of the organizers (May 2009)

- proposed that the conference be postponed (May 2009)

- proposed that the postponement period be used, among other things, for efforts to reach an accommodation on the conference program with two critics of the existing program (May 2009)

- did not disclose to the organizers that criticism of the conference in the media and representations to the government against their SSHRC grant—the Steinberg op-ed—were impending (May 2009).

Accounts of the Dean's Involvements. I have reviewed six successive accounts of various aspects of the dean's involvement:

1. A response to a draft of Drummond's "Field Notes" article, undated and unsigned but provided to her by Monahan in a meeting with Shoukri on July 13, 2009 (six pages)

2. York University's submission to this Inquiry, dated October 16, 2009, and provided by University Secretary and General Counsel Harriet I. Lewis (six pages, plus copies of the president's public statements of May and June 2009)

3. Professor Monahan's letter to the Executive Committee of OHFA, dated June 30, 2010 (three pages)

4. Professor Monahan's submission to this Inquiry dated February 11, 2011, and provided through his legal counsel Ms. Linda Rothstein (an eighteen-page brief, plus fifty-three pages of supporting documents)

5. Professor Monahan's supplementary submission to this Inquiry, dated July 15, 2011, and sent directly by him (a one-page covering letter plus a thirty-four-page document titled "The Mapping Models Conference," dated July 2011)

6. Professor Monahan's second supplementary submission to this Inquiry, dated July 22, 2011, and sent directly by him (a two-page covering letter plus a thirteen-page decision, dated July 13, 2011, by an adjudicator appointed under the *Freedom of*

Information and Protection of Privacy Act of Ontario, pertaining to
a request for "copies of all submissions made to the Iacobucci
Review" submitted by "an [un-named] individual").

Each of the first three did not address some of the issues, and ques-
tions remained in regard to certain matters Monahan did address in them.
For example, in response to Monahan's letter to OHFA (June 30, 2010),
Drummond wrote to Monahan on July 5, 2010:

> I very much disagree with your assessment that the conference
> organizing committee welcomed your suggestions and was
> solicitous of your advice. While we tried assiduously to be polite
> and collegial and deferential to the office, your interventions were
> felt to be heavy-handed by more than one of us on the organizing
> committee, impelled by your own set of urgencies, not ours.

Both the outgoing and incoming OHFA executive committees also replied
to Monahan's letter of June 30, 2010, expressing dissatisfaction with his
account of events.

The fourth and fifth accounts are more comprehensive, both in detail
and range of matters addressed. The fourth was received in response to a
series of matters raised with Professor Monahan by CAUT on behalf of this
Inquiry. The fifth was prepared in response to a "Factual Summary" document Professor Monahan had received from Professor Drummond in June
2011 in connection with her book manuscript on the conference that was
being considered by the University of British Columbia Press. There is substantial similarity between the two accounts in regard to the matters raised by
CAUT, and so the following discussion cites the fourth account more extensively. However, in regard to certain events, there are differences in wording
between the two accounts. The differences are noted in the discussion.

The sixth account in effect invited me to consider the July 13 decision by
the adjudicator and implications it may have for "the independence of Mr.
Iacobucci." In his July 22 covering letter Professor Monahan also mentioned
material in his previous submissions to this Inquiry pertaining to "meetings which took place involving Professor Ryder, Professor Drummond and
myself."[16]

Elements of Professor Monahan's Position
Reasons for the Dean's Involvements. Monahan's February 2011 account

of his involvements in the particular events discussed here is based on information and arguments that may be grouped into three overlapping categories: academic, administrative, and collegial

In the academic category, his position was that the committee membership lacked balance and the program of speakers selected by the organizers lacked balance.

In the administrative category, Monahan's position was that:

- the conference organizers had, in some sense, entered into a quasi-contract (implicit or explicit) with the corporate community York University, under which they were obligated to deliver not only an international conference as outlined in their U50 application, but one that "would be a high quality academic event" and one which would have a "balanced" program;

- compliance with the quasi-contract as to quality and balance for U50 events would appropriately be assessed by the dean of the relevant academic unit, and so, as Dean of Osgoode Hall Law School, he had a "responsibility to attempt to address questions or difficulties that arose in relation to the event";

- "I was at all times acting in accordance with the instructions of the President."

In the collegial category, his position was that:

- "While we did not always agree, the discussions [with conference organizers] throughout were collegial, respectful and appropriate."

- "It was at all times up to the organizers, and not the administration, to determine the program and the focus of the conference. This was always clearly understood by everyone involved, and is precisely what occurred."

- The "alternative narrative" put forward by the conference organizers and their supporters in Osgoode Hall has resulted in "harm" being "cause[d] to the law school, to collegial relationships, and to York University itself."

Conference Success. Another element of Monahan's position is that the event, which he said he supported from the outset, and assisted substantially at various times and in various ways, was a "success." He wrote: "This conference was a success and demonstrated once again that York University is committed to an open dialogue on difficult issues," and that it was "a successful academic event."

He confirmed his significant role in securing key support for the event:

> After meeting with Bruce and Susan in early 2008, and reviewing their proposal, I suggested it would be ideal as a York 50th event. I signed and submitted the application for the Mapping Models conference on April 11, 2008.

He summarized his overall involvement as follows: "I privately and publicly supported the organizers throughout and contributed to the success of the conference." He also stated that "the conference proceeded in the manner determined by the organizers, with my and the university's support, despite many pressures to the contrary."

With regard to administrative matters, Monahan relied on generally understood responsibilities of deans, two specific documents pertaining to U50 funding support for the conference that he had signed, and his assertion concerning instructions of the president in matters pertaining to the conference.

Responsibilities of Deans. In Canadian universities, it is generally accepted that one of the responsibilities of deans is to assist members of their faculties in efforts to obtain resources for research. Another is to assist faculty members in defending their academic freedom and the integrity of their research programs. Reciprocally, it is generally accepted that, as Monahan noted, a dean has the "responsibility to attempt to address questions or difficulties," if and when they arise, in relation to research activities, "on behalf of and at the direction of the President and the administration of the university."

The documentary record establishes that, in a number of ways and in a variety of circumstances, Monahan fulfilled these responsibilities in connection with the York/Queen's conference. At issue is whether, in the course of carrying out what he considered to be his responsibilities, he conducted his office in ways that were at *all times* appropriate. Also at issue is whether certain documents from 2008 and 2009 on which he relied in his February 2011 brief actually support his position.

Balance. There is no general requirement in Canadian universities that the membership of a research team be balanced or that a research project be balanced in a political or ideological sense, nor is there any such requirement in SSHRC regulations. In some cases there may be balance, but often there is not. However, it is possible that a team could give an undertaking to ensure such balance in its work. This would appear to be the contention of Monahan in documentation from October 2008 and in April and May 2009, and in his submission to this Inquiry in February 2011.

Regarding the contention that the organizing committee composition lacked balance, or did not have "a sufficiently broad range of perspectives that would be required if they were to achieve the ambitious goals that had been set for the event," Monahan provided no supporting documentation. Regarding the contention that the program lacked balance, he relied on two documents he provided. However, he neither provided nor discussed a third, relevant document: the organizers' application to SSHRC.

The Quasi-Contractual Element of Professor Monahan's Position. The two documents relied on by Monahan were the organizers' application to the U50 committee, signed by the dean (U50 Application), and a U50 Memorandum of Understanding (MoU), signed by the dean and Ryder.

The U50 MoU. There was no reference to the Memorandum of Understanding (MoU) in either the first or the third account of the dean's involvements—the account provided to Drummond in a meeting on July 13, 2009, and the account provided in a letter to the OHFA executive committee on June 30, 2010. However, the MoU was referred to and relied on in the second and fourth accounts, and a copy was provided to this Inquiry on February 11, 2011, as Schedule 2 in Monahan's submission.

The second in the series of accounts of the dean's involvements was York University's submission to this Inquiry, dated October 16, 2009. It stated:

> Both the President and the Dean were concerned this conference would not meet the standards expected of a York 50th event, as reflected in the Memorandum of Understanding with the organizers.

The fourth account, Monahan's brief of February 2011, stated:

> Because this particular conference was approved and sponsored by the University as one of the select number of York 50th events, the University had an interest in its conduct and success. It was for

this reason that all York 50th events had to be approved by the Dean of the relevant faculty, and that all event organizers were to report regularly to their Dean on their plans and progress. These commitments were understood and accepted, as set out in a July 18, 2008 Memorandum of Understanding signed by Bruce and me, setting out administrative arrangements, planning time-lines and reporting expectations (See Schedule 2, attached).

However, from a review of the MoU, it is clear that this was a generic document for U50 events, concerned with administrative matters to help ensure timely and successful mounting of each event. It was not concerned with the academic standards or program content of the particular event.

Therefore, I conclude that the MoU provides no effective support for Professor Monahan's position.

For purposes of general interest and completeness, I note that, as to the reporting and other procedural or administrative requirements that were the actual content of the MoU, the university's own inquiry—the Iacobucci Review—appears to have confirmed that the organizers of the York/ Queen's conference (Mapping Conference) had met these:

> The Conference participated fully in this [U50] oversight
> process—Professor D'Agostino, the Osgoode faculty
> representative, came to each [U50] Campus Committee meeting
> with a report that included details on the progress of the
> Mapping Conference. [...] The organizers continued to participate
> in other meetings organized by the U50 Office, including a series
> of media relations and security meetings, and an event planning
> session.[17]

The U50 Application. In his February 2011 brief, Monahan emphasized a specific reason for his particular interest and involvements with respect to the conference, namely, a need for balance. He also had invoked this criterion in discussions with, or email messages to, the organizers in autumn 2008 and spring 2009. In his brief he relied especially on the U50 Application and a discussion pertaining to it in spring 2008, contending in effect that these amounted to a quasi-contractual requirement. The discussion occurred in a meeting on March 26, 2008, when Ryder and Drummond met with Monahan to explain their conference proposal and request his support in obtaining funds for it. The dean proposed that they apply to the U50 Committee and indicated he would support their application. The organizers subsequently submitted a detailed proposal to the dean, the U50 Application, which is dated April 11, 2008, when the dean signed it.[18]

In his brief Monahan wrote:

> At all times the organizers and I were aware that issues relating to statehood in the Middle East are extraordinarily complex and arouse strong emotion from those involved. Thus any effort to promote genuine academic debate and dialogue needs to be sensitive to the range of competing academic perspectives on these matters. This need for 'balance', in the sense of ensuring a wide range of scholarly perspectives on the issues, had been accepted and understood from the very beginning of the discussions with the conference organizers in spring 2008. This was set out in the original York 50 Application, and was repeatedly affirmed by the conference organizers themselves [...]
>
> [T]he need for balance in the program and speakers [...] was the accepted basis upon which the conference had been accepted as a York 50 Event, and guided the efforts of the conference organizers throughout the process.

There is a fundamental weakness in this central element of his position. The U50 Application did not speak of balance. Also, in the sense Monahan used the term in autumn 2009 and thereafter, it did not imply balance.

Before discussing this important detail, a secondary difficulty should be noted, namely, that the importance the dean attributed to his approval of the U50 application varied with the time and the audience. The passages quoted above from his brief suggest greater significance should be attributed to his approval than in the account he gave in an email reply to conference critics on April 24, 2009:

> I supported their application, based on the vision statement. And really I had no other realistic choice but to support them. I supported every application that was put forward by my faculty members. (There were 7 applications and all of them got money from the York 50th fund.) So that is what "sponsorship" consists of.[19]

Monahan appended a copy of the U50 Application prepared by Ryder, Drummond, Aiken, and Masri—the one signed by himself as dean on April 11, 2008—as Schedule 1 to his submission. Its twenty-one pages include a vision statement; a tentative conference title; a draft conference program, setting out in some detail main subtopics and titles for possible talks or panel discussions under these headings; biographical summaries on each of the seven members of the conference's International Advisory Board who had agreed by that date to serve (called an advisory committee at the time); a proposed budget; and a list of possible funding sources in addition to the U50 fund—those already committed, along with those to be approached. In particular, the U50 Application stated explicitly that an application would be made to SSHRC for a "conference grant." The U50 Application was not balanced between the one-state and two-state models. As indicated by the proposed conference title—"Imagining a Bi-national Constitutional Democracy in Israel/Palestine"—far from being balanced, the program approved by Monahan was focused on the one-state model.

Although the proposed program included some discussion of the two-state model, that this was a secondary component is clear from the draft included as part of the U50 Application. Only part of a single hour-and-a-half session in the planned two-and-a-half-day conference would include a discussion of the two-state model. Although the "current prospects" of the two-state model would "be examined in detail" in this session, they would be discussed from the perspective that "the prospects of a lasting peace under the two-state model appear increasingly remote, if not impossible." Moreover, the two proposed components in this single session dealing with the two-state model were titled "The Dusk of the Two State Solution," and "Finding the Pulse of the Two State Solution."

Thus instead of "'balance', in the sense of ensuring a wide range of scholarly perspectives on the issues," as Monahan contended in his brief, the U50 Application focused on a single issue, the one-state, bi-national model in which all citizens would enjoy equal rights: "equal rights to dignity and fundamental justice for Jews and Palestinians [in the combined territory Israel/Palestine]."

A revised program giving approximately equal prominence to the two models of statehood was developed during the period from April to September 2008 by the organizers as a result of discussions with their International Advisory Board (Professor Kretzmer, Mr. Abunimah, and others), without involvement by the dean. This was reflected in the new title, "Israel/Palestine: One State or Two," and in the vision statement published with the call for papers in September 2008.

In his July 2011 supplementary submission (at page 7) Monahan appeared to suggest that, notwithstanding the actual content of the U50 Application he signed in April 2008, he anticipated at that time the conference program would be balanced in the sense he used the term in autumn 2008 and spring 2009. However, as noted above, the conference proposal outlined in the U50 Application was clearly focused on the one-state binational model.

In his February 2011 submission, Monahan relied also on the discussion he had in a meeting with the organizers in March 2008, which was held before he signed the detailed written proposal. Drummond's recollection is that the dean clearly understood the nature of the proposal as it was explained to him in that meeting:

> The only comment that he [Dean Monahan] made about the substance of our conference was that he, personally, thought that the only realistic option in the Middle East was a two state solution; but that if we thought that it was worth exploring the one state model, then he would support that in our U50 application. There was absolutely no discussion at this juncture about "genuine forums for scholarly dialogue and discussion" nor any stress or requirement that the conference have "internationally recognized scholars or public figures." There was certainly no discussion about the conference representing a "balanced range of opinion on the issues to be discussed."[20]

Monahan relied, in addition, on certain statements concerning balance made to him by the organizers. The statements he quoted were made in a memo sent to him much later, on October 10, 2008, after the draft program had been revised so as to give comparable prominence to both the one- and two-state models, and after the call for papers was published on this revised basis. The memo was sent to the dean following the meeting he had with the organizers on October 9, in which he suggested that the organizing committee lacked balance and requested the committee membership be adjusted.

Although in his submission Monahan included the full October memo from the organizers as Schedule 11, in his accompanying brief he quoted only phrases from sentences in the memo. The complete passage in the organizers' memo said:

> We should reiterate that we have long been aware of the need
> for balance with respect to perspectives and politics in the
> conference planning process and have been working extremely
> hard in pulling together a high profile advisory committee [the
> International Advisory Board] that we think is best place to meet
> the goal of balance. As we indicated, the peer review process for
> selecting speakers for the conference will be governed by input
> from this committee [their advisory board].[21]

Thus, in October 2008, the organizers wrote of "balance" in "the conference planning process" with respect to a "goal of balance" for the revised
conference topic and title published in September 2008—not the conference topic approved by the dean in April 2008. They also stated—appropriately—that "balance" was reflected in the composition of the advisory
board of experts who would be assisting them in determining appropriate
"balance." From the text of this memo and the context of communications
between the dean and the organizers during October 9–10, the clear implication of this passage in the memo is that "balance" should be determined
by the organizers and their expert advisory board, not by Dean Monahan.
It remained the case throughout the period from October 2008 to June
2009, when the event was held, that the selection of speakers was made
by the organizers with advice from their advisory board, notwithstanding
the dean's involvements. Indeed Monahan himself acknowledged in his
brief that "the conference proceeded in the manner determined by the
organizers."

The Application to SSHRC. The third document approved by York
University's administration and relevant to this discussion is Ryder's successful application to SSHRC on behalf of the organizing committee.[22] In
his brief, Monahan did not address the detailed conference proposal set
out in this application. He said only that "in early June [2009] I worked
with the Office of Vice President Research and Innovation to ensure that
the conference funding from SSHRC was confirmed (with the SSHRC
specifically referencing my support as being significant in their decision to
confirm the funding)."

Findings in Regard to Balance and Related Matters
On the basis of the foregoing discussion, I conclude that the U50
Application provides no effective support for Professor Monahan's pos-
ition. In particular, I conclude that the U50 Application does not provide

an effective basis for his assertions in regard to the purported need for balance in either the organizing committee membership, or the program of conference speakers. As discussed earlier, a similar conclusion applies to the U50 MoU.

As noted above, Monahan also relied on the discussion about the conference that he and the organizers had in a meeting in spring 2008. However, the only such meeting of the dean and Ryder and Drummond was held on March 26, 2008, and hence before April 11, 2008, when the dean signed and submitted the application to the U50 Committee.

I conclude that the discussion about U50 Application also does not provide effective support for Professor Monahan's position.

In regard to the organizers' statements about program balance made in October 2008 or later, these were related to the draft program of September 2008, instead of the draft program of April 2008 signed by the dean. Moreover, the dean and the organizers had different conceptions of balance and of which persons should appropriately determine the need for balance, if any, in regard to an academic research project.

I conclude that the organizers' October 2008 statements about program balance do not provide effective support for Professor Monahan's position.

Finally, on the matter of purported quasi-contractual obligations, there was no requirement for balance associated with the peer-reviewed SSHRC grant. Thus I conclude that the application to SSHRC for a conference grant provides no effective support for Professor Monahan's position.

The Administrative Neutrality Principle. Deans may appropriately raise questions with researchers or research teams in response to concerns brought to their attention. However, academic content decisions regarding a research project are properly those of the researchers, not an administrator.

An exception would be a case in which the researcher(s) had voluntarily undertaken to accept academic assessment of the project and academic involvement in it by an administrator. In the case of the York/Queen's conference, there was no such undertaking. Yet Monahan made academic assessments regarding "balance" for both the research team (in October 2008) and the program of speakers (in April and May 2009). Moreover, he involved himself academically on the basis of this assessment.

I conclude that Dean Monahan did not respect the principle of administrative neutrality in specific instances as discussed here.

I note that the dean acknowledged (in email messages and in discussions with Ryder and Drummond cited in Chapter 5) that he lacked expertise in the specific topics of the conference. Thus he had no direct academic basis on which to come to his conclusions as to need for balance in either the committee or the conference program. Even if he had such expertise, he was not a member of the specific research team, and so his comments about the academic content of the project would still be contrary to the principle of administrative neutrality.

The Defence of Acting on Instructions. The other administrative element of Monahan's position is his statement that he was "at all times acting in accordance with the instructions of the President." In my view, if the president had instructed the dean to take an inappropriate action and he carried out such an instruction, the dean would still bear responsibility.

Therefore, I conclude that this is not an effective defence against a finding of inappropriateness, although potentially it could be viewed as a mitigating factor. However, I have seen no evidence whatever that the president gave the dean any such instruction.

In summary, the administrative elements of Monahan's position do not provide effective support for the statements or actions by him that are matters of contention.

The Collegial Element. Monahan stated that his discussions with the organizers "throughout were collegial." In addition, it "was always clearly understood by everyone involved" that "it was at all times up to the organizers [...] to determine the program." However, the "alternative narrative" of events, put forward by the organizers and their supporters in Osgoode Hall, has resulted in "harm" to "collegial relationships." The problems with this defence are that there is great variability in university communities as to what constitutes collegial discourse, and that the organizers felt in certain instances the discussions with the dean were not collegial in that he had administrative authority as dean and they had no comparable administrative authority or counterweight (such as a comprehensive grievance procedure). As to the latter point, some specific comments by Drummond, reflecting concerns of other organizing committee members, are cited below.

I conclude that, regardless of whether these discussions were collegial, or which persons may be seen to have caused harm to collegial relationships, this has no effective bearing on questions of whether certain statements or actions by the dean were appropriate or inappropriate.

My overall conclusion is that Dean Monahan did not have a significant, appropriate academic, administrative, or collegial reason for the views he developed to the effect that the committee lacked balance in its composition or that the conference program lacked balance.

The Dean's Request for an Adjustment to the Committee

Controversy over the conference began to emerge not long after the call for papers was issued in September 2008, although the intensity did not begin to escalate rapidly until the spring of 2009. It was in this context that Monahan met with Ryder and Drummond on October 9, at his request. At the meeting, the dean requested that Masri be removed from the committee. Ryder and Drummond resisted, and the dean proposed as an alternative that someone like Morgan be added to the committee so as to balance Masri's presence. In an email message on October 10, the dean informed Ryder and Drummond he would be discussing his request with the president.

In his July 2011 supplementary submission, Monahan explained the basis for his request:

> I was surprised to learn at this time that the organizing
> committee included Mazen Masri, a graduate student who had
> played a prominent and public role in various organizations that
> are politically active in relation to the politics of the Middle East.
> It was evident to me that his participation would likely lead to
> criticism of the event on the grounds that it was a political rather
> than an academic exercise; this might jeopardize the willingness
> of some scholars to participate, and could undermine the goal
> of creating a robust scholarly dialogue at the conference. I raised
> these concerns with Bruce and Susan in what I intended to be
> a collegial manner, in a good faith attempt to assist them in
> planning a successful event that would achieve the ambitious
> goals they had established.[23]

He did not offer an explanation as to the implications of this reasoning in regard to his own proposal to the organizers in April 2009 that one or both of two serving politicians, MPs Bob Rae and Irwin Cotler, be invited as plenary or keynote speakers for the conference.

Ryder and Drummond sent a three-page memo to the dean on October 10, outlining progress in planning for the conference and giving specific reasons why they opposed any adjustment to the committee and, in particular, why Masri should remain a member. They considered the dean's request academically inappropriate. Subsequently, the dean did not insist on changes and the committee membership remained the same. The organizers' perspective on these events was expressed in Drummond's "Field Notes" paper, where she also explained why, at the time, they did not strongly protest the dean's request for an adjustment to the committee membership:

> As any serious scholars would be, we were gravely concerned about a Dean's suggestion that we remove one of the conference Organizing Committee members and were not prepared to entertain it. However, beyond the ordinary deference that is shown to Deans and the ordinary dependencies (such as merit pay and promotion) implicit in the background of such requests, we were well aware that we were also dependent on the Dean for ongoing support of the conference in tangible ways such as research assistance and institutional sponsorship. [...]

> Despite such worrying pressures, we were determined not to remove an excellently qualified doctoral student from our committee nor to include a further member to the committee to meet what the Dean perceived as a lack of "balance", as if an academic conference were a news broadcast. After the meeting, the Organizing Committee regrouped and assessed what accommodations we could make without violating the academic integrity of the whole project.[24]

The committee membership was the same in October 2008 as it was in April 2008 when Monahan approved the U50 Application, a document on which he substantially relied in his February 2011 brief. (The document named Ryder, Drummond, and Aiken, and said that the fourth member was an Osgoode Hall doctoral student, although it did not give Masri's name explicitly.) Removing the one Palestinian Israeli lawyer on the committee could reasonably have been seen as narrowing, not broadening, the range of perspectives.

Findings in Regard to the Request for an Adjustment to the Committee

I conclude that there was no appropriate academic or administrative reason for the dean's request for an adjustment to the organizing committee membership. In addition, and notwithstanding the fact that the dean ultimately did not insist on removal of Mr. Masri, I conclude also that this specific aspect of the dean's request was inappropriate for the following reasons.

First, to propose removing the one Palestinian Israeli member was inappropriate. Second, Masri had been working with Ryder, Drummond, and Aiken on the conference topics for a year (starting with their reading/ study group in the autumn of 2007), the topics were related to his doctoral research, being on the committee was a significant opportunity for him in terms of career development, and SSHRC encourages involvement of graduate students in faculty research endeavours (including conferences it funds). Third, the dean's request potentially infringed the academic freedom of Ryder and Drummond to form a research team they considered academically appropriate.

The Dean's Academic Assessment: Origins and Consequences

In mid-April 2009, by which time approximately four dozen speakers had been confirmed, Monahan made an adverse academic assessment about the academic content of the conference program, specifically in regard to some of the confirmed speakers and the abstracts of their talks. He initially communicated his concerns in two email messages to Ryder and Drummond on April 15, saying, among other things, that:

> If you look at your website and review the abstracts I have to tell you that this comes across as not particularly balanced. [...] This is shaping up as a major event that could spin very badly out of control.[25]

Only a few days earlier (April 11), Monahan had defended the event to a conference critic, writing that it was "a serious academic conference" and adding that the SSHRC grant provided "evidence of the scholarly character of the conference."[26] The dean's reliance on the SSHRC grant for this purpose was especially appropriate because he lacked expertise in the conference topic. Notwithstanding this lack, he made the adverse assessment he communicated on April 15. He appeared also to have made a political assessment to the effect that the organizers, through faulty academic judgment, had created a political problem for the university. Significant consequences flowed from these assessments, both immediately and later.

Among the consequences were that during the next several days, the dean directly involved himself in academic matters pertaining to the conference program, and communicated to the president and the board chair that there was "damage" to be "mitigated" and that "rebalancing" of the program was needed to "ensure that the conference is a legitimate academic conference."[27] During this period also, he considered that he had reached what he termed "an agreement" with the organizers to the effect that their consideration of program changes he proposed was reciprocated by the re-securing of the Glendon College venue.

As concluded earlier, there was no appropriate academic or administrative basis for such involvements by the dean. Moreover, subsequent actions or statements by the dean served to undermine his contentions in the spring of 2009, and in his submissions of February 2011, that these and certain other interventions were warranted and appropriate. In this connection I note the following:

- On June 11, 2009, Monahan (along with Shapson) supported Ryder's report to SSHRC that there had been no major changes to the conference program subsequent to the application to SSHRC in autumn 2009.

- The list of speakers for the actual conference program of June 22–24, 2009, had only minor changes from the list in mid-April 2009 when the dean had concluded the program lacked balance and there was damage to be mitigated.

- In his February 2011 submission, Monahan wrote that "the conference proceeded in the manner determined by the organizers," notwithstanding his adverse academic assessment in mid-April 2009 and his subsequent proposals regarding the academic content of the program.

- In his February 2011 submission, he stated that "this conference was a success," and that it was "a successful academic event."

- In his July 15 submission, he again stated that the conference was "a success."

In other words, Monahan appeared to acknowledge in February and July 2011 that his assessment in April 2009 that the conference was not a "legitimate" academic event was not well founded academically.

I turn next to possible academic origins of the dean's adverse assessment of April 15, 2009. In his February 2011 submission, the only academic (other than Ryder and Drummond) with whom Monahan acknowledged discussing the conference in mid-April was Irving Abella. He said he had known Abella "for many years as a colleague," and that he had spoken with him at the request of the president, with whom Abella had been in communication about the conference. This was confirmed by university email records from the time. In early April Dewitt had informed the organizers that Abella "was leading the campaign against the conference."[28]

It was appropriate for the dean to have spoken with Abella. Also, Abella had the academic freedom to hold the views on the conference that he held, and to express them to the president, the dean, or anyone. He was not serving in a relevant university administrative office at the time, and so was entirely free *not* to be neutral in this matter. The issue is not Abella's position on the conference; the issue is the involvement of a dean in academic aspects of a research project.

In his July 2011 submission, Monahan also acknowledged discussing the conference with David Dewitt, and this was confirmed by contemporaneous email records. This too was appropriate. Dewitt was the senior administrator with responsibilities for matters in the SSHRC disciplines, and as a professor he had relevant expertise. By mid-April both Abella and Dewitt were strongly critical of aspects of the conference program, but an important distinction was that the latter was a representative of the York University corporate community. In other words, Monahan and Dewitt had responsibilities to uphold and protect the academic freedom of the organizers.

On April 14, there was an email exchange between Abella and Monahan. On the following day, the dean sent an email message to Abella, saying, "Irv I have looked at the website in more detail and understand the concerns."[29] Thus, on April 15 the dean considered that a problem had been identified, following one or more communications he had with Abella and his own subsequent, non-expert assessment of material posted on the conference website.

The Approach Adopted. The approach Monahan adopted to solve the perceived problem or, in his words, to "mitigate the damage," included trying to add additional academic speakers to the program who would be strong supporters of the two-state model, or strong supporters of Israel, in order to provide "balance" he considered was needed. He asked Abella, and later also Dewitt, to provide him with advice on the conference program. Of these two professors, he wrote in emails to Shoukri: "This [conference topic] is not an area of [Abella's] expertise," and "The topic of the conference is not really in [Dewitt's] area."[30]

It was open to Monahan—who by April 15, 2009, doubted the

judgment of the members of the organizing committee in selecting some of the speakers they had selected—to have consulted with one or more members of their International Advisory Board. Its members had been asked to serve because, to a greater or lesser extent, the conference topic *was* in their area of expertise. The dean knew, or should have known, that there was an advisory board, because the U50 application he reviewed and signed in April 2008 included biographical summaries of the members who had agreed by that date to serve. Ryder and Drummond had explicitly reminded him of this board in their memo on October 10, 2008. In addition, it would have been prudent for him to have so consulted, especially in light of the controversy that had already begun to intensify. He might thereby have gained a more broadly informed perspective on the program.

Monahan was asked on behalf of this Inquiry why he had not earlier consulted Ian Lustick or other experts involved in the development of the conference program. He responded:

> I was at all times dealing directly with Bruce and Susan,
> who were the persons responsible within the faculty for the
> conference. This was in accordance with my instructions from
> the President. I have never had any contact with Professor
> Lustick, and was not aware of any involvement he may have
> had in the conference planning. I do not recall Bruce or Susan
> ever suggesting that I should contact Professor Lustick and, in
> any event, do not understand what purpose would have been
> accomplished by my contacting him.

It is hard to believe that Shoukri (or indeed the president of any other major Canadian university) would have expressly instructed a dean *not* to consult with others involved in a research project, particularly when that dean was entertaining doubts about the academic judgment of the two persons expressly mentioned. Therefore, I stand by my observation that it was open to the dean to consult one or more members of the advisory board and that it would have been prudent for him to have done so.

Although Lustick was not on the list he had reviewed and approved in April 2008, seven others were, including Professor Kretzmer who, like Professor Monahan, was a senior member of an internationally known faculty of law. The dean appeared to have been aware on or before April 27, 2009, that Lustick was involved, at least to the extent that he was a participant in the conference, since he mentioned "Lustick" in an email message to AVPR Dewitt on April 27 discussing possible keynote or plenary speakers.[31]

If the dean had consulted Kretzmer or others from the list of seven members of the advisory board on file in the dean's office (and which he included with his submission to this Inquiry), or independent experts, he might have learned that Lustick was an authority on aspects of the conference topic. From Kretzmer or others on the advisory board, the dean also might have gained an understanding of the criteria and process by which speakers were selected, and the appropriateness of their selection, which would have been independent of the perspectives of Abella, Dewitt, Drummond, or Ryder.

Finally, I note that, had the dean consulted Ryder's application to SSHRC in mid-April, he might have appreciated that the April list of confirmed speakers was consistent with the program set out in detail in that application. In his brief to this Inquiry, Monahan did not indicate whether or not he had consulted the application, although in his April 11 email reply to a conference critic he had cited the success of the application as favourable evidence of the conference's quality.

Findings in Regard to the Dean's Information Base for his Academic Assessments

I conclude that Dean Monahan relied at least in part on the views of Professor Abella in arriving on April 15 at an adverse academic judgment concerning aspects of the conference program.

There is no evidence in the documentation available to this Inquiry (including Monahan's three 2011 submissions) that the dean consulted experts who were independent, or, alternatively, experts who supported the conference program (such as members of the advisory board).

I conclude that between April 15 and May 12, 2009, Dean Monahan should have made an effort to consult with at least one expert involved in the development of the program, or with an independent expert. This would have been important because he himself was not an expert, he doubted the judgment of Professors Ryder and Drummond, and Professors Abella and Dewitt were strong critics of the program.

Community Pressure

Dean Monahan, along with the president and the board chair, had another factor under consideration—one that was not academic in its essence—as he acknowledged in email messages at the time. This was the mounting pressure on the university from elements of the Jewish community. For example, by April 14 the board chair, Marshall Cohen, had become very concerned about community reaction against the conference, and expressed his heightened concern to the president and the dean on April 14 and 15.

Their concerns about mounting community pressure were certainly understandable. However, had the dean sought a broader range of advice, such as from members of the conference advisory board, he might have gained not only a more informed academic perspective on the program—he might have learned also that similar pressures had already been experienced at some major universities in the United States (such as Columbia University), which had developed successful approaches for contending with them. The intense campaigns by Israel lobby organizations and their supporters against academic events or programs, or individual academics in the United States, had became increasingly widely known after 2006–2007 as a result of publications by Mearsheimer and Walt, and other scholars.

In accordance with standard procedures in universities, the president and the board chair relied on the dean of the relevant faculty for advice in this matter. Monahan did provide advice, but it appears not to have been as fully informed as it could have been.

The Glendon Venue and Program Changes

Dean Monahan and the Glendon Venue. Ryder and Drummond met with the dean on April 17. He reiterated concerns about the conference program expressed in his April 15 email messages to them, notably the perceived lack of balance. Also in this meeting, he gave the organizers to understand that it now was unlikely that the conference could be held at *any* campus venue, because it was the wish of the board of governors that the conference be held off campus.

Monahan and Ryder and Drummond met again on April 23, when the dean made detailed proposals for program changes. He gave the organizers to understand that if they would agree to his program proposals, he would endeavour to re-secure the cancelled Glendon campus reservation. The organizers agreed only to discuss his proposals with their committee colleagues and report back as to which changes they would accept.

A Question Regarding Pressure on the Organizers. This chain of events raised a question as to whether the dean was attempting to bargain program changes for restoration of the Glendon venue. In his February 2011 brief, Monahan stated: "During this period I did receive a number of emails from Board Chair Cohen with respect to moving the conference off campus. However I supported the organizers in their desire to remain on the Glendon campus, and did not attempt to 'bargain' the availability of space for changes in the program." Later in the brief, he repeated the gist of this statement: "No such 'bargaining' occurred." Nevertheless, York University email records from April and May 2009 pertaining to discussions on a campus venue disclose the following statements:

i) Dean Monahan to the president and board chair, April 25: "With the [program] changes discussed above, I have indicated they can go ahead at Glendon. […] I have to say that I pushed them very hard […]."

ii) Dean Monahan to the president, May 9 (7:49 AM): "Without further consultation or discussion with me, the organizers decided that they are not going to add any speakers to the conference program, contrary to what they agreed with me last week. Instead they are going to have one of their existing speakers, (Ian Lustick), serve as a keynote. They proceeded to invite Lustick and presented that to me last night as a fait accompli."

iii) Dean Monahan to Professors Drummond and Ryder, May 10:

> [A]dding a new speaker as a keynote was a very important and constructive decision on your part. I was encouraged by your agreement with this and, based on that, (as well as on the idea of plenary sessions to highlight the strongest scholars) I facilitated the securing of the space in Glendon for the conference.
>
> What your email now indicates is that you are not in fact going to add another speaker but, instead, have decided to elevate one of your existing speakers to be a keynote. This is not what we agreed in my office. […]
>
> I would have thought it appropriate and necessary to

at least discuss this revised plan with me before acting
on it, particularly since it was inconsistent with what
we had agreed.[32]

Regarding his April 25 email message to the president and the board
chair, and his May 10, 2009, email message to the organizers, Monahan
stated in his February 2011 brief that:

> The first, an April 25, 2009 email from me to Board Chair Cohen
> and President Shoukri, provides an update on positive steps that
> have been taken with respect to the conference and, amongst
> other things, attempts to explain why I was supporting the desire
> of the organizers to hold the event at Glendon. The second
> email, sent by me to Bruce and Susan on May 10, 2009, reminds
> them (in passing) of the fact that I had earlier supported their
> desire to hold the conference at Glendon. But I make it clear that
> all decisions regarding the conference are for them to make, and
> there is no suggestion that the Glendon space is to be bargained
> in return for changes in the program, nor did I ever intend such
> a suggestion.

For their part, the testimonies of Ryder and Drummond were that they,
too, did not consider they were bargaining with the dean. They had agreed
to certain of his proposals on academic program content, provided all
members of the organizing committee agreed. They considered that they
were accommodating the dean's proposals under duress, because he had
given them to understand that the board of governors might deprive them
of any campus venue if they did not cooperate. The email records reflect
their uncertainty in the circumstances—for example, they initially agreed
to invite one or both of MPs Bob Rae and Irwin Cotler to speak, but later
refused. Ryder also agreed to work with an Osgoode Hall staff-person in
exploring prospects for an off-campus venue for the conference.

However, regardless of whether a term such as "bargaining" or some
other word or phrase is used to characterize the sequence of events concerning the organizers' objective to have the Glendon reservation re-instat-
ed and the dean's objective to have program changes made, the statements
quoted above pertain to a process involving two parties that culminated in
an outcome.

In his supplementary submission of July 15, 2011, Monahan discussed the events between April 17 and 23 and "the agreement" at greater length than in his February submission. However, none of the six accounts by Monahan of his involvements as dean that I have reviewed addressed directly the testimony of the organizers to the effect that, on April 17, he gave them to understand that it was the wish of the board of governors that the conference not be held on university premises. As in earlier accounts, he suggested that the venue issue had arisen solely from scheduling problems at Glendon College. In his July 2011 account, he disputed significant aspects of the summary Drummond had provided to him in connection with her book manuscript. His July 2011 account suggested that the organizers' concern was that the Keele campus was inconveniently located and as a result they appreciated his offer of assistance in seeking an off-campus hotel venue. He suggested he was surprised on April 22 by email communications from Drummond saying she and Ryder were "troubled" by recent developments.

When the three of them met on April 23, Ryder and Drummond both expressed opposition to moving off campus. Monahan made more specific suggestions about program changes than he had made on April 17, and the organizers agreed to discuss them with their fellow committee members. In his July 2011 supplementary submission he said he had undertaken to assist them in re-securing the Glendon venue, "as expression of goodwill" that "was not in any sense intended to somehow 'bargain' the availability of space in return for changes in the conference program."[33] He added, "if there is any doubt on this particular issue, I would suggest that Bruce be consulted for his view of the matter."[34]

I interviewed Ryder on October 2009, and he spoke of his surprise and dismay on being informed by the dean that the board wished to move the conference off-campus:

On April 17th Susan and I had lunch with the dean and he said to us, listen, the problem, it turns out, isn't holding the conference at Glendon [...] they [the university] wondered if we would hold it elsewhere. [...] there was no plausible explanation for why we were threatened with removal from campus entirely. [...] And, so, the Dean said to us, I mean I really think we need to start exploring other options off campus [...] so let's start exploring hotel venues. [...] This was April 17th; the conference was June 22nd. So we were extraordinarily upset, distraught about this. [...] The getting booted off campus, so to speak, the

threat of getting booted off campus is, I'm not sure where it
came from [...] I don't think he [the Dean] was the [original]
source of the pressure.[35]

Monahan suggested that contemporaneous email records from April 23
"confirmed the suggestions I was making to the organizers were consistent
with their own goals, and were in no way inappropriate or unwelcome."[36]
Yet in the same document he wrote that in the meeting that day, "Susan
had threatened to complain to CAUT."[37] In his own email summary of the
April 23 meeting to the president and the board chair, he reported "I have
to say that I pushed them very hard, even to the point where Drummond
said that I was pressuring them inappropriately and infringing their academic freedom," while earlier in the same message he reported, "With the
[program] changes discussed above, I have indicated they can go ahead at
Glendon."[38]

In his February 11 and July 15 submissions, Monahan emphasized that
the organizers agreed with some of his suggested program changes and
welcomed his assistance. A notable example was in their joint efforts to
persuade Michael Bell to be a keynote speaker. However, notwithstanding accord on certain matters, the organizers were deeply distressed about
what they considered to be inappropriate pressures. Their uncertainty and
anxiety over university support, including the Glendon venue, were not
dispelled until they met with the president on May 13.

This was the meeting about which the dean had written to the president
on May 9 advising him *not* to agree to because the organizers had not lived
up to "what they agreed with me last week."[39] On May 10, the dean wrote
to the organizers expressing displeasure that they had not lived up to their
agreement with him. In a May 11 email to the dean, AVPR Dewitt gave as
one of his reasons they should not disclose the draft Steinberg op-ed to
the organizers that "they have not kept one or more aspects of the agreement you thought you had with them."[40] Thus the "agreement" between
the dean and the organizers had an operational significance for the two
senior administrators most directly responsible for matters pertaining to
the conference. Correspondingly, the organizers were potentially placed at
a disadvantage.

Findings in Regard to the "Agreement" with the Dean
I conclude that, regardless of what his intentions may have been, or the
particular words used to characterize his involvement, Dean Monahan

conducted through the senior administrative office he held a process wherein two professors in his faculty were given to understand that the prospect of the university's withholding a campus venue—a prospect he communicated to them in meetings—could be avoided through his intercession, subject to their acceptance of program changes he proposed. He himself termed the outcome of this process an "agreement." I further conclude that his action in this matter was inappropriate.

The status on April 23, 2009, of the campus venue—which during the meeting with the organizers that morning the dean undertook to facilitate securing—is also of interest. This is because, three days earlier, on April 20, the president had directed that the Glendon venue be secured for the conference. The president's directive was recorded in an email message between senior support staff reporting to him.[41] Monahan was asked about the temporal sequence of these events. In his February 2011 brief he wrote: "With respect to the April 20, 2009 email from the President's Office, this was not sent to me and I was unaware of its existence at the time. Thus I could not and did not withhold any such information from the organizers." I make no finding with respect to this detail. Although in his clarification Monahan correctly stated that the April 20, 2009, email was not sent to him, he did not state whether by some other means of communication he did or did not learn of the president's directive concerning the Glendon venue, at that time or at some later time in 2009.

Non-disclosure of Steinberg's Draft Op-Ed
In his February 2011 brief, Monahan gave an account of the basis of his agreement not to disclose to the organizers the existence of the Steinberg draft op-ed. In the first part he wrote:

> In my May 12 meeting with Bruce and Susan, I did review with
> them some of the criticisms that had been raised by various
> external critics of the event. This included the criticisms that were
> set out in a draft opinion piece by Professor Steinberg, of which
> I had become aware (although the name of this individual was
> not shared at the May 12 meeting).

If is of note that in this statement Monahan did not claim that he gave any information to the organizers in the May 12 meeting that there might be criticism of their project in the media, or complaints to SSHRC or the federal government about it. The testimony of the organizers to this

Inquiry is that indeed the dean provided no such information in that meeting. In the second part of his account, Monahan wrote:

> Professor Dewitt provided me with the Steinberg opinion piece in confidence, and breaching that confidence would have been inappropriate. Further, in all likelihood it would not have been constructive to have done so, since the criticisms were well understood and we were making good faith attempts to address them in a constructive fashion.
>
> The Steinberg article simply repeated criticisms that had been circulating in the public domain for many months. When I received it, it was in draft form, and I was unaware of whether in fact it would be published, and in what form. [...]
>
> In short, in my view the Steinberg article had no particular significance.

There is a difference between the accounts provided by Monahan and Dewitt on the issue of disclosure of information about the Steinberg article, although both were dated February 11, 2011, and submitted through the same legal counsel. As cited earlier, Dewitt wrote:

> I passed on his draft op-ed to Patrick because as the Dean of the sponsoring faculty of a U50 event, he was the key central administration person in this matter. He deserved to be kept informed on matters that could involve his Faculty and the University. [...] I did what was necessary and appropriate to ensure that my colleagues in the senior administration and their colleagues as the conference planners were aware of the fact that there may be an adverse op-ed piece published, thereby allowing them to be in a position to prevent unfair criticism of their work.

Dewitt requested of the dean that he not disclose the document, and the dean agreed. As a result, neither of the officers of the corporate community of York University most immediately responsible for administrative matters pertaining to the conference acted so as "to ensure" that "their colleagues as the conference planners were aware of the fact that there may be an adverse op-ed piece published."

The Dean's Reasons for Non-disclosure. The fact that Dewitt requested of the dean that the existence of the Steinberg article not be disclosed did not, in my opinion, absolve the dean of responsibility, because, as Dewitt noted, the dean was "the key central administration person in this matter." The dean intended to use the substance of the draft op-ed in his meeting with the organizers, as he informed the AVPR at the time, and by his own account he did use it. The non-disclosure deprived the organizers of an opportunity to consider in advance how they might contend with public criticism of their conference and an attempt to undermine their SSHRC award.

If the assertion that "the Steinberg article simply repeated" well-known criticisms is correct, then the dean's specific resolve—stated to AVPR Dewitt that morning, prior to the meeting—to "use the substantive points [in the Steinberg article] as the basis of my discussion" remains unexplained because he and the organizers would have already been aware of the criticisms.

The additional assertion that in the May 12 meeting "we were making good faith attempts to address" well-known criticisms is also unexplained in Monahan's brief. He was using "the substantive points" from a document of whose existence Ryder and Drummond were unaware.

The assertion that "the Steinberg article had no particular significance" might be reasonable and acceptable, *if* it referred to the period after mid-June 2009, when a version of it was published by the *National Post*, that newspaper published a reply by Lustick, and SSHRC agreed to accept Ryder's report that there had been no major changes in the conference program. My interest, for purposes of this Inquiry, is in its significance for Monahan in May 2009. Notably, on the morning of May 12 and prior to his meeting with the organizers, he wrote to Dewitt stating, among other things, "They may be feeling the pressure. I sent them a strong email over the weekend and [...] the armour may be cracking."

Later that month (May 21), Monahan sent an email message to Dewitt concerning the public statement by the president web-posted earlier that day, saying, "See below. David as per our discussion can you follow with GS? Thanks."[42] The president later explained to Drummond that he had authorized this communication to Steinberg through Dewitt because he "hoped [Gerald] Steinberg would consider modifying his article." Therefore, it is reasonable to infer that, between May 11 and May 22 at least, the dean's own email messages from that period suggest the Steinberg article had particular significance not only for the dean and the AVPR, but also for the president.

Findings in Regard to Non-Disclosure of Steinberg's Draft Op-Ed

In summary, I consider Monahan's account of this matter unpersuasive. I conclude that Dean Monahan had a responsibility to ensure that, in AVPR Dewitt's words, "the conference planners were aware of the fact that there may be an adverse op-ed piece published, thereby allowing them to be in a position to prevent unfair criticism of their work." Monahan should have ensured that, at a minimum, the conference organizers were informed that there might be an adverse op-ed piece published, the gist of the draft op-ed, and that the author would "be sending it to Jason Kenney and Irwin Cotler in the context of the SSHRC funding issues." Such information could have been communicated by the dean without disclosing the name of the author.

I conclude that Dean Monahan failed to live up to a responsibility of his office and, therefore, that he acted inappropriately.

Events of May 12, 2009

Events of the Day. A number of events pertaining to the conference and Monahan's involvement occurred on May 12, between early morning and late evening, including the meeting of Ryder and Drummond with Monahan in the morning, a subsequent meeting between the dean and the president, the public statement critical of the conference issued by CIJA around mid-day, a telephone call from the dean to Ryder in the evening, and an email message from the dean to the president following his telephone discussion with Ryder.

After the CIJA statement was issued, Dewitt emailed a copy of the statement to Shapson and Monahan (at 1:11 PM). It is not known to this Inquiry whether any of York University's senior academic administrators had advance notice that CIJA would be issuing a statement against the conference that day.

Immediate Background to the May 12 Meeting. In his February 2011 brief, Monahan outlined his understanding of circumstances around that time:

> By mid-May of 2009 progress had been made in addressing
> some of the academic concerns regarding the conference.
> However, as described above, my efforts on behalf of the
> conference organizers to recruit additional keynote speakers had
> been unsuccessful; the event was then a little more than one
> month away and prominent individuals who might be suitable

for this role had conflicts in their schedules.

He also outlined his proposed solution to the problem of shortness of time:

> I discussed with President Shoukri the possibility of asking the conference organizers to postpone the conference until the fall in order to provide additional time to recruit additional speakers; the President and I agreed that I would raise the possibility with the conference organizers. This was done at the May 12, 2009 meeting with Bruce and Susan, as well as during a telephone discussion with Bruce that evening.

The May 12 Morning Meeting of the Dean with the Organizers
The Dean's Assertions about Some Speakers and about the Organizers. In the May 12 meeting with Ryder and Drummond, after reviewing his concerns that the conference might be perceived as one-sided, Monahan made more detailed criticisms. He asserted that some of the confirmed speakers were not serious academics (or words to that effect), and that some were "activists" or "polemicists," or "anti-Israeli." He specifically mentioned Ali Abunimah and Jeff Halper as being in this category, and suggested Abunimah's presence on the program should be balanced by an author of a book promoting the two-state model. (It is relevant to note that Halper is an Israeli, and that both he and Abunimah are authors of scholarly books on topics relevant to the conference program. Also, Abunimah was listed as a member of the conference advisory board in the April 2008 U50 Application the dean had approved.) As an additional criticism, the dean said that some confirmed speakers were graduate students, suggesting he had not expected this.

Monahan next asserted that Ryder, Drummond, and Aiken did not have the relevant academic credentials to organize the conference, outlining why, in his view, this was true of each of them. The dean also expressly noted that Masri was a graduate student, thereby suggesting that for this reason he too lacked credentials.

In support of his assertions, Monahan suggested that respected scholars of the Middle East (whom he did not name) held the opinions he was expressing. It is of note that, in all three published versions of his op-ed article denouncing the conference, Steinberg also had denounced some of the speakers as "activists," and specifically named Abunimah and Halper. It is relevant to recall that a suggestion that Drummond lacked relevant credentials had been made in early March 2009, by Dewitt in an email message to Professor Aiken.[43]

In his February 2011 brief, Monahan gave the following account:

> In my May 12 meeting with Bruce and Susan, I did review with them [...] the criticisms that were set out in a draft opinion piece by Professor Steinberg, of which I had become aware (although the name of this individual was not shared at the May 12 meeting). This discussion was difficult and challenging, since it involved a frank and candid exchange of views. [...] The discussion was at all times conducted in a civil and respectful manner.

He stated also that:

> It is difficult to recall the precise comments that were made during this meeting, which took place almost two years ago. [...]

> Some months later I was made aware that one of the organizers who was present may have interpreted certain comments made at this meeting as personally insulting, but that was certainly not intended, was never expressed to me at the meeting by the individual in question, or at any other time up to and including the conference itself in late June 2009.

Professor Drummond's Meeting Notes. After their April 17 meeting with the dean, the organizers kept a detailed account of discussions in their subsequent meetings with him, which was maintained by Professor Drummond. Her meeting notes constituted part of the basis for concerns she later expressed, and summaries based on them were included in her "Field Notes" paper. It is a relevant consideration that Monahan had earlier opportunities to correct the record, if he believed correction was warranted.

The first opportunity was in July 2009, when Drummond gave copies of her "Field Notes" paper to Monahan and to the president. The second was in spring 2010, when she posted summaries on a website, including a summary of the discussion in the May 12, 2009, meeting; this material was publicly accessible for many months, but Monahan did not contact her with any corrections to her account of the meeting. In his June 30,

2010, letter to the OHFA executive committee, Monahan acknowledged there had been a meeting with the organizers "in early May" (his meetings with them in early May were on May 12 and on May 13, the latter with the president). In the letter to OHFA he did not dispute the specific details in Drummond's web-posted summaries of his statements during the May 12, 2009, discussion.

The Dean's Proposal about Compromise with Professors Dewitt and Adelman. After asserting that the organizers lacked relevant academic credentials, the dean proposed that the conference be postponed for "a couple of months" (according to Drummond's meeting notes). He indicated that he would be advising the president that the conference should be postponed.

The dean then made a further proposal, to the effect that during the postponement period the organizers should meet with Dewitt and Adelman for the purpose of reaching a compromise on the conference program, such that they would then agree to participate. The dean suggested also that the president would want such a compromise to be reached. As noted earlier, Dewitt and Adelman strongly objected to some of the confirmed speakers. Therefore, it is a reasonable inference that any such compromise probably would involve disinviting some speakers, as Dewitt had in effect proposed on April 15. Indeed, the dean acknowledged in the meeting that Dewitt and Adelman might say that certain of the confirmed speakers should not be on the final program when the conference actually was held.

According to Drummond's notes, in this phase of the meeting the dean said that Dewitt was "knowledgeable in the area" of the conference topic and, after proposing that the organizers work toward a compromise with him and Adelman, the dean repeated his opinion that the organizers lacked appropriate credentials.

In his brief of February 2011, Monahan made the following statement about this phase of the May 12, 2009, meeting: "[T]he purpose of proposing that the organizers consider whether to postpone the conference was so as to permit additional time to better plan the conference, and there was never any suggestion that the organizers required the approval of Professors Dewitt or Adelman."

This was the only reference in the brief to involving Dewitt or Adelman in conference program discussions during the proposed postponement. I accept the statement that "there was never any suggestion that the organizers *required* the approval of Professors Dewitt or Adelman." (Italics added.) However, the concern of the organizing committee at the time, and subsequently, was that the dean had challenged their academic credentials and had proposed they use a postponement period not only to attract speakers who could meet his "balance" criterion, but also to work toward a compromise with two professors whose strong opposition to aspects of the program was known to all three persons present in the May 12 meeting.

Although words such as "required" or "approval" were not used in the meeting, the conference organizers were cognizant of the fact that that the dean had given them to understand that he was expressing the wishes of the president. Also, on May 12 they remained under the apprehension that university resources might still be withheld, especially in light of the dean's email message of May 10 expressing displeasure that they had not yet lived up to what he considered to have been an "agreement" reached with them, following which he had "facilitated securing of the space in Glendon."

Notwithstanding their apprehensions, Ryder and Drummond did not agree to postpone the conference.

Monahan's Overview of the Meeting. As stated in his brief, Monahan's position was as follows: "It was clear that it was up to the organizers to decide whether they wished to postpone or not. [...] My overall recollection is that the meeting was conducted throughout in a collegial and respectful manner and I do not recall the organizers expressing any offence at anything that was said. The conclusion of the meeting was positive and constructive [...]."

The Evening of May 12

The Dean Repeats His Postponement Proposal. Notwithstanding Monahan's assertion quoted above as to what was "clear" after the organizers had that morning stated their wish not to postpone the conference, the dean telephoned Ryder in the evening and urged that the conference be postponed. Ryder's information is that the Dean spoke in forceful terms. The result of the telephone discussion was that Ryder refused to agree to postpone the conference.

The Dean's New Approach. The dean emailed the president later that evening, reporting Ryder's refusal. In the email message, captioned "possible solution," the dean continued, "We can't force them to delay it. That will only hurt us," and proposed a new approach, namely, to issue a public "disclaimer." He suggested that in the disclaimer:

In effect we would say that this is an independently organized academic event; the views expressed at the conference are those of the participants and will reflect a range of opinion; and that these views do not necessarily refect those of the university.

The dean added: "If we put out such a statement, then we would just let them proceed with their event as they wish, without attempting to make any further changes."[44]

However, the dean did not communicate this "possible solution" to the organizers that night. As a result of his telephone discussion with Ryder, they experienced a night of anxiety, as Drummond expressed it, until the next morning when she, Ryder, and Masri met with the president, with the dean also present.

It was only in this May 13 meeting with Dr. Shoukri—in which he assured them of the university's support for the conference and their academic freedom—that it became "clear" to the organizers that they could refuse to postpone the conference, and that the university would nevertheless provide the resources it had committed.

Findings in Regard to the Dean's Involvements on May 12

The Postponement Proposal. Monahan wrote in his brief that:

> The suggestion that the organizers be asked to consider postponing the Conference had been discussed with the President in early May and it had been jointly agreed that I would raise this possibility at my May 12 meeting with the conference organizers. The President did not disagree with the suggestion that it be raised for discussion; [...]

> The suggestion was offered in good faith as a way to provide additional time for the efforts underway to improve the academic quality of the event; [...]

> The president did not disagree with or reject my advice, and there was in fact no difference of opinion between me and the President on the matter.

I accept that it was reasonable to "raise the possibility" of postponement, provided "it was clear that it was up to the organizers to decide whether they wished to postpone or not," as Monahan asserted, but here

I mean clear to the organizers. In complex circumstances, many questions can be raised for purposes of open discussion, provided that raising them is not followed by actions or utterances that potentially or actually infringe academic freedom.

However, Monahan did not limit his actions or utterances to "raising the possibility." Instead, in his administrative capacity he also proposed postponement; gave the organizers to understand that the president likely would support his proposal; proposed that the organizers use the delay to make an effort to reach a compromise with Dewitt and Adelman, each of whom was strongly opposed to some confirmed speakers; did not make clear to the organizers that it was up to them to decide on postponement; did not disclose to the organizers that the president's position was to the effect that the question of postponement could be raised for discussion but that, because of their right to academic freedom, it was up to the organizers to decide; and made a further effort to obtain agreement of the organizers to postponement through his strongly worded telephone call to Ryder.

It is relevant to recall President Shoukri's position as he himself described it in writing to Drummond in July 2009:

> With my complete knowledge, the role of Dean Monahan was
> to attempt—while protecting academic freedom—to examine
> ways to alleviate possible concerns and to assure the external
> communities of our commitment to excellence and fairness.
> Although the Dean shared various suggestions with the
> committee, it was always up to the committee to accept or reject
> his suggestions while the university continued to provide all the
> logistical and financial support [...].

I conclude that the dean's telephoned reiteration of his postponement proposal was inappropriate, even though raising the question of postponement as a topic for discussion in the morning meeting of May 12 was not inappropriate.

Observations on the Stated Reason for Postponement. As stated in the dean's February 2011 brief, the reason was "to provide additional time for the efforts underway to improve the academic quality of the event." In his July 2009 "Preliminary Review" of Drummond's "Field Notes" paper, Monahan gave a more detailed statement. He wrote that, by the second week in May:

It was clear that it would be impossible to add any additional
internationally recognized scholars or public figures at this stage.
The Dean suggested that it might be desirable to postpone the
conference until the fall in order to provide sufficient time to
ensure that the conference was planned properly, and so that the
original goals and objectives could be met.[45]

Specifically, Monahan justified his involvements as dean in the academic content of the program from April 15 to May 12 on the basis of
his understanding of "the original goals and objectives" of the conference.
These were described to him by the organizers when they approached
him for support in spring 2008, and were "set out in the original York 50
Application." In his brief, he described his understanding of these goals and
objectives as including, notably, (i) "balance" in the selection of speakers
who would be selected so as to represent a "wide range of perspectives and
viewpoints," and (ii) speakers who would be "internationally recognized
scholars." Unfortunately, his understanding was substantially inaccurate.

Balance was not part of the conference proposal the dean approved in
April 2008. A second respect in which the dean's understanding was substantially inaccurate was his view that all (or almost all) the speakers would
be "internationally recognized scholars." This view may have been reflected
in the remarks he made in the May 12 meeting that some speakers were
not serious academics (or words to that effect). This view appears to stem
from a misunderstanding of the U50 Application and of the application to
SSHRC. Monahan's brief stated:

> The York 50 Application indicated that the event was intended
> to draw together "internationally recognized scholars" from
> a variety of disciplines and generate a "high profile; highly
> prestigious conference on a topic of widespread topical interest."

The relevant passage in the York 50 (U50) Application was: "We have
a preliminary list of internationally recognized scholars to whom we are
about to send out invitations for participation." Thus the U50 Application
did not say that all (or almost all) speakers would be "internationally
recognized scholars," but only that some speakers of this stature would
be invited. There was no basis in the application for misunderstanding
the meaning, because on the next page the applicants stated they would
"be applying for a SSHRC conference grant." Some speakers indeed were

internationally recognized scholars, such as Webber, Lustick, Bisharat, Kretzmer, and Smooha, but there was no reasonable basis to expect that all (or almost all) speakers must be of similar stature.

Monahan wrote in his brief that he "regarded" the conference "as a successful academic event." Therefore, it may reasonably be inferred that it met its goals and objectives as set out in the published vision statement and in the application to SSHRC, having "proceeded in the manner determined by the organizers," without any postponement. I conclude that Professor Monahan's argument was unpersuasive and that there was no appropriate academic or administrative basis for postponement.

The Dean's Labelling of Some Speakers as Polemicists, Activists, or Not Academics. It was clear and explicit in the U50 Application and the application to SSHRC that participants would include political activists, both academics such as Uri Davis and non-academics such as Ali Abunimah. It would have been appropriate and prudent for the dean, in mid-April 2009, to have reviewed both of these application documents before he began to criticize the program and the organizers. If he did review them, he substantially misunderstood the contents.

I conclude that the dean either made a significant error in administrative judgment if he did not carefully review these documents in April 2009, or (if he did review them) he made a significant error in interpretation regarding their contents.

The dean expressed as a criticism that some speakers were polemicists, activists, or not academics. In his opening remarks to conference participants on June 22, the dean quoted a passage from J. S. Mill's *Essay on Liberty*, emphasizing the importance of freedom of speech. As is well known, Mill was an outspoken activist, and for most of his life a non-academic.

I conclude that, in Laskin's terms, the dean as an officer of the corporate community was not neutral. He was in effect repeating and giving undue weight to criticisms that, regardless of the number of persons who made them, or their stations in life, were the opinions of individuals, when he knew or should have known that others had different opinions.

Thus, I conclude that the dean's criticisms of confirmed conference speakers had no appropriate academic basis and, in the context in which he made them, they were inappropriate.

The Assertion that the Organizers Lacked Credentials. In its October 16, 2009, brief to this Inquiry, York University stated that the dean "was well acquainted with the organizers and considered them academic colleagues."

Among other things, as dean he had access to their CVs. They provided him with a lengthy and detailed conference proposal (the U50 Application). By his own account, the dean reviewed it, before signing it and submitting it to the U50 Committee on behalf of the organizers. It was assessed and funded by the U50 Committee. Subsequently, the organizers submitted a revised and more detailed proposal to SSHRC for a conference grant. This was assessed by a SSHRC peer-review committee and funded by SSHRC. In his April 11 email message to a conference critic, the dean himself cited in defence of the conference the fact that "the SSHRC committee, which is made up of scholars from other universities, gave the conference the highest possible ranking as a scholarly conference."[46]

Therefore, I conclude that the dean had no appropriate academic basis for his May 12 assertions to the organizers that they lacked credentials to organize the conference, and that his assertions were inappropriate.

I conclude also that in making these assertions the dean, regardless of whatever his intent may have been, was in effect expressing disregard for SSHRC and its peer-review process, and disregard for the U50 Committee and its review process.

I conclude, in addition, that the dean's unwarranted assertions about credentials (both of the organizers and of the speakers) continued a pattern of events involving the dean and the organizers that he initiated through email messages on April 15, and extended through several meetings and email messages up to and including May 12. These were events in which the dean subjected the organizers to what he himself acknowledged in email messages were pressures. This pattern of events continued through the dean's telephone call to Ryder in the evening of May 12.

The Dean's Proposal about Compromise with Professors Dewitt and Adelman. The dean proposed that in the postponement period the organizers should meet with Dewitt and Adelman in an effort to reach a compromise over the program. I conclude that the dean's May 12 proposal about compromise with Professors Adelman and Dewitt must be seen as a departure from his previous approach (endeavouring to add balance to the program) and toward an approach related to the April 15 approach of AVPR Dewitt (in effect to disinvite some speakers).

I conclude also that the proposal about compromise was inappropriate in that it in effect expressed disregard for the credentials and academic judgment of the organizers, and also because it had the potential to infringe their academic freedom in regard to their research activity.

The Defence of Acting in Accordance with Instructions

In his February 11, 2007, brief, Monahan based his position also on the following categorical assertion: "I was at *all times* acting in accordance with the instructions of the President, and we were both equally committed to protecting the academic freedom of the organizers." (Italics added.)

It is convenient to discuss the two components of this assertion together with related, but not necessarily equivalent, statements by President Shoukri in his one-page letter to me of February 17, 2011. Among other things, the president wrote:

> I, as the university President, was in close touch with Dean Monahan and together we established an overall strategy that was based on ensuring success of the conference, and protecting academic freedom and the university's role as an institution of free inquiry.

> Dean Monahan kept me informed regularly of his conversations with his colleagues. Our conversations were always guided by the aforementioned principles. [...]

> Dean Monahan and Associate Vice-President Dewitt, as members of the university's senior administration were working in a manner consistent with protecting academic freedom and the university's role as an institution of free inquiry. I hope that your deliberations will be consistent with this understanding of their role.

The categorical character of Monahan's assertion gives rise to the question as to whether the assertion was completely and literally accurate at "all times," or whether there was some elasticity in the meaning of the term "instructions," as used in 2011 by Monahan, or as interpreted and carried out by him in 2009. He did not describe the level of detail or specificity of the president's instructions in regard to events discussed in this chapter. The president did not provide explicit wording of any such instructions in his letter to me. For example, neither of them provided evidence that the president instructed the dean to challenge the organizers' credentials in the May 12 meeting.

The record from 2009 raises questions about the phrase "at all times." For instance, on April 20 the president had directed that the Glendon College venue be secured for the conference. Yet three days later, in meeting with the organizers, the dean gave them to understand that provision of a campus venue was in some sense conditional on their agreeing to certain program changes he was proposing. On May 9, the dean had advised the president against meeting with the organizers, yet the president nevertheless met with them. In addition, the question as to possible elasticity in the dean's interpretation of presidential "instructions" must be considered in light of the president's July 2009 statement on his instructions to the dean, in which he assured Drummond that "it was always up to the committee to accept or reject his [the dean's] suggestions." The testimony of the organizers was to the effect that the dean did not make this clear, and it became clear to them only when they met with the president on May 13. This uncertainty in their minds was a reason why they wrote directly to the president asking him to meet with them—the "end-run" as the dean termed it.

I conclude that Professor Monahan's assertion that "I was at all times acting in accordance with the instructions of the President" is not established by information available to this Inquiry, including Professor Monahan's submission of February 2011.

With regard to the other component of Monahan's assertion, that the president and he "were both equally committed to protecting the academic freedom of the organizers," I conclude that the president was consistently committed to academic freedom, and that he consistently acted to protect it throughout the relevant time period. I conclude that certain actions or utterances by the dean on October 9, 2008, and at various times between April 15 and May 12, 2009, discussed above, would have resulted in academic freedom violations had the organizers not resisted them and had they and their conference not had the support of the president at critical junctures.

President Shoukri wrote to me that "together," he and the dean "established an overall strategy that was based on ensuring success of the conference, and protecting academic freedom." I am aware that, as usual in a large university, the president must rely on information and advice provided by the relevant dean. In this instance, as discussed earlier, Monahan appears to have had a substantially inaccurate understanding of important details in the U50 Application and in the application to SSHRC. Moreover, he was not an expert on the conference topic and, as established in documents, he relied on the opinions of academics such as Abella, Dewitt, and Steinberg. There is no evidence available to this Inquiry that he consulted other academics with substantially different opinions regarding the conference program. In other words, he did not ensure that he as dean developed a fully informed perspective on the program.

I conclude, therefore, that the information and advice the dean gave to the president was substantially incomplete in its content, although I have no doubt that the dean provided it in good faith and with the sincere belief it was accurate and sufficient.

This incompleteness in information and advice may have influenced the conception of "success of the conference" that the president, the dean, or both developed from mid-April to mid-May 2009. It may also have influenced the conception one or both administrators developed during that period regarding possible "ways to alleviate possible concerns and to assure the external communities of our commitment to excellence and fairness" (quoting from Shoukri's letter to Drummond of July 2009, cited above).

The record available to this Inquiry supports my conclusion that, *except* for October 9, 2008, and at certain times between April 15 and May 12, 2009, as discussed above, Dean Monahan was "working in a manner consistent with protecting academic freedom and the university's role as an institution of free inquiry," as Dr. Shoukri wrote. Regrettably, however, and for the reasons discussed here, I have concluded that this was not the case with the dean's involvement in specific instances as noted. I therefore differ with the president in this limited, but significant respect.

Events Between May 13 and June 24, 2009

From May 13 through to the conference itself, Monahan was actively and significantly engaged in institutional efforts to defend the principle of academic freedom and to secure logistical and financial support to the conference. Among other things, he assisted substantially with the drafting of the president's two public statements on academic freedom and the conference, and wrote about the importance of academic freedom in reply to at least one conference critic. He also provided timely and appropriate advice on media strategy.

In his memo to all faculty members in Osgoode Hall on June 15, the dean commended Ryder and Drummond for their efforts during "an extraordinarily difficult undertaking" and expressed his "personal support" for them. In his address of welcome, opening the conference, he spoke eloquently of the university's commitment to freedom of expression "no matter how sensitive or controversial the subject matter." He read one of the most stirring passages in Mill's *Essay on Liberty* and again commended Ryder and Drummond for their efforts.

York University more than doubled its original financial commitment to the conference, largely because it absorbed substantial and unbudgeted security costs for the event. These extraordinary provisions were made because university officials and the conference organizers had serious concerns about the character of demonstrations JDL Canada, and possibly other organizations, were expected to mount.

THE INTERFERENCE BY THE HARPER GOVERNMENT IN SSHRC

There were two aspects to the interference, both plainly stated in Minister Goodyear's media release of June 5, 2009:

- I have spoken to the president of the Social Sciences and Humanities Research Council to bring these concerns to his immediate attention and asked that Council give them full consideration.

- In particular, I asked that the Council, once they have seen this information, to consider conducting a second peer review of the application to determine whether or not the conference still meets SSHRC's criteria for funding of an academic conference.

The minister's statement said "these concerns" were that "several individuals and organizations have expressed their grave concerns that some of the speakers have, in the past, made comments that have been seen to be anti-Israeli and anti-Semitic. Some have also expressed concerns that the event is no longer an academic research-focussed event." The action came despite the statement in the same media release that, "our government is committed to the principle of academic independence and the independent, arm's-length, peer review process for assessing applications for research grants."[47]

The minister's statement was first sent, not to the media generally, but to "the Jewish-Canadian media," and did not become fully public until a few days later. In the meantime, B'nai Brith had sent an "Action Alert" to its supporters with a copy of the minister's statement, asking them to thank the minister for his action, and to urge him to interfere more strongly by "direct[ing] SSHRC to immediately withdraw its funding."[48] In other words, a group that had asked for government interference, expressed appreciation for the interference, and then urged its supporters to request stronger interference.

In addition to the unprecedented interference as such, the minister's two requests quoted above also, potentially, have wider adverse implications. First, asking a research council president to give consideration to unsubstantiated allegations made by a group or groups from the public at large sends by implication a message to all three arm's-length granting councils and the research communities they support. The message is that this government is willing to interfere in the work of the councils—and hence in the work of researchers—when representatives of a sufficiently numerous voting bloc, or otherwise influential group, complain about an activity (such as a research program or conference). There are topics within the purview of each of three councils that could potentially precipitate such interference by the Harper government in future, in light of its positions on these topics, or the positions of some of its MPs or supporters: for example, topics related to climate change, environmental degradation, abortion, biological evolution, or criminal justice.

Second, requesting SSHRC "to consider conducting a second peer review" is an even more direct and specific type of interference because there is no existing procedural provision in SSHRC policy for such action. In other words, the government asked SSHRC to consider acting outside its own rules.

I note that there is a record dating from September and October 2009 (when the controversy over interference was raised in Parliament), documenting that the government issued "PCO-approved" media lines to SSHRC in early October 2009. These set out assertions the agency could make to the public, one of which was to the effect that SSHRC was arm's-length, and another of which was to assert that "there was no ministerial interference."[49]

Notwithstanding such after-the-fact assertions, on the basis of the documentary record from June 2009, including the minister's media release of June 5, I conclude there was government interference in the arm's-length agency SSHRC through the action and statement by Minister Goodyear. I conclude also that the government's interference was inappropriate and constituted a serious adverse precedent for the independence and integrity of academic research in Canada, with potential adverse implications for all three granting councils and the research communities they support.

Among such implications is an atmosphere of uncertainty as to which type of research project might next bring interference.

A difference between the approach of the Progressive Conservatives who held power in Ottawa several times in the post-war period and the Conservatives now in power may be illustrated by comparing statements in Minister Goodyear's media release of June 5, 2009, with a statement by MP Ray Hnatyshyn in 1977 when SSHRC was being established. Speaking for the Progressive Conservatives, Mr. Hnatyshyn (later a federal minister and subsequently Governor General) said:

> [T]he Council [...] must be independent to support the
> research it feels—through its own elaborate evaluation system,
> I grant you—warrants support on the basis of this evaluation
> process, rather than whatever government of the day decides is
> appropriate research to be carried out by council.[50]

THE SSHRC RESPONSE TO GOVERNMENT INTERFERENCE

In the light of Chapter 6, there are unanswered questions regarding the minister's requests to SSHRC: in communications with the minister or his staff, did President Gaffield suggest a second peer review as an option, or as one of a group of options SSHRC would be willing to consider, and did President Gaffield indicate to the minister his degree of comfort, or discomfort, with considering a second peer review?

Subsequent to interventions by CAUT, SSHRC did not arrange a second peer review of the conference application. Instead, on June 10, 2009, it issued a demand to Ryder, the grant holder, that he "identify any changes in your conference [...] since the time of your application, by close of business tomorrow."[51] There was no provision in SSHRC policy for the making of such a demand. SSHRC has not yet responded directly to the concerns expressed by the CAUT executive committee on June 12, 2009, by members of the Osgoode Hall faculty on June 14, 2009, and by members of the Queen's law faculty on the following day. Instead, SSHRC issued a statement to the effect that its actions were appropriate.

The Osgoode Hall faculty members wrote, "We believe that SSHRC made a serious error in acceding to political interference in this manner," and the CAUT executive committee expressed similar concerns. President Gaffield replied to the CAUT letter on July 16, 2009, saying among other things that

I am fully satisfied that our handling of the matter, as an arm's
length agency, is consistent with relevant SSHRC policies and
procedures and with our responsibilities as stewards of public
funds under the mandate of the SSHRC Act.[52]

Notwithstanding Gaffield's expression of satisfaction, his letter did
not directly address facts and concerns set out in the letters by CAUT or
the law professors. Instead, he asserted, first, that "the peer review of the
grant-in-aid application has never been in question at SSHRC"; second,
that "SSHRC is expected and committed to look into concerns about how
awards are being administered"; and, third, that "In this case, the result is
that SSHRC—as well as the public—has timely assurance that conference
planning is proceeding in a manner consistent with the provisions of the
Grant Holder's Guide for the program."

As to the first assertion, according to the minister's statement the
president of SSHRC was asked "to consider conducting a second peer
review of the application." Subsequently, as recorded in SSHRC email records, senior staff-persons were discussing a range of options that included
subjecting the successfully peer-reviewed conference to investigations.
Possible "ethical," "integrity," and "hate crime" investigations were mentioned. In this connection, SSHRC also sought legal advice through staff
counsel in government departments, one of which pertained to the legal
implications of "Withdrawal of SSHRC Funding" for this conference.[53] As
a result, the precise meaning and the significance of this assertion by Dr.
Gaffield remain unclear.

As to the second assertion, SSHRC staff had already looked into "concerns" about how this award was "being administered"—on May 25,
2009—more than a week before the minister interfered. This is documented
through internal SSHRC email messages, notably the message sent by program officer Craig McNaughton to other SSHRC staff-persons that day, in
response to a complaint made by JDL Canada, and McNaughton noted that
all of the relevant information was on the conference website. He suggested
that complaints could be addressed by "simply pointing people" who complained to the vision statement on the conference website.

A difference between May 25, when the JDL complaint was discussed
by SSHRC staff-persons, and June 4, when the minister interfered, may
have been a complaint (or complaints) by one or more other Israel lobby
organizations, or other groups or individuals opposed to the conference. In
this regard it is of note that B'nai Brith, in an email communication to its

supporters, said that the minister's action followed its appeal to the government about the conference.

As to the third assertion, McNaughton had by June 10 compiled tables summarizing information about confirmed speakers and topics from the conference website, in comparison to Ryder's November 2008 application. His tables appeared to indicate there had been no major changes to the program since Ryder submitted the grant application in autumn 2008. Therefore, it appears from its own records that in effect SSHRC may already have known the answer to the question it demanded Ryder answer. After it received the reply from Ryder, detailing as demanded all changes—none of them major—SSHRC "reviewed" his letter and replied several days later that it "accept[ed] this assurance."[54]

On the basis of this information, I conclude that SSHRC acted outside of its own procedures, and that this followed the government's interference. It is to SSHRC's credit that it did not conduct a second peer review, but there also was no basis in its policy for it to have demanded a pre-conference account from the grant-holder. I conclude that this demand by SSHRC to Professor Ryder was inappropriate.

As to Gaffield's comment that SSHRC is "an arm's length agency," we know that it was established as such by Parliament in 1978. Notwithstanding the statements by Gaffield and the government, there is an unresolved and ongoing concern: the Harper government interfered in the agency, the agency subsequently took inappropriate action, and then—in the letter of June 16, 2009, to CAUT—SSHRC appeared to have suggested in effect that such had not been the case.

During the weekend of June 13–14, senior SSHRC staff-persons were discussing possible explanations both for the granting agency's response to the government interference and its haste in responding. In this context, McNaughton drafted a note to his colleagues saying, among other things, "We need to explain why the speed was needed," and "It does not matter that the Minister relayed the concerns (save in the sense that his statement complicates matters in relation to principles of arm's length and peer review)." McNaughton's parenthetical remark acknowledged that SSHRC appeared to have acted in response to government interference. An email message SSHRC Corporate Secretary Trauttmansdorff sent to SSHRC Vice-Presidents Yasmeen and Charette on June 14, 2009, appeared to confirm this. Trauttmansdorff said: "In the normal course of things, questions or concerns about projects we fund are directed to the grant holder and the institution and that's the end of it. This case is outside the norm."[55]

In summary, Gaffield's letter and the internal correspondence among senior staff have not dispelled uncertainty as to how SSHRC would respond in the event of future interference by the government.

THE IACOBUCCI REPORT

The background to York University's commissioning of the Iacobucci Review was outlined in Chapter 7, and the statement by President Shoukri announcing the review with its terms of reference is in Appendix V.

Assurances about the Review. When Monahan was assisting the president with drafts of the review's terms of reference for Shoukri's approval, the president sent an email message to Monahan saying, "I just want to avoid the impression that we are looking for something that was done wrongly." After he had begun his work, the Honourable Mr. Iacobucci issued a "clarification" of his terms of reference saying that, "following further discussions with President Shoukri and with his agreement,"

> I wish to make it clear that my review does not in any way mean
> that I will be making findings against any individual, group,
> or organization [...] I am not conducting an inquiry into past
> events [...] My review is intended to provide forward-looking
> recommendations [...] that respect the University's commitment
> to academic freedom.[56]

Overview of the Report. Notwithstanding the "clarification," the Iacobucci report included extensive criticism of the conference organizers, in the form of summaries of testimony by unnamed persons. The report did not characterize the criticisms as "findings." The report also included some criticism of the dean of Osgoode Hall Law School, in the form of summaries of testimony by the two members of the conference organizing committee who participated in the review, identified in the report as organizer A and organizer B. However, regardless of his intent, the structure of Iacobucci's report was such that insufficiently attentive readers could be left with the impression that some of these criticisms were, in some sense, findings.[57]

There is no evidence of any significant examination of any of the testimony provided to the review. It is simply reported in summary form and then used as a significant part of the basis for the report's recommendations. In other words, the structure and content of the report suggest that the summaries of testimony in effect were treated by Iacobucci himself as if they constituted findings.

The Iacobucci report also promoted a restrictive conception of academic freedom significantly at variance with the definition in the York/YUFA collective agreement. This conception, eccentric in the modern Canadian context, is justified in the report on the basis of the author's conception of academic freedom and his inferences from the summaries of testimony. If adopted as policy, the recommendations would infringe or potentially infringe existing rights to academic freedom at York University.

Use of Unmediated Assertions in the Report. In a letter to officers of the York University senate dated April 26, 2010, Professors Joan Gilmour, Shin Imai, and Gus van Harten, in their capacity as the members of the executive committee of the Osgoode Hall Faculty Association (OHFA), stated, "The Association considers the Iacobucci Report to be unsound and unreliable." Among the reasons for their conclusion was:

> The Report claims not to make findings of fact or fault. However, it presents a series of anonymous and unmediated assertions about the merits of the conference and its organizers. The Report draws on its "perspectives on the conference" section to support its recommendations on regulating future academic events at York University.[58]

The "perspectives on the conference" section of the Iacobucci report contained the anonymous and unmediated assertions, and two examples are given here by way of illustration. At page 30 Iacobucci wrote, "It was suggested that the Conference organizers were not experienced in the subject matter of the Conference." This unmediated assertion had been made by several conference critics in the months immediately preceding the conference, notwithstanding the facts that the organizers had been awarded a large SSHRC conference grant on the basis of the detailed program they submitted, along with their own scholarly credentials and a detailed list of proposed speakers, and that they had the assistance of an eleven-person International Advisory Board, including very senior, internationally distinguished scholars, in developing the program. Arguably, this unmediated assertion had the effect of personally and professionally discrediting the organizers.

At page 32 Iacobucci wrote, "Many [participants in the Iacobucci review] also expressed surprise that the organizers had not consulted more broadly and had not, for example, sought the assistance of any member of York's Centre for Jewish Studies." This unmediated assertion ignored or disregarded the involvement of the International Advisory Board. In addition, it appears to have been factually incorrect. Drummond informed me that the organizers had sought the assistance of members of York's Centre for Jewish Studies, including an invitation to serve on the conference's Advisory Board. She also informed me that no such assistance was provided.

Implicit in this unmediated assertion is that participation in conference planning or in the conference by one or more faculty members from a Jewish Studies group or an academic group with similar expertise was essential for a conference on statehood models for Israel/Palestine. The conference's International Advisory Board included distinguished experts on the conference topic such as Ian Lustick, a former president of the Association for Israel Studies, who was one of the keynote speakers. The conference speakers included Marc Ellis, University Professor of Jewish Studies at Baylor University. This unmediated assertion leaves the impression that those who made it did not agree with the views of such distinguished scholars as Lustick and Ellis. Anyone may disagree with the views of any scholars, but such disagreement does not by itself establish superiority of the views of critics.

Academic Freedom in the Iacobucci Report. The other main pillar supporting Iacobucci's recommendations is a diminished—indeed reactionary—conception of academic freedom, As discussed below, his adherence to such a conception is clear, despite the fact his report does include a number of quotations from a variety of books, reports, policy statements, collective agreements, and *ad hoc* statements defining, explaining, or defending academic freedom, some of which are relatively recent. The array of quotations and related discussions on academic freedom occupies approximately nineteen pages of the report, amounting to slightly more than the space occupied by the "perspectives on the conference" section. It is not clear from the text of the report whether the near equality of these two space allocations was intended as a measure of balance, or had some significant purpose that was not cosmetic. In any case, the array of quotations and related discussions on academic freedom creates, at first reading, the impression that the recommendations to which it leads will be supported by a current and widely accepted understanding of this right of faculty members in Canada.

For example, Iacobucci quoted remarks by former university president James Downey:

> The primary mission of the university is not to train but to educate [...] Through teaching and research the university must cultivate a spirit of intellectual dissent. Not for its own sake, but in the interests of a free, tolerant, enlightened, and improving society.[59]

He also cited the 1969 report to York University by Bora Laskin that emphasized the importance in a university of toleration of unsettling opinions (cited also in the present report). Yet, Iacobucci opened his report with the comment that the conference "str[uck] at the heart of deeply held religious and political beliefs," thereby giving the impression that if an academic event offends the religious or political beliefs of some person or group, the university may reasonably be expected to direct that the event be either modified or cancelled, so as to eliminate the claimed (perhaps, even, potentially claimed) offence. A reasonable inference is that the beliefs of some persons may trump the rights, possibly even the beliefs, of others in the academy. This impression is borne out by the full report. As Professor Jamie Cameron of Osgoode Hall had predicted in a brief submitted to this Inquiry, Iacobucci's report culminated with recommendations to the effect that York University establish a system of prior approval and restraint for academic events. In other words, his report recommended a mechanism of institutional censorship, despite sporadic assurances that such was not his intent.

Iacobucci appeared to rely also on *For the Common Good* (2009) by Professors Finkin and Post in support of his conception of academic freedom. For instance, at page 53, in a section advocating that "limits and qualifications" to academic freedom, as well as "responsibilities" and "accountability" in relation to "professional standards" in the exercise of this right, should be "spelled out," Iacobucci asserted that "these responsibilities are alluded to but not spelled out as clearly as they might be in York's various policies and statements."[60] Apparently in support of this position, he included a passage from page 154 of *For the Common Good*, but on the same page Finkin and Post made an additional statement, one not cited by Iacobucci:

> Even though institutions of higher education in fact rely on public acceptance, they cannot shackle scholars to the "generally accepted beliefs" of those "persons, private or official, through whom society provides the means for the maintenance of universities." Used in the wrong way, catchphrases of

responsibility and restraint can "become a negation, rather than a complement, of academic freedom."[61]

A basic problem with Iacobucci's prescription for perceived ills of the academy is that he conceives of it as being possible—indeed, recommends—that catchphrases such as "responsibilities" can be "spelled out" in a way that, for example, fulfil a purported "obligation to be sensitive to equality issues such as those relating to gender, religion, race and the dignity of the individual in general," without becoming a negation of academic freedom.[62] There is a reason, with a long and storied history, why such things are not spelled out, except in general terms: spelling them out would almost certainly invite their use by some person or group displeased by discussion of some topic in an effort to limit or prevent such discussion, thereby infringing academic freedom.

Fundamentalism. Mr. Iacobucci's report bolstered the case for his conception by a time-honoured device: academic fundamentalism—reliance on a highly selective reading of a text from an earlier time, combined with inferences supported neither by the text nor the intent of its authors. The text is the 1915 *Declaration of Principles on Academic Freedom and Academic Tenure* of the American Association of University Professors (AAUP).

The 1915 *Declaration* is venerable, and substantial parts of it remain highly relevant. At issue are the manner and purpose for which Iacobucci used the short passage he quoted in support of his recommendations to York University, as well as the relevance of passages he did not quote to the circumstances he addresses and to his argument. It is important to have an understanding and appreciation of the social and political context in which this nearly century-old document was drafted, from which the intent of the authors can reasonably be inferred. For this purpose, *The Development of Academic Freedom in the United States* (1955) by Hofstadter and Metzger is a valuable resource. It is also important that in the intervening century the conception of academic freedom has substantially broadened in the USA, and even more so in Canada, as outlined in Chapter 8.

The 1915 *Declaration* is approximately ten pages in length (in the format presented on the AAUP website), and from it Iacobucci selected part of one paragraph. The centre (and centrepiece) of the passage he quoted (at page 38 of his report) is the following:

> So far as the university teacher's independence of thought and utterance is concerned—though not in other regards—the

> relationship of professor to trustees may be compared to that
> between judges of the federal courts and the executive who
> appoints them [63]

The context when this passage was drafted was that there was no effective right to academic freedom and no effective tenure in the USA in 1915,
so that an appeal to an existing model of independence of thought and
security of employment was natural. However, it is abundantly clear from
other passages in the *Declaration* that the qualifier "though not in other
regards" was of fundamental importance to the drafting committee and the
new association that adopted it. This document was drafted by a committee that included some of the most outspoken professors of the day, and
some of the most active defenders of their outspoken colleagues.

There are passages especially relevant to a controversial event such as the
one at hand, and the *Declaration* spoke specifically of "the special dangers
to freedom of teaching in the domain of the social sciences." It observed
that "the most serious difficulty" arose from

> the dangers connected with the existence in a democracy of an
> overwhelming and concentrated public opinion. The tendency
> of modern democracy is for men to think alike, to feel alike, and
> to speak alike. Any departure from the conventional standards is
> apt to be regarded with suspicion. Public opinion is at once the
> chief safeguard of a democracy, and the chief menace to the real
> liberty of the individual. [...] in a democracy there is political
> freedom, but there is likely to be a tyranny of public opinion.

The *Declaration* then proposed a solution to this problem:

> An inviolable refuge from such tyranny should be found in
> the university. It should be an intellectual experiment station,
> where new ideas may germinate and where their fruit, though
> still distasteful to the community as a whole, may be allowed
> to ripen until finally, perchance, it may become a part of the
> accepted intellectual food of the nation or of the world. [...]
> One of its most characteristic functions in a democratic society
> is to help make public opinion more self-critical and more
> circumspect, to check the more hasty and unconsidered impulses
> of popular feeling, to train the democracy to the habit of looking

before and after. It is precisely this function of the university
which is most injured by any restriction upon academic freedom;
and it is precisely those who most value this aspect of the
university's work who should most earnestly protest against any
such restriction.

These passages are as timely today as in 1915. It is unclear from his report
whether Iacobucci did not cite passages such as the foregoing because they
would have undermined his argument, or for some other reason.

In any case, in his "Recommendations" Iacobucci returned to the passage he had earlier cited and regarding which he had said, "That statement
is an eloquent articulation of what I believe lies behind the concept of
academic freedom."[64] However, in this second, more significant reference he used different wording when leading into one of his key recommendations. Instead of the phrase, "though not in other regards" in the
Declaration as he had correctly quoted at his page 38, he wrote at page 61,
"in some respects," that is, he substituted a flexible phrase for the comprehensively exclusive phrase in the original AAUP document.

Iacobucci's complete statement was:

As I noted above [Iacobucci report, p. 38–40], the 1915
Declaration of Principles on Academic Freedom and Academic Tenure
draws an analogy in some respects between the duties and
professional self-regulation of academics and judges. I agree
with and endorse that analogy. There is a similarity in rationale
between the independence of the judiciary in the fulfilling of
its role, particularly in the rendering of its decisions, and the
academic freedom of the professoriate to pursue their teaching,
research, and academic activities.[65]

From this he not unreasonably inferred, "Just as guidelines for the
conduct of individual judges come from other judges, so too must the
standards to which academics should aspire be set by fellow academics."[66]
However, his very next sentence constituted a conceptual leap:

Flowing from this is the requirement that academics, themselves,
conduct the necessary work to instigate changes to the academic
freedom policies and procedures at York, and to establish a set of
best practices.[67]

In other words, the report in effect recommended to professors at York University that they engage in an exercise of producing self-censorship guidelines. As to what a "Statement of Best Practices" should include, he explained his view with such words and phrases as "civil discourse," "respect," "dignity," "obligation to be sensitive," and "responsibility." For example:

> The concept of civil discourse is expressly and impliedly
> intended to be present in academic discussion. Likewise, mutual
> respect for those who are spoken with or listened to in academic
> settings is highlighted.[68]

As to the meaning of such assertions, it is reasonable to take Iacobucci at his word: academics should in controversial matters behave like judges. However, in the academy there has always been, and there will continue to be, a variety of controversial matters. Discourse in the academy is characteristically disputatious and may often appear (and occasionally may even be) somewhat uncivil. He cites no significant document in support of his assertion that "civil discourse is expressly and impliedly intended to be present in academic discussion," possibly because the history of academic freedom does not provide support.

Society has expectations regarding the behaviour and discourse of judges because they have the power to deprive people of their liberty or property—a power not normally possessed by academics. It is abundantly clear that this is not what the drafters of the 1915 *Declaration* and founders of the AAUP had in mind. They organized themselves into an association in order to better defend outspoken professors, including very outspoken ones, such as the economist and sociologist Edward A. Ross, whose dismissal by Stanford University was one of the events stimulating both the founding of the AAUP and the drafting of the 1915 *Declaration*. In summary, Iacobucci represented the content of the AAUP 1915 *Declaration*, and the intent of its framers, in ways that were inaccurate.

Iacobucci suggested that it will be possible, through his proposed "best practices" exercise, to develop a "shared understanding about the meaning of academic freedom." This is not only improbable, but such an enterprise would pose a potential danger to academic freedom. Professors need academic freedom as a defence against those wish to circumscribe dissent.

Deep disagreements over the meaning of academic freedom are unavoidable. However, contrary to what Iacobucci suggests, strong disagreement, strongly expressed, does not necessarily entail lack of professional respect. The recent exchange between Professors Ze'ev Sternhell and Gabriel Piterberg on Zionist ideology and colonialism provides an instructive illustration.[69] Many other examples could be given, such as the criticism of each other's work by historians A. J. P. Taylor and Hugh Trevor-Roper.

In 1971 Yale University president Kingman Brewster wrote:

> This spirit of academic freedom within the university has a value
> which goes beyond protecting the individual's broad scope
> of thought and inquiry. It bears crucially upon the distinctive
> quality of the university as a community. If a university is alive
> and productive it is a place where colleagues are in constant
> dispute; defending their latest intellectual enthusiasm, attacking
> the contrary views of others. From this trial by intellectual
> combat emerges a sharper insight, later to be blunted by other,
> sharper minds. It is vital that this contest be uninhibited by fear
> of reprisal.[70]

In the closing pages of his report, Iacobucci provided reassurances to the effect that his recommendations did not mean what they plainly said. For example, they were "not intended to be restrictive of academic freedom." Presumably his comment that the intent of a "Statement of Best Practices" on the exercise of academic freedom "would not be to create any binding provisions for faculty members that would be accompanied by sanctions" also was intended to be helpful to readers. All he intended, he wrote, is that "the Best Practices would serve as reminders."[71]

In a late addition to his report (inserted between its release in draft form to a limited audience and its public release in final form), he provided an additional reassurance. He said that none of his recommended actions would be "intended to circumvent or interfere with normal collective bargaining processes." Instead he proposed that the university's senate carry out the tasks he recommended, and the fruits of its labour could then be brought to "the parties to the collective agreements."[72]

I do not question Iacobucci's sincerity in putting forward his reassurances. In view of the diminished conception of academic freedom he advanced, and the standards of evidence and reasoning by which his report is characterized, it would have been logically consistent for him to have affirmed that his recommendations were "not intended to be restrictive of academic freedom."

However, any "Best Practices" document, or even a "Handbook on Academic Freedom" (another of the recommendations), could in practice be considered by someone, sometime, as an interpretive manual for the YUFA collective agreement. It would thus increase the probability that infringements of academic freedom would occur that otherwise might not occur, as well as encouraging eventual demands for renegotiation of collective agreement articles pertaining directly or indirectly to academic freedom. In brief, such a document would provide recipes for future trouble.

The modern American source cited in the Iacobucci report, *For the Common Good*, is well written and informative. However, it is a book about academic freedom in the USA, where the prevailing definition (in the 1940 joint AAUP–AAC *Statement*, amended subsequently by a series of clarifications) is less comprehensive than the one prevailing in Canada (the CAUT definition, as reflected in the York/YUFA collective agreement and similar documents Canada-wide). No less importantly, the right to academic freedom is less well protected in the USA than in Canada. As a result, some American experts, such as these two authors, set out a conservative view of the right that can be more effectively defended in specific cases in their legal/quasi-legal/political context. It is not clear from his report that Iacobucci understood or appreciated such differences.

I conclude that the recommendations in the Iacobucci report pertaining to academic freedom were not well-founded and not appropriate for a Canadian university. I further conclude that, if implemented, such recommendations could lead to circumstances in which academic freedom at York University would be seriously diminished from the right currently prevailing and, moreover, if implemented at York, they could represent a serious adverse precedent for academic freedom in Canada.

LIMITS TO COLLEGIALITY

The faculty members in Osgoode Hall Law School do not have procedural protections available to other faculty members at York University. They do not have a comprehensive document on terms and conditions of employment that is comparable to the York/YUFA collective agreement. In particular, they do not have access to the type of grievance and arbitration procedures available to other university faculty members in Canada. As a result, their faculty association, OHFA, although vigilant and vigorous, lacks effective means to enforce rights and maintain principles, means available to faculty in other law schools in Canada, as well as to all members of the YUFA bargaining unit.

There are historical reasons why faculty in the school were not included in the YUFA bargaining unit in the 1970s, and an earlier type of collegial model was retained in Osgoode Hall. Collegial models of the university employment relationship were a considerable advance over the models prevalent before the 1960s. However, they were more highly dependent on personal approaches than on more modern structured models in which rights and principles are defined and enforceable—with a substantial measure of procedural equality—by both faculty and administrators.

In significant respects, faculty in Osgoode Hall Law School are in a situation similar to clinical faculty in many medical schools—decades behind York University colleagues in other faculties in regard to procedural protections. The situation in medical schools also has a historical basis, but with the additional complications that clinical professors' financial compensation comes largely through the hospitals instead of the universities, and they are in effect employed by two employers (the university and the affiliated health-care institution) that are legally separate corporate entities. These impediments are not present in the case of Osgoode Hall faculty members.

From my discussions with representatives of OHFA, it was clear that they understood that their members were at a procedural disadvantage in relation to colleagues in other York faculties and in other faculties of law in Canada.

10
LESSONS AND RECOMMENDATIONS

LESSONS

In his 1995 remarks to an audience of academic administrators, former York University president Harry Arthurs said that "academic freedom is a central value, arguably the central value of university life." It also has been and remains important to the maintenance of a free and democratic society. Noting that in any democracy there are frequent occurrences of "overwhelming and concentrated public opinion," the AAUP 1915 *Declaration* said freedom of expression for university professors is necessary in the ongoing task of helping to "train the democracy to look before and after." It is for the common good.

Although it is better protected in Canada than in any other country, and better protected here now than it was a few decades ago, academic freedom remains a fragile right. Governments have the power to infringe on this right in many significant ways for which there is no direct procedural recourse, but broad-based collective political action can sometimes be effective. The era of McCarthyism in the United States provided many examples in which the academic community largely acquiesced, although coordinated resistance was possible and might have been effective. Actions by the Bennett (Social Credit) provincial government in British Columbia in the 1980s and by the recent Graham (Liberal) provincial government in New Brunswick had potentially serious adverse consequences for academic freedom and university autonomy. In both these instances, the potential effects were limited or deflected as a result of large-scale political-action campaigns involving not only academics but—significantly and importantly—many other civil society organizations.

The York/Queen's conference was successfully held as planned and scheduled; however, the fact that a campaign of the type mounted against it by Israel lobby groups could arise in Canada nearly three-quarters of a century after the similar campaign by Christian groups in New York City against the appointment of Bertrand Russell to the City College serves to emphasize the perpetual vulnerability of academic freedom and the need for ongoing vigilance to protect it.

It is reasonable to infer that the favourable outcome in the case of the York/Queen's conference resulted at least in part from academic freedom being at present widely accepted and respected in Canada, and threats to it having been vigorously opposed by the organizers and some of their colleagues, along with CAUT, which made the Harper government's interference with SSHRC into a public issue. These factors may have served as informal restraints on the government, so that its interference was limited—on this occasion. In contrast, the power of the state exercised through the courts and the city government in the 1940 Russell case and by congressional committees during the era of McCarthyism was unbridled.

A related lesson to be drawn is that a robust national organization, with established and respected policies and procedures, and with the resources to provide prompt and effective assistance, is indispensable to the maintenance of academic freedom. There have been several recent incidents in the United States, the United Kingdom, and France, in which Israel lobby groups and their supporters succeeded in having academic events cancelled—in none of these countries is there a faculty organization comparable in effectiveness to CAUT in Canada.

CAUT is only as strong as the majority of its local associations. Moreover, its strength and effectiveness are enhanced when existing campus affiliates are strengthened, or through new affiliations. CAUT and the Osgoode Hall Faculty Association would be mutually strengthened by OHFA affiliation with CAUT, and by the provision to OHFA members of the robust procedural protections available to other university faculty members in Toronto and elsewhere, through a new arrangement between OHFA and York University.

As always in such matters, personal courage is indispensable, and this was displayed throughout the controversy by a number of individuals, including the four members of the organizing committee and several university administrators.

Finally, while academic freedom developed in part out of relatively ancient traditions, its modern forms developed from the Enlightenment, along with broader rights and freedoms. Periods of reaction against these rights and freedoms are recurrent, and a new reactionary period appears to be emerging world-wide. Ze'ev Sternhell closed his analysis of these phenomena with the observation that "to prevent people of the twenty-first century from sinking into a new ice age of resignation, the Enlightenment vision of the individual as creative of his or her present and hence his or her future is irreplaceable."[1]

RECOMMENDATIONS

The terms of reference for this Inquiry included a request to "make recommendations as to policies and procedures that will safeguard academic freedom and the integrity of educational work."

Recommendation 1. The York University Faculty Association and the Osgoode Hall Faculty Association should endeavour to ensure that the currently accepted definition of academic freedom at York University (deemed to be that provided by Article 10 in the York/YUFA collective agreement), and the means of protecting the right to academic freedom, are not diminished or otherwise restricted by senate or other processes arising from recommendations in the Iacobucci report. CAUT should offer assistance to both associations in such efforts, even though OHFA is not currently affiliated with it.

Recommendation 2. The Osgoode Hall Faculty Association should take steps to provide itself and its members with modern procedural protections, including an enforceable definition of and right to academic freedom, as well as other terms and conditions of academic employment, such as a grievance and arbitration procedure covering all significant matters, comparable to the protections available to members of YUFA or to those available to faculty members in other faculties of law in Canada. There are several possible avenues by which OHFA could achieve this recommended objective, including a merger with YUFA to form a single, larger bargaining unit; an application for separate certification as a collective bargaining agent under the Ontario labour code; a request to the board of governors for voluntary recognition as a bargaining agent; or through negotiation of a comprehensive agreement on terms and conditions along the lines of the Memorandum of Agreement between the University of Toronto and UTFA. CAUT should offer assistance to OHFA in this matter.

Changes in the general political, economic, and other circumstances in which universities and academics sometimes find themselves cannot always be successfully addressed through university policies and procedures, as historical events in Canada and elsewhere illustrate. Events such as government actions or large-scale political currents can render procedural protections ineffective. In the present instance, the Conservative government's inference in the work of SSHRC and SSHRC's response posed a threat to academic freedom and integrity that was unprecedented and significant in the post-war Canadian context. Even though the interference and its immediate effects were limited, it may have adverse longer-term effects on how all three federal granting councils conduct their work in future, not least because of the climate of uncertainty brought on by these events. The government may possibly have felt constrained by its minority status and its perception of its prospects for achieving a majority in Parliament in a future election. Having achieved majority status in May 2011, it is no longer constrained in that respect.

In many circumstances, the only possible constraint on arbitrary or ill-advised government actions, however limited in its effectiveness, would be a greater understanding and an appreciation of academic freedom and the integrity of educational work by the public. To this end, development of an increased sense of social and political solidarity between the Canadian academic community and society at large would be essential.

Regardless of which party or parties may be in power federally or provincially in Canada during the next decade or so, the social atomization processes of recent decades—in Canada and internationally—that are in significant measure the result of neoliberal political economies, may continue. Increasingly, the public interest—including individual and collective rights—is being pushed aside by measures giving primacy to private profit. Democracy, as we have known it in the past half-century, is being eroded.

In particular, the systemic problems now faced by university communities, such as erosions of academic integrity and infringements of academic freedom due to increasing commercialization of the academy and casualization of academic work, are direct or indirect consequences of neoliberal government policies, or in some instances also neoconservative policies. Continuation of such government policies is, in principle, neither inevitable nor inexorable, but they will continue and become more severe in their adverse effects unless actively countered by an engaged citizenry through electoral and other democratic means.

Without significant collective citizen actions on many fronts, Canadians can expect that the existing frameworks that protect the public interest will continue to be eroded, as part of an international trend as well as a national one. For Canadian academics, an important area of erosion is that of the context for collective bargaining on which our robust right to academic freedom significantly depends at present.[2]

CAUT has already been active in developing informal coalitions with other civil-society organizations. For example, it collaborated with diverse groups in 2010 in connection with protests over the cancellation of the mandatory long form in the census. This campaign was not successful, but such is often the case with public-interest campaigns against arbitrary measures by governments. The important point is that there is no significant practical alternative to such broad-based coalitions in the present political economy, and even if such campaigns are only rarely successful, they are worthwhile in that they can help build social and political solidarity for the future. Everyone should bear in mind that it took three decades of citizen effort through many channels before the social programs we currently still enjoy in Canada were instituted in the 1960s, and that a number of academics played prominent roles in this process. In addition to helping to broaden and strengthen CAUT's public information work on the importance of academic freedom and the integrity of educational work, such efforts would help create informal alliances for broader endeavours.

Recommendation 3. CAUT should expand its efforts, particularly through engaging more of its individual members through their local faculty associations and through cooperation with their learned societies, in creating and developing informal coalitions with civil-society organizations.

The Harry Crowe Foundation has organized conferences on several current issues affecting academic freedom and the integrity of academic work, each of which had an international dimension. Recent events strongly suggest that the coming years will see deteriorations in one or more of our climatic, environmental, economic, social, and political circumstances, globally as well as nationally. There is uncertainty, as always, but the larger uncertainties may pertain to whether such evolutions will be gradual or rapid.

Recommendation 4. The Board of Directors of the Harry Crowe Foundation should be approached to consider organizing an international conference on the implications of the evolving political circumstances for the protection of academic freedom and the integrity of academic work, and how to contend effectively with the effects of significant changes in the circumstances in which universities find themselves. A conference cannot by itself make a major difference, but catalytic events and organizational nuclei are needed.

APPENDICES

Appendix A – The Members of the Conference Organizing Committee
http://www.caut.ca/thompson-report/appendix-a.aspx

Appendix B – List of Sponsors and Advisory Board Members
http://www.caut.ca/thompson-report/appendix-b.aspx

Appendix C – Conference Vision Statement
http://www.caut.ca/thompson-report/appendix-c.aspx

Appendix D – JDL Boycott Warning, October 4, 2008
http://www.caut.ca/thompson-report/appendix-d.aspx

Appendix E – Suggestion by Board Chair Marshall Cohen, April 15, 2009
http://www.caut.ca/thompson-report/appendix-e.aspx

Appendix F – Message from Dean Monahan to Irving and Rosalie Abella, April 15, 2009
http://www.caut.ca/thompson-report/appendix-f.aspx

Appendix G – AVPR Dewitt's Email to the Organizers, April 15, 2009
http://www.caut.ca/thompson-report/appendix-g.aspx

Appendix H – Keynote Speakers
http://www.caut.ca/thompson-report/appendix-h.aspx

Appendix I – Views Expressed by Dean Monahan, May 9–10, 2009
http://www.caut.ca/thompson-report/appendix-i.aspx

Appendix J – An Agreement between the AVPR and Dean, May 11–12, 2009
http://www.caut.ca/thompson-report/appendix-j.aspx

Appendix K – CIJA Statement, May 12, 2009
http://www.caut.ca/thompson-report/appendix-k.aspx

Appendix L – President Shoukri's Statement, May 21, 2009
http://www.caut.ca/thompson-report/appendix-l.aspx

Appendix M – Statement by the Honourable Gary Goodyear, June 5, 2009
http://www.caut.ca/thompson-report/appendix-m.aspx

Appendix N – SSHRC Correspondence with Conference Organizers
http://www.caut.ca/thompson-report/appendix-n.aspx

Appendix O – Letter from McNaughton to Yasmeen re: Draft to Ryder
http://www.caut.ca/thompson-report/appendix-o.aspx

Appendix P – Steinberg Op-ed, June 9, 2009
http://www.caut.ca/thompson-report/appendix-p.aspx

Appendix Q – Lustick Op-ed, June 11, 2009
http://www.caut.ca/thompson-report/appendix-q.aspx

Appendix R – Open Letters by Osgoode Hall and Queen's Law Faculty Members
http://www.caut.ca/thompson-report/appendix-r.aspx

Appendix S – Statement by President Shoukri and Board Chairs, June 15, 2009
http://www.caut.ca/thompson-report/appendix-s.aspx

Appendix T – Remarks by Deans Monahan and Flanagan, June 22, 2009
http://www.caut.ca/thompson-report/appendix-t.aspx

Appendix U – Open Letter by York Faculty and Students
http://www.caut.ca/thompson-report/appendix-u.aspx

Appendix V – Iacobucci Review Terms of Reference
http://www.caut.ca/thompson-report/appendix-v.aspx

Appendix W – CAUT Policy Statement on Academic Freedom and Academic Freedom Clause (Article 10) from the YUFA Collective Agreement
http://www.caut.ca/thompson-report/appendix-w.aspx

Appendix X – Contributions to Inquiry
http://www.caut.ca/thompson-report/appendix-x.aspx

Appendix Y – York U50 Application, April 2008
http://www.caut.ca/thompson-report/appendix-y.aspx

ENDNOTES

FOREWORD

1   Harry Arthurs, "Academic Freedom: When and Where?" Notes for a Panel Discussion at the Annual Conference of the Association of Universities and Colleges of Canada. Halifax, N.S., October 5, 1995, p. 1.

2   Ibid.

3   Jon Thompson, Patricia Baird and Jocelyn Downie, The Olivieri Report: The Complete Text of the Report of the independent commission of inquiry by the Canadian Association of University Teachers. Toronto: James Lorimer & Co., 2001

4   See Ellen W. Schrecker, No Ivory Tower: McCarthyism & The Universities. New York: Oxford University Press, 1986.

5   K. Brewster, Annual Report, 1971, quoted in W. Van Alstyne, "The Meaning of Tenure" in M. W. Finkin, ed., The Case for Tenure (Ithaca: Cornell University Press, 1996), p. 62.

CHAPTER 1

1   A. Eban, "Our Place in the Human Scheme," Congress Bi-Weekly, March 30, 1973, p. 5–9.

2   J. Mearsheimer, "Israel and American Academia," text of comments in a symposium on "Freedom and the University," Columbia University, October 30, 2007.

3   The AAUP's 1915 Declaration: http://www.aaup.org/AAUP/pubsres/policydocs/contents/1915.htm.

4   Z. Sternhell, The Anti-Enlightenment Tradition (New Haven, CT: Yale University Press, 2010).

5   This statement opens Chapter 21, "The Problem of Equality" in Israel's Enlightenment Contested: Philosophy, Modernity, and the Emancipation of Man, 1670–1752 (New York: Oxford University Press, 2006), p. 545. Israel has explained that by the term Radical Enlightenment he meant "a set of basic principles that can be summed up concisely as: racial and sexual equality; individual liberty of lifestyle; full freedom of thought, expression, and the press; eradication of religious authority from the legislative process and education; and full separation of church and state." (J. Israel, A Revolution of the Mind: Radical Enlightenment and the intellectual Origins of Modern Democracy [Princeton: Princeton University Press, 2010], p. vii–viii).

6   Z. Sternhell, "In Defence of Liberal Zionism," New Left Review 62, March/April 2010, p. 107.

7   This observation was made by Richard Hofstadter and Walter P. Metzger, summarizing the views of economists Richard T. Ely and Edward W. Bemis, who were subjected to dismissal proceedings in the mid-1890s, in The Development of Academic Freedom in the United States

(New York: Columbia University Press, 1955), p. 425.

8   A. Judt, reply to letters in response to his "Israel: The Alternative," *New York Review of Books*, December 4, 2003, p. 19 (www.nybooks.com/articles/16824, accessed October 27, 2009).

9   The full text is in Appendix S at http://www.caut.ca/thompson-report/appendix-s.aspx.

CHAPTER 2

1   *Commons Debates*, 30th Canadian Parliament, 3rd session, December 13, 1976, p. 1,938.

2   *Commons Debates*, 30th Canadian Parliament, 3rd session, April 22, 1977, p. 4,913.

3   Email, L. Chiv (Industry Canada) to T. Lynn, U. Gobel, and D. Holton (SSHRC), October 5, 2009, with Media Lines attached (ATI 2009–2010 16), p. 51–54.

4   Letter, T. Clement, replying to an email message dated June 15, 2009, from a person whose name is redacted on the copy released to CAUT by the Privy Council Office through Industry Canada (reply undated) (PCO ATI release pages 000025–000026).

5   M. Wente, *Globe and Mail*, September 19, 2009, p. A21.

6   A. Oz, from the text of his 2005 Goethe Prize lecture, quoted in Y. Laor, *The Myths of Liberal Zionism* (London: Verso, 2009), p. 104–105.

7   G. Myrdal, *An American Dilemma: The Negro Problem and Modern Democracy*, Twentieth Anniversary Edition (New York: Harper & Row, 1964), p. 1016. (Originally published by Harper & Bros., 1944.)

8   F. P. Keppel, 1944 Foreword to *An American Dilemma*.

9   Ibid.

10   D. H. Price, *Threatening Anthropology: McCarthyism and the FBI's Surveillance of Activist Anthropologists* (Durham: Duke University Press, 2004), p. 35.

11   C. Robin, "Conservatism and Counterrevolution," *Raritan* 30, no.1 (June 1, 2010).

12   I. Abella and H. Troper, *None is Too Many* (Toronto: Lester & Orpen Dennys, 1986; first published in 1983), p. 64.

13   Ibid., p. 178.

14   Ibid., p. 283.

15   J. J. Mearsheimer and S. M. Walt, *The Israel Lobby and U.S. Foreign Policy* (New York: Farrar, Strauss and Giroux, 2007), p. 355.

16   Ibid., p. 341.

17   Among earlier discussions were the book *The Lobby: Jewish Political Power and American Foreign Policy* by E. Tivnan (New York: Simon and Schuster, 1987), and two articles in the *New York Times*, July 6 and 7, 1987, by D. K. Shipler, and R. Pear and R. L. Berke, respectively.

18   Mearsheimer and Walt, *Israel Lobby*, p. vii.

19   Ibid., p. viii.

20   Ibid., p. ix.

21   Ibid., p. 191.

22   Ibid., p. 193.

23   J. J. Mearsheimer and S. M. Walt, "The Israel Lobby and U.S. Foreign Policy." A Working Paper available at http://web.hks.harvard.edu/publications/workingpapers/citation. aspx?PubId=3670, p. 24. Accessed on November 4, 2009.

24   Mearsheimer and Walt, *Israel Lobby* (book), p. 185.

25   Ibid., p. 191–192, 196.

26   Ibid., p. 188, 190.

27   N. Chomsky, transcript of a talk given October 11, 2002, http://www.fromoccupiedpalestine. org/node/116.

28   Published discussions of Israel lobby organizations in Canada and their political influence

can be found in: Marci McDonald, "The Heather and Gerry Show," *Toronto Life* (June 2005) and her book *The Armageddon Factor* (Toronto: Random House, 2010); Daniel Freeman-Maloy "AIPAC North," ZNet, June 26, 2006 (http://www.zcommunications.org/aipac-north-by-dan-freeman-maloy); and David Noble, "The New Israel Lobby in Action," *Canadian Dimension*, November-December 2005 (http://canadiandimension.com/articles/1890/).

29   The organizers were Professors Joan W. Scott, Jeremy Adelman, Edmund Burke III, Steven Caton, and Jonathan R. Cole. Professor Scott is a former chair of the AAUP's Committee A; Professor Cole is provost emeritus of Columbia University.

30   J. W. Scott, et al., petition at http://sites.google.com/site/defenduniversity/home.

31   Ibid.

32   See, for example, A. R. D. Matthias, "The Ignorance of Bourabaki," *Mathematical Intelligencer* 14 (1992), p. 3–14.

33   F. Stern, *Five Germanys I Have Known* (New York: Farrar, Strauss and Giroux, 2006), p. 203, 298.

34   Z. Sternhell, *The Founding Myths of Israel: Nationalism, Socialism, and the Making of the Jewish State* (Princeton: Princeton University Press, 1998), p. x. See also G. Piterberg, *The Returns of Zionism: Myths, Politics and Scholarship in Israel* (New York: Verso, 2008), and S. Sand, *The Invention of the Jewish People* (New York: Verso, 2009).

35   N. Chomsky, *On Power and Ideology: The Managua Lectures* (Boston: South End Press, 1987), p. 69.

36   See W. Leontieff, "Academic Economics," letter to the editor, *Science*, July 9, 1982, p. 106–107; W. Vickrey, "Fifteen fatal fallacies of financial fundamentalism: A disquisition on demand-side economics," *Proc. Nat. Acad. Sci. USA* 95, February 1998, p. 1340–1347; J. Stiglitz. *Free Fall: America, Free Markets, and the Sinking of the World Economy* (New York: W. W. Norton, 2010), p. 238. See also M. Angell, "The Epidemic of Mental Illness: Why?" and "The Illusions of Psychiatry," *New York Review of Books*, June 23 and July 14, 2011.

37   J. Lehrer, "The Truth Wears Off," *New Yorker*, December 13, 2010.

CHAPTER 3

1   The Oslo Accords (officially, the *Declaration of Principles on Interim Self-Government Arrangements*) were negotiated subsequent to the 1988 announcement by PLO Chair Yasser Arafat that his organization was prepared to accept UN Security Council Resolution 242, adopted unanimously in 1967, following the Six-Day War. Among other things, this meant recognition of the State of Israel by the PLO—a reversal of its long-standing position.

2   A different type of one-state model also was under active consideration from the 1920s onward, one in which all of Palestine would become a Jewish state. It had substantial support among the Jewish community in Palestine, but with the UN decision on partition of the territory it, too, did not come to fruition. However, a variant has recently become a topic of public discussion in Israel.

3   A. J. Mayer, *The Furies: Violence and Terror in the French and Russian Revolutions* (Princeton: Princeton University Press, 2000), p. 483.

4   G. Lefebvre, *The French Revolution* (London: Routledge, 2004), p. 141.

5   A. J. Mayer, *Plowshares into Swords* (New York: Verso, 2008), p. 103.

6   N. Chomsky, "Breaking the Israel-Palestinian Deadlock," *ZNet*, January 4, 2011 (http://www.zcommunications.org/breaking-the-israel-palestine-deadlock-by-noam-chomsky). A discussion of apparent influences of Christian Zionism on Herzl and other Zionists can be found in *The Returns of Zionism* by Gabriel Piterberg (New York: Verso, 2008), Chapter 7.

7   A. J. Mayer, *Why Did the Heavens Not Darken?* (New York: Verso, 1990), p. 5.

8   Ibid., p. 6–7.

9   Z. Sternhell, *The Anti-Enlightenment Tradition* (New Haven, CT: Yale University Press, 2010), p. 439.

10 A. J. Mayer, *Why Did the Heavens Not Darken?* (New York: Verso, 1990), p. 113–114. In *The Origins of the Second World War*, A. J. P. Taylor wrote that Hitler "did not 'seize' power. He waited for it to be thrust upon him by the men who had previously tried to keep him out. In January 1933 Papen and Hindenburg were imploring him to become Chancellor; and he

graciously consented." (New York: Touchstone, 1996, p. 71; first published in 1961.)

11   Ibid. p. 216–218.

12   F. Stern, "A Fundamental History Lesson: The Rise of National Socialism Proved Politics and Religion Don't Mix," *In These Times*, October 10, 2005.

13   F. Stern, "Imperial Hubris: A German Tale," *Lapham's Quarterly* 1, no. 1 (Winter 2008), p. 205–210.

14   A. J. Mayer, *Plowshares into Swords: From Zionism to Israel* (New York: Verso, 2008), p. 7.

15   Z. Sternhell, *The Anti-Enlightenment Tradition*, p. 441.

16   Z. Sternhell, "In Defence of Liberal Zionism," *New Left Review* 62, March–April 2010, p. 111.

17   An outline of the commitments, with a summary of modern scholarship concerning them, can be found in Avi Shlaim, *Israel and Palestine* (New York: Verso, 2009).

18   J. Scheer, *The Balfour Declaration: The Origins of the Arab-Israeli Conflict* (Toronto: Bond Street Books, 2010), p. 347.

19   Ibid., p. 361.

20   B. Morris, *Righteous Victims: A History of the Zionist-Arab Conflict, 1881–2001* (New York: Vintage Books, 2001), p. 73.

21   Mayer, *Plowshares into Swords*, p. xi.

22   Ibid.

23   Ibid., p. 178, quoting J. Magnes.

24   Ibid., p. 198, quoting J. Magnes.

25   Ibid., p. 8–9.

26   The territory of the original (1920) Palestine Mandate accorded to Britain by the League of Nations included Transjordan. In 1922, the mandate was altered so that the region now called Palestine remained under direct British rule, while Transjordan became an autonomous Hashemite kingdom, and "the east bank of the Jordan river was closed to Jewish colonization." (Mayer, *Plowshares into Swords*, p. 118).

27   A. Shlaim, *The Iron Wall: Israel and the Arab World* (New York: W. W. Norton, 2001), p. 11–12.

28   Ibid., p. 12.

29   Ibid.

30   Mayer, *Plowshares into Swords*, p. 9.

31   Ibid., p. 125.

32   Shlaim, *The Iron Wall*, p. 16–17.

33   Quoted by Noam Chomsky in "Middle East Terrorism and the American Ideological System," Chapter 5 of *Blaming the Victims*, edited by E. W. Said and C. Hitchens (New York: Verso, 1991), p. 98 and 140n2.

34   A. Shlaim, *Israel and Palestine* (New York: Verso, 2009), p. 259.

35   Ibid.

36   Ibid., p. 259–260.

37   Mayer, *Plowshares into Swords*, p. 378.

38   I. Pappé, "The Deadly Closing of the Israeli Mind," *Independent*, June 6, 2010 (http://www.independent.co.uk/opinion/commentators/ilan-papp-the-deadly-closing-of-the-israeli-mind-1992471.html).

39   Ibid.

40   H. Siegman, "The Great Middle East Peace Process Scam," *London Review of Books*, August 16, 2007.

41   M. Arens, "Is There Another Option?" *Haaretz*, June 2, 2010 (http://www.haaretz.com/print-edition/opinion/is-there-another-option-1.293670).

42   Ibid.

43   R. Falk, transcript of a talk, "Imaging Israel-Palestine Peace: Why International Law Matters" at The Palestine Centre in Washington, DC in October 2009 (http://www.thejerusalemfund. org/ht/display/ContentDetails/i/7143/pid/897).

44   Shlaim, *Israel and Palestine*, p. 353.

45   T. Judt, "Israel: The Alternative," *New York Review of Books*, October 23, 2003 (www.nybooks. com/articles/16671, accessed October 27, 2009).

46   Ibid.

47   Ibid.

48   Mearsheimer and Walt, *The Israel Lobby*, p. 345–346.

49   Judt, reply to letters in response to his "Israel: The Alternative," *New York Review of Books*, December 4, 2003, p. 19 (www.nybooks.com/articles/16824, accessed October 27, 2009).

50   Benny Morris, *One State, Two States* (New Haven, CT: Yale University Press, 2009), p. 196.

51   Ibid., p. 199. During the past several years Professor Morris has promoted other solutions to political problems of the Middle East, in addition to the two in the closing pages of his 2009 book. In news media interviews and articles in 2004 he suggested that ethnic cleansing of Palestinians from their territory could be the best solution under certain conditions. More recently, he advocated another type of solution, namely, an Israeli military strike against Iran (preferably with American approval and assistance), "despite the likely devastating repercussions—regional and global." (http://www.guardian.co.uk/commentisfree/ cifamerica/2009/nov/24/obama-nuclear-spring-israel-iran).

CHAPTER 4

1   Biographical summaries of the four organizers are given in Appendix A at http://www.caut.ca/ thompson-report/appendix-a.aspx.

2   S. Drummond and B. Ryder, application ("Event Proposal") to the York U50 Committee, endorsed by P. Monahan, April 11, 2008. The application is in Appendix Y at http://www. caut.ca/thompson-report/appendix-y.aspx.

3   Morgan taught international and constitutional law, including legal aspects of the Middle East conflict. He was aware of "the ongoing controversies surrounding the Middle East conflict on the York campus," having served as legal counsel to the campus chapter of the Hasbara Fellowships, as he wrote to Frank Iacobucci on August 7, 2009. He had been president of the Canadian Jewish Congress (2004–2007) and was the founding National Chair of Canadian Academic Friends of Israel (CAFI).

4   Monahan "is widely regarded as one of Canada's leading constitutional experts." He served as dean from 2003 to 2009. In the academic year 2008–2009, he was a candidate for the position of Vice-President Academic and Provost of York University. He was appointed to this position effective July 1, 2009. He had served as a senior policy advisor to the Ontario government and "played a key role in the negotiation of the 1987 Meech Lake Accord." (http://vpacademic.yorku.ca/office/bio_monahan.php)

5   S. Drummond and B. Ryder, application ("Event Proposal") to the York U50 Committee, endorsed by P. Monahan, April 11, 2008. The application is in Appendix Y at http://www. caut.ca/thompson-report/appendix-y.aspx.

6   Appendix B at http://www.caut.ca/thompson-report/appendix-b.aspx lists all of the conference sponsors, as well as the final membership of the International Advisory Board.

7   The final program as mounted in June 2009 can be found at http://www.yorku.ca/ipconf/.

8   The full text of the vision statement is in Appendix C at http://www.caut.ca/thompson-report/ appendix-c.aspx.

9   Email, E. Morgan to S. Aiken, September 27, 2008.

10   Ibid.

11   Email, B. Geva to P. Monahan, copied to B. Ryder, S. Drummond, and others, October 2, 2008.

12   Later, the words "Prospects for" were changed to "Paths to."

13   Email, P. Monahan to B. Geva, B. Ryder, and S. Drummond, October 19, 2008.

14   Mamdouh Shoukri became York University's seventh president and vice-chancellor on

July 1, 2007. Prior to accepting the York presidency, Shoukri was Vice-President Research and International Affairs at McMaster University, where he was a professor of mechanical engineering, and also had served as dean of the Faculty of Engineering.

15 Appendix D at http://www.caut.ca/thompson-report/appendix-d.aspx contains the full text of the email from the JDL.

16 The JDL had posted its warning letter on a public website. The conference organizers learned of it from Susan Davis, executive vice-president of the Canadian Council for Israel and Jewish Advocacy (CIJA), who had been informed of it by the CEO of the Canadian Jewish Congress (CJC), Bernie M. Farber.

17 Email, P. Monahan to M. Shoukri, October 9, 2008. The term "balanced" came to be used by Monahan in particular ways at various times between October 2008 and May 2009, in discussions regarding the conference.

18 Email, M. Shoukri to M. Weinstein, October 24, 2008.

19 Email, P. Zumbansen to M. Masri, October 6, 2008.

20 Email, P. Zumbansen to M. Masri, October 14, 2008.

21 Masri held an LLB from Hebrew University and an LLM from the University of Toronto, and was a member of the Israeli Bar Association. He was fluent in Arabic, Hebrew, and English. In addition to these credentials, he had contacts with a number of the academics in Israel/Palestine who were expert in the conference topics. Thus he was a significant member of the committee, not merely a graduate student assistant, as the dean suggested in the meeting, and he had been involved from the outset (among other things, he was the "doctoral candidate" referred to in the U50 application as a committee member). Also, like Monahan, Masri had served as an advisor to a governmental agency—in his case, as a legal advisor to the Negotiations Affairs Department of the Palestine Liberation Organization (PLO). The PLO remains the only Palestinian political party recognized by Israel and the United States as representing the Palestinian people.

22 S. Drummond, "Field Notes from a Conference," October 2009 draft, provided to this Inquiry by the author, p. 14.

23 Like Professor Morgan, Professor Aiken was a Jewish professor of law at a Canadian university.

24 Email, P. Monahan to B. Ryder and S. Drummond, October 10, 2008.

25 These emails are included in Appendix D at http://www.caut.ca/thompson-report/appendix-d. aspx.

26 E. Morgan, letter to Hon. F. Iacobucci, August 7, 2009 (copy forwarded to this Inquiry by Professor Morgan, October 29, 2009).

27 E. Morgan, email to B. Ryder, November 9, 2008.

28 B. Ryder, email reply to E. Morgan, November 9, 2008.

29 E. Morgan, "Fight Bad Speech with Good Speech," *National Post*, November 4, 2008.

30 Ibid.

31 Ibid.

32 E. Morgan, letter to Hon. F. Iacobucci, August 7, 2009 (copy forwarded to this Inquiry by Professor Morgan, October 29, 2009).

33 Under SSHRC policy (available at www.sshrc.ca), "Workshops must [...] be invitational," and "Conferences must [...] be open to all interested and qualified researchers, i.e., involve a call for papers."

34 B. Ryder, Application for a Grant, identification number 646-08-1073, October 28, 2008 (ATI 2009–2010 8), p. 1–45.

35 At this stage the university financial commitments included $10,000 from Queen's and $23,500 from York, plus nearly $14,000 "in kind" from York in the form of graduate student assistants' time.

36 For instance, among those in the first list was Uri Davis (an Israeli academic and human-rights activist), and among those on the third list was Ali Abunimah (an American writer and activist for Palestinian rights), both of whom spoke at the conference. Both also were mentioned by some conference opponents among their reasons for denouncing the

conference. The lists of speakers also included several doctoral students.

37   SSHRC conference grant award notification to B. Ryder, March 2009.

CHAPTER 5

1   Barghouti is a founding member of the Palestinian civil-society group called Boycott, Divestment and Sanctions Campaign (www.pacbi.org). He has published academic articles drawing comparisons between Israel's administration of the occupied Palestinian territory and South Africa under the apartheid regime.

2   M. Shoukri, address to senate, February 26, 2009. The events referred to by the president involved demonstrations on campus by rival student groups: pro-Palestinian, and pro-Israeli.

3   Ibid.

4   Dewitt is a member of the Department of Political Science and of YCISS, and was the founding director of YCISS. His research interests include Middle East and Asia Pacific security politics, and Canadian security policy.

5   Email, D. Dewitt to S. Aiken, March 1, 2009 (forwarded by S. Aiken to the other conference organizers).

6   Ibid.

7   Beck was a co-founder and then-president emeritus of Scholars for Peace in the Middle East. He had affiliate appointments at Haifa and Bar-Ilan universities, and had been active in several Jewish-American community organizations, including AIPAC and the Anti-Defamation League.

8   The Program Manager of CAFI was Dylan Hanley, who was also associated with CIJA.

9   Adelman was a professor emeritus of philosophy at York and a member of YCISS. He had written extensively on topics such as refugees, genocide, immigration, and the Middle East.

10   H. Adelman, memo (unaddressed), March 20, 2009.

11   Ibid.

12   Email, M. Weinstein to JDL supporters, March 5, 2009.

13   M. Weinstein, open letter to M. Shoukri, March 22, 2009.

14   Email thread involving I. Maxwell Rodrigues and P. Monahan, March 26, 2009.

15   I. Abella and H. Troper, *None Is Too Many* (Toronto: Lester & Orpen Dennys, 1986).

16   Abella sent an email message to the president on March 25, and he replied on March 27.

17   M. Masri, "A Tale of Two Conferences: On Power, Identity, and Academic Freedom," *Journal of Academic Freedom* 2 (2011). (http://www.academicfreedomjournal.org/VolumeTwo/Masri.pdf)

18   Other CIJA documents relevant to this Inquiry and obtained under FIPPA had been forwarded to Dewitt by Davis. "Created in January 2004, CIJA is an umbrella organization coordinating the advocacy work of established Jewish organizations." (www.cija.ca)

19   Email thread involving P. Monahan, D. Dewitt, "iabella," and S. Davis, April 1, 2009, with attached memo dated March 20, 2009, by H. Adelman.

20   Email reply, P. Monahan to a person whose name is redacted on the copy released to CAUT, April 1, 2009, 6:28 PM.

21   Email, P. Monahan to B. Ryder and S. Drummond, April 1, 2009, 6:27 PM.

22   B. Ryder, S. Drummond, S. Aiken, and M. Masri, memo to P. Monahan, April 3, 2009.

23   Ibid.

24   Email, P. Monahan to M. Shoukri, April 11, 2009, 6:58 AM.

25   Ibid.

26   Email, M. Cohen to M. Shoukri, April 12, 2009.

27   Email, M. Shoukri to P. Monahan, April 12, 2009.

28   Email, P. Monahan to a person whose name is redacted in the copy released to CAUT under

FIPPA, April 11, 2009, 6:51 AM.

29 Email, P. Monahan to M. Shoukri, April 12, 2009, 10:12 PM.

30 Email, M. Shoukri to P. Monahan, April 12, 2009, 11:23 PM.

31 Email, M. Cohen to M. Shoukri, April 14, 2009, 5:22 PM.

32 Email, M. Shoukri to P. Monahan, April 14, 2009, 6:34 PM.

33 Email. M. Cohen to M. Shoukri and P. Monahan, April 15, 2009, 3:41 PM. The full text is in Appendix E at http://www.caut.ca/thompson-report/appendix-e.aspx.

34 "The Ferman incident" refers to an incident on the York campus involving students.

35 Email memo, M. Cohen to file, forwarded to M. Shoukri and P. Monahan, April 15, 2009. The full text is in Appendix E at http://www.caut.ca/thompson-report/appendix-e.aspx. The square brackets around "You have heard this too" and "JDL, maybe B'nai Brith" are in the original.

36 Ibid.

37 Email, S. Drummond to P. Monahan, April 15, 2009, 11:26 AM.

38 Email, S. Drummond to D. Dewitt, April 15, 2009, 11:12 AM. Ryder and Drummond met with Abella on April 30.

39 Ibid.

40 Email, S. Drummond to P. Monahan, April 15, 2009, 11:26 AM.

41 Email thread between I. Abella and P. Monahan, April 14, 2009, texts redacted, provided to CAUT with covering letter, C. Heald to K. Rubin, November 24, 2010.

42 Email, P. Monahan to I. Abella, copied to "Rosalie Abella" at scc-csc.gc.ca, April 15, 2009, 6:30 PM. This email message is in Appendix F at http://www.caut.ca/thompson-report/appendix-f.aspx.

43 Email, P. Monahan to M. Shoukri, copied to M. Cohen, April 15, 2009, 9:29 PM.

44 Email, P. Monahan to two persons whose names are redacted in the copy released to CAUT under FIPPA, April 24, 2009 (9:08 PM).

45 For example, on April 25 the dean reported to the president and the chair of the board, "I pushed them [Professors Ryder and Drummond] very hard." In this instance, the dean appeared to be responding to an email from the board chair on April 17, in which the chair had written, "I can only assume that you put the fear of all 3 gods involved here into them!" Email, P. Monahan to M. Shoukri and M. Cohen, April 25, 2009. Email, M. Cohen to P. Monahan, M. Shoukri, and S. Shapson, April 17, 2009, 4:54 PM.

46 Email, P. Monahan to B. Ryder and S. Drummond, April 15, 2009, 10:55 AM.

47 Email reply, B. Ryder to P. Monahan, copied to S. Drummond, April 15, 2009, 12:59 PM.

48 Email, D. Dewitt to MappingModels@osgoode.yorku.ca (the conference email address), copied to S. Drummond (who had sent an email message to D. Dewitt earlier in the day— cited above), April 15, 2009. The full text of the email is in Appendix G at http://www.caut.ca/thompson-report/appendix-g.aspx.

49 Ibid.

50 Ibid.

51 Ibid.

52 Email, P. Monahan to B. Ryder and S. Drummond, April 15, 2009, 9:44 PM.

53 Email, S. Brathwaite to B. Ryder, March 2, 2009. Pascal Lewin was coordinator of hospitality and conference services at Glendon College.

54 Email, B. Ryder to S. Brathwaite, April 14, 2009, 12:25 PM.

55 It appears that the decision by U50 staff to move the conference venue from the Glendon campus to the Keele campus resulted from a perceived scheduling conflict with Convocation events at Glendon (arising from the delays caused by the three-month strike by contract academic staff), and was unrelated to Cohen's suggestion to consider moving the conference to an off-campus venue. Emails among U50 staff from April 2 and 3 already referred to moving the venue from Glendon to suitable but as yet undetermined space at Keele. Cohen's

suggestion ("this idea" as the Dean termed it) was made to the president and the dean on April 15. The U50 staff did not contact Ryder again until April 14, after the Keele space had been arranged. The conference organizers did not gain access to the email messages among Cohen, Shoukri, and Monahan cited here until many months after the conference. It was unclear to them at the time whether or not the dean's information of April 17 and the information from the U50 committee on April 14 were coordinated or otherwise related.

56　Email, P. Monahan to M. Cohen, M. Shoukri, and S. Shapson, April 17, 2009, 3:23 PM. For April 15 email from Cohen to Shoukri and Monahan, see Appendix E at http://www.caut.ca/thompson-report/appendix-e.aspx.

57　Email, P. Monahan to M. Cohen, M. Shoukri, and S. Shapson, April 17, 2009, 3:23 PM.

58　Email, M. Cohen to P. Monahan, M. Shoukri, and S. Shapson, April 17, 2009, 4:54 PM. The square brackets around "i.e. no marches etc" and the last two sentences are in the original.

59　In 2001 the *World Conference against Racism, Racial Discrimination, Xenophobia and Related Intolerance* was held in Durban. Among issues raised were reparations to Africa for the centuries of European exploitation of its people and resources, and criticism of Israel. This was the third in a series of four World Conferences against Racism, under UN auspices. The fourth was held in Geneva in April 2009 and came to be known by detractors as Durban II. A discussion of what actually happened in the 2001 and 2009 conferences, with comparisons to what detractors claimed, can be found in Naomi Klein, "Minority Death Match: Jews, Blacks and the 'Post-racial' Presidency," *Harper's Magazine*, September 2009, p. 53–67.

60　Email, M. Cohen to M. Shoukri and P. Monahan, April 21, 2009, 2:54 PM. The square brackets around "physical" and "Roy McMurtry?" are in the original.

61　Email, M. Shoukri to M. Cohen and P. Monahan, April 21, 2009, 3:29 PM. Professor John McCamus (faculty member and former dean, Osgoode Hall) was chair of the U50 Campus Committee.

62　Email, P. Monahan to M. Shoukri and M. Cohen, April 21, 2009, 5:59 PM.

63　Email, P. Monahan to M. Shoukri and M. Cohen, April 25, 2009. Email, D. Dewitt to MappingModels@osgoode.yorku.ca, copied to S. Drummond, April 15, 2009. The full text of the Dewitt email is in Appendix G at http://www.caut.ca/thompson-report/appendix-g.aspx.

64　Faculty members in Osgoode Hall were not members of the York University Faculty Association and the Osgoode Hall Faculty Association was not affiliated with CAUT.

65　Email, P. Monahan to M. Shoukri and M. Cohen, April 25, 2009.

66　Email, P. Monahan to B. Ryder and S. Drummond, May 10, 2009. The full text is in Appendix I at http://www.caut.ca/thompson-report/appendix-i.aspx.

67　Email reply, D. Dewitt to P. Monahan, May 11, 2009, 10:50 PM AST.

68　P. Monahan, submission to this Inquiry, February 11, 2011, p. 10.

69　Email, I. Maxwell Rodrigues to H. Lewis, April 20, 2009.

70　Email, P. Monahan to M. Shoukri and M. Cohen, April 25, 2009.

71　Ibid.

72　Email, P. Monahan to a person whose name is redacted in the copy released to CAUT under FIPPA, April 24, 2009, 8:02 PM.

73　Email, P. Monahan to a person whose name is redacted in the copy released to CAUT under FIPPA, April 24, 2009, 9:08 PM.

74　Ibid.

75　Email, D. Dewitt to MappingModels@osgoode.yorku.ca, copied to S. Drummond, April 15, 2009. The full text of the email is in Appendix G at http://www.caut.ca/thompson-report/appendix-g.aspx.

76　Email, P. Monahan to D. Dewitt, May 2, 2009, 7:47 AM.

77　Email, B. Ryder to P. Monahan, May 1, 2009, 2:04 PM.

78　Ibid.

79　Ibid.

80 In the original conference program, only one keynote speaker was scheduled—Professor Jeremy Webber (Canada Research Chair in Law and Society, University of Victoria), who would open the conference on June 22 with an address titled "Past Injustice, Agonistic Encounter, and the Construction of Community among Those Who Have Nothing in Common." The two additional keynote addresses would be scheduled for mid-day on June 23 and 24.

81 Email reply, P. Monahan to B. Ryder, copied to the other organizers, April 23, 2009, 3:58 PM.

82 Letter of invitation, from all four organizers to M. Bell, April 27, 2009, sent by email at 6:00 PM.

83 Email reply, D. Dewitt to P. Monahan, April 27, 2009, 9:28 PM.

84 Ibid.

85 Email, P. Monahan to D. Dewitt, April 27, 2009, 10:08 PM.

86 P. Monahan, submission to this Inquiry, February 11, 2011, p. 9.

87 Rae and Cotler were members of the Canadian Parliamentary Coalition to Combat Antisemitism (www.cpcca.ca).

88 Email, B. Ryder to P. Monahan, copied to S. Drummond, S. Aiken, and M. Masri, April 23, 2009, 3:49 PM.

89 B. Ryder, S. Drummond, S. Aiken, and M. Masri, memo to P. Monahan, April 3, 2009.

90 They did not learn until many months after the conference (when CAUT provided a copy of the relevant university email message to them) that the president had already, on April 20, directed that the Glendon venue be secured for the conference.

91 Email, P. Monahan to B. Ryder, May 8, 2009, 8:02 AM.

92 From information on their university webpages, it may reasonably be inferred that Professor Lustick's credentials were in significant respects similar to those of Professor Dowty, whom the dean had mentioned on May 8 as someone who might be considered as a keynote speaker.

93 Additional biographical details on the keynote speakers are given in Appendix H at http://www.caut.ca/thompson-report/appendix-h.aspx.

94 The dean wrote to AVPR Dewitt two days later, "I sent them a strong email over the weekend." Email, P. Monahan to D. Dewitt, May 12, 2009.

95 Email, P. Monahan to S. Drummond and B. Ryder, May 10, 2009. The full text of the dean's May 10 email message is in Appendix I at http://www.caut.ca/thompson-report/appendix-i.aspx.

96 Ibid.

97 The conference organizers had emailed the president on May 8, requesting a meeting. On May 9 the dean emailed the president, advising him not to meet with them because, in his view, they had not lived up to their purported agreement (of April 23) with him and were now proposing an "end-run around" him. These emails are in Appendix I at http://www.caut.ca/thompson-report/appendix-i.aspx.

98 Email, P. Monahan to S. Drummond and B. Ryder, May 10, 2009. The full text of the dean's May 10 email message is in Appendix I at http://www.caut.ca/thompson-report/appendix-i.aspx.

99 Email, D. Dewitt to P. Monahan, May 9, 2009.

100 Email reply, P. Monahan to M. Shoukri, May 9, 2009. This email exchange is included in Appendix I at http://www.caut.ca/thompson-report/appendix-i.aspx.

101 Email, P. Monahan to D. Dewitt, copied to S. Shapson, May 10, 2009. The conference, titled "One State for Palestine/Israel: A Country for All Its Citizens?" was held at the Boston campus of the University of Massachusetts, March 28–29, 2009, with more than 500 people attending.

102 Email, D. Dewitt to P. Monahan, May 11, 2009, 4:21 PM.

103 Email, D. Dewitt to P. Monahan, May 11, 2009, 12:39 PM. Jason Kenney and Irwin Cotler were members of the Canadian Parliamentary Coalition to Combat Antisemitism (www.cpcca.ca).

104 Email reply, P. Monahan to D. Dewitt, May 11, 2009.

105 Email reply, D. Dewitt to P. Monahan, May 11, 2009, 10:50 PM AST.

106 Ibid.

107 Email, P. Monahan to D. Dewitt, May 12, 2009. Copies of the email messages about the draft op-ed are in Appendix J at http://www.caut.ca/thompson-report/appendix-j.aspx.

108 Y. Alpher, "NGO Monitor Needs a Monitor," *Forward*, December 25, 2009 (http://www.forward.com/articles/121170/).

109 On May 9 Dean Monahan had informed President Shoukri that "the conference is not really in his [Professor Dewitt's] area." (The full text is in Appendix I at http://www.caut.ca/thompson-report/appendix-i.aspx.)

110 Email, C. Morrow (CIJA) to CIJA University Outreach Committee, May 12, 2009, 11:43 AM.

111 The CIJA statement was by its CEO Hershell Ezrin and was posted on the website of the Canada Israel Committee. It listed CIJA Executive Vice-President Susan Davis as the person to contact for clarification. Dewitt forwarded a copy of it to Vice-President Research Stan Shapson and Dean Monahan at 1:11 PM on May 12.

112 CIJA Statement, May 12, 2009. The full text is in Appendix K at http://www.caut.ca/thompson-report/appendix-k.aspx.

113 Ibid.

114 L. Green, May 15, 2009, online response to CIJA statement of May 12, 2009.

115 C. Scott, May 17, 2009, online response to CIJA statement of May 12, 2009.

116 Ibid.

117 Email, P. Monahan to M. Shoukri, May 12, 2009, 10:42 PM.

118 Ibid.

119 Email, P. Monahan to a person whose name is redacted in the copy released to CAUT under FIPPA, April 11, 2009, 6:51 AM. In this message he cited the SSHRC grant as evidence of the quality of the conference.

120 S. Drummond, "Field Notes from a Conference: A Case Study in the Fragility of Academic Freedom," October 2009 (unpublished draft manuscript, cited with permission from the author), p. 25–26. Drummond prepared this draft of her "Field Notes" paper in October 2009, before York University had released the email message of April 20, 2009, between senior support staff confirming that the president had directed the Glendon venue be secured for the conference. In October 2009, the only information she had about the venue was that provided by Dean Monahan and U50 staff in April 2009.

121 Email, P. Monahan to M. Shoukri, May 9, 2009, 7:04 AM. The full texts of the relevant email messages from the period May 8 to May 10 are in Appendix I at http://www.caut.ca/thompson-report/appendix-i.aspx.

122 Email, I. Lustick to MappingModels, copied to M. Shoukri, P. Monahan, and S. Davis (CIJA), May 13, 2009, 11:22 AM.

123 The full text of the CIJA statement is in Appendix K at http://www.caut.ca/thompson-report/appendix-k.aspx.

124 Email, I. Lustick to MappingModels, copied to M. Shoukri, P. Monahan, and S. Davis (CIJA), May 13, 2009, 11:22 AM.

125 Ibid.

126 Ibid.

127 Email, P. Monahan to D. Dewitt, May 13, 2009, 11:58 AM.

128 Email from a York supporter addressed to M. Shoukri and forwarded to him by P. Marcus, May 12, 2009, released to CAUT under FIPPA with portions redacted.

129 Email, M. Shoukri to P. Marcus, May 12, 2009.

130 Email, D. Dewitt to P. Monahan, May 13, 2009.

131 Email, M.Shoukri to R. Fisher, copied to P. Monahan, May 14, 2009.

132 Email, P. Monahan to R. Fisher and M. Shoukri, May 14, 2009.

133 Email, R. Fisher to J. Shapiro, May 15, 2009.

134 Email from a person whose name is redacted on the copy released to CAUT under FIPPA, to

M. Shoukri and P. Monahan, May 18, 2009.

135 Email, P. Monahan to R. Fisher and J. Shapiro, May 18, 2009.

136 Email, M. Shoukri to P. Monahan, J. Shapiro, and R. Fisher, May 18, 2009, 11:57 PM.

137 Email, P. Monahan to D. Dewitt, May 14, 2009.

138 Email, P. Monahan to D. Dewitt, copied to S. Shapson, May 20, 2009, 9:04 AM

139 Email, D. Dewitt to S. Shapson and P. Monahan, May 20, 2009, 8:17 AM.

140 G. Steinberg, "YORK UNIVERSITY'S ANTI-PEACE CONFERENCE: IMMORAL, NAÏVE, OR BOTH," dated May 21, 2009, and available at www.isranet.org vol. 9, no. 2,097, Thursday, May 28, 2009 (http://www.isranet.org/isranetbriefings/Permanent-2009/Permanent_May_2009.htm#2097).

141 M. Shoukri, Presidential Statement, May 21, 2009. Appendix L at http://www.caut.ca/thompson-report/appendix-l.aspx contains the full text of the president's statement.

142 Ibid.

143 Ibid.

144 Email, P. Monahan to D. Dewitt and S. Shapson, May 21, 2009, 10:14 AM.

145 Email, D. Dewitt to P. Monahan and S. Shapson, May 22, 2009, 9:37 AM.

146 G. Steinberg, "York University vs. Israel; 'Academic Freedom' or Academic Farce?" dated May 22, 2009, and available on the website http://faculty.biu.ac.il/~steing/index.shtml.

147 Email, M. Shoukri to S. Drummond, April 20, 2010.

148 B'nai Brith, news release, May 22, 2009.

149 Email, from a person whose name is redacted on the copy released to CAUT under FIPPA, to M. Shoukri, May 27, 2009 (sent as a follow-up to a meeting the day before).

150 Ibid.

151 Excerpts from the proposal by the Committee in Support of the Speakers' Series at York, discussed in a meeting with M. Shoukri, May 26, 2009.

152 Email from a person whose name is redacted on the copy released to CAUT under FIPPA, to M. Shoukri, May 27, 2009 (sent as a follow-up to a meeting the day before).

153 Email reply, M. Shoukri to a person whose name is redacted on the copy released to CAUT under FIPPA, May 27, 2009.

154 Email from a person whose name is redacted on the copy released to CAUT under FIPPA, to P. Monahan, May 12, 2009.

155 Email reply, P. Monahan to a message he received on May 5 (from a person whose name is redacted on the copy released to CAUT under FIPPA), May 27, 2009.

156 Email, S. Aiken to D. Dewitt, June 1, 2009.

157 In contrast, the large conference on a similar topic held at the University of Massachusetts (Boston campus) in March 2009 did permit some media access.

CHAPTER 6

1 Email, M. Weinstein to M. Shoukri, March 22, 2009.

2 SSHRC reports to Parliament through the minister of Industry Canada. Email, Trevor Lynn to Ursula Gobel and others at SSHRC, May 25, 2009, enclosing JDL complaint to Industry Canada (ATI 2009–2010 10), pages 1–3. NOTE: here and in subsequent endnote references to documents released to CAUT following an application under the federal *Access to Information Act*, the designations are those printed on the released material. Thus "ATI," the year and number of the application, and the page numbers are included to identify the specific document.

3 Ibid.

4 Ibid.

5 Ibid. Another approach to disrupting the conference was proposed by a person who wrote to the Prime Minister of Canada on June 15, requesting that some of those scheduled to speak

at the conference be barred from entering the country. The government did not grant this person's request.

6   Email thread involving T. Lynn, U. Gobel and others, May 25, 2009 (ATI 2009–2010 10), pages 9–10.

7   Ibid.

8   Ibid.

9   Email, C. McNaughton to T. Lynn, copied to C. Charette, G. Yasmeen, U. Gobel, and others, May 25, 2009, 4:31 PM (ATI 2009–2010 10), page 12.

10   Email, T. Lynn to C. Charette, G. Yasmeen, U. Gobel, C. McNaughton, and others, May 25, 2009, 3:34 PM (ATI 2009–2010 10), page 29.

11   SSHRC tables compiling details about conference participants, dated June 10, 2009, by SSHRC Program Director Craig McNaughton (ATI 2009–2010 10), pages 30–36.

12   Ibid.

13   The Ministry of State (Science and Technology) is a sub-department of Industry Canada. Email, U. Gobel to T. Lynn and others, June 9, 2009 (ATI 2009–2010 10), page 115.

14   An email on June 9 from York's government relations officer to senior administrators, reporting on a discussion with ministerial staff, indicates at least one of the expressions of concern to the federal government came by way of conversation, as distinct from letters or email messages (such as the email from JDL), and hence was not accessible under access to information legislation.

15   Statement from the Hon. Gary Goodyear, dated June 5, 2009. The full text of the ministerial statement is in Appendix M, at http://www.caut.ca/thompson-report/appendix-m.aspx.

16   Email, G. Toft to T. Lynn, June 5, 2009, 1:04 PM (ATI 2009–2010 10), page 37.

17   "Phil" is Phillip Welford, chief of staff to Minister of State Goodyear. (The last four digits of his phone number have been redacted for this Inquiry report.) Email, T. Lynn to C. Gaffield, June 5, 2009 (ATI 2009–2010 10), page 42.

18   After CAUT received a copy of this email message under the *Access to Information Act*, and issued a press release about it on September 28, SSHRC issued a public statement the same day that the "internal email regarding comments by the Minister's Chief of Staff is inaccurate." When Opposition science and technology critic Marc Garneau questioned Minister Goodyear about the email in the House of Commons on September 29, Goodyear replied, "The member will be happy to know that the social sciences council has clearly stated that the email is inaccurate." Lynn was subsequently contacted by a reporter for *Le Devoir* and questioned about the nature of the claimed inaccuracy, but he declined to provide details (CAUT *Bulletin*, October 2009, p. A1, A9).

19   Email thread, I. Stewart to C. Fox to I. Stewart, June 8, 2009 (ATI 2009–2010 10), pages 56, 58.

20   T. Belman, blog www.israpundit.com/2008/?p=14002.

21   Email, J. Turk to C. Gaffield, June 7, 2009, 8:43 PM (ATI 2009–2010 10), page 59.

22   Email, G. Yasmeen to S. Shapson, 8 June 2009 (ATI 2009–2010 10), page 63.

23   Email thread involving D. Dewitt (whose name is redacted on the SSHRC copy released to CAUT), S. Shapson, and G. Yasmeen, June 8, 9, 2009 (ATI 2009–2010 10), pages 73–79 and 101; also, email, D. Dewitt to S. Shapson, June 8, 2009, 5:20 PM, released to CAUT under FIPPA. The email from Dewitt to Shapson included another copy of Minister Goodyear's June 5 statement, but this copy of it was issued by Adam Blinick, Special Assistant, Office of the Prime Minister.

24   Abunimah also was on a very different list—a list of possible speakers provided on Professor Ryder's November grant application to SSHRC.

25   Email, Jewish Canada (B'nai Brith) to supporters, June 8, 2009 (ATI 2009–2010 10), pages 113–114.

26   Ibid.

27   Email, M. Papadopoulos to M. Shoukri, P. Monahan, and others, June 9, 2009.

28   Email thread involving C. McNaughton, G. Yasmeen, and C. Charette, June 9, 2009 (ATI

2009–2010 10), page 99–100.

29   Email thread between C. McNaughton and G. Yasmeen, June 9, 2009, 8:01–8:25 AM (ATI 2009–2010 10), pages 99–100.

30   Email thread between C. Trauttmansdorff and C. Charette, June 9, 2009 (ATI 2009–2010 10), page 87–88.

31   Email thread among C. Charette, C. Trauttmansdorff, and others, June 9, 2009 (ATI 2009–2010 10), pages 116–124.

32   Ibid.

33   Email, E. Skrapek to G. Yasmeen and C. McNaughton, June 10, 2009 (ATI 2009–2010 10), page 135.

34   Email thread among C. Trauttmansdorff, C. Charette, and G. Yasmeen, June 14, 2009 (ATI 2009–2010 10), page 481.

35   Email, C. Trauttmansdorff to H. Beaton, June 14, 2009 (ATI 2009–2010 10), page 465.

36   Email thread, N. Girard to H. Beaton to C. Trauttmansdorff to C. Charette and G. Yasmeen, June 15–16, 2009 (ATI 2009–2010 10), page 656–657.

37   Ibid.

38   SSHRC media release, June 9, 2009.

39   SSHRC media release, June 10, 2009.

40   SSHRC media release, June 11, 2009.

41   The precise wording of the policy was included in the letter sent to Professor Ryder, dated June 10, included here in Appendix N, at http://www.caut.ca/thompson-report/appendix-n.aspx.

42   Email, C. McNaughton to G. Yasmeen, June 10, 2009, 2:53 PM (ATI 2009–2010 10), page 136.

43   Email, C. McNaughton to B. Ryder, June 10, 2009, 5:22 PM (ATI 2009–2010 10), page 181.

44   Email, J. Turk to C. Gaffield, June 10, 2009.

45   Ibid.

46   Email correspondence among B. Ryder, S. Drummond, S. Aiken, S. Shapson, and P. Monahan, June 11, 2009.

47   Email, B. Ryder to C. McNaughton, June 11, 2009 (ATI 2009–2010 10), pages 178–179. The full text of Professor Ryder's letter is included in Appendix N, at http://www.caut.ca/thompson-report/appendix-n.aspx.

48   Ibid.

49   Ibid.

50   Email, S. Drummond to C. McNaughton, June 13, 2009 (ATI 2009–2010 10), pages 405–407. The full text is included in Appendix N, at http://www.caut.ca/thompson-report/appendix-n.aspx.

51   Email, C. Christie to C. Gaffield, June 12, 2009 (ATI 2009–2010 10), pages 502–503.

52   An email message sent to Minister Goodyear on June 12, which was re-sent to SSHRC on June 14 by the original sender after receiving a reply from the Minister's Office, and an email message sent to SSHRC Executive Vice-President Carmen Charette on June 15 (ATI 2009–2010 10), pages 556–558 and 483–485.

53   Draft of a letter to be sent by C. McNaughton to B. Ryder, June 13, 2009 (ATI 2009–2010 10), page 426.

54   Email, C. Trauttmansdorff to G. Yasmeen and C. Charette, copied to C. McNaughton and others, June 14, 2009 (ATI 2009–2010 10), page 476.

55   Regarding the "need" for "speed": in fact, as noted earlier, a complaint had been brought to SSHRC's attention by Industry Canada on May 25. Yet it was not until June 8, a full two weeks later—following the minister's talk with the president of SSHRC on June 4 and his chief of staff's talk with SSHRC's communications manager on June 5—that SSHRC began to take the actions protested against by the academic community. Moreover, McNaughton had himself suggested to other senior SSHRC staff on May 25 that the complaints could reasonably be addressed by referring complainants to the website, which made it clear that

the conference was neither anti-Semitic nor anti-Israel. He had made essentially the same suggestion on June 9, after the minister's interference.

56 The available record indicates that the applicant was the last, or one of the last, to be checked with; first the Jewish-Canadian media were notified of the minister's intervention by his staff, then Shapson was notified by SSHRC, and then the public at large were notified of these matters by a wider release of the minister's statement. SSHRC did not contact Ryder, the applicant, until June 10. Letter, C. McNaughton to G. Yasmeen, undated, but likely June 13 or 14, 2009 (ATI 2009–2010 10), pages 427–428. The full text of this letter is included in Appendix O, at http://www.caut.ca/thompson-report/appendix-o.aspx.

57 Letter, C. McNaughton to B. Ryder, June 15, 2009 (ATI 2009–2010 10), page 650. See Appendix N at http://www.caut.ca/thompson-report/appendix-n.aspx.

58 SSHRC media release, June 15, 2009.

59 Email, C. Trauttmansdorff to T. Kierans, copied to C. Gaffield and others, June 14, 2009 (ATI 2009–2010 10), pages 490–493.

60 CAUT media release, June 10, 2009.

61 Open letter, CAUT Executive Committee to C. Gaffield, June 12, 2009.

62 Letter, C. Gaffield to J. Turk, June 16, 2009.

63 Lynn's email was to the effect that the minister's concerns over the grant to the York conference might be reflected in future SSHRC budget allocations.

64 Email, D. Holton to T. Bercier, September 30, 2009 (ATI 2009–2010 16), pages 49–50.

65 Email, L. Chiv to T. Lynn, U. Gobel, and D. Holton, October 5, 2009, with Media Lines attached (ATI 2009–2010 16), pages 51–54.

66 Ibid.

67 Ibid.

68 P. Martin, "Has The Two-State Ship Sailed?" *Globe and Mail*, June 5, 2009.

69 Ibid.

70 Ibid. In 1996, during Netanyahu's previous time as prime minister, a spokesperson in his office, David Bar-Illan, said Netanyahu did not favour a Palestinian state as such, but instead an entity with limited sovereignty. Bar-Illan added that semantics were unimportant, and that, so long as its sovereignty was sufficiently limited, whether the entity was called a "state" or "fried chicken" did not matter. (Cited in Noam Chomsky, *Failed States* [New York: Metropolitan Books, 2006], p. 178. A more complete quotation of Bar-Illan can be found at www.distantocean.com/2009/06/everything-old.html.)

71 The citation of Phineas T. Barnum in the May 22 version did not appear in the June 9 version. In an email message to the dean, the president, and others on June 9, sent after the article appeared in the *National Post*, York's Chief Marketing Officer Richard Fisher commented, "this is a slightly sanitized version of an article that has been doing the rounds on the internet. [...] I suggest we put the President's statement [of May 21] back on the homepage asap and consider a response from the organisers to this op ed now that it has gone public."

72 G. Steinberg, "York University Sinks Deeper in the Mire," op-ed article, *National Post*, June 9, 2009. The full text of this op-ed is in Appendix P at http://www.caut.ca/thompson-report/appendix-p.aspx.

73 Ibid.

74 Ibid.

75 Ibid.

76 Ibid.

77 C. Scott, comment on the *National Post* website, June 10, 2009.

78 I. Lustick, "The Conference Must Go On," op-ed article, *National Post*, June 11, 2009. The full text of this op-ed is in Appendix Q at http://www.caut.ca/thompson-report/appendix-q.aspx.

79 Email, P. Monahan to D. Dewitt, June 7, 2009.

80 Email, D. Dewitt to P. Monahan, June 7, 2009.

81 Email, D. Dewitt to P. Monahan, copied to S. Shapson, June 8, 2009, 5:38 PM.

82 Ibid. It is unclear, from the email record available to this Inquiry, which "previous email" to the dean is referred to here by the AVPR. One possibility is the email message he sent to VP Shapson and Dean Monahan a few minutes earlier on June 8, enclosing the four-page denunciation of the conference and fifteen of its speakers on the letterhead of NGO Monitor, the organization headed by Professor Gerald Steinberg.

83 Ibid.

84 Email thread, between a person whose name is redacted on the copy released to CAUT under FIPPA and M. Shoukri, June 9–10, 2009.

85 Ibid.

86 Ibid.

87 Email, D. Dewitt to a person whose name is redacted on the copy released by York to CAUT under FIPPA, June 12, 2009.

88 Letter, F. Dimant to M. Shoukri, June 12, 2009.

89 B'nai Brith Canada, public statement, June 12, 2009.

90 Ibid.

91 Email, C. Scott to J. Thompson, January 31, 2010. The "sentences" misattributed to Abunimah are actually phrases cut and pasted from two long sentences in an undated three-page article by Amayreh, accessed on February 11, 2010, at http://www.themodernreligion.com/jihad/holocaust-lie.html.

92 The "sentences" in question, still incorrectly attributed to Abunimah, were available on the website www.discoverthenetworks.org on February 11, 2010, in a "profile" of Abunimah, one in a very long list of profiles of individuals disliked by some person or persons. Those on the list (some of whom are deceased) include Jimmy Carter, Hugo Chavez, Rachel Corrie, Ayatollah Khomeini, Joan Wallach Scott, George Soros, and Ted Turner. This website was launched several years ago by a well-known list compiler, David Horowitz, author of *The Professors: The 101 Most Dangerous Academics in America* (Washington, DC: Regnery, 2006).

93 The relevant paragraphs from the B'nai Brith retraction and apology statement can be found at http://www.yorku.ca/yfile/archive/index.asp?Article=12819.

94 Dimant of B'nai Brith had previously faxed a brief letter to President Shoukri, acknowledging the "Holocaust denial" allegation against Abu Nimah "does appear to be attributed to him erroneously." Although it was dated June 12, 2009, the fax printout bore the date and time 06/15/2009 02:43. The unequivocal acknowledgement and apology were made public on June 22, 2009, the opening day of the conference.

95 Email thread, June 12–17, provided to this Inquiry to illustrate the manner in which Queen's administrators handled criticisms of the conference.

96 Letter, from a person (whose name is redacted) to the Prime Minister, June 15, 2009 (PCO Access pages 00022–000024).

97 Email, P. Monahan to M. Shoukri and R. Fisher, June 13, 2009, 7:37 AM.

98 Email, R. Fisher to P. Monahan and M. Shoukri, June 13, 2009, 8:23 AM.

99 Email, M. Shoukri to R. Fisher, copied to P. Monahan and others, June 13, 2009, 10:18 AM.

100 Email, P. Monahan to M. Shoukri and R. Fisher, June 13, 2009, 10:28 AM.

101 Copies of these letters are in Appendix R at http://www.caut.ca/thompson-report/appendix-r.aspx.

102 Email, P. Monahan to Osgoode Hall faculty members, June 15, 2009.

103 Public statement by M. Shoukri, M. Cohen, and P. Cantor, June 15, 2009. The full text of the statement is in Appendix S at http://www.caut.ca/thompson-report/appendix-s.aspx.

104 Ibid.

105 Ibid.

106 Email, B. Geva to Osgoode colleagues and President of SSHRC, June 16, 2009.

107 Email, B. Geva to Osgoode colleagues and President of SSHRC, June 18, 2009.

108 Ibid.

109 Ibid.

110 Ibid.

111 Ibid.

112 Email, M. Lockshin to B. Ryder, copied to Osgoode Hall faculty members, July 1, 2009.

113 Ibid.

114 M. Lockshin, "You Don't Need Credentials to Bash Israel," *National Post*, May 26, 2009, p. A18.

115 Open letter, M. Weinstein to C. Charette, June 21, 2009 (ATI 2009–2010 10), page 771.

116 Email thread among SSHRC staff, June 22, 2009 (ATI 2009–2010 10), pages 772–774. Gary Toft was communications director at Industry Canada.

Chapter 7

1 Email thread between R. Fisher and A. Bilyk, June 22, 2009. Hasbara is a Jewish student organization.

2 P. Monahan, "Opening Remarks for Israel/Palestine Conference," copy provided to this Inquiry by P. Monahan, quoting from J. S. Mill, *On Liberty*. The text of the remarks, together with the text of Flanagan's remarks, is in Appendix T at http://www.caut.ca/thompson-report/appendix-t.aspx.

3 Ibid.

4 Email, S. Aiken to M. Shoukri, copied to others, August 5, 2009.

5 Ibid.

6 Ibid.

7 Ibid.

8 Email, D. Dewitt to P. Monahan, copied to S. Shapson, August 6, 2009.

9 UJA Federation and CIJA, public statement, June 26, 2009 (copy distributed to SSHRC staff through an email by D. Holton) (ATI 2009–2010 10), p. 788. The conference organizers report that CIJA observers registered for the conference as students.

10 Ibid.

11 B'nai Brith statement, Jewish Canada network, June 26, 2009 (ATI 2009–2010 10), pages 799–802.

12 T. Cheifetz, "Twittering Canadian Students Rebut Anti-Israel Message of York U Conference," *Jerusalem Post*, June 24, 2009 (copy distributed to SSHRC staff through an email by D. Holton on June 26 (ATI 2009–2010 10), p. 782–783.

13 H. Siddiqui, "What's Discussed Openly in Israel is Toxic in Toronto," *Toronto Star*, June 28, 2009.

14 N. Carmi, "Middle East Conference Anything But Academic," *Toronto Star*, June 30, 2009.

15 Ibid. Members of the organizing committee reported that the interlocutor who made the offensive remark was a person who registered for the conference but was not one of the presenters or organizers. (Under SSHRC guidelines, conferences it sponsors are open to interested scholars who register, such as this interlocutor and the three CIJA observers who registered.) After the incident, Professor Drummond asked the interlocutor to offer an apology to Carmi, but the interlocutor refused. Drummond then apologized to Carmi on behalf of the conference.

16 L. Panitch, email to the editor, *Toronto Star*, July 2, 2009.

17 F. Iacobucci, "The Mapping Conference and Academic Freedom," (York University, March 2010), p. 25. Iacobucci did not identify his sources of information by name.

18 D. Naaman, "Coordinated Campaign Aimed to Stifle Academic Discussion about Israel Raises Critical Questions," CAUT *Bulletin*, October 2009.

19 B'nai Brith advertisement, *National Post*, September 12, 2009.

20 York faculty and students, public statement issued by I. Kapoor, L. Panitch, and many others, October 2009. The full text of the statement is in Appendix U at http://www.caut.ca/thompson-report/appendix-u.aspx.

21 "Rights and Responsibilities within the University: Report of the Presidential Task Force on Student Life, Learning and Community" (York University, August 2009), p. 22.

22 Ibid., p. 12.

23 E. Lackie et al., brief submitted to the York Task Force on Student Life, Learning, and Community on behalf of the United Jewish Appeal Federation of Greater Toronto and other organizations. The brief was posted on the website of the Canada Israel Committee (accessed March 15, 2010), at http://www.cicweb.ca/scene/2009/07/submission-to-the-york-u-task-force-on-student-life-learning-and-community/. The posted copy was dated July 28, 2009, but the date of submission to the Task Force is not indicated. Since the June 29 submission to the Task Force by the organizers of the York/Queen's conference was cited in this brief, it may reasonably be inferred that its submission date was on or before June 29. The copy posted on the CIC website did not include any of the several appendices referred to in the text of the brief. The Canada-Israel Committee (CIC) was the official representative of the organized Canadian Jewish community on matters pertaining to Canada-Israel relations. It was an agency funded by the Canadian Council for Israel and Jewish Advocacy (CIJA), the advocacy arm of United Israel Appeal Canada (UIAC).

24 Ibid.

25 Ibid.

26 See, for example, the text titled, "Keep Us Informed," on the webpage www.campus-watch.org/incident.php.

27 S. Drummond, B. Ryder, S. Aiken, and M. Masri, "Report of the Organizing Committee for the Conference: 'Israel/Palestine: Mapping Models of Statehood and Paths to Peace,'" submitted to York Task Force, June 29, 2009, p.1.

28 Ibid., p. 2.

29 Ibid., p. 21.

30 Ibid., p. 21–22.

31 E. Morgan, "Re: Anti-Israel Activism at York," submitted to York Task Force, July 3, 2009, p. 6.

32 Ibid.

33 Ibid., p. 6–7.

34 Ibid., p. 7.

35 C. Ehrlich, S. Horowitz, E. Lawee, and M. Lockshin, "Comments on the Report of the Organizing Committee for the Conference: 'Israel/Palestine: Mapping Models of Statehood and Paths to Peace'," submitted to York Task Force, undated, p. 1.

36 Ibid., p. 2–3.

37 Ibid., p. 3–4.

38 Ibid., p. 4.

39 L. Green, submission to York Task Force, July 13, 2009, p. 3.

40 Ibid., p. 4–5.

41 Ibid., p. 7.

42 Ibid., p. 7–8.

43 Ibid., p. 8.

44 Ibid., p. 9.

45 Ibid.

46 Ibid., p. 10.

47 Ibid., p. 10. The quotation "so long as..." is from the email message sent by AVPR Dewitt to the conference organizers on April 15, 2009. The full text of that email is in Appendix G at

http://www.caut.ca/thompson-report/appendix-g.aspx.

48   M. Shoukri, public statement, July 31, 2009. The full text of the statement is in Appendix V at
      http://www.caut.ca/thompson-report/appendix-v.aspx.

49   Ibid.

50   Email thread between P. Monahan and M. Shoukri, July 20, 2009.

51   Email, M. Shoukri to S. Drummond, July 16, 2009.

52   Ibid.

53   Ibid.

54   F. Iacobucci, "Clarification of Mandate," undated copy (in the form of a print-out from the
      University's website), provided to CAUT pursuant to a request under the FIPPA legislation.

55   Ibid.

56   Letter, A. Hutchinson, J. Gilmour, and G. Van Harten to F. Iacobucci, October 17, 2009.

57   As noted in Chapter 1, I attended this session of the 2010 Toronto Group conference.

58   Ryder made a similar comment to the Iacobucci review, as mentioned in its report.

CHAPTER 8

1   Walter Benjamin, *Gesammelte Briefe*, vol. 1 (Frankfurt: Suhrkamp Verlag, 1995), p. 182
      (as quoted in S. Žižek, *First as Tragedy, Then as Farce* [New York: Verso, 2009], p. 3).

2   F. Iacobucci, "The Mapping Conference and Academic Freedom," York University, March
      2010, p. 1.

3   R. Hofstadter and W. P. Metzger, *The Development of Academic Freedom in the United States*
      (New York: Columbia University Press, 1955), p. 42–43.

4   M. White, *Isaac Newton: The Last Sorcerer* (Reading, MA: Perseus Books, 1997), p. 150–151.

5   M. W. Finkin and R. C. Post, *For the Common Good: Principles of American Academic Freedom*
      (New Haven, CT: Yale University Press, 2009), p. 19, citing several German sources on Wolff.

6   Hofstadter and Metzger, *Development of Academic Freedom*, p. 385n59.

7   Ibid., n60.

8   Finkin and Post, *For the Common Good*, p. 19.

9   Ibid., p. 22.

10   Ibid., p. 23.

11   Hofstadter and Metzger, *Development of Academic Freedom*, p. 389.

12   Hofstadter and Metzger, op. cit., p. 390.

13   Ibid., p. 386–387.

14   Ibid., p. 387.

15   Ibid., p. 371.

16   Ibid., p. 377.

17   Report of the Investigating Committee, Board of Regents, University of Wisconsin, in the
      dismissal trial of Richard T. Ely, September 18, 1894, cited in R. Hofstadter and W. Smith,
      eds., *American Higher Education* (Chicago: University of Chicago Press, 1961), vol. 2,
      p. 859–860.

18   Hofstadter and Metzger, *Development of Academic Freedom*, p. 437.

19   Ibid., p. 392.

20   At that time, Americans' beliefs in their right to freedom of speech were based more on
      mythology around the meaning of the First Amendment to the American Constitution than
      on jurisprudence. Reviewing the history of freedom of speech in the United States, David
      Kairys wrote that "no free speech as we know it existed, either in law or practice [...] until
      the period from about 1919 to 1940," and that, "the expansion of speech rights, after a
      regression in the 1950s, resumed in the 1960s and early 1970s, when the civil rights and

antiwar movements demanded and received heightened enforcement and a substantial enlargement in speech rights." He added that, prior to the 1930s, "Federal and state courts [...] repeatedly refused to protect any form of speech." (Chapter 8, "Freedom of Speech," in *The Politics of Law: A Progressive Critique*, David Kairys, ed., [New York: Basic Books, 1998; originally published in 1982].)

21   It is of note that the committee was chaired by Professor Seligman of Columbia, who had chaired the AEA committee of inquiry on the Ross case, and included philosopher Arthur O. Lovejoy of Johns Hopkins, one of those who had resigned from Stanford in protest over the Ross dismissal, as well as Richard T. Ely. Seligman and Lovejoy were the principal drafters of the *Declaration*.

22   AAUP, 1915 *Declaration of Principles on Academic Freedom and Academic Tenure* (http://www.aaup.org/AAUP/pubsres/policydocs/contents/1915.htm).

23   Ibid.

24   The 1940 *Statement* can be found at http://www.aaup.org/AAUP/pubsres/policydocs/contents/1940statement.htm.

25   C. Russell, *Academic Freedom* (New York: Routledge, 1993), p. 2. Lord Jenkins of Hillhead, chancellor of Oxford University, introduced an "Academic Freedom" amendment to the *Education Reform Bill of 1988*, providing to academics, "the freedom within the law to question and test received wisdom, and to put forward ideas and controversial or unpopular opinions without placing themselves in jeopardy of losing their jobs or privileges they may have at their institutions."

26   G. H. Hardy, *Bertrand Russell and Trinity* (1942; New York: Arno Press, 1977), p. 47–48.

27   In addition to the diplomatic but forceful wording of the petition signed by so many Fellows, it also may have helped that there had been some turnover in council membership, including appointment of a new master of the college in 1918, Sir Joseph John "J. J." Thomson (1906 winner of the Nobel Prize in physics), who had not been on the council in 1916 and who favoured reinstatement.

28   G. H. Hardy, *Bertrand Russell and Trinity*, p. 46.

29   In recent times it again became fashionable to discount the impact of the peace terms on Germany. Thus, "historians are increasingly coming to the conclusion that the burden was never as great as Germany and her sympathizers claimed," historian Margaret McMillan wrote in her book *Paris, 1919* (New York: Random House, 2003), at p. 181. This recent "conclusion," as McMillan called it, was in essence a revival of Allied propaganda of the day, identified as such by Keynes. It misses an essential point that he made: the problem lay not only with the magnitude of the reparations, but also with some provisions in the treaty that were deeply and gratuitously humiliating to Germany. In any case, the perceived economic burden and the humiliation together enabled Hitler to exploit public resentment of the Versailles *Diktat*. This, along with social distress caused by the Depression and strong, pre-existing anti-democratic and anti-Semitic currents in substantial parts of the German population, helped fuel his rise to power. In *Five Germanys I Have Known* (New York: Farrar, Strauss and Giroux, 2006), Professor Fritz Stern, an authority on the history of modern Germany wrote, "The Treaty of Versailles was meant to be harsh, but, worse perhaps, it was humiliating in style and substance" (p. 57).

30   Finkin and Post, *For the Common Good*, p. 5.

31   Ibid., p. 51–52.

32   Ibid., p. 2–3.

33   Noam Chomsky, "The Responsibility of Intellectuals," *New York Review of Books*, February 23, 1967.

34   Finkin and Post, *For the Common Good*, p. 125.

35   Hofstadter and Metzger, *Development of Academic Freedom*, p. 495–496.

36   Ibid., p. 504. Among those dismissed was the outspoken and academically distinguished Columbia psychologist James McKeen Cattell (one of the AAUP's charter members), who had written to three congressmen urging them not to vote for a bill to authorize the use of American conscripts in Europe.

37   E. Schrecker, *No Ivory Tower: McCarthyism and the Universities* (New York: Oxford University Press, 1986), p. 8.

38   Ibid., p. 340–341.

39   These events were discussed in essays by Richard C. Lewontin and Noam Chomsky in the
      collection *The Cold War and the University*, edited by André Schiffrin (New York: New Press,
      1997). Chomsky recalled that in the 1960s, ironically, faculty at universities with strong
      Pentagon connections, such as MIT, had more academic freedom than faculty at other
      universities, such as Harvard, especially in extramural speech. He attributed this to the especially
      great prestige that science and engineering acquired during World War II and the Cold War.

40   Not all constraints are purely ideological. During the past two decades, the increasing
      dependence of medical research on funding by the pharmaceutical industry has resulted in
      serious erosions in academic freedom and academic integrity. Several academic freedom cases
      in medical faculties in the United States, Canada, and the United Kingdom have received
      international attention and illustrate the point. The problems caused by increasing reliance
      on corporate funding for research are, of course, not limited to the medical sciences, and
      have been discussed in a number of books and symposia in recent years. The scope of these
      challenges can be seen in, for example, *Universities in the Marketplace: The Commercialization of
      Higher Education* by Derek Bok (Princeton: Princeton University Press, 2003), and *Universities
      at Risk: How Politics, Special Interests and Corporatization Threaten Academic Integrity* edited by
      James L. Turk (Toronto: James Lorimer, 2008).

41   Noam Chomsky, *Towards a New Cold War* (New York: Pantheon, 1982), p. 14.

42   Nadia Abu El-Haj, *Facts on the Ground: Archaeological Practice and Territorial Self-Fashioning in
      Israeli Society* (Chicago: University of Chicago Press, 2001), p. 2.

43   Ibid., p. 280–281.

44   The quotations in this and the following two paragraphs are from J. Kramer, "The Petition,"
      New Yorker, April 14, 2008, p. 50–59.

45   D. Rabinowitz and R. Shamir, "Who Got to Decide on Nadia Abu El-Haj's Tenure?" (http://
      www.aaup.org/AAUP/pubsres/academe/2008/JF/Feat/rabi.htm?PF=1).

46   Ibid.

47   Ibid.

48   I. Gilmour and D. Gilmour, "Pseudo-Travellers," (a review of *From Time Immemorial*), *London
      Review of Books*, February 7, 1985.

49   N. Chomsky, *Understanding Power* (New York: New Press, 2002), p. 244.

50   A. Hourani, *Observer*, March 5, 1985; and Ian and David Gilmour, *LRB*, February 7, 1985—
      cited by E. Said, "Conspiracy of Praise," in E. W. Said and C. Hitchens, eds., *Blaming the Victims:
      Spurious Scholarship and the Palestinian Question* (1988; New York: Verso, 2001), p. 27–28.

51   N. Finkelstein, *Beyond Chuzpah: On the Misuse of Anti-Semitism and the Abuse of History*
      (Berkeley: University of California Press, 2005), p. 2.

52   N. Finkelstein, *Beyond Chutzpah*, p. 17.

53   A. Shlaim, *Israel and Palestine: Reappraisals, Revisions, Refutations* (New York: Verso, 2009),
      p. 369. Harvard University investigated the specific charge of plagiarism and exonerated
      Professor Dershowitz, as noted on p. 254 of *Beyond Chutzpah*. Professor Dershowitz also
      publicly defended himself—on the basis of, among other things, the *Chicago Manual of Style*.
      The effectiveness of his defence was disputed by journalist Alexander Cockburn, who assessed
      it against both the *Chicago Manual of Style* and the section of a Harvard student guidebook on
      "Writing with Sources" (*The Nation*, vol. 277, issue 13, October 27, 2003).

54   A. Shlaim, *Israel and Palestine: Reappraisals, Revisions, Refutations*, p. 371.

55   Ibid., p. 368.

56   Ibid.

57   E. W. Said and C. Hitchens, eds., *Blaming the Victims: Spurious Scholarship and the Palestinian
      Question* (1988; New York: Verso, 2001), p. 11.

58   The essential reference work is *Academic Freedom in Canada* (Toronto: University of Toronto
      Press, 1999) by historian Michiel Horn, where more details on the cases mentioned in this
      section can be found.

59   M. Horn, *Academic Freedom in Canada*, Chapters 5 and 7.

60 Dunning's remark is quoted in Horn, *Academic Freedom*, p. 186.

61 Halperin and Infeld were Jewish and academically distinguished but, in those times, "widespread anti-Semitism [...] made it very difficult for even the most promising Jewish scholars to find university positions in Canada," as Professor Horn wrote in *Academic Freedom in Canada*. Thus it is not inconceivable that anti-Semitism may also have been a factor in considering actions against those Jewish scholars who had been hired. Their hiring prospects appear to have depended on particularities, such as the discipline, or the academic pedigree, or imposition of a special condition. In the years when Infeld and Halperin were being hired, Bora Laskin was refused a position in Law at the University of Manitoba, but later appointed at the University of Toronto under a special condition: a loyalty test—he had to declare that he had no connection of any kind with "Communism, Fascism or any other subversive movement" (cited in Horn, p. 165).

62 Horn, *Academic Freedom*, p. 224.

63 V. C. Fowke and B. Laskin, "Report of the Investigation by the Committee of the Canadian Association of University Teachers into the Dismissal of Professor H.S. Crowe by United College, Winnipeg, Manitoba." *CAUT Bulletin*, 7, 3, January 1959, p. 68–69.

64 Ibid., p. 45, 47.

65 Ibid., p. 49.

66 Ibid., p. 50.

67 Ibid.

68 The facts of the Crowe case and the Fowke–Laskin report remain of interest, in the context of the informal jurisprudence that has developed through the work of CAUT, its investigating committees, and records of settlements or decisions of adjudicators. For example, in 2006 the author of the present report discussed the Crowe case in his expert witness brief (and appended thereto a copy of the Fowke–Laskin report), when appearing on behalf of YUFA in an arbitration between York University and YUFA in the matter of a grievance by Professor David Noble. The arbitrator found that the university had violated Professor Noble's academic freedom and awarded him a remedy. (Award by arbitrator Russell Goodfellow, 2007 CanLII 50108 [ON L.A.], http://www.canlii.org/en/on/onla/doc/2007/2007canlii50108 /2007canlii50108.html).

69 The current form of the CAUT definition is in Appendix W at http://www.caut.ca/thompson-report/appendix-w.aspx.

70 B. Laskin. *Freedom and Responsibility in the University* (Toronto: University of Toronto Press, 1970).

71 The AAUP also encouraged collective bargaining, but its efforts have been impeded by the unevenness among state labour codes, and by the fact that at many universities it does not have active chapters.

72 Letter, H. Adelman to A. Dershowitz, June 30, 1982.

73 HCF website: www.crowefoundation.ca. The author of the present report is a member of the board of directors of the Harry Crowe Foundation.

74 J. Thompson, P. Baird, and J. Downie, *The Olivieri Report* (Toronto: James Lorimer and Co., 2001; available electronically at http://www.caut.ca/uploads/OlivieriInquiryReport.pdf), p. 401.

75 A. McIlroy, "Olivieri, supporters win settlement," *Globe and Mail*, November 13, 2002, p. A4.

76 Statement of Claim by D. Healy against CAMH and others, filed September 24, 2001 in the Superior Court of Justics of Ontario, quoting from a University publication dated on or about June 21, 2001.

77 The rights and obligations of clinical professors are discussed in the 2001 report of the CAUT Committee of Inquiry into the Olivieri case: J. Thompson , P. Baird, and J. Downie, *The Olivieri Report*.

78 See http://www.ahrp.org/risks/MHRAssri0903.php and http://www.fda.gov/Drugs/DrugSafety/ InformationbyDrugClass/UCM096273?sms_ss=email&at_xt=4dbded900d69c9c0%2C0.

79 J. Thompson, P. Baird, and J. Downie, *The Olivieri Report*, p. 447.

80 J. Thompson, P. Baird, and J. Downie, *The Olivieri Report*, p. 89.

81 In December 1998, after Dr. Olivieri published her findings of risks of Apotex's drug deferiprone—despite warnings from Apotex of legal action against her should she do so—

President J. Robert S. Prichard issued a public statement that, "As a faculty member of the University of Toronto, Dr. Olivieri is entitled to the full freedoms, rights and privileges of all members of the faculty including vigilant protection of her academic freedom." However, until CAUT and its local affiliate UTFA intervened, neither the university nor HSC provided effective assistance to her. Details can be found at p. 239 and elsewhere in the report of the CAUT Committee of Inquiry.

82 Fowke and Laskin, "Report of the Investigation by the Committee of the Canadian Association of University Teachers into the Dismissal of Professor H.S. Crowe," p. 39.

83 R. Post, "The Structure of Academic Freedom," in *Academic Freedom after September 11*, edited by B. Doumani (Brooklyn: Zone Books, 2006), p. 69.

84 B. Laskin, *Freedom and Responsibility in the University* (Toronto: University of Toronto Press, 1970), p. 3.

85 The CAUT definition is in Appendix W at http://www.caut.ca/thompson-report/appendix-w.aspx.

86 H. W. Arthurs, "Notes for Panel Discussion at Annual Conference of AUCC, October 5, 1995." (Professor Arthur gave copies of these Notes to various individuals, including a copy to the author of this Report in the 1990s.)

87 See note 68, above.

88 P. Edwards, "The Bertrand Russell Case," an Appendix to B. Russell, *Why I am Not a Christian and Other Essays on Religion and Related Subjects* (New York: Simon and Schuster, 1957), p. 207–259; the quotations are taken from p. 209–213.

89 J. Dewey and H. M. Kallen, eds., *The Bertrand Russell Case* (New York: Viking Press, 1941; reprinted by Da Capo Press, 1972), p. 20.

90 Ibid., p. 22 and p. 213–225, where Justice McGeehan's decision is reproduced in its entirety.

91 Ibid., p. 9.

92 L. H. Lapham, "Tentacles of Rage: The Republican Propaganda Mill, A Brief History," *Harper's Magazine*, September 2004, p. 31–41.

93 N. Chomsky, "Intellectuals and the State," Chapter 1 in *Towards a New Cold War* (New York: Pantheon, 1982), p. 68.

94 J. Rancière, *Hatred of Democracy* (New York: Verso, 2006), p. 85.

95 Ibid., p. 84.

96 J. K. Galbraith, *The Predator State: How Conservatives Abandoned the Free Market and Why Liberals Should Too* (New York: Free Press, 2008), p. xiii and 131.

97 P. Krugman, "Wisconsin Power Play," *New York Times*, February 21, 2011.

98 H. Arthurs, "Labour Law After Labour," Osgoode CLPE Research Paper No. 15/2011, March 21, 2011, p. 20 (available electronically at http://ssrn.com/abstract=1791868).

99 J. K. Galbraith, *The Predator State*, p. 42.

100 H. Arthurs, "Labour Law After Labour," p. 20.

101 Ibid.

CHAPTER 9

1 The full text of Article 10 of the York-YUFA collective agreement is in Appendix W at http://www.caut.ca/thompson-report/appendix-w.aspx.

2 B. Laskin. *Freedom and Responsibility in the University* (Toronto: University of Toronto Press, 1970), p. 3.

3 Email, I. Lustick to MappingModels, copied to M. Shoukri, P. Monahan, and S. Davis (CIJA), May 13, 2009, 11:22 AM.

4 The protest letter to SSHRC is in Appendix R at http://www.caut.ca/thompson-report/appendix-r.aspx.

5 Letter, C. Heald to K. Rubin, November 12, 2009.

6 Email, M. Shoukri to S. Drummond, June 16, 2009 (quoted more fully in Chapter 7).

7   Email reply, M. Shoukri to a person whose name is redacted on the copy released to CAUT under FIPPA, May 27, 2009.

8   The full text of the June 15, 2009 statement by Shoukri and board chairs is in Appendix S at http://www.caut.ca/thompson-report/appendix-s.aspx.

9   In this discussion quotations refer to Dr. Dewitt's submission to this Inquiry, dated February 11, 2011, unless otherwise specified.

10 The full text of Dewitt's April 15, 2009, email is included in Appendix G at http://www.caut. ca/thompson-report/appendix-g.aspx.

11 G. Piterberg, "Settlers and Their States," *New Left Review* 62, March–April 2010, p. 123.

12 The email messages quoted here are included in Appendix J, http://www.caut.ca/thompson-report/appendix-j.aspx.

13 Letter, M. Shoukri to J. Thompson, February 17, 2011.

14 In this discussion quotations refer to Professor Monahan's submission to this Inquiry, dated February 11, 2011, unless otherwise specified.

15 Email, B. Ryder to S. Brathwaite, April 14, 2009, 12:25 PM.

16 Letter, P. Monahan to J. Thompson, July 22, 2011.

17 F. Iacobucci, "The Mapping Models Conference and Academic Freedom: A Report to President Mamdouh Shoukri," March 2010, p. 10–11.

18 The full U50 Application is included in Appendix Y at http://www.caut.ca/thompson-report/appendix-y.aspx.

19 Email, P. Monahan to a person whose name is redacted in the copy released to CAUT under FIPPA, April 24, 2009, 9:08 PM.

20 S. Drummond, written submission to this Inquiry, October 16, 2009.

21 Memo, B. Ryder and S. Drummond to P. Monahan, October 10, 2008.

22 In accordance with standard procedures, Professor Ryder's application was approved by the Director of the Office of Research Services, York University, Dr. David Phipps (on November 3, 2008).

23 P. Monahan, "The Mapping Models Conference," July 2011, p. 7–8.

24 S. Drummond, "Field Notes," draft dated October 2009, p. 14–15.

25 Email, P. Monahan to B. Ryder and S. Drummond, April 15, 2009 (9:44 PM).

26 Email, P. Monahan to a person whose name is redacted in the copy released to CAUT under FIPPA, April 11, 2009, 6:51 AM.

27 Emails, P. Monahan to M. Shoukri and M. Cohen, April 21 and 25, 2009.

28 This quotation is from an email message from Professor Drummond to Dean Monahan on April 15, 2009, cited in Chapter 5.

29 Email, P. Monahan to I. Abella, copied to "Rosalie Abella" at scc-csc.gc.ca, April 15, 2009, 6:30 PM. Appendix F at http://www.caut.ca/thompson-report/appendix-f.aspx.

30 Emails, P. Monahan to M. Shoukri, April 15 and May 9, 2009.

31 Email reply, D. Dewitt to P. Monahan, April 27, 2009, 9:28 PM.

32 These three emails are cited in Chapter 5; the full texts of the second and third are in Appendix I at http://www.caut.ca/thompson-report/appendix-i.aspx.

33 P. Monahan, "The Mapping Models Conference," July 2011, p. 13.

34 Ibid.

35 B. Ryder, testimony in recorded interview with J. Thompson, October 15, 2009. At the time of this interview, Ryder had not yet seen any of the email messages among the dean, the president, and the board chair, or between senior staff-persons in the president's office in which the matter of a campus venue was discussed. These emails were obtained later in 2009 and in 2010 though requests under freedom-of-information legislation.

36 P. Monahan, "The Mapping Models Conference," July 2011, p. 14 (enclosed with his

submission to this Inquiry, July 15, 2011).

37   Ibid., p. 16.

38   Email, P.Monahan to M. Shoukri and M. Cohen, April 25, 2009.

39   Email, P. Monahan to M. Shoukri, May 9, 2009 (included in Appendix I).

40   Email, D. Dewitt to P. Monahan, May 11, 2009.

41   Email, I. Maxwell Rodrigues to H. Lewis, April 20, 2009.

42   Email, P. Monahan to D. Dewitt and S. Shapson, May 21, 2009, 10:14 AM.

43   Email, D. Dewitt to S. Aiken, March 1, 2009 (forwarded by S. Aiken to the other conference organizers).

44   Email, P. Monahan to M. Shoukri, May 12, 2009, 10:42 PM.

45   Page 4, Provost Monahan's "Preliminary Review" of S. Drummond's "Field Notes,"undated but given to Professor Drummond on July 13, 2009, by the provost.

46   Email, P. Monahan to a person whose name is redacted in the copy released to CAUT under FIPPA, April 11, 2009, 6:51 AM.

47   The full text of the minister's media statement is in Appendix M at http://www.caut.ca/thompson-report/appendix-m.aspx.

48   The B'nai Brith statement is cited in Chapter 6, "SSHRC Responds to the Minster's Request."

49   The PCO-approved media lines issued October 5, 2009, are cited in Chapter 6, in section "Actions by CAUT, June 7–15."

50   Commons Debates, 30th Canadian Parliament, 3rd session, April 22, 1977, p. 4,913.

51   The letter from SSHRC to Professor Ryder is in Appendix N at http://www.caut.ca/thompson-report/appendix-n.aspx.

52   Dr. Gaffield's letter is quoted more fully in Chapter 6.

53   The internal SSHRC email records are cited in Chapter 6.

54   The correspondence between SSHRC and Professor Ryder is in Appendix N at http://www.caut.ca/thompson-report/appendix-n.aspx.

55   The internal SSHRC communications of the weekend of June 13–14 are cited in Chapter 6.

56   F. Iacobucci, "Clarification of Mandate," undated copy (in the form of a print-out from the University's website), provided to CAUT pursuant to a request under the FIPPA legislation. A similar statement appears in the Iacobucci report, at page 19, where the author included the more explicit reassurance that the report did not "provide any findings of fact against any person or group."

57   Writing about the report in the *Toronto Star* on May 11, 2010, under the heading, "York Mideast debate a debacle," columnist Martin Regg Cohn concluded that "the 68-page report comes across as an indictment of acute Ivory Tower syndrome and profound obtuseness by tenured academics. And while there is no evidence that the conference organizers were motivated by malice, they were afflicted by an astonishing naïveté that put York on a course for a public relations disaster—and prompted the damage-control exercise that led to Iacobucci's report."

58   Letter, J. Gilmour, S. Imai, and G. Van Harten to C. Haig Brown, S. Dimock, and L. Sanders (copied to M. Shoukri, P. Monahan, D. Dewitt, and P. Cantor), April 26, 2010.

59   J. Downey, "The Consent University and Dissenting Academy," AUCC, April 9, 2003.

60   F. Iacobucci, p. 53.

61   M. W. Finkin and R. C. Post, *For the Common Good* (New Haven, CT: Yale University Press, 2009), p. 154.

62   F. Iacobucci, p. 53, 60.

63   AAUP, 1915 *Declaration of Principles on Academic Freedom and Academic Tenure.* (http://www.aaup.org/NR/rdonlyres/A6520A9D-0A9A-47B3-B550-C006B5B224E7/0/1915Declaration.pdf).

64   F. Iacobucci, p. 38.

65   F. Iacobucci, p. 61.

66   Ibid.

67   Ibid.

68   Ibid., p. 60.

69   Z. Sternhell, "In Defence of Liberal Zionism" and G. Piterberg, "Settlers and Their States," *New Left Review* 62, March–April 2010.

70   K. Brewster, *Annual Report, 1971*, quoted in W. Van Alstyne, "The Meaning of Tenure" in M. W. Finkin, ed., *The Case for Tenure* (Ithaca: Cornell University Press, 1996), p. 62.

71   F. Iacobucci, p. 60, 62.

72   Ibid., p. 58.

Chapter 10

1   Z. Sternhell, *The Anti-Enlightenment Tradition* (New Haven, CT: Yale University Press, 2010), p. 443.

2   This erosion process—already underway—was discussed by Professor Arthurs in his article "Labour Law After Labour," Osgoode CLPE Research Paper No. 15/2011, March 21, 2011.

INDEX